HERITAGE OF WESTERN CIVILIZATION

—— VOLUME I ——

Ancient Civilizations and the Emergence of the West

NINTH EDITION

John L. Beatty ◆ Oliver A. Johnson
John Reisbord ◆ Mita Choudhury

PEARSON

Prentice
Hall

Upper Saddle River, NJ 07458

Library of Congress Cataloging-in-Publication Data

Heritage of Western civilization/edited by John L. Beatty, Oliver A.
Johnson.—9th ed./[newly edited by] John Reisbord, Mita Choudhury.
p.   cm.
ISBN 0-13-034127-4 (v. 1)—ISBN 0-13-034128-2 (v. 2)
1. Civilization, Western—History—Sources. 2. Civilization—
History—Sources. I. Beatty, John Louis. II. Johnson, Oliver A.
III. Reisbord, John. IV. Choudhury, Mita.
CB245.H428   2004
909'.09821—dc21   2002044570

Acquisitions Editor: Charles Cavaliere
Editor-in-Chief: Charlyce Jones Owen
Associate Editor: Emsal Hasan
Editorial Assistant: Adrienne Paul
Marketing Manager: Heather Shelstad
Marketing Assistant: Jennifer Bryant
Production Editor: Laura A. Lawrie
Manufacturing Buyer: Tricia Kenny
Cover Design: Kiwi Design

Cover Illustration/Photo: German peasant
women in the Rhineland, medieval agricul-
ture. (Einrelblatt eines Jungfrauenspiegels.
Eindebilder)./Braunschweig Landesmuseum
Composition: This book was set in 10/12
Palatino by Preparé Inc.
Printer/Binder: Interior printed by Courier
Companies, Inc. The cover was printed by
Coral Graphics.

Credits and acknowledgments borrowed from other sources and reproduced, with permission,
in this textbook appear on appropriate page within text.

Pearson Education LTD.
Pearson Education Singapore, Pte. Ltd.
Pearson Education Canada, Ltd.
Pearson Education—Japan

Pearson Education Australia PTY, Limited
Pearson Education North Asia, Ltd.
Pearson Educación de Mexico, S.A. de C.V.
Pearson Education Malaysia, Pte. Ltd.

10 9 8 7 6 5 4 3 2 1
ISBN 0-13-034127-4

In memory of John W. Olmsted

Contents

Contents

RENAISSANCE AND REFORMATION

Preface

The editor assigned to a work entering its Ninth Edition takes on a special obligation. Since 1958, John Beatty and Oliver Johnson's *Heritage of Western Civilization* has proved a valuable tool for countless students and instructors. Our revision of the Eighth Edition was carried out with full knowledge and respect for the fact that we were working on a book that has stood the test of time. Still, no work such as this reaches a Ninth Edition unless its editors are constantly on the lookout for ways to improve on past efforts.

In a sense, our challenge was very much like that facing any teacher of Western Civilization. Given limited time, or in our case limited space, what should the instructor include and what must he or she leave out? The latter task was at least as difficult as the former. A strong argument could be made for the retention of every selection in the Eighth Edition. However, our mandate was to broaden the range of topics and authors included in this anthology without increasing its length and, in service of that goal, tough choices had to be made. We hope that the inclusion of authors such as the Muslim warrior and courtier Usāmah Ibn-Munqidh, the Italian matriarch Alessandra Strozzi, and the Dominican witch hunters Heinrich Kramer and James Sprenger will provide readers with a richer, more complex picture of Western history.

Changes to the Ninth Edition:
The most important change to the Ninth Edition of the *Heritage of Western Civilization* is the inclusion of fourteen new selections, six of which were authored by women. New sources include:

Volume I
- Esarhaddon, "Second Inscription of Esarhaddon"
- Xenophon, "The Character of Cyrus"
- Aristotle, "The Care of Infancy"
- Plutarch, "The Insurrection of the Gladiators"
- Hildegard of Bingen, *Letters*
- Usāmah Ibn-Munqidh, "An Appreciation of the Frankish Character"
- Laura Cereta, *Letters*
- Alessandra Strozzi, *Letters*

Volume II
- *Malleus Malificarum*
- Olympe de Gouges, "Declaration of the Rights of Women"
- Henry Mayhew, *London Labour and the London Poor*
- Catherine Booth, "God of Education"
- W.E.B. Du Bois, *The Souls of Black Folk*
- Gusta Dawidson-Draenger, *Justina's Diary*

In addition, the introductions to every source in both volumes of *Heritage* have been revised with an eye to providing students with the necessary context to explore the selection in question, while avoiding the imposition of any particular analytical framework on the material. Finally, in an effort to help facilitate student's close reading and critique of the selections, questions for consideration have been added to the introduction to each source and at the end of the general introduction to each major section.

John Reisbord

Mita Choudhury

Heritage
of Western
Civilization

Assyrian kings used public art to immortalize their deeds. In this example, Assyrian warriors fight their enemies in a battle scene from a palace wall at Nineveh.

THE ANCIENT
NEAR EAST

The source of Western civilization, the ancient Near East, lies in a relatively small area of land where three continents—Asia, Africa, and Europe—come together. It is difficult to state with precision just when Western civilization began. Two quite different kinds of problems stand in our way. An obvious difficulty is that in very early times people had not developed the art of writing and so could not preserve a detailed or reliable account of their deeds. A more formidable obstacle lies in determining just what constitutes civilization. Clearly we cannot decide when a civilization began until after we have determined what a civilization is. Historians, generally, have solved this problem by dating the birth of civilization from the time people first began to live together in cities. Accepting this criterion, we can date the beginning of Western civilization in the fifth millennium B.C., when inhabitants of the ancient Near East began drifting down from the hills into the fertile river bottoms, abandoning their nomadic existence as herders for a more settled life in towns.

Some historians, however, believe that civilization demands more than city life; in particular, they insist on the necessity of permanent, accurate records. This criterion implies the ability to write. Those who base civilization on the existence of written records have an additional point in their argument, for almost concurrent with the invention of writing at the end of the fourth millennium B.C. there occurred a second event of epochal significance. Usually called the *copper revolution*, this development is important not only because it introduced a metal as the main constituent of arms and implements in place of stone, but also because it led to a vast expansion of commerce. Since few localities possessed copper deposits, it was necessary to transport the supplies long distances from their sources to their destinations. Extensive commerce required larger political units, more complex commercial organization, and better means of transportation and communication. All of these are basic ingredients of civilized life.

Whether we accept the notion that civilized life begins with life in the city or only with the development of a written language, we must recognize a fact often overlooked—that the portion of Western history occupied by the civilizations of the ancient Near East is a large one indeed. If we take as a dividing line the year 500 B.C.—when classical Greece, entered its period of greatness—we find that we have cut Western civilization almost exactly in half. And, if we mark the beginning of civilization by the development of city life, we must tip the temporal balance in favor of the pre-Greek world.

Our knowledge of the ancient Near East comes from many sources. Important among these, of course, are written records. The Old Testament, for instance, is a treasure house of information about every facet of life in ancient times, revealing intimate details of the daily life not only of the tribes of Israel but also of their neighbors from Egypt to Mesopotamia. For those periods of history in which no written records exist, our most important sources of information are the findings of archaeologists. Since the romantic discovery of the city of Troy a century ago by a German amateur, Heinrich Schliemann, archaeologists have systematically dug up the sites where ancient people had built and lived. They have been aided in their researches in various unexpected ways. For example, the most essential item in an ancient household, the clay pot, is almost indestructible. Although it may be broken and cast on a dump heap, the shards remain through the millennia, waiting to be put together again. When archaeologists of the twentieth century reassemble this humble object, they can learn much about its original owners from its composition, its shape, and its decoration. In addition, they can make shrewd deductions about the time it was originally molded, from the relative depth of the layer in the dump from which they dug it up.

Archaeologists are also greatly indebted to the ancient Egyptians for their faith in immortality. Believing in a life after death much like that on earth, the Egyptians filled the tombs of their deceased with everything necessary for a prosperous, happy existence. Preserved intact through the ages in the dry air of the Egyptian desert, ancient tombs such as that of the pharaoh Tutenkhamon, who reigned in the fourteenth century B.C., have yielded dazzling treasures to the picks and shovels of modern diggers.

Because it spanned several millennia, the history of the ancient Near East is a complex affair. Nevertheless it is possible to distinguish four major Near Eastern centers of civilization: Mesopotamia, Egypt, Asia Minor and Syria, and the eastern Mediterranean Sea. Of these, Mesopotamia is generally conceded to have the oldest civilization. At a very early date people were attracted by the deep, rich soils created by the annual flooding of two great rivers, the Tigris and the Euphrates, as they flowed in a generally eastward direction to their ultimate destination in the Persian Gulf. The long history of Mesopotamia witnessed a succession of peoples gaining political domination over the land, only to be overcome and superseded by another group. A twofold reason lies behind this turbulent history. The fertile land was extremely attractive and hence considered a worthy prize. In addition, it was very difficult to defend against invasions because it offered few natural barriers to attackers.

To reap maximum benefit from the fertile soil of the river valley, it was necessary to develop extensive systems of irrigation. Such an endeavor required large-scale cooperation, which in turn encouraged the development of legal relationships. The result was an early elaboration of a complex legal system, which was codified by the Babylonian king Hammurabi around

1700 B.C. and became one of the most important bequests of Mesopotamia to Western civilization.

Ancient Egypt, like Mesopotamia, was a civilization based on a river. To reach its mouth at the southeast corner of the Mediterranean Sea, the Nile meanders for nearly a thousand miles from its first cataract in upper Egypt. Most of the life of ancient Egypt was concentrated in a narrow strip of fertile land, 10 to 20 miles wide, along the banks of the river. Egypt differed from Mesopotamia, however, in having a relatively tranquil history. Indeed, it was one of the most stable societies in the history of the world. The reason, again, was mainly geographical. Relatively isolated and protected from potential invaders by barriers of mountain and desert, the Egyptians were able to go about their affairs century after century unmolested by foreign intruders.

The third general area of the ancient Near East, Asia Minor and Syria, is more difficult to characterize briefly because its history was quite diverse. Including the Anatolian peninsula between the eastern Mediterranean and the Black Sea as well as the narrow strip of land between the eastern end of the Mediterranean and the desert of Arabia, this land was the home of many very diverse groups of people. Because of their strategic location along the shores of the Mediterranean and astride the main overland routes connecting Egypt and Mesopotamia, the peoples of the area turned naturally to trade as a way of life. One group, the Phoenicians, took to the sea, sending their ships far and wide across the Mediterranean and even venturing beyond the Straits of Gibraltar into the Atlantic. Others turned to trade by land; a group known as Aramaeans dominated commerce in the Near East from their trading city of Damascus for centuries. Among the smallest, weakest, yet most influential of all Near Eastern peoples was a group of wandering tribes who presumably originated near the mouth of the Tigris and Euphrates and, after many vicissitudes, settled in the land of Canaan, on a thin coastal strip at the southeast corner of the Mediterranean. These were the Jewish people.

The final important ancient Near Eastern civilization had its center in the islands of the eastern Mediterranean and Aegean seas and along the coastal strips of the adjacent mainland, in Greece and Asia Minor. Of particular significance was the island of Crete, just off the southern tip of Greece. Here an advanced society developed, especially at the city of Cnossus, where an enormous and elaborate palace was built to house the royal family and its retainers. The Minoans, as the members of this civilization are generally called, naturally took to the sea and for centuries dominated the commerce of the Aegean area, from seaports on Crete, on other islands, and on the mainland. Although Minoan civilization declined after some unknown force attacked and destroyed the great palace at Cnossus around 1400 B.C., this city and the civilization it represented achieved a high level of wealth, splendor, and sophistication. In addition, it provided a link between the older civilizations in the ancient Near East and classical Greece.

During the last thousand years of its period of greatness, civilization in the ancient Near East was characterized by the appearance of successive empires. Among the first of these was the Babylonian Empire of Hammurabi, which took shape in Mesopotamia around 1700 B.C. There followed the Egyptian Empire and the Empire of the Hittites, centered in Anatolia. Overshadowing all of these in extent and influence were the last two imperial powers, the Assyrians and then the Persians. Under their great leaders, Cyrus and Darius, the Persians gained control of all the ancient Near East from the Mediterranean shores in the west to the banks of the Indus River in India in the east. Around 500 B.C. they began to move through the strait called the Dardanelles into Europe. Here they were met by the Greeks in a series of decisive encounters, which were to shape the course of Western history to our own day.

LOOKING AHEAD

As you learn about the Ancient Near East, consider the following questions.

1. What are the essential characteristics of a civilization?

2. Why is it so important to begin a study of Western Civilization with an exploration of the history of the Near East?

3. Compare and contrast the civilizations of the Babylonians, the Egyptians, and the Hebrews. What did these three societies have in common?

The Code of Hammurabi

Hammurabi (whose tribe, the Amorites, had occupied the middle Euphrates valley), established himself in power and founded the city of Babylon along the lower river, then reigned as king of Babylonia from 1728 to 1686 B.C. Although he was responsible for formulating and publishing the Code, he did not originate the laws it contains. Rather, the Code is a compilation and revision of older laws of the Sumerians and Akkadians (tribes occupying the same general region). These deal with almost every facet of life in the ancient Near East, including marriage and the family, relationships among social classes, regulations concerning land and business, labor relations, military service, religion, and crime. They are important not only for the light they shed on the quite complex society of that time but also for the influence they had on later Near Eastern law codes. In this regard it is instructive to compare the Code with the Mosaic law as it appears in the Old Testament. Both reveal, particularly in their sanction of the *lex talionis*, something of the cruelty and violence that was endemic throughout the ancient world.

Consider the following questions as you study the text below.

1. Did the Code treat men and women differently? In what ways? Were all of Hammurabi's subjects, rich and poor alike, equal before the law?

2. What was the role of government in the Babylonian economy? How did the Code help define that role?

The Code of Hammurabi

1.   If a man has accused another of laying a death spell upon him, but has not proved it, he shall be put to death.

2.   If a man has accused another of laying a spell upon him, but has not proved it, the accused shall go to the sacred river, he shall plunge into the sacred river, and if the sacred river shall conquer him, he that accused him shall take possession of his house. If the sacred river shall show his innocence and he is saved, his accuser shall be put to death. He that plunged into the sacred river shall appropriate the house of him that accused him.

Trans. C. H. W. Johns.

3.   If a man has borne false witness in a trial, or has not established the statement that he has made, if that case be a capital trial, that man shall be put to death.

6.   If a man has stolen goods from a temple, or house, he shall be put to death; and he that has received the stolen property from him shall be put to death.

14.   If a man has stolen a child, he shall be put to death.

15.   If a man has induced either a male or female slave from the house of a patrician, or plebeian, to leave the city, he shall be put to death.

16.   If a man has harbored in his house a male or female slave from a patrician's or plebeian's house, and has not caused the fugitive to leave on the demand of the officer over the slaves condemned to public forced labor, that householder shall be put to death.

22.   If a man has committed highway robbery and has been caught, that man shall be put to death.

23.   If the highwayman has not been caught, the man that has been robbed shall state on oath what he has lost and the city or district governor in whose territory or district the robbery took place shall restore to him what he has lost.

25.   If a fire has broken out in a man's house and one who has come to put it out has coveted the property of the householder and appropriated any of it, that man shall be cast into the self-same fire.

26.   If a levy-master, or warrant-officer, who has been detailed on the king's service, has not gone, or has hired a substitute in his place, that levy-master, or warrant-officer, shall be put to death and the hired substitute shall take his office.

34.   If either a governor, or a prefect, has appropriated the property of a levy-master, has hired him out, has robbed him by high-handedness at a trial, has taken the salary which the king gave to him, that governor, or prefect, shall be put to death.

45.   If a man has let his field to a farmer and has received his rent for the field but afterward the field has been flooded by rain, or a storm has carried off the crop, the loss shall be the farmer's.

46.   If he has not received the rent of his field, whether he let it for a half, or for a third, of the crop, the farmer and the owner of the field shall share the corn that is left in the field, according to their agreement.

53, 54.   If a man has neglected to strengthen his dike and has not kept his dike strong, and a breach has broken out in his dike, and the waters have flooded the meadow, the man in whose dike the breach has broken out shall restore the corn he has caused to be lost. [54]. If he be not able to restore the corn, he and his goods shall be sold, and the owners of the meadow whose corn the water has carried away shall share the money.

100. [If an agent has received money of a merchant, he shall write down the amount] and [what is to be] the interest of the money, and when his time is up, he shall settle with his merchant.

102, 103. If the merchant has given money, as a speculation, to the agent, who during his travels has met with misfortune, he shall return the full sum to the merchant. [103]. If, on his travels, an enemy has forced him to give up some of the goods he was carrying, the agent shall specify the amount on oath and shall be acquitted.

108. If the mistress of a beer-shop has not received corn as the price of beer or has demanded silver on an excessive scale, and has made the measure of beer less than the measure of corn, that beer-seller shall be prosecuted and drowned.

109. If the mistress of a beer-shop has assembled seditious slanderers in her house and those seditious persons have not been captured and have not been haled to the palace, that beer-seller shall be put to death.

110. If a votary, who is not living in the convent, open a beer-shop, or enter a beer-shop for drink, that woman shall be put to death.

122. If a man has given another gold, silver, or any goods whatever, on deposit, all that he gives shall he show to witnesses, and take a bond and so give on deposit.

123. If he has given on deposit without witnesses and bonds, and has been defrauded where he made his deposit, he has no claim to prosecute.

124. If a man has given on deposit to another, before witnesses, gold, silver, or any goods whatever, and his claim has been contested, he shall prosecute that man, and [the man] shall return double what he disputed.

125. If a man has given anything whatever on deposit, and, where he has made his deposit, something of his has been lost together with something belonging to the owner of the house, either by house-breaking or a rebellion, the owner of the house who is in default shall make good all that has been given him on deposit, which he has lost, and shall return it to the owner of the goods. The owner of the house shall look after what he has lost and recover it from the thief.

128. If a man has taken a wife and has not executed a marriage-contract, that woman is not a wife.

129. If a man's wife be caught lying with another, they shall be strangled and cast into the water. If the wife's husband would save his wife, the king can save his servant.

130. If a man has ravished another's betrothed wife, who is a virgin, while still living in her father's house, and has been caught in the act, that man shall be put to death; the woman shall go free.

131. If a man's wife has been accused by her husband, and has not been caught lying with another, she shall swear her innocence, and return to her house.

132.   If a man's wife has the finger pointed at her on account of another, but has not been caught lying with him, for her husband's sake she shall plunge into the sacred river.

138.   If a man has divorced his wife, who has not borne him children, he shall pay over to her as much money as was given for her bride-price and the marriage-portion which she brought from her father's house, and so shall divorce her.

141.   If a man's wife, living in her husband's house, has persisted in going out, has acted the fool, has wasted her house, has belittled her husband, he shall prosecute her. If her husband has said, "I divorce her," she shall go her way; he shall give her nothing as her price of divorce. If her husband has said, "I will not divorce her," he may take another woman to wife; the wife shall live as a slave in her husband's house.

142.   If a woman has hated her husband and has said, "You shall not possess me," her past shall be inquired into, as to what she lacks. If she has been discreet, and has no vice, and her husband has gone out, and has greatly belittled her, that woman has no blame, she shall take her marriage-portion and go off to her father's house.

143.   If she has not been discreet, has gone out, ruined her house, belittled her husband, she shall be drowned.

150.   If a man has presented field, garden, house, or goods to his wife, has granted her a deed of gift, her children, after her husband's death, shall not dispute her right; the mother shall leave it after her death to that one of her children whom she loves best. She shall not leave it to her kindred.

152.   From the time that that woman entered into the man's house they together shall be liable for all debts subsequently incurred.

153.   If a man's wife, for the sake of another, has caused her husband to be killed, that woman shall be impaled.

154.   If a man has committed incest with his daughter, that man shall be banished from the city.

155.   If a man has betrothed a maiden to his son and his son has known her, and afterward the man has lain in her bosom, and been caught, that man shall be strangled and she shall be cast into the water.

156.   If a man has betrothed a maiden to his son, and his son has not known her, and that man has lain in her bosom, he shall pay her half a mina of silver, and shall pay over to her whatever she brought from her father's house, and the husband of her choice shall marry her.

157.   If a man, after his father's death, has lain in the bosom of his mother, they shall both of them be burnt together.

159.   If a man, who has presented a gift to the house of his prospective father-in-law and has given the bride-price, has afterward looked upon another woman and has said to his father-in-law, "I will not marry

your daughter"; the father of the girl shall keep whatever he has brought as a present.

160. If a man has presented a gift to the house of his prospective father-in-law, and has given the bride-price, but the father of the girl has said, "I will not give you my daughter," the father shall return double all that was presented him.

168. If a man has determined to disinherit his son and has declared before the judge, "I cut off my son," the judge shall inquire into the son's past, and, if the son has not committed a grave misdemeanor such as should cut him off from sonship, the father shall not disinherit his son.

169. If he has committed a grave crime against his father, which cuts off from sonship, for the first offence he shall pardon him. If he has committed a grave crime a second time, the father shall cut off his son from sonship.

170. If a man has had children borne to him by his wife, and also by a maid, if the father in his lifetime has said, "My sons," to the children whom his maid bore him, and has reckoned them with the sons of his wife; then after the father has gone to his fate, the children of the wife and of the maid shall share equally. The children of the wife shall apportion the shares and make their own selections.

171. And if the father, in his lifetime, has not said, "My sons," to the children whom the maid bore him, after the father has gone to his fate, the children of the maid shall not share with the children of the wife in the goods of their father's house. The maid and her children, however, shall obtain their freedom. The children of the wife have no claim for service on the children of the maid.

The wife shall take her marriage-portion, and any gift that her husband has given her and for which he has written a deed of gift and she shall dwell in her husband's house; as long as she lives, she shall enjoy it, she shall not sell it. After her death it is indeed her children's.

175. If either a slave of a patrician, or of a plebeian, has married the daughter of a free man, and she has borne children, the owner of the slave shall have no claim for service on the children of a free woman. And if a slave, either of a patrician or of a plebeian, has married a free woman and when he married her she entered the slave's house with a marriage-portion from her father's estate, be he slave of a patrician or of a plebeian, and from the time that they started to keep house, they have acquired property; after the slave, whether of a patrician or of a plebeian, has gone to his fate, the free woman shall take her marriage-portion, and whatever her husband and she acquired, since they started house-keeping. She shall divide it into two portions. The master of the slave shall take one half, the other half the free woman shall take for her children.

176. If the free woman had no marriage-portion, whatever her husband and she acquired since they started house-keeping he shall divide into

two portions. The owner of the slave shall take one half, the other half the free woman shall take for her children.

177.   If a widow, whose children are young, has determined to marry again, she shall not marry without consent of the judge. When she is allowed to remarry, the judge shall inquire as to what remains of the property of her former husband, and shall intrust the property of her former husband to that woman and her second husband. He shall give them an inventory. They shall watch over the property, and bring up the children. Not a utensil shall they sell. A buyer of any utensil belonging to the widow's children shall lose his money and shall return the article to its owners.

186.   If a man has taken a young child to be his son, and after he has taken him, the child discover his own parents, he shall return to his father's house.

188, 189.   If a craftsman has taken a child to bring up and has taught him his handicraft, he shall not be reclaimed. If he has not taught him his handicraft that foster child shall return to his father's house.

195.   If a son has struck his father, his hands shall be cut off.
196.   If a man has knocked out the eye of a patrician, his eye shall be knocked out.
197.   If he has broken the limb of a patrician, his limb shall be broken.
198.   If he has knocked out the eye of a plebeian or has broken the limb of a plebeian, he shall pay one mina of silver.
199.   If he has knocked out the eye of a patrician's servant, or broken the limb of a patrician's servant, he shall pay half his value.
200.   If a patrician has knocked out the tooth of a man that is his equal, his tooth shall be knocked out.
201.   If he has knocked out the tooth of a plebeian, he shall pay one-third of a mina of silver.
202.   If a man has smitten the privates of a man, higher in rank than he, he shall be scourged with sixty blows of an ox-hide scourge, in the assembly.

209.   If a man has struck a free woman with child, and has caused her to miscarry, he shall pay ten shekels for her miscarriage.
210.   If that woman die, his daughter shall be killed.

215.   If a surgeon has operated with the bronze lancet on a patrician for a serious injury, and has cured him, or has removed with a bronze lancet a cataract for a patrician, and has cured his eye, he shall take ten shekels of silver.

218.   If a surgeon has operated with the bronze lancet on a patrician for a serious injury, and has caused his death, or has removed a cataract for a patrician, with the bronze lancet, and has made him lose his eye, his hands shall be cut off.

224.   If a veterinary surgeon has treated an ox, or an ass, for a severe injury, and cured it, the owner of the ox, or the ass, shall pay the surgeon one-sixth of a shekel of silver, as his fee.

225.   If he has treated an ox, or an ass, for a severe injury, and caused it to die, he shall pay one-quarter of its value to the owner of the ox, or the ass.

226.   If a brander has cut out a mark on a slave, without the consent of his owner, that brander shall have his hands cut off.

229.   If a builder has built a house for a man, and has not made his work sound, and the house he built has fallen, and caused the death of its owner, that builder shall be put to death.

230.   If it is the owner's son that is killed, the builder's son shall be put to death.

231.   If it is the slave of the owner that is killed, the builder shall give slave for slave to the owner of the house.

236.   If a man has let his boat to a boatman, and the boatman has been careless and the boat has been sunk or lost, the boatman shall restore a boat to the owner.

237.   If a man has hired a boat and boatman, and loaded it with corn, wool, oil, or dates, or whatever it be, and the boatman has been careless, and sunk the boat, or lost what is in it, the boatman shall restore the boat which he sank, and whatever he lost that was in it.

244.   If a man has hired an ox, or an ass, and a lion has killed it in the open field, the loss falls on its owner.

245.   If a man has hired an ox and has caused its death, by carelessness, or blows, he shall restore ox for ox, to the owner of the ox.

249.   If a man has hired an ox, and God has struck it, and it has died, the man that hired the ox shall make affidavit and go free.

250.   If a bull has gone wild and gored a man, and caused his death, there can be no suit against the owner.

251.   If a man's ox be a gorer, and has revealed its evil propensity as a gorer, and he has not blunted its horn, or shut up the ox, and then that ox has gored a free man, and caused his death, the owner shall pay half a mina of silver.

265.   If a herdsman, to whom oxen or sheep have been given, has defaulted, has altered the price, or sold them, he shall be prosecuted, and shall restore oxen, or sheep, tenfold, to their owner.

266.   If lightning has struck a fold, or a lion has made a slaughter, the herdsman shall purge himself by oath, and the owner of the fold shall bear the loss of the fold.

267.   If the herdsman has been careless, and a loss has occurred in the fold, the herdsman shall make good the loss in the fold; he shall repay the oxen, or sheep, to their owner.

278.   If a man has bought a male or female slave and the slave has not fulfilled his month, but the *bennu* disease has fallen upon him, he shall return the slave to the seller and the buyer shall take back the money he paid.

280.   If a man, in a foreign land, has bought a male, or female, slave of another, and if when he has come home the owner of the male or female slave has recognized his slave, and if the slave be a native of the land, he shall grant him his liberty without money.

281.   If the slave was a native of another country, the buyer shall declare on oath the amount of money he paid, and the owner of the slave shall repay the merchant what he paid and keep his slave.

282.   If a slave has said to his master, "You are not my master," he shall be brought to account as his slave, and his master shall cut off his ear.

Egyptian Religion

In their worship of the Nile and the sun, the ancient Egyptians were exemplifying a form of religious belief common among early civilizations—*animism*, or the deification of objects of nature. Nevertheless, a close reading of the two hymns reveals differences between them. It is clear from the first that the Nile is being worshiped as only one of many gods, so the religion is not only animistic but also polytheistic. In the second, however, the worshiper makes it plain, as he says, that the sun is the "sole god." Thus, we have in this hymn an expression of monotheism. Indeed, it is generally considered to be among the earliest statements of a monotheistic theology in history. And, more subtly, there are indications in the hymn that the object of worship is not the physical sun itself but some power more fundamental and pervasive than any single natural object. So we find in it the beginnings of a departure from simple animism.

The date of the "Hymn to the Nile" is not known, but scholars believe that it was sung during an annual festival held at Thebes (in upper Egypt) that celebrated the inundation of the land by the river. It has, unfortunately, not survived intact, but it is sufficiently complete so that its content is clear. The "Hymn to the Sun" is known to be the work of the Pharoah Ikhnaton, who reigned in the early part of the fourteenth century B.C. Ikhnaton attempted to transform Egyptian religion; his attempt, however, proved to be unsuccessful, for after his death the Egyptians returned to their old beliefs.

Consider the following questions as you study the text below.

1. What was the relationship of the Egyptians to their environment? How was this relationship expressed in the "Hymn to the Nile"?

2. Compare and contrast the two hymns. What evidence do you find to support the notion that the "Hymn to the Nile" was a reflection of polytheism and the "Hymn to the Sun" a reflection of monotheism? What other differences do you see between the two hymns?

Hymn to the Nile

Praise to thee, O Nile, that issueth from the earth, and cometh to nourish Egypt. Of hidden nature, a darkness in the daytime. . . .

Adolph Erman, *The Literature of the Ancient Egyptians*, trans. A. M. Blackman (London: Methuen & Co., Ltd., 1927), pp. 146–49. Courtesy of Methuen & Co., Ltd.

That watereth the meadows, he that Rē [1] hath created to nourish all cattle.
That giveth drink to the desert places, which are far from water; it is his
dew that falleth from heaven.
Beloved of Kēb,[2] director of the corn-god; that maketh to flourish every
workshop of Ptah.[3]
Lord of fish, that maketh the water-fowl to go upstream. ...
That maketh barley and createth wheat, so that he may cause the temples to
keep festivals.
If he be sluggish,[4] the nostrils are stopped up,[5] and all men are impoverished;
the victuals of the gods are diminished, and millions of men perish.
If he be niggardly the whole land is in terror and great and small lament. ...
Khnum[6] hath fashioned him. When he riseth, the land is in exultation and
every body is in joy. All jaws begin to laugh and every tooth is revealed.
He that bringeth victuals and is rich in food, that createth all that is good.
The revered, sweet-smelling. ... That createth herbage for the cattle,
and giveth sacrifice to every god, be he in the underworld, in heaven,
or upon earth. ... That filleth the storehouses, and maketh wide the
granaries, that giveth things to the poor.
He that maketh trees to grow according to every wish, and men have no lack
thereof; the ship is built by his power, for there is no joinery with
stones. ...
... thy young folk and thy children shout for joy over thee, and men hail
thee as king. Unchanging of laws, when he cometh forth in the presence of Upper and Lower Egypt. Men drink the water. ...
He that was in sorrow is become glad, and every heart is joyful. Sobk,[7] the child
of Neith, laugheth, and the divine Ennead, that is in thee, is glorious.
Thou that vomitest forth, giving the fields to drink and making strong the
people. He that maketh the one rich and loveth the other. He maketh
no distinctions, and boundaries are not made for him.
Thou light, that cometh from the darkness! Thou fat for his cattle. He is a
strong one, that createth. ...
... one beholdeth the wealthy as him that is full of care, one beholdeth each
one with his implements. ... None that (otherwise) goeth clad, is
clad,[8] and the children of notables are unadorned. ...
He that establisheth right, whom men love. ... It would be but lies to compare thee with the sea, that bringeth no corn. ... no bird descendeth in
the desert. ...

---

[1] The sun-god.
[2] The earth-god.
[3] Ptah, the craftsman, who fashions everything, could effect nothing without the Nile.
[4] On the occasion of a deficient inundation.
[5] Men no longer breathe and live.
[6] The ram-headed god, who fashions all that is.
[7] Sobk has the form of a crocodile and will originally have been a water-god, who rejoices in the
inundation.
[8] For hard work, clothes are taken off.

Men begin to play to thee on the harp, and men sing to thee with the hand.[9]
Thy young folk and thy children shout for joy over thee, and deputations to thee are appointed.

He that cometh with splendid things and adorneth the earth! That causeth the ship to prosper before men; that quickeneth the hearts in them that are with child; that would fain have there be a multitude of all kinds of cattle.

When thou art risen in the city of the sovereign, then men are satisfied with a goodly list.[10] "I would like lotus flowers," saith the little one, "and all manner of things," saith the ... commander, "and all manner of herbs," say the children. Eating bringeth forgetfulness of him.[11] Good things are scattered over the dwelling. ...

When the Nile floodeth, offering is made to thee, cattle are slaughtered for thee, a great oblation is made for thee. Birds are fattened for thee, antelopes are hunted for thee in the desert. Good is recompensed unto thee.

Offering is also made to every other god, even as is done for the Nile, with incense, oxen, cattle, and birds (upon) the flame. The Nile hath made him his cave in Thebes, and his name shall be known no more in the underworld. ...

All ye men, extol the Nine Gods, and stand in awe of the might which his son, the Lord of All, hath displayed, even he that maketh green the Two River-banks. Thou art verdant, O Nile, thou art verdant. He that maketh man to live on his cattle, and his cattle on the meadow! Thou art verdant, thou art verdant: O Nile, thou art verdant.

Hymn to the Sun

Thy dawning is beautiful in the horizon of heaven,
O living Aton,[1] Beginning of life!
When thou risest in the eastern horizon of heaven,
Thou fillest every land with thy beauty;
For thou art beautiful, great, glittering, high over the earth;
Thy rays, they encompass the lands, even all thou hast made.
Thou art Rē, and thou hast carried them all away captive;
Thou bindest them by thy love.
Though thou art afar, thy rays are on earth;
Though thou art on high, thy footprints are the day.

---

[9] It is an old custom to beat time with the hand while singing.
[10] *I.e.*, a multitude of good things.
[11] The Nile.

Trans. James H. Breasted.

[1] [One of the names given to the sun god—*Ed.*]

When thou settest in the western horizon of heaven,
The world is in darkness like the dead.
They sleep in their chambers,
Their heads are wrapt up,
Their nostrils stopped, and none seeth the other.
Stolen are all their things, that are under their heads,
While they know it not.
Every lion cometh forth from his den,
All serpents, they sting.
Darkness reigns,
The world is in silence,
He that made them has gone to rest in his horizon.

Bright is the earth,
When thou risest in the horizon,
When thou shinest as Aton by day.
The darkness is banished,
When thou sendest forth thy rays,
The Two Lands[2] are in daily festivity,
Awake and standing upon their feet,
For thou hast raised them up.
Their limbs bathed, they take their clothing;
Their arms uplifted in adoration to thy dawning.
Then in all the world, they do their work.

All cattle rest upon their herbage,
All trees and plants flourish,
The birds flutter in their marshes.
Their wings uplifted in adoration to thee.
All the sheep dance upon their feet,
All winged things fly,
They live when thou hast shone upon them.

The barques sail up-stream and down-stream alike.
Every highway is open because thou hast dawned.
The fish in the river leap up before thee,
And thy rays are in the midst of the great sea.

Thou art he who createst the manchild in woman,
Who makest seed in man,
Who giveth life to the son in the body of his mother,
Who soothest him that he may not weep,
A nurse even in the womb.
Who giveth breath to animate every one that he maketh.
When he cometh forth from the body

[2] [Upper and Lower Egypt—*Ed.*]

. . . on the day of his birth,
Thou openest his mouth in speech.
Thou suppliest his necessities.
When the chicklet crieth in the eggshell,
Thou givest him breath therein, to preserve him alive.
When thou hast perfected him
That he may pierce the egg,
He cometh forth from the egg,
To chirp with all his might;
He runneth about upon his two feet,
When he hath come forth therefrom.
How manifold are all thy works!
They are hidden from before us,
O thou sole god, whose powers no other possesseth.
Thou didst create the earth according to thy desire.
While thou wast alone:
Men, all cattle large and small,
All that are upon the earth,
That go about upon their feet;
All that are on high,
That fly with their wings.
The countries of Syria and Nubia,
The land of Egypt;
Thou settest every man in his place,
Thou suppliest their necessities.
Every one has his possessions,
And his days are reckoned.
Their tongues are divers in speech,
Their forms likewise and their skins,
For thou divider, hast divided the peoples.

Thou makest the Nile in the Nether World,
Thou bringest it at thy desire, to preserve the people alive.
O lord of them all, when feebleness is in them,
O lord of every house, who risest for them,
O son of day, the fear of every distant land,
Thou makest also their life.
Thou has set a Nile in heaven,
That it may fall for them,
Making floods upon the mountains, like the great sea;
And watering their fields among their towns.
How excellent are thy designs, O lord of eternity!
The Nile in heaven is for the strangers,
And for the cattle of every land, that go upon their feet;
But the Nile, it cometh from the Nether World for Egypt.

Thus thy rays nourish every garden,
When thou risest they live, and grow by thee.
Thou makest the seasons, in order to create all thy works:
Winter bringing them coolness,
And the heat of summer likewise.
Thou hast made the distant heaven to rise therein,
In order to behold all that thou didst make,
While thou wast alone,
Rising in thy form as living Aton,
Dawning, shining afar off and returning.
Thou makest the beauty of form, through thyself alone.
Cities, towns and settlements,
On highway or on river,
All eyes see thee before them.
For thou art Aton of the day over the earth.

Thou art in my heart,
There is no other that knoweth thee,
Save thy son Ikhnaton.
Thou hast made him wise in thy designs
And in thy might.
The world is in thy hand,
Even as thou hast made them.
When thou hast risen, they live:
When thou settest, they die.
For thou art duration, beyond thy mere limbs,
By thee man liveth,
And their eyes look upon thy beauty.
Until thou settest.
All labour is laid aside,
When thou settest in the west;
When thou risest, they are made to grow
. . . for the king.

Since thou didst establish the earth,
Thou hast raised them up for thy son,
Who came forth from thy limbs,
The king, living in truth,
The lord of the Two Lands Nefer-khepru-Rë, Wan-Rë,
The son of Rë, living in truth, lord of diadems,
Ikhnaton, whose life is long;
And for the great royal wife, his beloved,
Mistress of the Two Lands, Nefer nefru aton, Nofretete,
Living and flourishing for ever and ever.

Assyrian Conquest

The Assyrians were not the only Iron Age empire to use terror and intimidation to expand and control their territories. That warfare was the rightful occupation of a king was an accepted fact throughout the ancient world. The Assyrians, however, acquired a reputation for particular brutality and ruthlessness. Whether this reputation was deserved or not, the Assyrians themselves did nothing to discourage the notion that their opponents were much better off surrendering to Assyrian armies than opposing them and, in so doing, risking the full force of the Assyrian's wrath.

The passages that follow were recorded on clay tablets found near the Assyrian capital of Nineveh. They tell of the deeds and accomplishments of the Assyrian king Esarhaddon. Writing in the first person, Esarhaddon boasted of his victories in battle, the cities and territories he added to his kingdom, and the magnificent palace he had built in honor of himself, his ancestors, and his gods. As you read his words, pay close attention to the way in which he characterized his own actions. What justified his conquests? How did he want to be remembered by generations to come?

Consider the following questions as you study the text below.

1. What role did religion play in Esarhaddon's sense of himself as king? In Esarhaddon's view, how did loyalty to the gods of Assyria inspire and even require the conquest of his neighbors?

2. Why did Esarhaddon expand the royal palace at Nineveh? Was he motivated primarily by practical concerns, religious obligations, or the desire for glory? What connections do you see between his conquests and his massive building project?

Second Inscription of Esarhaddon

1. (ESARHADDON King of Sumir) and Accad,
2. (son of SENNACHERIB King of) Assyria,
3. (son of SARGON) King of Assyria,
4. (who in the name of ASSUR, BEL,) the MOON, the SUN,

From *Records of the Past: Being English Translations of the Assyrian and Egyptian Monuments*, Vol. III (1874–1881).

5. NEBO, MARDUK, ISHTAR of Niniveh,
6. and ISHTAR of Arbela, the great gods his lords
7. from the rising of the sun to the setting of the sun
8. marched victorious without a rival.

---

9. Conqueror of the city Sidon, which is on the sea,
10. sweeper away of all its villages,
11. its citadel and residence I rooted up,
12. and into the sea I flung them.
13. Its place of *justice* I destroyed.
14. ABDIMILKUTTI its king
15. who away from my arms
16. into the middle of the sea had fled
17. like a fish from out of the sea
18. I caught him, and I cut off his head.
19. His treasure, his goods, gold and silver and precious stones
20. skins of *elephants*, teeth of *elephants*, *dan* wood, *ku* wood,
21. cloths, died purple and yellow, of every description
22. and the regalia of his palace
23. I carried off as my spoil.
24. Men and women without number
25. oxen and sheep and mules
26. I swept them all off to Assyria.
27. I assembled the Kings of Syria
28. and the sea coast, all of them.
29. (The city of Sidon) I built anew,
30. and I called it "The City of ESARHADDON."
31. Men, captured by my arms, natives of the lands
32. and seas of the East
33. within it I placed to dwell
34. and I set my own officers in authority over them.

---

35. And SANDUARRI
36. King of Kundi and Sitzu
37. an enemy and heretic, not honouring my majesty
38. who had abandoned the worship of the gods
39. trusted to his rocky stronghold
40. and ABDIMILKUTTI King of Sidon
41. took for his ally.
42. The names of the great gods side by side he wrote
43. and to their power he trusted;
44. but I trusted to ASHUR my Lord.
45. Like a bird, from out of the mountains
46. I took him, and I cut off his head.

47. I wrought the judgment of ASHUR my Lord
48. on the men who were criminals.
49. The heads of SANDUARRI
50. and ABDIMILKUTTI
51. by the side of those of their Chiefs I, hung up:
52. and with captives young and old; male and female,
53. to the gate of Niniveh I marched.

The first lines are broken off: it appears that the King had taken some prisoners, to whom he was resolved to show no mercy.

1. . . . I collected them:
2. to Assyria I carried them off:
3. and in front of the great entrance gate of Niniveh
4. along with *bears*, dogs, and . . .
5. I left then to stay for ever.

———————

6. And TIUSPA the Cimmerian
7. a roving warrior, whose own country was remote
8. in the province of Khubusna
9. him and all his army I destroyed with the sword.

———————

10. Trampler on the heads of the men of Khilakki
11. and Duhuka, who dwell in the mountains,
12. which front the land of Tabal,
13. who trusted to their mountains
14. and from days of old never submitted to my yoke:
15. twenty-one of their strong cities
16. and smaller towns in their neighbourhood
17. I attacked captured and carried off their spoil
18. I ruined destroyed and burnt them with fire.
19. The rest of the men, who crimes
20. and *murders* had not committed
21. I only placed the yoke of my empire heavily upon them.

———————

49. In those same days, the royal palace
50. of the centre of Niniveh
51. which the Kings my fathers who went before me
52. had made, for the protection of a camp
53. the care of horses, mares,
54. chariots able to carry munitions of war
55. and foreign spoil of every kind
56. which ASHUR King of the gods
57. had given to my arms. . . .

1.   (*I brought captives from lands which had warred against me*)
2.   I caused crowds of them to work in fetters
3.   in making bricks.
4.   That small palace
5.   I pulled down the whole of it.
6.   Much earth in baskets
7.   from the fields I brought away
8.   and threw it upon that spot,
9.   and with stones of great size
10.   I completed the mound.

---

11.   I assembled 22 Kings, of the land of Syria
12.   and of the sea coast and the islands, all of them
13.   and I passed them in review.
14.   Great beams and rafters
15.   of *abimi* wood cedar and cypress
16.   from the mountains of Sirar and Lebanon,
17.   divine images, has reliefs,
18.   stone *ilu*, slabs
19.   of *granite* and *alabaster*
20.   and of various other stones
21.   *ditto.   ditto.*
22.   from the mountain quarries
23.   the place of their origin
24.   for the adornment of my palace
25.   with labour and difficulty
26.   unto Niniveh they brought along with them.

---

27.   In a fortunate month, and on a holy day,
28.   upon that mound
29.   great palaces
30.   for the residence of my Majesty
31.   I began to build.
32.   A great building of 95 measures in length
33.   and 31 in breadth
34.   which in the days of the Kings my fathers who went before me
35.   none ever had made, I made.
36.   With beams of lofty cedar trees
37.   I laid its roof
38.   doors of *cypress* whose wood is excellent
39.   with cunning work of silver and copper I inlaid
40.   and fitted them to the gates.
41.   Bulls and lions, carved in stone
42.   which with their majestic mien
43.   deter wicked enemies from approaching,

44. the guardians of the footsteps, the saviours
45. of the path, of the King who constructed them
46. right and left I placed them
47. at the gates.
48. A palace of stone and cedar wood
49. of well contrived dimensions
50. for the *repose* of my Majesty
51. artistically I made.
52. Lionesses of bronze, painted
53. on the *hither* side, and before, and behind,
54. *on sculptured bases* I placed within it.

1. Of fine cedar wood and *ebony*
2. I made the ceilings of the apartments.
3. The whole of that palace
4. with *veneered* slabs of ivory and *alabaster*
5. I embellished, and I embroidered its tapestries.
6. With flat roofs, like *floor* of lead,
7. I covered the whole building
8. and with plates of pure silver and bright copper
9. I lined its interior.

---

10. The mighty deeds of ASHUR my lord
11. which in foreign hostile lands
12. he had done
13. by the skill of sculptors I erected within it.
14. Cedars, like those of the land of Khamana
15. which all other shrubs and trees
16. excel, I planted around it.
17. Its courts greatly I enlarged,
18. its stalls very much I improved
19. for the stabling of horses within it.
20. Wells I skilfully made
21. and I *covered* them properly.
22. That great building from its foundation
23. to its summit
24. I built and I finished. I filled with beauties
25. the Great Palace of my Empire,
26. and I called it "The Palace which rivals the world."

---

27. ASHUR, ISHTAR of Niniveh, and the gods of Assyria
28. all of them, I feasted within it:
29. victims precious and beautiful
30. I sacrificed before them
31. and I caused them to receive my *gifts*.

32. I did for those gods whatever they wished.
33. The great Assembly of my kingdom
34. the Chiefs, and the people of the land, all of them,
35. according to their tribes and cities
36. on lofty seats
37. I seated within it
38. and I made the company joyful.
39. With the wine of grapes I furnished their tables
40. and I let martial music resound among them.

———————

41. In the name of ASHUR King of the gods, and the gods of Assyria
42. all of them, with sound limbs, cheerful mind,
43. brightness of heart, and a numerous offspring
44. within it long may I continue to dwell!
45. and long may its glory endure!
46. In the . . . a fine race of horses
47. mares, mules, and camels,
48. able to carry munitions of war
49. for a whole army, with its foreign spoils:
50. every year without fail
51. may it receive them within it!
52. Within this Palace
53. may the bull of good fortune, the genius of good fortune
54. the guardian of the footsteps of my Majesty
55. the giver of joy to my heart
56. for ever watch over it! Never more
57. may its care cease!

———————

58. In future days, under the Kings my sons
59. whom ASHUR and ISHTAR to the government of this land and people
60. shall name their names,
61. when this Palace
62. shall grow old and decay,
63. the man who shall repair its injuries,
64. and in like manner as I the tablet written
65. with the name of the King my father, along with the tablet written
     with my own name
66. have placed, so do Thou after my example
67. read aloud the tablet written with my name
68. then pour a libation on the altar! sacrifice a victim!
69. and place it with the tablet written with thy own name!
70. so shall ASHUR and ISHTAR
71. hear thy prayers!

The Old Testament

The Old Testament, one of the greatest creations of the human mind, was the product of a weak, relatively insignificant nation that was regularly exploited and overrun by its more powerful Near Eastern neighbors. Although we usually think of it as a religious document, it is much more than that, for its pages record, in infinite variety and rich detail, the full range of the historical experience of the ancient Jewish people.

Rather than attempting the impossible task of encompassing the wealth of the Old Testament in the selection that follows, just two of its main themes have been chosen for illustration—the belief in one God (monotheism) and the concept of God as a moral being (standing in a personal relationship to every human being).

We'll explore these themes through four selections from the Old Testament. The source for the Christian doctrine of original sin is found in the Book of Genesis, with its account of God's creation of Adam and Eve in his own image, his placing them in the idyllic Garden of Eden, and their sin of disobedience against him. Another kind of problem is expressed in the encounter between God and Abraham on the mountain, also taken from Genesis. Should God have tempted Abraham's faith in the way he did? Should Abraham have had such faith? In Exodus, God presents Moses with the Ten Commandments, laws that are to provide the moral foundation of Jewish society. It is Moses' responsibility to communicate God's will to his people. A final moral problem of the most profound significance is found in the Book of Job. The issue concerns the question of divine justice. If God is just, why, Job asks, should the wicked of this world so often prosper and the good suffer?

Consider the following questions as you study the text below.

1. What light does the Old Testament shed on ancient Jewish society? How did the Jews see themselves? How did they see themselves in relation to the other societies with which they came in contact?

2. Does a single conception of God run through all four passages? If so, how would you describe that conception? If not, what differences do you note?

Genesis

In the beginning God created the heaven and the earth. And the earth was without form, and void; and darkness was upon the face of the deep. And the Spirit of God moved upon the face of the waters. And God said,

"Let there be light": and there was light. And God saw the light, that it was good and God divided the light from the darkness. And God called the light Day, and the darkness he called Night. And the evening and the morning were the first day.

And God said, "Let there be a firmament in the midst of the waters, and let it divide the waters from the waters." And God made the firmament, and divided the waters which were under the firmament from the waters which were above the firmament; and it was so. And God called the firmament Heaven. And the evening and the morning were the second day.

And God said, "Let the waters under the heaven be gathered together unto one place, and let the dry land appear": and it was so. And God called the dry land Earth; and the gathering together of the waters called he Seas; and God saw that it was good. And God said, "Let the earth bring forth grass, the herb yielding seed, and the fruit tree yielding fruit after his kind, whose seed is in itself, upon the earth": and it was so. And the earth brought forth grass, and herb yielding seed after his kind, and the tree yielding fruit, whose seed was in itself, after his kind: and God saw that it was good. And the evening and the morning were the third day.

And God said, "Let there be lights in the firmament of the heaven to divide the day from the night; and let them be for signs, and for seasons, and for days, and years: and let them be for lights in the firmament of the heaven to give light upon the earth": and it was so. And God made two great lights; the greater light to rule the day, and the lesser light to rule the night: he made the stars also. And God set them in the firmament of the heaven to give light upon the earth. And to rule over the day and over the night, and to divide the light from darkness: and God saw that it was good. And the evening and the morning were the fourth day.

And God said, "Let the waters bring forth abundantly the moving creature that hath life, and fowl that may fly above the earth in the open firmament of heaven." And God created great whales, and every living creature that moveth, which the water brought forth abundantly, after their kind, and every winged fowl after his kind: and God saw that it was good. And God blessed them, saying, "Be fruitful, and multiply, and fill the water in the seas, and let fowl multiply in the earth." And the evening and the morning were the fifth day.

And God said, "Let the earth bring forth the living creature after his kind, cattle, and creeping thing, and beast of the earth after his kind": and it was so. And God made the beast of the earth after his kind, and cattle after their kind, and every thing that creepeth upon the earth after his kind: and God saw that it was good.

And God said, "Let us make man in our image, after our likeness: and let them have dominion over the fish of the sea, and over the fowl of the air, and over the cattle, and over all the earth, and over every creeping thing that creepeth upon the earth." So God created man in his own image, in the image of God created he him: male and female created he them. And God blessed them and God said unto them, "Be fruitful, and multiply, and re- plenish the earth, and subdue it: and have dominion over the fish of the sea, and over the fowl of the air, and over every living thing that moveth upon the earth."

And God said, "Behold, I have given you every herb bearing seed, which is upon the face of all the earth, and every tree, in the which is the fruit of a tree yielding seed; to you it shall be for meat. And to every beast of the earth, and to every fowl of the air, and to every thing that creepeth upon the earth, wherein there is life, I have given every green herb for meat": and it was so. And God saw every thing that he had made, and, behold, it was very good. And the evening and the morning were the sixth day.

Thus the heavens and the earth were finished, and all the host of them. And on the seventh day God ended his work which he had made; and he rested on the seventh day from all his work which he had made. And God blessed the seventh day, and sanctified it: because that in it he had rested from all his work which God created and made.

These are the generations of the heavens and of the earth when they were created, in the day that the LORD God made the earth and the heavens. And every plant of the field before it was in the earth, and every herb of the field before it grew: for the LORD God had not caused it to rain upon the earth, and there was not a man to till the ground. But there went up a mist from the earth, and watered the whole face of the ground. And the LORD God formed man of the dust of the ground, and breathed into his nostrils the breath of life; and man became a living soul.

And the LORD God planted a garden eastward in Eden; and there he put the man whom he had formed. And out of the ground made the LORD God to grow every tree that is pleasant to the sight, and good for food; the tree of life also in the midst of the garden, and the tree of knowledge of good and evil. And a river went out of Eden to water a garden; and from thence it was parted, and became into four heads. The name of the first is Pison: that is it which compasseth the whole land of Havilah, where there is gold; and the gold of that land is good: there is bdellium and the onyx stone. And the name of the second river is Gihon: the same is it that compasseth the whole land of Ethiopia. And the name of the third river is Hiddekel: that is it which goeth toward the east of Assyria. And the fourth river is Euphrates. And the LORD God took the man, and put him into the garden of Eden to dress it and to keep it. And the LORD God commanded the man, saying, "Of every tree of the garden thou mayest freely eat: But of the tree of the knowledge of good and evil, thou shalt not eat of it: for in the day that thou eatest thereof thou shalt surely die."

And the LORD God said, "It is not good that the man should be alone; I will make an help meet for him." And out of the ground the LORD God formed every beast of the field, and every fowl of the air; and brought them unto Adam to see what he would call them: and whatsoever Adam called every living creature, that was the name thereof. And Adam gave names to all cattle, and to the fowl of the air, and to every beast of the field; but for Adam there was not found an help meet for him. And the LORD God caused a deep sleep to fall upon Adam, and he slept: and he took one of his ribs, and closed up the flesh instead thereof. And the rib, which the LORD God had taken from man, made he a woman, and brought her unto the man. And Adam said, "This is now bone of my bones, and flesh of my flesh: she shall be called Woman, because she was taken out of Man. Therefore shall a man leave his father and his mother, and shall cleave unto his wife: and they shall be one flesh." And they were both naked, the man and his wife, and were not ashamed.

Now the serpent was more subtle than any beast of the field which the LORD God had made. And he said unto the woman, "Yea, hath God said, 'Ye shall not eat of every tree of the garden'?" And the woman said unto the serpent, "We may eat of the fruit of the trees of the garden: But of the fruit of the tree which is in the midst of the garden God hath said, 'Ye shall not eat of it, neither shall ye touch it, lest ye die.' " And the serpent said unto the woman, "Ye shall not surely die: For God doth know that in the day ye eat thereof, then your eyes shall be opened, and ye shall be as gods, knowing good and evil." And when the woman saw that the tree was good for food, and that it was pleasant to the eyes, and a tree to be desired to make one wise, she took of the fruit thereof, and did eat, and gave also unto her husband with her and he did eat. And the eyes of them both were opened, and they knew that they were naked; and they sewed fig leaves together, and made themselves aprons.

And they heard the voice of the LORD God walking in the garden in the cool of the day: and Adam and his wife hid themselves from the presence of the LORD God amongst the trees of the garden. And the LORD God called unto Adam, and said unto him, "Where art thou?" And he said, "I heard thy voice in the garden, and I was afraid, because I was naked; and I hid myself." And he said, "Who told thee that thou wast naked? Hast thou eaten of the tree, whereof I commanded thee that thou shouldest not eat?" And the man said, "The woman whom thou gavest to be with me, she gave me of the tree, and I did eat." And the LORD God said unto the woman, "What is this that thou hast done?" And the woman said, "The serpent beguiled me, and I did eat." And the LORD God said unto the serpent, "Because thou hast done this, thou art cursed above all cattle, and above every beast of the field; upon thy belly shalt thou go, and dust shalt thou eat all the days of thy life: And I will put enmity between thee and the woman, and between thy seed and her seed; it shall bruise thy head, and thou shalt bruise his heel." Unto the woman he said, "I will greatly multiply thy sorrow and thy conception; in sorrow thou shalt bring forth children; and thy desire shall be to thy husband, and he shall rule over thee." And unto Adam he said, "Because thou hast harkened unto the voice of thy wife, and hast eaten of the tree, of which I commanded thee, saying 'Thou shalt not eat of it': cursed is the ground for thy sake; in sorrow shalt thou eat of it all the days of thy life; thorns also and thistles shall it bring forth to thee; and thou shalt eat the herb of the field; in the sweat of thy face shalt thou eat bread, till thou return unto the ground; for out of it wast thou taken: for dust thou art and unto dust shalt thou return." And Adam called his wife's name Eve; because she was the mother of all living. Unto Adam also and to his wife did the LORD God make coats of skins, and clothed them.

And the LORD God said, "Behold, the man is become as one of us, to know good and evil: and now, lest he put forth his hand, and take also of the tree of life, and eat, and live for ever": Therefore the LORD God sent him forth from the garden of Eden, to till the ground from whence he was taken. So he drove out the man; and he placed at the east of the garden of Eden Cherubim and a flaming sword which turned every way, to keep the way of the tree of life.

. . .

[Abraham and Isaac]

And it came to pass after these things that God did tempt Abraham, and said unto him, "Abraham." And he said, "Behold, here I am." And He said, "Take now thy son, thine only son Isaac, whom thou lovest, and get thee into the land of Moriah, and offer him there for a burnt offering upon one of the mountains which I will tell thee of."

And Abraham rose up early in the morning, and saddled his ass, and took two of his young men with him, and Isaac his son, and clove the wood for the burnt offering, and rose up and went unto the place of which God had told him. Then on the third day Abraham lifted up his eyes and saw the place afar off. And Abraham said unto his young men, "Abide ye here with the ass and I and the lad will go yonder and worship, and come again to you."

And Abraham took the wood of the burnt offering and laid it upon Isaac his son, and he took the fire in his hand, and a knife, and they went both of them together. And Isaac spake unto Abraham his father and said, "My father." And he said, "Here I am, my son." And he said, "Behold the fire and the wood, but where is the lamb for a burnt offering?" And Abraham said, "My son, God will provide Himself a lamb for a burnt offering." So they went, both of them together. And they came to the place which God had told him of, and Abraham built an altar there, and laid wood in order, and bound Isaac his son, and laid him on the altar upon the wood. And Abraham stretched forth his hand, and took the knife to slay his son.

And the Angel of the Lord called unto him out of heaven and said, "Abraham, Abraham." And he said, "Here am I." And He said, "Lay not thine hand upon the lad, neither do thou anything to him, for now I know that thou fearest God seeing thou has not withheld thy son, thine only son, from me." And Abraham lifted up his eyes, and looked, and beheld behind him a ram caught in a thicket by his horns. And Abraham went and took the ram, and offered him up for a burnt offering in the stead of his son.

Exodus

In the third month, when the children of Israel were gone forth out of the land of Egypt, the same day came they into the wilderness of Sinai. For they were departed from Rephidim, and were come to the desert of Sinai, and had pitched in the wilderness; and there Israel camped before the mount. And Moses went up unto God, and the LORD called unto him out of the mountain, saying, "Thus shalt thou say to the house of Jacob, and tell the children of Israel; 'Ye have seen what I did unto the Egyptians, and how I bare you on eagles' wings, and brought you unto myself. Now, therefore, if ye will obey my voice indeed, and keep my covenant, then ye shall be a peculiar treasure unto me above all people: for all the earth is mine: And ye be unto me a kingdom of priests, and an holy nation.' These are the words which thou shalt speak unto the children of Israel."

And Moses came and called for the elders of the people, and laid before their faces all these words which the LORD commanded him. And all the people answered together, and said, "All that the LORD hath spoken we will do." And Moses returned the words of the people unto the LORD. And the LORD said unto Moses, "Lo, I come unto thee in a thick cloud, that the people may hear when I speak with thee, and believe thee for ever." And Moses told the words of the people unto the LORD.

And the LORD said unto Moses, "Go unto the people, and sanctify them to day and to morrow, and let them wash their clothes. And be ready against the third day: for the third day the LORD will come down in the sight of all the people upon mount Sinai. And thou shalt set bounds unto the people round about, saying 'Take heed to yourselves, that ye go not up into the mount, or touch the border of it: whosoever toucheth the mount shall be surely put to death: There shall not an hand touch it, but he shall surely be stoned, or shot through; whether it be beast or man, it shall not live: when the trumpet soundeth long, they shall come up to the mount."

And Moses went down from the mount unto the people, and sanctified the people; and they washed their clothes. And he said unto the people, "Be ready against the third day: come not at your wives."

And it came to pass on the third day in the morning, that there were thunders and lightnings, and a thick cloud upon the mount, and the voice of the trumpet exceeding loud; so that all the people that was in the camp trembled. And Moses brought forth the people out of the camp to meet with God; and they stood at the nether part of the mount. And mount Sinai was altogether on a smoke, because the LORD descended upon it in fire: and the smoke thereof ascended as the smoke of a furnace, and the whole mount

Chapters 19; 20:1–17; 21:1–25.

quaked greatly. And when the voice of the trumpet sounded long, and waxed louder and louder, Moses spake and God answered him by a voice. And the LORD came down upon the mount Sinai, on the top of the mount: and the LORD called Moses up to the top of the mount; and Moses went up. And the LORD said unto Moses, "Go down, charge the people, lest they break through unto the LORD to gaze, and many of them perish. Let the priests also, which come near to the LORD, sanctify themselves, lest the LORD break forth upon them." And Moses said unto the LORD, "The people cannot come up to mount Sinai: for thou chargest us, saying, 'Set bounds about the mount, and sanctify it.' " And the LORD said unto him, "Away, get thee down, and thou shalt come up, thou, and Aaron with thee: but let not the priests and the people break through to come up unto the LORD, lest he break forth upon them." So Moses went down unto the people, and spake unto them.

And God spake all these words, saying, "I am the LORD thy God, which have brought thee out of the land of Egypt, out of the house of bondage. Thou shalt have no other gods before me. Thou shall not make unto thee any graven image, or any likeness of any thing that is in heaven above, or that is in the earth beneath, or that is in the water under the earth. Thou shalt not bow down thyself to them, nor serve them: for I the LORD thy God am a jealous God, visiting the iniquity of the fathers upon the children unto the third and fourth generation of them that hate me: And shewing mercy unto thousands of them that love me, and keep my commandments. Thou shalt not take the name of the LORD thy God in vain; for the LORD will not hold him guiltless that taketh his name in vain. Remember the sabbath day, to keep it holy. Six days shalt thou labour, and do all thy work: But the seventh day is the sabbath of the LORD thy God; in it thou shalt not do any work, thou, nor thy son, nor thy daughter, thy manservant, nor thy maidservant, nor thy cattle, nor the stranger that is within thy gates. For in six days the LORD made heaven and earth, the sea, and all that in them is, and rested the seventh day: wherefore the LORD blessed the sabbath day, and hallowed it. Honour thy father and thy mother: that thy days may be long upon the land which the LORD thy God giveth thee. Thou shalt not kill. Thou shalt not commit adultery. Thou shalt not steal. Thou shalt not bear false witness against thy neighbour. Thou shalt not covet thy neighbour's house, thou shalt not covet thy neighbour's wife, nor his manservant, nor his maidservant, nor his ox, nor his ass, nor any thing that is thy neighbour's.

. . .

"Now these are the judgments which thou shalt set before them.

"If thou buy an Hebrew servant, six years he shall serve: and in the seventh he shall go out free for nothing. If he came in by himself, he shall go out by himself: if he were married, then his wife shall go out with him. If his master have given him a wife, and she have borne him sons or daughters; the wife and her children shall be her master's, and he shall go out by himself.

And if the servant shall plainly say, 'I love my master, my wife, and my children; I will not go out free': Then his master shall bring him unto the judges; he shall also bring him to the door, or unto the door post; and his master shall bore his ear through with an awl; and he shall serve him for ever.

"And if a man sell his daughter to be a maidservant, she shall not go out as the menservants do. If she please not her master, who hath betrothed her to himself, then shall he let her be redeemed: to sell her unto a strange nation he shall have no power, seeing he hath dealt deceitfully with her. And if he have betrothed her unto his son, he shall deal with her after the manner of daughters. If he take him another wife; her food, her raiment, and her duty of marriage, shall he not diminish. And if he do not these three unto her, then shall she go out free without money.

"He that smiteth a man so that he die, shall be surely put to death. And if a man lie not in wait, but God deliver him into his hand; then I will appoint thee a place whither he shall flee. But if a man come presumptuously upon his neighbour to slay him with guile; thou shalt take him from mine altar, and he may die.

"And he that smiteth his father, or his mother, shall be surely put to death.

"And he that stealeth a man, and selleth him, or if he be found in his hand, he shall surely be put to death.

"And he that curseth his father, or his mother, shall surely be put to death.

"And if men strive together, and one smite another with a stone, or with his fist, and he die not, but keepeth his bed: If he rise again, and walk abroad upon his staff, then shall he that smote him be quit: only he shall pay for the loss of his time, and shall cause him to be thoroughly healed.

"And if a man smite his servant, or his maid, with a rod, and he die under his hand; he shall be surely punished. Notwithstanding, if he continue a day or two, he shall not be punished: for he is his money.

"If men strive, and hurt a woman with child, so that her fruit depart from her, and yet no mischief follow: he shall be surely punished, according as the woman's husband will lay upon him; and he shall pay as the judges determine. And if any mischief follow, then thou shalt give life for life. Eye for eye, tooth for tooth, hand for hand, foot for foot. Burning for burning, wound for wound, stripe for stripe."

The Book of Job

There was a man in the land of Uz, whose name was Job; and that man was perfect and upright, and one that feared God, and eschewed evil. And there were born unto him seven sons and three daughters. His substance also was seven thousand sheep, and three thousand camels, and five hun-

Chapters 1; 2:1–10; 21:7–15; 23:2–12; 38; 40:1–14; 42:1–6, 10–17.

dred yoke of oxen, and five hundred she asses, and a very great household; so that this man was the greatest of all the men of the east. And his sons went and feasted in their houses, every one his day; and sent and called for their three sisters to eat and to drink with them. And it was so, when the days of their feasting were gone about, that Job sent and sanctified them, and rose up early in the morning, and offered burnt offerings according to the number of them all: for Job said, "It may be that my sons have sinned, and cursed God in their hearts." Thus did Job continually.

Now there was a day when the sons of God came to present themselves before the LORD, and Satan came also among them. And the LORD said unto Satan, "Whence comest thou?" Then Satan answered the LORD, and said, "From going to and fro in the earth, and from walking up and down in it." And the LORD said unto Satan, "Hast thou considered my servant Job, that there is none like him in the earth, a perfect and an upright man, one that feareth God, and escheweth evil?" Then Satan answered the LORD, and said, "Doth Job fear God for nought? Hast not thou made an hedge about him, and about his house, and about all that he hath on every side? Thou hast blessed the work of his hands, and his substance is increased in the land. But put forth thine hand now, and touch all that he hath and he will curse thee to thy face." And the LORD said unto Satan, "Behold, all that he hath is in thy power; only upon himself put not forth thine hand." So Satan went forth from the presence of the LORD.

And there was a day when his sons and his daughters were eating and drinking wine in their eldest brother's house. And there came a messenger unto Job, and said, "The oxen are plowing, and the asses feeding beside them: And the Sabeans fell upon them, and took them away; yea, they have slain the servants with the edge of the sword; and I only am escaped alone to tell thee." While he was yet speaking there came also another, and said, "The fire of God is fallen from heaven, and hath burned up the sheep, and the servants, and consumed them; and I only escaped alone to tell thee." While he was yet speaking, there came also another, and said, "The Chaldeans made out three bands, and fell upon the camels, and have carried them away, yea, and slain the servants with the edge of the sword; and I only am escaped alone to tell thee." While he was yet speaking, there came also another, and said, "Thy sons and thy daughters were eating and drinking wine in their eldest brother's house: And, behold, there came a great wind from the wilderness, and smote the four corners of the house, and it fell upon the young men, and they are dead; and I only am escaped alone to tell thee." Then Job arose, and rent his mantle, and shaved his head, and fell down upon the ground, and worshipped. And said, "Naked came I out of my mother's womb, and naked shall I return thither: the LORD gave, and the LORD hath taken away; blessed be the name of the LORD." In all this Job sinned not, nor charged God foolishly.

Again there was a day when the sons of God came to present themselves before the LORD, and Satan came also among them to present himself before the LORD. And the LORD said unto Satan, "From whence comest thou?" And Satan answered the LORD, and said, "From going to and fro in the earth, and from walking up and down in it." And the LORD said unto Satan, "Hath thou considered my servant Job, that there is none like him in the earth, a perfect and an upright man, one that feareth God, and escheweth evil? And still he holdeth fast his integrity, although thou movedst me against him, to destroy him without cause." And Satan answered the LORD, and said, "Skin for skin, yea, all that a man hath will he give for his life. But put forth thine hand now, and touch his bone and his flesh, and he will curse thee to thy face." And the LORD said unto Satan, "Behold, he is in thine hand; but save his life."

So went Satan forth from the presence of the LORD, and smote Job with sore boils from the sole of his foot unto his crown. And he took him a potsherd to scrape himself withal; and he sat down among the ashes.

Then said his wife unto him, "Dost thou still retain thine integrity? Curse God, and die." But he said unto her. "Thou speakest as one of the foolish women speaketh. What? shall we receive good at the hand of God, and shall we not receive evil?" In all this did not Job sin with his lips.

.   .   .

[*And Job spake, and said*] "My soul is weary of my life; I will leave my complaint upon myself; I will speak in the bitterness of my soul, I will say unto God, 'Do not condemn me; shew me wherefore thou contendest with me. Is it good unto thee that thou shouldest oppress, that thou shouldest despise the work of thine hands, and shine upon the counsel of the wicked? Hast thou eyes of flesh? or seest thou as man seeth? Are thy days as the days of man? Are thy years as man's days, that thou enquirest after mine iniquity, and searchest after my sin? Thou knowest that I am not wicked; and there is none that can deliver out of thine hand. Thine hands have made me and fashioned me together round about; yet thou dost destroy me. Remember, I beseech thee, that thou hast made me as the clay; and wilt thou bring me into dust again? Hast thou not poured me out as milk, and curdled me like cheese? Thou hast clothed me with skin and flesh, and hast fenced me with bones and sinews. Thou hast granted me life and favour, and thy visitation hath preserved my spirit. And these things hast thou hid in thine heart; I know that this is with thee.

'If I sin, then thou markest me, and thou wilt not acquit me from mine iniquity. If I be wicked, woe unto me; and if I be righteous, yet will I not lift up my head. I am full of confusion; therefore see thou mine affliction; for it increaseth. Thou huntest me as a fierce lion: and again thou shewest thyself marvellous upon me. Thou renewest thy witnesses against me, and increasest thine indignation upon me; changes and war are against me. Wherefore then hast thou brought me forth out of the womb? Oh that I had given up the ghost, and no eye had seen me! I should have been as though I had not been; I should have been carried from the womb to the grave. Are not my days few? Cease then, and let me alone, that I may take comfort a little, before I go whence I shall not return, even to the land of darkness and the shadow of death; a land of darkness, as darkness itself; and of the shadow of death, without any order, and where the light is as darkness.'

·   ·   ·

"Wherefore do the wicked live, become old, yea, are mighty in power? Their seed is established in their sight with them, and their offspring before their eyes. Their houses are safe from fear, neither is the rod of God upon them. Their bull gendereth, and faileth not; their cow calveth, and casteth not her calf. They send forth their little ones like a flock, and their children dance. They take the timbrel and harp, and rejoice at the sound of the organ. They spend their days in wealth, and in a moment go down to the grave. Therefore they say unto God, 'Depart from us; for we desire not the knowledge of thy ways. What is the Almighty, that we should serve him? And what profit should we have, if we pray unto him?'

·   ·   ·

"Even to day is my complaint bitter: my stroke is heavier than my groaning. Oh that I knew where I might find him! that I might come even unto his seat! I would order my cause before him, and fill my mouth with arguments. I would know the words which he would answer me, and understand what he would say unto me. Will he plead against me with his great power? No, but he would put strength in me. There the righteous might dispute with him; so should I be delivered for ever from my judge. Behold, I go forward, but he is not there; and backward, but I cannot perceive him: On the left hand, where he doth work, but I cannot behold him: he hideth himself on the right hand, that I cannot see him. But he knoweth the way that I take: when he hath tried me, I shall come forth as gold. My foot hath held his steps, his way have I kept, and not declined. Neither have I gone back from the commandment of his lips; I have esteemed the words of his mouth more than my necessary food."

·   ·   ·

Then the LORD answered Job out of the whirlwind, and said "Who is this that darkeneth counsel by words without knowledge? Gird up now thy loins like a man; for I will demand of thee, and answer thou me. Where wast thou when I laid the foundations of the earth? Declare, if thou hast understanding. Who hath laid the measures thereof, if thou knowest? Or who hath stretched the line upon it? Whereupon are the foundations thereof fastened?

Or who laid the corner stone thereof; when the morning stars sang together, and all the sons of God shouted for joy? Or who shut up the sea with doors, when it brake forth, as if it had issued out of the womb? When I made the cloud the garment thereof, and thick darkness a swaddling band for it, and brake up for it my decreed place, and set bars and doors, and said, 'Hitherto shalt thou come, but no further: and here shall thy proud waves be stayed'? Hast thou commanded the morning since thy days; and caused the dayspring to know his place; that it might take hold of the end of the earth, that the wicked might be shaken out of it? It is turned as clay to the seal; and they stand as a garment. And from the wicked their light is withholden, and the high arm shall be broken. Hast thou entered into the springs of the sea? Or hast thou walked in the search of the depth? Have the gates of death been opened unto thee? Or hast thou seen the doors of the shadow of death? Hast thou perceived the breadth of the earth? Declare if thou knowest it all.

"Where is the way where light dwelleth? And as for darkness, where is the place thereof, that thou shouldest take it to the bound thereof, and that thou shouldest know the paths to the house thereof? Knowest thou it, because thou wast then born? Or because the number of thy days is great? Hast thou entered into the treasures of the snow? Or hast thou seen the treasures of the hail, which I have reserved against the time of trouble, against the day of battle and war? By what way is the light parted, which scattereth the east wind upon the earth? Who hath divided a watercourse for the overflowing of waters, or a way for the lightning or thunder; to cause it to rain on the earth, where no man is; on the Wilderness, wherein there is no man; to satisfy the desolate and waste ground; and to cause the bud of the tender herb to spring forth? Hath the rain a father? Or who hath begotten the drops of dew? Out of whose womb came the ice? And the hoary frost of heaven, who hath gendered it? The waters are hid as with a stone, and the face of the deep is frozen.

"Canst thou bind the sweet influences of Pleiades, or loose the bonds of Orion? Canst thou bring forth Massaroth in his season? Or canst thou guide Arcturus with his sons? Knowest thou the ordinances of heaven? Canst thou set the dominion thereof in the earth? Canst thou lift up thy voice to the clouds, that abundance of waters may cover thee? Canst thou send lightnings that they may go, and say unto thee, 'Here we are'? Who hath put wisdom in the inward parts? Or who hath given understanding to the heart? Who can number the clouds in wisdom? Or who can stay the bottles of heaven, when the dust groweth into hardness, and the clods cleave fast together? Wilt thou hunt the prey for the lion? Or fill the appetite of the young lions, when they couch in their dens, and abide in the covert to lie in wait? Who provideth for the raven his food? When his young ones cry unto God, they wander for lack of meat."

. . .

Moreover, the LORD answered Job, and said, "Shall he that contendeth with the Almighty instruct him? He that reproveth God, let him answer it."

Then Job answered the LORD, and said, "Behold, I am vile; what shall I answer thee? I will lay mine hand upon my mouth. Once have I spoken; but I will not answer: yea, twice, but I will proceed no further."

Then answered the LORD unto Job out of the whirlwind, and said, "Gird up thy loins now like a man: I will demand of thee, and declare thou unto me. Wilt thou also disannul my judgment? Wilt thou condemn me, that thou mayest be righteous? Hast thou an arm like God? Or canst thou thunder with a voice like him? Deck thyself now with majesty and excellency; and array thyself with glory and beauty. Cast abroad the rage of thy wrath: and behold every one that is proud, and abase him. Look on every one that is proud, and bring him low; and tread down the wicked in their place. Hide them in the dust together; and bind their faces in secret. Then will I also confess unto thee that thine own right hand can save thee."

·   ·   ·

Then Job answered the LORD, and said, "I know that thou canst do every thing, and that no thought can be witholden from thee. Who is he that hideth counsel without knowledge? Therefore have I uttered that I understood not; things too wonderful for me, which I knew not. Hear, I beseech thee, and I will speak: I will demand of thee, and declare thou unto me. I have heard of thee by the hearing of the ear: but now mine eye seeth thee. Wherefore I abhor myself, and repent in dust and ashes."

·   ·   ·

And the LORD turned the captivity of Job, when he prayed for his friends: also the LORD gave Job twice as much as he had before. Then came there unto him all his brethren, and all his sisters, and all they that had been of his acquaintance before, and did eat bread with him in his house: and they bemoaned him, and comforted him over all the evil that the LORD had brought upon him: every man also gave him a piece of money, and every one an earring of gold. So the LORD blessed the latter end of Job more than his beginning: for he had fourteen thousand sheep, and six thousand camels, and a thousand yoke of oxen, and a thousand she asses. He had also seven sons and three daughters. And he called the name of the first, Jemima; and the name of the second, Kezia; and the name of the third, Kerenhappuch. And in all the land were no women found so fair as the daughters of Job: and their father gave them inheritance among their brethren. After this lived Job an hundred and forty years, and saw his sons, and his son's sons, even four generations. So Job died, being old and full of days.

ΠΕΡΙΚΛΗΣ
ΞΑΝΘΙΠΠΟΥ
ΑΘΗΝΑΙΟΣ

This Greek bust memorializes Pericles, one of Athens' greatest statesmen and a leader of the Athenians during the Peloponnesian War. He is shown wearing his battle helmet.

GREECE

The center of classical Greek civilization was the *polis*, or city-state. Ancient Greece was divided into hundreds of *poleis*, each a tiny unit politically independent and culturally unique. Athens, for example, one of the largest of the *poleis*, had a population of just over three hundred thousand and an area roughly equal to that of Rhode Island. The forms of government varied widely from *polis* to *polis*, and even within the same *polis* at different times.

By far the most important form—at least as far as later Western history is concerned—was the Athenian democracy, particularly as it flourished in the Age of Pericles during the fifth century B.C. Although the Athenians shared with us the belief that democratic government means rule by the people, their democracy differed from ours in one important respect: Because of the very size and complexity of the nation in which we live, we must exercise our sovereignty through representatives, but in Athens the people could rule directly. Every adult male citizen was a member of the Assembly, the sole legislative body of the city-state. From the ranks of the assembly a Council of Five Hundred was chosen annually to supervise the administrative affairs of the *polis*. From the Council, in turn, an executive committee of fifty was chosen to conduct the day-to-day business of administration for a term lasting one-tenth of one year. One member of this committee was then chosen as chairman for each twenty-four-hour period. Since all these selections were made by lot, any citizen of the *polis* might be called on to serve as the chief administrative officer of Athens for a day.

But for the average Greek male the *polis* was more than just the political unit within which he happened to live. It was also the center of his social, intellectual, aesthetic, and religious life. Aristotle, in the beginning of his work on political theory, the *Politics*, takes a typically Greek attitude toward the *polis* in a statement usually translated, "Man is a political animal." But in the original Greek this statement reads, "Man is by nature an animal intended to live in a *polis*." Here Aristotle is implying that only within the *polis* can one live a truly human life. The philosopher Socrates expressed a similar feeling toward the *polis*. Though unjustly condemned to death by an Athenian court, he rejected a chance to escape from prison, insisting that, because he owed his very being to his *polis*, he must accept whatever Athens decreed for him, even execution.

One of the finest appreciations of Athens's achievements was made by a great Athenian leader—Pericles. The occasion was a funeral oration that he delivered in 431 B.C. just outside the city walls, to honor the Athenian soldiers who had fallen in the first year of the Peloponnesian War. For Pericles, the highest honor that could be paid to the dead was to say that they "were worthy of Athens." By Athens he referred not just to the city in which they had lived, but to the way of life that they, as Athenians, had shared. The

Athenians, Pericles told his audience, are "lovers of the beautiful." The truth of Pericles's claim was self-evident; anyone listening to him could have verified it simply by gazing back at the city itself. The view would have been dominated by the Acropolis, rising high above the plain and crowned with temples. In the center stood the Parthenon, completed less than a decade before Pericles delivered his oration. Dedicated to Athena, goddess of wisdom and protectress of Athens, the Parthenon embodied an ideal of beauty based on architectural symmetry or balance.

The ideal of balance so completely realized in the Parthenon was pursued in all forms of Greek art. And, outside the aesthetic realm, it was an ideal that pervaded Greek civilization. Just as Greeks experienced pleasure in a well-proportioned building, so they delighted in a well-balanced personality and tried in their lives to follow the path of moderation. The life of moderation is summed up in Aristotle's famous doctrine of the Golden Mean, perhaps the most clearly reasoned defense ever made of a civilization and its way of life. Behind the Greek ideal of moderation and balance stands the belief that the universe is a rational order, operating according to fixed laws. The orderliness of the universe, the Greeks argued, is good; hence order anywhere must be good, and disorder evil. When the Greeks translated this belief into aesthetic and moral terms, they found their ideal of beauty in the symmetry of the Parthenon, and their conception of the good life in the moderation of the Golden Mean.

Because they were convinced that humans are capable of reasoning, the Greeks concluded that we can comprehend the world in which we live. The Greeks' faith in reason permeated their entire intellectual and cultural life. To take the most obvious example, it made possible their phenomenal achievements in science. Earlier civilizations in the ancient Near East had developed advanced technologies, but the Greeks were the first theoretical scientists in Western history. What set them apart from their predecessors was their ability to generalize, to see an object or event not simply in its individuality but as an instance of a universal rule or pattern. They were led to seek the general laws governing natural events—in other words, to become theoretical scientists—by their conviction that people can use their reasoning powers to discover the rational pattern of the universe.

This tendency to generalize shows itself over and over again in Greek thought. Thucydides, in the introduction to his *History of the Peloponnesian War*, states that he is interested not just in recounting the events of the war but in revealing the general pattern of war. The Greek tragedians attempted to trace the patterns in which universal moral law revealed itself in people's lives. Greek generalization reached its highest expression in Plato's Form of the Good, one of the most difficult concepts in Western thought. For Plato's belief that the Form of the Good is the heart of reality is really a philosophical formulation of the Greek faith in the ultimate unity, rationality, and goodness of the universe.

LOOKING AHEAD

As you learn about Greek civilization, consider the following questions.

1. Describe the values with which the Greeks imbued the city-state or *polis*. What did the members of a *polis* owe to the community? What did the community owe to its members?

2. How did male domination of Greek society shape Greek civilization? What role, if any, did women play in Greek public life?

3. Describe the qualities of a Greek hero. What personal characteristics did the Greeks admire most?

Sophocles

The life of Sophocles, the tragic poet, spanned the fifth century B.C. Born in 496 B.C., he was just old enough to remember the battle of Marathon, and in 480 he led a chorus of Athenian youths in the ceremonial celebration of the naval victory at Salamis. He reached the height of his creative powers in the Age of Pericles. His *Antigone* was produced in 441, three years before the completion of the Parthenon, and his *King Oedipus* was produced around 430, the year before the death of Pericles. Sophocles lived to witness the end of the Golden Age, dying in 406 at the age of ninety, two years before the Athenian defeat in the Peloponnesian War.

To understand the tragic drama *Antigone*, we must realize that, according to Greek religion, the body of a deceased person had to be buried before the soul could enter Hades. Thus, Antigone had a sacred duty to bury her brother, a duty that she believed took precedence over all others, even obedience to the decrees of the state. Creon, on the other hand, placed political considerations before religious, thus looked on Polynices as an enemy, to be treated as such. The tragedy, therefore, can be interpreted as a clash between divine law, championed by Antigone, and human or political law, championed by Creon. Such an interpretation, however, does not exhaust the meaning of the play, which may also be viewed as a dramatic portrayal of human character. The tragedy that destroys Antigone and Creon becomes the inevitable result of a clash between two strong-willed individuals, each dedicated to an ideal in itself good, but neither willing either to compromise that ideal or to recognize the merits of the opposed ideal.

Consider the following questions as you study the text below.

1. How might Antigone have defined honor and duty? How might her definitions have differed from those of Creon?

2. Does it matter to the play that Antigone is a woman? How might the play have been different if Antigone was a man?

Antigone

CHARACTERS

ISMENE ⎱
ANTIGONE ⎰ *daughters of Oedipus*

CREON, *King of Thebes*

HAEMON, *son of* CREON

TEIRESIAS, *a blind prophet*

SENTRY

MESSENGER

EURYDICE, *wife of* CREON

CHORUS *of Theban elders*

　　　King's attendants

　　　Queen's attendants

BOY *leading* TEIRESIAS

SOLDIERS

SCENE: Before the Palace at Thebes

Enter ISMENE *from the central door of the Palace.* ANTIGONE *follows, anxious and urgent; she closes the door carefully, and comes to join her sister.*

ANTIGONE:　O sister! Ismene dear, dear sister Ismene!
　　You know how heavy the hand of God is upon us;
　　How we who are left must suffer for our father, Oedipus.
　　There is no pain, no sorrow, no suffering, no dishonour
　　We have not shared together, you and I.
　　And now there is something more. Have you heard this order,
　　This latest order that the King has proclaimed to the city?
　　Have you heard how our dearest are being treated like enemies?
ISMENE:　I have heard nothing about any of those we love,
　　Neither good nor evil—not, I mean, since the death
　　Of our two brothers, both fallen in a day.
　　The Argive army, I hear, was withdrawn last night.
　　I know no more to make me sad or glad.
ANTIGONE:　I thought you did not. That's why I brought you out here,
　　Where we shan't be heard, to tell you something alone.
ISMENE:　What is it, Antigone? Black news, I can see already.
ANTIGONE:　O Ismene, what do you think? Our two dear brothers . . .
　　Creon has given funeral honours to one,
　　And not to the other; nothing but shame and ignominy.
　　Eteocles has been buried, they tell me, in state,

Sophocles, "Antigone," in *The Theban Plays*, trans. E. F. Watling (Harmondsworth, Middlesex: Penguin Books, Ltd., 1947), pp. 126–62. Courtesy of Penguin Books, Ltd.

With all honourable observances due to the dead.
But Polynices, just as unhappily fallen—the order
Says he is not to be buried, not to be mourned;
To be left unburied, unwept, a feast of flesh
For keen-eyed carrion birds. The noble Creon!
It is against you and me he has made this order.
Yes, against me. And soon he will be here himself
To make it plain to those that have not heard it,
And to enforce it. This is no idle threat;
The punishment for disobedience is death by stoning.
So now you know. And now is the time to show
Whether or not you are worthy of your high blood.

ISMENE: My poor Antigone, if this is really true,
What more can I do, or undo, to help you?

ANTIGONE: Will you help me? Will you do something with me? Will you?

ISMENE: Help you do what, Antigone? What do you mean?

ANTIGONE: Would you help me lift the body . . . you and me?

ISMENE: You cannot mean . . . to bury him? Against the order?

ANTIGONE: Is he not my brother, and yours, whether you like it
Or not? I shall never desert him, never.

ISMENE: How could you dare, when Creon has expressly forbidden it?

ANTIGONE: He has no right to keep me from my own.

ISMENE: O sister, sister, do you forget how our father
Perished in shame and misery, his awful sin
Self-proved, blinded by his own self-mutilation?
And then his mother, his wife—for she was both—
Destroyed herself in a noose of her own making
And now our brothers, both in a single day
Fallen in an awful exaction of death for death.
Blood for blood, each slain by the other's hand.
Now we two left; and what will be the end of us,
If we transgress the law and defy our king?
O think, Antigone; we are women; it is not for us
To fight against men; our rulers are stronger than we,
And we must obey in this, or in worse than this.
May the dead forgive me, I can do no other
But as I am commanded; to do more is madness.

ANTIGONE: No; then I will not ask you for your help.
Nor would I thank you for it, if you gave it.
Go your own way: I will bury my brother;
And if I die for it, what happiness!
Convicted of reverence—I shall be content
To lie beside a brother whom I love.
We have only a little time to please the living.
But all eternity to love the dead.

There I shall lie for ever. Live, if you will;
Live, and defy the holiest laws of heaven.
ISMENE: I do not defy them; but I cannot act
Against the State. I am not strong enough.
ANTIGONE: Let that be your excuse, then I will go
And heap a mound of earth over my brother.
ISMENE: I fear for you, Antigone; I fear—
ANTIGONE: You need not fear for me. Fear for yourself.
ISMENE: At least be secret. Do not breathe a word.
I'll not betray your secret.
ANTIGONE: Publish it
To all the world! Else I shall hate you the more.
ISMENE: Your heart burns! Mine is frozen at the thought.
ANTIGONE: I know my duty, where true duty lies.
ISMENE: If you can do it; but you're bound to fail.
ANTIGONE: When I have tried and failed, I shall have failed.
ISMENE: No sense in starting on a hopeless task.
ANTIGONE: Oh, I shall hate you if you talk like that!
And he will hate you, rightly. Leave me alone
With my own madness. There is no punishment
Can rob me of my honourable death.
ISMENE: Go then, if you are determined, to your folly.
But remember that those who love you . . . love you still.

ISMENE *goes into the Palace.*

ANTIGONE *leaves the stage by a side exit. Enter the* CHORUS *of Theban elders.*

CHORUS: Hail the sun! the brightest of all that ever
Dawned on the City of Seven Gates, City of Thebes!
Hail the golden dawn over Dirce's river
Rising to speed the flight of the white invaders
Homeward in full retreat!
The army of Polynices was gathered against us,
In angry dispute his voice was lifted against us.
Like a ravening bird of prey he swooped around us
With white wings flashing, with flying plumes,
With armed hosts ranked in thousands.
At the threshold of seven gates in a circle of blood
His swords stood round us, his jaws were opened against us;
But before he could taste our blood, or consume us with fire,
He fled, fled with the roar of the dragon behind him
And thunder of war in his ears.
The Father of Heaven abhors the proud tongue's boasting;
He marked the oncoming torrent, the flashing stream
Of their golden harness, the clash of their battle gear;
He heard the invader cry Victory over our ramparts,
And smote him with fire to the ground.

Down to the ground from the crest of his hurricane onslaught
He swung, with the fiery brands of his hate brought low:
Each and all to their doom of destruction appointed
By the god that fighteth for us.
Seven invaders at seven gates, seven defenders
Spoiled of their bronze for a tribute to Zeus; save two
Luckless brothers in one fight matched together
And in one death laid low.
Great is the victory, great be the joy
In the city of Thebes, the city of chariots.
Now is the time to fill the temples
With glad thanksgiving for warfare ended;
Shake the ground with the night-long dances.
Bacchus afoot and delight abounding.
But see, the King comes here,
Creon, the son of Menoeceus,
Whom the gods have appointed for us
In our recent change of fortune.
What matter is it, I wonder,
That has led him to call us together
By his special proclamation?
The central door is opened, and CREON *enters.*

CREON: My councillors: now that the gods have brought our city
Safe through a storm of trouble to tranquillity,
I have called you especially out of all my people
To conference together, knowing that you
Were loyal subjects when King Laius reigned,
And when King Oedipus so wisely ruled us,
And again, upon his death, faithfully served
His sons, till they in turn fell—both slayers, both slain,
Both stained with brother-blood, dead in a day—
And I, their next of kin, inherited
The throne and kingdom which I now possess.
No other touchstone can test the heart of a man,
The temper of his mind and spirit, til he be tried
In the practice of authority and rule.
For my part, I have always held the view,
And hold it still, that a king whose lips are sealed
By fear, unwilling to seek advice, is damned.
And no less damned is he who puts a friend
Above his country: I have no good word for him.
As God above is my witness, who sees all,
When I see any danger threatening my people,
Whatever it may be, I shall declare it.

No man who is his country's enemy
Shall call himself my friend. Of this I am sure—
Our country is our life; only when she
Rides safely, have we any friends at all.
Such is my policy for our common weal.
In pursuance of this, I have made a proclamation
Concerning the sons of Oedipus, as follows:
Eteocles, who fell fighting in defense of the city,
Fighting gallantly, is to be honoured with burial
And with all the rites due to the noble dead.
The other—you know whom I mean—his brother Polynices,
Who came back from exile intending to burn and destroy
His fatherland and the gods of his fatherland,
To drink the blood of his kin, to make them slaves—
He is to have no grave, no burial,
No mourning from anyone; it is forbidden.
He is to be left unburied, left to be eaten
By dogs and vultures, a horror for all to see.
I am determined that never, if I can help it,
Shall evil triumph over good. Alive
Or dead, the faithful servant of his country
Shall be rewarded.

CHORUS: Creon, son of Menoeceus,
You have given your judgment for the friend and for the enemy.
As for those that are dead, so for us who remain,
Your will is law.

CREON: See then that it be kept.

CHORUS: My lord, some younger would be fitter for that task.

CREON: Watchers are already set over the corpse.

CHORUS: What other duty then remains for us?

CREON: Not to connive at any disobedience.

CHORUS: If there were any so mad as to ask for death—

CREON: Ay, that is the penalty. There is always someone
Ready to be lured to ruin by hope of gain.

He turns to go. A SENTRY *enters from the side of the stage.* CREON *pauses at the palace door.*

SENTRY: My lord: if I am out of breath, it is not from haste.
I have not been running. On the contrary, many a time
I stopped to think and loitered on the way,
Saying to myself, 'Why hurry to your doom,
Poor fool?' and then I said 'Hurry, you fool.
If Creon hears this from another man,
Your head's as good as off.' So here I am,
As quick as my unwilling haste could bring me;

    In no great hurry, in fact. So now I am here . . .
    But I'll tell my story . . . though it may be nothing after all.
    And whatever I have to suffer, it can't be more
    Than what God wills, so I cling to that for my comfort.
CREON: Good heavens, man, whatever is the matter?
SENTRY: To speak of myself first—I never did it, sir;
    Nor saw who did; no one can punish me for that.
CREON: You tell your story with a deal of artful precaution.
    It's evidently something strange.
SENTRY: It is. So strange, it's very difficult to tell.
CREON: Well, out with it, and let's be done with you.
SENTRY: It's this, sir, The corpse . . . someone has just
    Buried it and gone. Dry dust over the body
    They scattered, in the manner of holy burial.
CREON: What! Who dared to do it?
SENTRY: I don't know, sir.
    There was no sign of a pick, no scratch of a shovel;
    The ground was hard and dry—no trace of a wheel;
    Whoever it was has left no clues behind him.
    When the sentry on the first watch showed it us,
    We were amazed. The corpse was covered from sight—
    Not with a proper grave—just a layer of earth—
    As it might be, the act of some pious passer-by.
    There were no tracks of an animal either, a dog
    Or anything that might have come and mauled the body.
    Of course we all started pitching in to each other,
    Accusing each other, and might have come to blows,
    With no one to stop us; for anyone might have done it,
    But it couldn't be proved against him, and all denied it.
    We were all ready to take hot iron in hand
    And go through fire and swear by God and heaven
    We hadn't done it, nor knew of anyone
    That could have thought of doing it, much less done it.
    Well, we could make nothing of it. Then one of our men
    Said something that made all our blood run cold—
    Something we could neither refuse to do, nor do,
    But at our own risk. What he said was 'This
    Must be reported to the King: we can't conceal it.'
    So it was agreed. We drew lots for it, and I,
    Such is my luck, was chosen. So here I am,
    As much against my will as yours, I'm sure;
    A bringer of bad news expects no welcome.
CHORUS: My lord, I fear—I feared it from the first—
    That this may prove to be an act of the gods.

CREON: Enough of that! Or I shall lose my patience.
     Don't talk like an old fool, old though you be.
     Blasphemy, to say the gods could give a thought
     To carrion flesh! Held him in high esteem,
     I suppose, and buried him like a benefactor—
     A man who came to burn their temples down,
     Ransack their holy shrines, their land, their laws?
     Is that the sort of man you think gods love?
     Not they. There's a party of malcontents
     In the city, rebels against my word and law,
     Shakers of heads in secret, impatient of rule:
     They are the people, I see it well enough,
     Who have bribed their instruments to do this thing.
     Money! Money's the curse of man, none greater.
     That's what wrecks cities, banishes men from home,
     Tempts and deludes the most well-meaning soul,
     Pointing out the way to infamy and shame.
     Well, they shall pay for their success.
     (*To the* SENTRY)
     See to it!
     See to it, you! Upon my oath, I swear,
     As Zeus is my god above: either you find
     The perpetrator of this burial
     And bring him here into my sight, or death—
     No, not your mere death shall pay the reckoning,
     But, for a living lesson against such infamy,
     You shall be racked and tortured till you tell
     The whole truth of this outrage; so you may learn
     To seek your gain where gain is yours to get,
     Not try to grasp it everywhere. In wickedness
     You'll find more loss than profit.
SENTRY: May I say more?
CREON: No more; each word you say but stings me more.
SENTRY: Stings in your ears, sir, or in your deeper feelings?
CREON: Don't bandy words, fellow, about my feelings.
SENTRY: Though I offend your ears, sir, it is not I
     But he that's guilty that offends your soul.
CREON: Oh, born to argue, were you?
SENTRY: Maybe so;
     But still not guilty in this business.
CREON: Doubly so, if you have sold your soul for money.
SENTRY: To think that thinking men should think so wrongly!
CREON: Think what you will. But if you fail to find
     The doer of this deed, you'll learn one thing:

Ill-gotten gain brings no one any good.
He goes into the Palace.
SENTRY: Well, heaven send they find him.
But whether or no,
They'll not find me again, that's sure. Once free,
Who never thought to see another day,
I'll thank my lucky stars, and keep away.
Exit.
CHORUS: Wonders are many on earth, and the greatest of these
Is man, who rides the ocean and takes his way
Through the deeps, through wind-swept valleys of perilous seas
That surge and sway.
He is master of ageless Earth, to his own will bending
The immortal mother of gods by the sweat of his brow,
As year succeeds to year; with toil unending
Of mule and plough.
He is lord of all things living: birds of the air,
Beasts of the field, all creatures of sea and land
He taketh, cunning to capture and ensnare
With sleight of hand;
Hunting the savage beast from the upland rocks,
Taming the mountain monarch in his lair,
Teaching the wild horse and the roaming ox
His yoke to bear.
The use of language, the wind-swift motion of brain
He learnt; found out the laws of living together
In cities, building him shelter against the rain
And wintry weather.
There is nothing beyond his power. His subtlety
Meeteth all chance, all danger conquereth.
For every ill he hath found its remedy,
Save only death.
O wondrous subtlety of man, that draws
To good or evil ways! Great honour is given
And power to him who upholdeth his country's laws.
And the justice of heaven.
But he that, too rashly daring, walks in sin
In solitary pride to his life's end,
At door of mine shall never enter in
To call me friend.
(*Severally, seeing some persons approach from a distance*)
O gods! a wonder to see!
Surely it cannot be—
It is no other—

Antigone!
Unhappy maid—
Unhappy Oedipus' daughter; it is she they bring.
Can she have rashly disobeyed
The order of our King?

Enter the SENTRY, *bringing* ANTIGONE *guarded by two more soldiers.*

SENTRY: We've got her. Here's the woman that did the deed.
We found her in the act of burying him. Where's the King?

CHORUS: He is just coming out of the palace now.

Enter CREON.

CREON: What's this? What am I just in time to see?

SENTRY: My lord, an oath's a very dangerous thing.
Second thoughts may prove us liars. Not long since
I swore I wouldn't trust myself again
To face your threats; you gave me a drubbing the first time.
But there's no pleasure like an unexpected pleasure,
Not by a long way. And so I've come again,
Though against my solemn oath. And I've brought this lady,
Who's been caught in the act of setting that grave in order.
And no casting lots for it this time—the prize is mine.
And no one else's. So take her; judge and convict her.
I'm free, I hope, and quit of the horrible business.

CREON: How did you find her? Where have you brought her from?

SENTRY: She was burying the man with her own hands, and that's the truth.

CREON: Are you in your senses? Do you know what you are saying?

SENTRY: I saw her myself, burying the body of the man
Whom you said not to bury. Don't I speak plain?

CREON: How did she come to be seen and taken in the act?

SENTRY: It was this way.
After I got back to the place,
With all your threats and curses ringing in my ears,
We swept off all the earth that covered the body,
And left it a sodden naked corpse again;
Then sat up on the hill, on the windward side,
Keeping clear of the stench of him, as far as we could;
All of us keeping each other up to the mark.
With pretty sharp speaking, not to be caught napping this time.
So this went on some hours, till the flaming sun
Was high in the top of the sky, and the heat was blazing.
Suddenly a storm of dust, like a plague from heaven,
Swept over the ground, stripping the trees stark bare,
Filling the sky; you had to shut your eyes
To stand against it. When at last it stopped,
There was the girl, screaming like an angry bird,

When it finds its nest left empty and little ones gone.
Just like that she screamed, seeing the body
Naked, crying and cursing the ones that had done it.
Then she picks up the dry earth in her hands,
And pouring out of a fine bronze urn she's brought
She makes her offering three times to the dead.
Soon as we saw it, down we came and caught her.
She wasn't at all frightened. And so we charged her
With what she'd done before, and this. She admitted it,
I'm glad to say—though sorry too, in a way.
It's good to save your own skin, but a pity
To have to see another get into trouble,
Whom you've no grudge against. However, I can't say
I've ever valued anyone else's life
More than my own, and that's the honest truth.

CREON (*to* ANTIGONE):   Well, what do you say—you, hiding your head there:
   Do you admit, or do you deny the deed?
ANTIGONE: I do admit it. I do not deny it.
CREON (*to the* SENTRY):   You—you may go. You are discharged from blame.
   Exit SENTRY.
   Now tell me, in as few words as you can,
   Did you know the order forbidding such an act?
ANTIGONE: I knew it, naturally. It was plain enough.
CREON: And yet you dared to contravene it?
ANTIGONE: Yes.
   That order did not come from God. Justice,
   That dwells with the gods below, knows no such law.
   I did not think your edicts strong enough
   To overrule the unwritten unalterable laws
   Of God and heaven, you being only a man.
   They are not of yesterday or to-day, but everlasting,
   Though where they came from, none of us can tell.
   Guilty of their transgression before God
   I cannot be, for any man on earth.
   I knew that I should have to die, of course,
   With or without your order. If it be soon,
   So much the better. Living in daily torment
   As I do, who would not be glad to die?
   This punishment will not be any pain,
   Only if I had let my mother's son
   Lie there unburied, then I could not have borne it.
   This I can bear. Does that seem foolish to you?
   Or is it you that are foolish to judge me so?
CHORUS: She shows her father's stubborn spirit: foolish

Not to give way when everything's against her.
CREON:　Ah, but you'll see. The over-obstinate spirit
　　Is soonest broken; as the strongest iron will snap
　　If over-tempered in the fire to brittleness.
　　A little halter is enough to break
　　The wildest horse. Proud thoughts do not sit well
　　Upon subordinates. This girl's proud spirit
　　Was first in evidence when she broke the law;
　　And now, to add insult to her injury,
　　She gloats over her deed. But, as I live,
　　She shall not flout my orders with impunity
　　My sister's child—ay, were she even nearer,
　　Nearest and dearest, she should not escape
　　Full punishment—she, and her sister too,
　　Her partner, doubtless, in this burying.
　　Let her be fetched! She was in the house just now;
　　I saw her, hardly in her right mind either.
　　Often the thoughts of those who plan dark deeds
　　Betray themselves before the deed is done.
　　The criminal who being caught still tries
　　To make a fair excuse, is damned indeed.
ANTIGONE:　Now you have caught, will you do more than kill me?
CREON:　No, nothing more; that is all I could wish.
ANTIGONE:　Why then delay? There is nothing that you can say
　　That I should wish to hear, as nothing I say
　　Can weigh with you. I have given my brother burial.
　　What greater honour could I wish? All these
　　Would say that what I did was honourable,
　　But fear locks up their lips. To speak and act
　　Just as he likes is a king's prerogative.
CREON:　You are wrong. None of my subjects thinks as you do.
ANTIGONE:　Yes, sir, they do; but dare not tell you so.
CREON:　And you are not only alone, but unashamed.
ANTIGONE:　There is no shame in honouring my brother.
CREON:　Was not his enemy, who died with him, your brother?
ANTIGONE:　Yes, both were brothers, both of the same parents.
CREON:　You honour one, and so insult the other.
ANTIGONE:　He that is dead will not accuse me of that.
CREON:　He will, if you honour him no more than the traitor.
ANTIGONE:　It was not a slave, but his brother, that died with him.
CREON:　Attacking his country, while the other defended it.
ANTIGONE:　Even so, we have a duty to the dead.
CREON:　Not to give equal honour to good and bad.
ANTIGONE:　Who knows? In the country of the dead that may be the law.

CREON: An enemy can't be a friend, even when dead.

ANTIGONE: My way is to share my love, not share my hate.

CREON: Go then, and share your love among the dead.
  We'll have no woman's law here, while I live.
  Enter ISMENE *from the Palace.*

CHORUS: Here comes Ismene, weeping
  In sisterly sorrow; a darkened brow,
  Flushed face, and the fair cheek marred
  With flooding rain.

CREON: You crawling viper! Lurking in my house
  To suck my blood! Two traitors unbeknown
  Plotting against my throne. Do you admit
  To a share in this burying, or deny all knowledge?

ISMENE: I did it—yes—if she will let me say so.
  I am as much to blame as she is.

ANTIGONE: No.
  That is not just. You would not lend a hand
  And I refused your help in what I did.

ISMENE: But I am not ashamed to stand beside you
  Now in the hour of trial, Antigone.

ANTIGONE: Whose was the deed, Death and the dead are witness.
  I love no friend whose love is only words.

ISMENE: O sister, sister, let me share your death,
  Share in the tribute of honour to him that is dead.

ANTIGONE: You shall not die with me. You shall not claim
  That which you would not touch. One death is enough.

ISMENE: How can I bear to live, if you must die?

ANTIGONE: Ask Creon. Is not he the one you care for?

ISMENE: You do yourself no good to taunt me so.

ANTIGONE: Indeed no: even my jests are bitter pains.

ISMENE: But how, O tell me, how can I still help you?

ANTIGONE: Help yourself. I shall not stand in your way.

ISMENE: For pity, Antigone—can I not die with you?

ANTIGONE: You chose; life was your choice, when mine was death.

ISMENE: Although I warned you that it would be so.

ANTIGONE: Your way seemed right to some, to others mine.

ISMENE: But now both in the wrong, and both condemned.

ANTIGONE: No, no. You live. My heart was long since dead,
  So it was right for me to help the dead.

CREON: I do believe the creatures both are mad,
  One lately crazed, the other from her birth.

ISMENE: Is it not likely, sir? The strongest mind
  Cannot but break under misfortune's blows.

CREON: Yours did, when you threw in your lot with hers.

ISMENE: How could I wish to live without my sister?

CREON: You have no sister. Count her dead already.

ISMENE: You could not take her—kill your own son's bride?

CREON: Oh, there are other fields for him to plough.

ISMENE: No truer troth was ever made than theirs.

CREON: No son of mine shall wed so vile a creature.

ANTIGONE: O Haemon, can your father spite you so?

CREON: You and your paramour, I hate you both.

CHORUS: Sir, would you take her from your own son's arms?

CREON: Not I, but death shall take her.

CHORUS: Be it so. Her death, it seems, is certain.

CREON: Certain it is.

No more delay. Take them, and keep them within—
The proper place for women. None so brave
As not to look for some way of escape
When they see life stand face to face with death.
The women are taken away.

CHORUS: Happy are they who know not the taste of evil.
From a house that heaven hath shaken
The curse departs not
But falls upon all of the blood,
Like the restless surge of the sea when the dark storm drives
The black sand hurled from the deeps
And the Thracian gales boom down
On the echoing shore.
In life and in death is the house of Labdacus stricken.
Generation to generation,
With no atonement,
It is scourged by the wrath of a god.
And now for the dead dust's sake is the light of promise,
The tree's last root, crushed out
By pride of heart and the sin
Of presumptuous tongue.
For what presumption of man can match thy power,
O Zeus, that art not subject to sleep or time
Or age, living for ever in bright Olympus?
To-morrow and for all time to come,
As in the past,
This law is immutable:
For mortals greatly to live is greatly to suffer.
Roving ambition helps many a man to good,
And many it falsely lures to light desires,
Till failure trips them unawares, and they fall
On the fire that consumes them. Well was it said,

Evil seems good
To him who is doomed to suffer;
And short is the time before that suffering comes. But here comes Haemon,
Your youngest son.
Does he come to speak his sorrow
For the doom of his promised bride,
The loss of his marriage hopes?

CREON: We shall know it soon, and need no prophet to tell us.

Enter HAEMON.

Son, you have heard, I think, our final judgment
On your late betrothed. No angry words, I hope?
Still friends, in spite of everything, my son?

HAEMON: I am your son, sir; by your wise decisions
My life is ruled, and them I shall always obey.
I cannot value any marriage-tie
Above your own good guidance.

CREON: Rightly said.
Your father's will should have your heart's first place.
Only for this do fathers pray for sons
Obedient, loyal, ready to strike down
Their father's foes, and love their fathers' friends.
To be the father of unprofitable sons
Is to be the father of sorrows, a laughingstock
To all one's enemies. Do not be fooled, my son,
By lust and the wiles of a woman. You'll have bought
Cold comfort if your wife's a worthless one.
No wound strikes deeper than love that is turned to hate.
This girl's an enemy; away with her,
And let her go and find a mate in Hades.
Once having caught her in a flagrant act—
The one and only traitor in our State—
I cannot make myself a traitor too;
So she must die. Well may she pray to Zeus,
The God of Family Love. How, if I tolerate
A traitor at home, shall I rule those abroad?
He that is a righteous master of his house
Will be a righteous statesman. To transgress
Or twist the law to one's own pleasures, presume
To order where one should obey, is sinful,
And I will have none of it.
He whom the State appoints must be obeyed
To the smallest matter, be it right—or wrong.
And he that rules his household, without a doubt,
Will make the wisest king, or, for that matter,

The staunchest subject. He will be the man
You can depend on in the storm of war,
The faithfullest comrade in the day of battle.
There is no more deadly peril than disobedience;
States are devoured by it, homes laid in ruins,
Armies defeated, victory turned to rout.
While simple obedience saves the lives of hundreds
Of honest folk. Therefore, I hold to the law,
And will never betray it—least of all for a woman.
Better be beaten, if need be, by a man,
Than let a woman get the better of us.

CHORUS: To me, as far as an old man can tell,
It seems your Majesty has spoken well.

HAEMON: Father, man's wisdom is the gift of heaven,
The greatest gift of all. I neither am
Nor wish to be clever enough to prove you wrong,
Though all men might not think the same as you do.
Nevertheless, I have to be your watchdog,
To know what others say and what they do,
And what they find to praise and what to blame.
Your frown is a sufficient silencer
Of any word that is not for your ears.
But I hear whispers spoken in the dark;
On every side I hear voices of pity
For this poor girl, doomed to the cruellest death,
And most unjust, that ever woman suffered
For an honourable action—burying a brother
Who was killed in a battle, rather than leave him naked
For dogs to maul and carrion birds to peck at.
Has she not rather earned a crown of gold?—
Such is the secret talk about the town.
Father, there is nothing I can prize above
Your happiness and well-being. What greater good
Can any son desire? Can any father
Desire more from his son? Therefore I say,
Let not your first thought be your only thought.
Think if there cannot be some other way.
Surely, to think your own the only wisdom,
And yours the only word, the only will,
Betrays a shallow spirit, an empty heart.
It is no weakness for the wisest man
To learn when he is wrong, know when to yield.
So, on the margin of a flooded river
Trees bending to the torrent live unbroken,

While those that strain against it are snapped off.
A sailor has to tack and slacken sheets
Before the gale, or find himself capsized.
So, father, pause, and put aside your anger.
I think, for what my young opinion's worth,
That, good as it is to have infallible wisdom,
Since this is rarely found, the next best thing
Is to be willing to listen to wise advice.

CHORUS: There is something to be said, my lord, for his point of view,
And for yours as well; there is much to be said on both sides.

CREON: Indeed! Am I to take lessons at my time of life
From a fellow of his age?

HAEMON: No lesson you need to be ashamed of.
It isn't a question of age, but of right and wrong.

CREON: Would you call it right to admire an act of disobedience?

HAEMON: Not if the act were also dishonourable.

CREON: And was not this woman's action dishonourable?

HAEMON: The people of Thebes think not.

CREON: The people of Thebes!
Since when do I take my orders from the people of Thebes?

HAEMON: Isn't that rather a childish thing to say?

CREON: No, I am king, and responsible only to myself.

HAEMON: A one-man state? What sort of a state is that?

CREON: Why, does not every state belong to its ruler?

HAEMON: You'd be an excellent king—on a desert island.

CREON: Of course, if you're on the woman's side—

HAEMON: No, no—
Unless you're the woman. It's you I'm fighting for.

CREON: What, villain, when every word you speak is against me?

HAEMON: Only because I know you are wrong, wrong.

CREON: Wrong? To respect my own authority?

HAEMON: What sort of respect tramples on all that is holy?

CREON: Despicable coward! No more will than a woman!

HAEMON: I have nothing to be ashamed of.

CREON: Yet you plead her cause.

HAEMON: No, yours, and mine, and that of the gods of the dead.

CREON: You'll never marry her this side of death.

HAEMON: Then, if she dies, she does not die alone.

CREON: Is that a threat, you impudent—

HAEMON: Is it a threat
To try to argue against wrong-headedness?

CREON: You'll learn what wrong-headedness is, my friend, to your cost.

HAEMON: O father, I could call you mad, were you not my father.

CREON: Don't toady me, boy; keep that for your lady-love.

HAEMON: You mean to have the last word then?
CREON: I do.
  And what is more, by all the gods in heaven,
  I'll make you sorry for your impudence.
  (Calling to those within)
  Bring out that she-devil, and let her die
  Now, with her bridegroom by to see it done!
HAEMON: That sight I'll never see. Nor from this hour
  Shall you see me again. Let those that will
  Be witness of your wickedness and folly.
  Exit.
CHORUS: He is gone, my lord, in very passionate haste.
  And who shall say what a young man's wrath may do?
CREON: Let him go! Let him do! Let him rage as never man raged,
  He shall not save those women from their doom.
CHORUS: You mean, then sire, to put them both to death?
CREON: No, not the one whose hand was innocent.
CHORUS: And to what death do you condemn the other?
CREON: I'll have her taken to a desert place
  Where no man ever walked, and there walled up
  Inside a cave, alive, with food enough
  To acquit ourselves of the blood-guiltiness
  That else would lie upon our commonwealth.
  There she may pray to Death, the god she loves,
  And ask release from death; or learn at last
  What hope there is for those who worship death.
  Exit.
CHORUS: Where is the equal of Love?
  Where is the battle he cannot win,
  The power he cannot outmatch?
  In the farthest corners of earth, in the midst of the sea,
  He is there; he is here
  In the bloom of a fair face
  Lying in wait;
  And the grip of his madness
  Spares not god or man, marring the righteous man,
  Driving his soul in mazes of sin
  And strife, dividing a house,
  For the light that burns in the eyes of a bride of desire
  Is a fire that consumes.
  At the side of the great gods
  Aphrodite immortal
  Works her will upon all.
  The doors are open and ANTIGONE *enters, guarded.*

But here is a sight beyond all bearing,
At which my eyes cannot but weep;
Antigone forth faring
To her bridal-bower of endless sleep.

ANTIGONE: You see me, countrymen, on my last journey,
Taking my last leave of the light of day;
Going to my rest, where death shall take me
Alive across the silent river.
No wedding-day; no marriage-music;
Death will be all my bridal dower.

CHORUS: But glory and praise go with you, lady.
To your resting-place. You go with your beauty
Unmarred by the hand of consuming sickness,
Untouched by the sword, living and free,
As none other that ever died before you.

ANTIGONE: The daughter of Tantalus, a Phrygian maid,
Was doomed to a piteous death on the rock
Of Sipylos, which embraced and imprisoned her,
Merciless as the ivy; rain and snow
Beat down upon her, mingled with her tears,
As she wasted and died. Such was her story,
And such is the sleep that I shall go to.

CHORUS: She was a goddess of immortal birth,
And we are mortals; the greater the glory,
To share the fate of a god-born maiden,
A living death, but a name undying.

ANTIGONE: Mockery, mockery! By the gods of our fathers,
Must you make me a laughing-stock while I yet live?
O lordly sons of my city! O Thebes!
Your valley of rivers, your chariots and horses!
No friend to weep at my banishment
To a rock-hewn chamber of endless durance,
In a strange cold tomb alone to linger
Lost between life and death for ever.

CHORUS: My child, you have gone your way
To the outermost limit of daring
And have stumbled against Law enthroned.
This is the expiation
You must make for the sin of your father.

ANTIGONE: My father—the thought that sears my soul—
The unending burden of the house of Labdacus.
Monstrous marriage of mother and son . . .
My father . . . my parents . . . O hideous shame!
Whom now I follow, unwed, curse-ridden,

Doomed to this death by the ill-starred marriage
That marred my brother's life.
CHORUS: An act of homage is good in itself, my daughter;
But authority cannot afford to connive at disobedience.
You are the victim of your own self-will.
ANTIGONE: And must go the way that lies before me.
No funeral hymn; no marriage-music;
No sun from this day forth, no light,
No friend to weep at my departing.
Enter CREON.
CREON: Weeping and wailing at the door of death!
There'd be no end of it, if it had force
To buy death off. Away with her at once,
And close her up in rock-vaulted tomb.
Leave her and let her die, if die she must,
Or live within her dungeon. Though on earth
Her life is ended from this day, her blood
Will not be on our hands.
ANTIGONE: So to my grave.
My bridal-bower, my everlasting prison,
I go, to join those many of my kinsmen
Who dwell in the mansions of Persephone,
Last and unhappiest, before my time.
Yet I believe my father will be there
To welcome me, my mother greet me gladly,
And you, my brother, gladly see me come.
Each one of you my hands have laid to rest,
Pouring the due libations on your graves.
It was by this service to your dear body, Polynices,
I earned the punishment which now I suffer,
Though all good people know it was for your honour.
O but I would not have done the forbidden thing
For any husband or for any son.
For why? I could have had another husband
And by him other sons, if one were lost;
But, father and mother lost, where would I get
Another brother? For thus preferring you
My brother, Creon condemns me and hales me away,
Never a bride, never a mother, unbefriended,
Condemned alive to solitary death.
What law of heaven have I transgressed? What god
Can save me now? What help or hope have I,
In whom devotion is deemed sacrilege?
If this is God's will, I shall learn my lesson

In death; but if my enemies are wrong,
    I wish them no worse punishment than mine.
CHORUS: Still the same tempest in the heart
    Torments her soul with angry gusts.
CREON: The more cause then have they that guard her
    To hasten their work; or they too suffer.
CHORUS: Alas, that word had the sound of death.
CREON: Indeed there is no more to hope for.
ANTIGONE: Gods of our fathers, my city, my home,
    Rulers of Thebes! Time stays no longer.
    Last daughter of your royal house
    Go I, his prisoner, because I honoured
    Those things to which honour truly belongs.
        ANTIGONE *is led away*.
CHORUS: Such as the fate, my child, of Danae
    Locked in a brazen bower,
    A prison secret as a tomb,
    Where was no day.
    Daughter of kings, her royal womb
    Garnered the golden shower
    Of life from Zeus. So strong is Destiny,
    No wealth, no armoury, no tower,
    No ship that rides the angry sea
    Her mastering hand can stay.
    And Dryas' son, the proud Edonian king,
    Pined in a stony cell
    At Dionysus' bidding pent
    To cool his fire
    Till, all his full-blown passion spent,
    He came to know right well
    What god his ribald tongue was challenging
    When he would break the fiery spell
    Of the wild Maenad's revelling
    And vex the Muses' choir. It was upon the side
    Of Bosporus, where the Black Rocks stand
    By Thracian Salmydessus over the twin tide,
    That Thracian Ares laughed to see
    How Phineus' angry wife most bloodily
    Blinded his two sons' eyes that mutely cried
    For vengeance; crazed with jealousy
    The woman smote them with the weaving-needle in her hand.
    Forlorn they wept away
    Their sad step-childhood's misery
    Predestined from their mother's ill-starred marriage-day.

She was of old Erechtheid blood,
Cave-dwelling daughter of the North-wind God;
On rocky steeps, as mountain ponies play,
The wild winds nursed her maidenhood.
On her, my child, the grey Fates laid hard hands, as upon thee.
Enter TEIRESIAS, *the blind prophet, led by a boy.*

TEIRESIAS: Gentlemen of Thebes, we greet you, my companion and I,
Who share one pair of eyes on our journeys together—
For the blind man goes where his leader tells him to.

CREON: You are welcome, father Teiresias. What's your news?

TEIRESIAS: Ay, news you shall have; and advice, if you can heed it.

CREON: There was never a time when I failed to heed it, father.

TEIRESIAS: And thereby have so far steered a steady course.

CREON: And gladly acknowledge the debt we owe to you.

TEIRESIAS: Then mark me now; for you stand on a razor's edge.

CREON: Indeed? Grave words from your lips, good priest. Say on.

TEIRESIAS: I will; and show you all that my skill reveals,
At my seat of divination, where I sit
These many years to read the signs of heaven,
An unfamiliar sound came to my ears
Of birds in vicious combat, savage cries
In strange outlandish language, and the whirr
Of flapping wings; from which I well could picture
The gruesome warfare of their deadly talons.
Full of foreboding then I made the test
Of sacrifice upon the altar fire.
There was no answering flame; only rank juice
Oozed from the flesh and dripped among the ashes,
Smouldering and sputtering; the gall vanished in a puff,
And the fat ran down and left the haunches bare.
Thus (through the eyes of my young acolyte,
Who sees for me, that I may see for others)
I read the signs of failure in my quest.
And why? The blight upon us is your doing
The blood that stains altars and our shrines,
The blood that dogs and vultures have licked up,
It is none other than the blood of Oedipus
Spilled from the veins of his ill-fated son.
Our fires, our sacrifices, and our prayers
The gods abominate. How should the birds
Give any other than ill-omened voices,
Gorged with the dregs of blood that man has shed?
Mark this, my son: all men fall into sin.
But sinning, he is not for ever lost

Hapless and helpless, who can make amends
And has not set his face against repentance.
Only a fool is governed by self-will. Pay to the dead his due. Wound not the
     fallen.
It is no glory to kill and kill again.
My words are for your good, as is my will,
And should be acceptable, being for your good.
CREON: You take me for your target, reverend sir.
Like all the rest. I know your art of old,
And how you make your commodity
To trade and traffic in for your advancement.
Trade as you will; but all the silver of Sardis
And all the gold of India will not buy
A tomb for yonder traitor. No. Let the eagles
Carry his carcass up to the throne of Zeus;
Even that would not be sacrilege enough
To frighten me from my determination
Not to allow this burial. No man's act
Has power enough to pollute the goodness of God.
But great and terrible is the fall, Teiresias,
Of mortal men who seek their own advantage
By uttering evil in the guise of good.
TEIRESIAS: Ah, is there any wisdom in the world?
CREON: Why, what is the meaning of that wide-flung taunt?
TEIRESIAS: What prize outweighs the priceless worth of prudence?
CREON: Ay, what indeed? What mischief matches the lack of it?
TEIRESIAS: And there you speak of your own symptom, sir.
CREON: I am loth to pick a quarrel with you, priest.
TEIRESIAS: You do so, calling my divination false.
CREON: I say all prophets seek their own advantage.
TEIRESIAS: All kings, say I, seek gain unrighteously.
CREON: Do you forget to whom you say it?
TEIRESIAS: No.
Our king and benefactor, by my guidance.
CREON: Clever you may be, but not therefore honest.
TEIRESIAS: Must I reveal my yet unspoken mind?
CREON: Reveal all; but expect no gain from it.
TEIRESIAS: Does that still seem to you my motive, then?
CREON: Nor is my will for sale, sir, in your market.
TEIRESIAS: Then hear this. Ere the chariot of the sun
Has rounded once or twice his wheeling way,
You shall have given a son of your own loins
To death, in payment for death—two debts to pay:
One for the life that you have sent to death,

The life you have abominably entombed;
One for the dead still lying above ground
Unburied, unhonoured, unblest by the gods below.
You cannot alter this. The gods themselves
Cannot undo it. It follows of necessity
From what you have done. Even now the avenging Furies,
The hunters of hell that follow and destroy,
Are lying in wait for you, and will have their prey,
When the evil you have worked for others fall on you.
Do I speak this for my gain? The time shall come,
And soon, when your house will be filled with the lamentation
Of men and women; and every neighboring city
Will be goaded to fury against you, for upon them
Too the pollution falls when the dogs and vultures
Bring the defilement of blood to their hearths and altars.
I have done. You pricked me, and these shafts of wrath
Will find their mark in your heart. You cannot escape
The sting of their sharpness.
Lead me home, my boy.
Let us leave him to vent his anger on younger ears,
Or school his mind and tongue to a milder mood
Than that which now possesses him.
Lead on.
Exit.

CHORUS: He has gone, my lord. He has prophesied terrible things.
And for my part, I that was young and now am old
Have never known his prophecies proved false.

CREON: It is true enough; and my heart is torn in two.
It is hard to give way, and hard to stand and abide
The coming of the curse. Both ways are hard.

CHORUS: It would be advised, my good lord, Creon—

CREON: What must I do? Tell me, and I will do it.

CHORUS: Release the woman from her rocky prison.
Set up a tomb for him that lies unburied.

CREON: Is it your wish that I consent to this?

CHORUS: It is, and quickly. The gods do not delay
The stroke of their swift vengeance on the sinner.

CREON: It is hard, but I must do it. Well I know
There is no armour against necessity.

CHORUS: Go. Let your own hand do it, and no other.

CREON: I will go this instant.
Slaves there! One and all.
Bring spades and mattocks out on the hill!
My mind is made; 'twas I imprisoned her,

And I will set her free. Now I believe
It is by the laws of heaven that man must live.
Exit.
CHORUS: O Thou whose name is many.
Son of the Thunderer, dear child of his Cadmean bride,
Whose hand is mighty
In Italia,
In the hospitable valley of Eleusis,
And in Thebes,
The mother-city of thy worshippers,
Where sweet Ismenus gently watereth
The soil whence sprang the harvest of the dragon's teeth;
Where torches on the crested mountains gleam,
And by Castalia's stream
The nymph-train in thy dance rejoices,
When from the ivy-tangled glens
Of Nysa and from vine-clad plains
Thou comest to Thebes where the immortal voices
Sing thy glad strains. Thebes, where thou lovest most to be,
With her, thy mother, the fire-stricken one,
Sickens for need of thee.
Healer of all her ills;
Come swiftly o'er the high Parnassian hills,
Come o'er the sighing sea.
The stars, whose breath is fire, delight
To dance for thee; the echoing night
Shall with thy praises ring.
Zeus-born, appear! With Thyiads revelling
Come, bountiful
Iacchus, King!
Enter a MESSENGER, *from the side of the stage.*
MESSENGER: Hear, men of Cadmus' city, hear and attend,
Men of the house of Amphion, people of Thebes!
What is the life of man? A thing not fixed
For good or evil, fashioned for praise or blame.
Chance raises a man to the heights, chance casts him down,
And none can foretell what will be from what is.
Creon was once an enviable man;
He saved his country from her enemies,
Assumed the sovereign power, and bore it well,
The honoured father of a royal house.
Now all is lost; for life without life's joys
Is living death; and such a life is his.
Riches and rank and show of majesty

And state, where no joy is, are empty, vain
And unsubstantial shadows, of no weight
To be compared with happiness of heart.

CHORUS: What is your news? Disaster in the royal house?

MESSENGER: Death; and the guilt of it on living heads.

CHORUS: Who dead? And by what hand?

MESSENGER: Haemon is dead. Slain by his own—

CHORUS: His father?

MESSENGER: His own hand.
His father's act it was that drove him to it.

CHORUS: Then all has happened as the prophet said.

MESSENGER: What's next to do, your worships will decide.

The Palace door opens.

CHORUS: Here comes the Queen, Eurydice.
Poor soul,
It may be she has heard about her son.

Enter EURYDICE, *attended by women.*

EURYDICE: My friends, I heard something of what you were saying
As I came to the door. I was on my way to prayer
At the temple of Pallas, and had barely turned the latch
When I caught your talk of some near calamity.
I was sick with fear and reeled in the arms of my women.
But tell me what is the matter, what have you heard?
I am not unacquainted with grief, and I can bear it.

MESSENGER: Madam, it was I that saw it, and will tell you all.
To try to make it any lighter now
Would be to prove myself a liar. Truth
Is always best.
It was thus. I attended your husband,
The King, to the edge of the field where lay the body
Of Polynices, in pitiable state, mauled by the dogs.
We prayed for him to the Goddess of the Roads, and to Pluto,
That they might have mercy upon him. We washed the remains
In holy water, and on a fire of fresh-cut branches
We burned all that was left of him, and raised
Over his ashes a mound of his native earth.
That done, we turned towards the deep rock-chamber
Of the maid that was married with death.
Before we reached it,
One that stood near the accursed place had heard
Loud cries of anguish, and came to tell King Creon.
As he approached, came strange uncertain sounds
Of lamentation, and he cried out aloud:
'Unhappy wretch! Is my foreboding true?

Is this the most sorrowful journey that ever I went?
My son's voice greets me. Go, some of you, quickly
Through the passage where the stones are thrown apart,
Into the mouth of the cave, and see if it be
My son, my own son Haemon that I hear.
If not, I am the sport of gods.'
We went
And looked, as bidden by our anxious master.
There in the furthest corner of the cave
We saw her hanging by the neck. The rope
Was of the woven linen of her dress.
And, with his arms about her, there stood he
Lamenting his lost bride, his luckless love,
His father's cruelty.
When Creon saw them,
Into the cave he went, moaning piteously.
'O my unhappy boy,' he cried again,
'What have you done? What madness brings you here
To your destruction? Come away, my son,
My son, I do beseech you, come away!'
His son looked at him with one angry stare,
Spat in his face, and then without a word
Drew sword and struck out. But his father fled
Unscathed. Whereon the poor demented boy
Leaned on his sword and thrust it deeply home
In his own side, and while his life ebbed out
Embraced the maid in loose-enfolding arms,
His spurting blood staining her pale cheeks red.
EURYDICE *goes quickly back into the Palace.*
Two bodies lie together, wedded in death,
Their bridal sleep a witness to the world
How great calamity can come to man
Through man's perversity.
CHORUS: But what is this?
The Queen has turned and gone without a word.
MESSENGER: Yes. It is strange. The best that I can hope
Is that she would not sorrow for her son
Before us all, but vents her grief in private
Among her women. She is too wise, I think,
To take a false step rashly.
CHORUS: It may be.
Yet there is danger in unnatural silence
No less than in excess of lamentation.
MESSENGER: I will go in and see, whether in truth

There is some fatal purpose in her grief.

Such silence, as you say, may well be dangerous.

He goes in.

Enter Attendants preceding the King.

CHORUS: The King comes here.

What the tongue scarce dares to tell

Must now be known

By the burden that proves too well

The guilt, no other man's

But his alone.

Enter CREON *with the body of* HAEMON.

CREON: The sin, the sin of the erring soul

Drives hard unto death.

Behold the slayer, the slain,

The father, the son.

O the curse of my stubborn will!

Son, newly cut off in the newness of youth,

Dead for my fault, not yours.

CHORUS: Alas, too late you have seen the truth.

CREON: I learn in sorrow. Upon my head God has delivered this heavy punishment,

Has struck me down in the ways of wickedness,

And trod my gladness under foot.

Such is the bitter affliction of mortal man.

Enter the MESSENGER *from the Palace.*

MESSENGER: Sir, you have this and more than this to bear.

Within there's more to know, more to your pain.

CREON: What more? What pain can overtop this pain?

MESSENGER: She is dead—your wife, the mother of him that is dead—

The death-wound fresh in her heart. Alas, poor lady!

CREON: Insatiable Death, wilt thou destroy me yet?

What say you, teller of evil?

I am already dead,

And is there more?

Blood upon blood?

More death? My wife?

The central doors open, revealing the body of EURYDICE.

CHORUS: Look then, and see; nothing is hidden now.

CREON: O second horror!

What fate awaits me now?

My child here in my arms . . . and there, the other . . .

The son . . . the mother . . .

MESSENGER: There at the altar with the whetted knife

She stood, and as the darkness dimmed her eyes

Called on the dead, her elder son and this,
And with her dying breath cursed you, their slayer.
CREON: O horrible . . .
    Is there no sword for me,
    To end this misery?
MESSENGER: Indeed you bear the burden of two deaths.
    It was her dying word.
CREON: And her last act?
MESSENGER: Hearing her son was dead, with her own hand
    She drove the sharp sword home into her heart.
CREON: There is no man can bear this guilt but I.
    It is true, I killed him.
    Lead me away, away, I live no longer.
CHORUS: 'Twere best, if anything is best in evil times.
    What's soonest done, is best, when all is ill.
CREON: Come, my last hour and fairest,
    My only happiness . . . come soon.
    Let me not see another day.
    Away . . . away . . .
CHORUS: The future is not to be known; our present care
    Is with the present; the rest is in other hands.
CREON: I ask no more than I have asked.
CHORUS: Ask nothing.
    What is to be, no mortal can escape.
CREON: I am nothing. I have no life.
    Lead me away . . .
    That have killed unwittingly
    My son, my wife.
    I know not where I should turn,
    Where look for help.
    My hands have done amiss, my head is bowed
    With fate too heavy for me.
    Exit.
CHORUS: Of happiness the crown
    And chiefest part
    Is wisdom, and to hold
    The gods in awe.
    This is the law
    That, seeing the stricken heart
    Of pride brought down,
    We learn when we are old.
    Exeunt.

Thucydides

The period of Athenian greatness did not last long. Only about seventy-five years lay between the time of Athens' victory over the Persians and their defeat by the Spartans and their allies in the Peloponnesian War. The two wars were causally connected together through a link that was both political and economic in nature. Even after their repulsion of the Persians, the Greeks were fearful of a return of the invaders, so Athens and other city-states of the Aegean Sea and the Ionian coast formed the Delian League for mutual self-defense. The League began as a voluntary and equitable association, but largely under the leadership of the great statesman, Pericles, Athens came to dominate the League, exacting heavy taxes from the other members (much of the money being used to beautify Athens) and refusing to allow any city-state to withdraw from the association. Thus the Delian League was transformed into an Athenian Empire. As a consequence the Spartans (as well as other Greek city-states) became alarmed and set out to stem the growing power of Athens. The result was the Peloponnesian War which raged intermittently during much of the latter part of the fifth century B.C.

Our great source of information about this war comes from the historian, Thucydides, who was born sometime around 470 and probably died soon after 400. Thucydides, a descendant of Miltiades—the victor of the battle of Marathon—was himself a soldier, but not a successful one. Early in the war he failed in his defense of a city against a Spartan force; for this failure he was stripped of his command and sent into exile from Athens for twenty years.

If not an outstanding military leader, Thucydides was a great historian. The qualities of his writing that are generally cited in support of this judgment are such attributes as his objectivity, his accuracy, his penetrating analyses of character, his appreciation of the demoralizing effects of warfare on society, and his recognition of the logical connections between events. Finally, he considered history to have a moral value, believing that events like wars, not being chance things but the results of causes, would recur in the future if similar conditions arose. From this one can infer that, if we are acquainted with history, and aware of the mistakes that our predecessors made, we can profit from our knowledge and avoid repeating the past. As Thucydides put it, "My history is an everlasting possession, not a prize composition which is heard and forgotten."

Consider the following questions as you study the text below.

1. According to Thucydides, what were Athens' key mistakes? What consequences flowed from them?

2. In Pericles' view, what were the strengths of the Athenian form of government? What was required of each Athenian if Athens was to retain its position in the Greek world?

History of the Peloponnesian War

Book I

1.   Thucydides, an Athenian, wrote the history of the war in which the Peloponnesians and the Athenians fought against one another. He began to write when they first took up arms, believing that it would be great and memorable above any previous war.[1] For he argued that both states were then at the full height of their military power, and he saw the rest of the Hellenes either siding or intending to side with one or the other of them. No movement ever stirred Hellas more deeply than this; it was shared by many of the Barbarians, and might be said even to affect the world at large.

22.   As to the speeches which were made either before or during the war, it was hard for me, and for others who reported them to me, to recollect the exact words. I have therefore put into the mouth of each speaker the sentiments proper to the occasion, expressed as I thought he would be likely to express them, while at the same time I endeavored, as nearly as I could, to give the general purport of what was actually said. Of the events of the war I have not ventured to speak from any chance information, nor according to any notion of my own; I have described nothing but what I either saw myself, or learned from others of whom I made the most careful and particular inquiry. The task was a laborious one, because eye-witnesses of the same occurrences gave different accounts of them, as they remembered or were interested in the actions of one side or the other. And very likely the strictly historical character of my narrative may be disappointing to the ear. But if he who desires to have before his eyes a true picture of the events which have happened, and of the like events which may be expected to happen hereafter in the order of human things, shall pronounce what I have written to be useful, then I shall be satisfied. My history is an everlasting possession, not a prize composition which is heard and forgotten.

.   .   .

[1][Thucydides is here referring to himself in the third person.—*Ed.*]

Thucydides, trans. B. Jowett, 2nd ed.

Book II

. . .

34.   During the same winter,[2] in accordance with an old national custom, the funeral of those who first fell in this war was celebrated by the Athenians at the public charge. The ceremony is as follows: Three days before the celebration they erect a tent in which the bones of the dead are laid out, and every one brings to his own dead any offering which he pleases. At the time of the funeral the bones are placed in chests of cypress wood, which are conveyed on hearses; there is one chest for each tribe. They also carry a single empty litter decked with a pall for all whose bodies are missing, and cannot be recovered after the battle. The procession is accompanied by any one who chooses, whether citizen or stranger, and the female relatives of the deceased are present at the place of interment and make lamentation. The public sepulchre is situated in the most beautiful spot outside the walls; there they always bury those who fall in war; only after the battle of Marathon the dead, in recognition of their preeminent valor, were interred on the field. When the remains have been laid in the earth, some man of known ability and high reputation, chosen by the city, delivers a suitable oration over them; after which the people depart. Such is the manner of interment; and the ceremony was repeated from time to time throughout the war. Over those who were the first buried, Pericles was chosen to speak. At the fitting moment he advanced from the sepulchre to a lofty stage, which had been erected in order that he might be heard as far as possible by the multitude, and spoke as follows:—

FUNERAL SPEECH

35.   "Most of those who have spoken here before me have commended the law-giver who added this oration to our other funeral customs; it seemed to them a worthy thing that such an honor should be given at their burial to the dead who have fallen on the field of battle. But I should have preferred that, when men's deeds have been brave, they should be honored in deed only, and with such an honor as this public funeral, which you are now witnessing. Then the reputation of many would not have been imperilled on the eloquence or want of eloquence of one and their virtues believed or not as he spoke well or ill. For it is difficult to say neither too little nor too much; and even moderation is apt not to give the impression of truthfulness. The friend of the dead who knows the facts is likely to think that the words of the speaker fall short of his knowledge and of his wishes; another who is not so well informed, when he hears of anything which surpasses his own powers, will be

---

[2][At the end of the first year of the Peloponnesian War, 431 B.C.—*Ed.*]

envious and will suspect exaggeration. Mankind are tolerant of the praises of others so long as each hearer thinks that he can do as well or nearly as well himself, but, when the speaker rises above him, jealousy is aroused and he begins to be incredulous. However, since our ancestors have set the seal of their approval upon the practice, I must obey, and to the utmost of my power shall endeavor to satisfy the wishes and beliefs of all who hear me.

36. "I will speak first of our ancestors, for it is right and becoming that now, when we are lamenting the dead, a tribute should be paid to their memory. There has never been a time when they did not inhabit this land, which by their valor they have handed down from generation to generation, and we have received from them a free state. But if they were worthy of praise, still more were our fathers, who added to their inheritance, and after many a struggle transmitted to us their sons this great empire. And we ourselves assembled here today, who are still most of us in the vigor of life, have chiefly done the work of improvement, and have richly endowed our city with all things, so that she is sufficient for herself both in peace and war. Of the military exploits by which our various possessions were acquired, or of the energy with which we or our fathers drove back the tide of war, Hellenic or Barbarian, I will not speak; for the tale would be long and is familiar to you. But before I praise the dead, I should like to point out by what principles of action we rose to power, and under what institutions and through what manner of life our empire became great. For I conceive that such thoughts are not unsuited to the occasion, and that this numerous assembly of citizens and strangers may profitably listen to them.

37. "Our form of government does not enter into rivalry with the institutions of others. We do not copy our neighbors, but are an example to them. It is true that we are called a democracy, for the administration is in the hands of the many and not of the few. But while the law secures equal justice to all alike in their private disputes, the claim of excellence is also recognized; and when a citizen is in any way distinguished, he is preferred to the public service, not as a matter of privilege, but as the reward of merit. Neither is poverty a bar, but a man may benefit his country whatever be the obscurity of his condition. There is no exclusiveness in our public life, and in our private intercourse we are not suspicious of one another, nor angry with our neighbor if he does what he likes; we do not put on sour looks at him which, though harmless, are not pleasant. While we are thus unconstrained in our private intercourse, a spirit of reverence pervades our public acts; we are prevented from doing wrong by respect for authority and for the laws, having an especial regard to those which are ordained for the protection of the injured as well as those unwritten laws which bring upon the transgressor of them the reprobation of the general sentiment.

38. "And we have not forgotten to provide for our weary spirits many relaxations from toil; we have regular games and sacrifices throughout the year; at home the style of our life is refined; and the delight which we

daily feel in all these things helps to banish melancholy. Because of the greatness of our city the fruits of the whole earth flow in upon us; so that we enjoy the goods of other countries as freely as of our own.

39. "Then, again, our military training is in many respects, superior to that of our adversaries. Our city is thrown open to the world, and we never expel a foreigner or prevent him from seeing or learning anything of which the secret if revealed to an enemy might profit him. We rely not upon management or trickery, but upon our own hearts and hands. And in the matter of education, whereas they from early youth are always undergoing laborious exercises which are to make them brave, we live at ease, and yet are equally ready to face the perils which they face. And here is the proof. The Lacedaemonians come into Attica not by themselves, but with their whole confederacy following; we go alone into a neighbor's country; and although our opponents are fighting for their homes and we on a foreign soil, we have seldom any difficulty in overcoming them. Our enemies have never yet felt our united strength; the care of a navy divides our attention, and on land we are obliged to send our own citizens everywhere. But they, if they meet and defeat a part of our army, are as proud as if they had routed us all, and when defeated they pretend to have been vanquished by us all.

40. "If then we prefer to meet danger with a light heart but without laborious training, and with a courage which is gained by habit and not enforced by law, are we not greatly the gainers? Since we do not anticipate the pain, although, when the hour comes, we can be as brave as those who never allow themselves to rest; and thus too our city is equally admirable in peace and in war. For we are lovers of the beautiful, yet simple in our tastes, and we cultivate the mind without a loss of manliness. Wealth we employ, not for talk and ostentation, but when there is a real use for it. To avow poverty with us is no disgrace: the true disgrace is in doing nothing to avoid it. An Athenian citizen does not neglect the state because he takes care of his own household; and even those of us who are engaged in business have a very fair idea of politics. We alone regard a man who takes no interest in public affairs, not as a harmless, but as a useless character; and if few of us are originators, we are all sound judges of a policy. The great impediment to action is, in our opinion, not discussion, but the want of that knowledge which is gained by discussion preparatory to action. For we have a peculiar power of thinking before we act and of acting too, whereas other men are courageous from ignorance but hesitate upon reflection. And they are surely to be esteemed the bravest spirits who, having the clearest sense both of the pains and pleasures of life, do not on that account shrink from danger. In doing good, again, we are unlike others; we make our friends by conferring, not by receiving favors. Now, he who confers a favor is the firmer friend, because he would fain by kindness keep alive the memory of an obligation; but the recipient is colder in his feelings, because he knows that in requiting another's generosity he will not be winning gratitude, but only paying a debt. We alone do good to

our neighbors not upon a calculation of interest, but in the confidence of freedom and in a frank and fearless spirit.

41.   "To sum up: I say that Athens is the school of Hellas, and that the individual Athenian in his own person seems to have the power of adapting himself to the most varied forms of action with the utmost versatility and grace. This is no passing and idle word, but truth and fact; and the assertion is verified by the position to which these qualities have raised the state. For in the hour of trial Athens alone among her contemporaries is superior to the report of her. No enemy who comes against her is indignant at the reverses which he sustains at the hands of such a city; no subject complains that his masters are unworthy of him. And we shall assuredly not be without witnesses; there are mighty monuments of our power which will make us the wonder of this and of succeeding ages; we shall not need the praises of Homer or of any other panegyrist whose poetry may please for the moment, although his representation of the facts will not bear the light of day. For we have compelled every land and every sea to open a path for our valor, and have everywhere planted eternal memorials of our friendship and of our enmity. Such is the city for whose sake these men nobly fought and died; they could not bear the thought that she might be taken from them; and every one of us who survive should gladly toil on her behalf.

42.   "I have dwelt upon the greatness of Athens because I want to show you that we are contending for a higher prize than those who enjoy none of these privileges, and to establish by manifest proof the merit of these men whom I am now commemorating. Their loftiest praise has been already spoken. For in magnifying the city I have magnified them, and men like them whose virtues made her glorious. And of how few Hellenes can it be said as of them, that their deeds when weighted in the balance have been found equal to their fame! Methinks that a death such as theirs has been given the true measure of a man's worth; it may be the first revelation of his virtues, but is at any rate their final seal. For even those who come short in other ways may justly plead the valor with which they have fought for their country; they have blotted out the evil with the good, and have benefited the state more by their public services than they have injured her by their private actions. None of these men were enervated by wealth or hesitated to resign the pleasures of life; none of them put off the evil day in the hope, natural to poverty, that a man, though poor, may one day become rich. But, deeming that the punishment of their enemies was sweeter than any of these things, and that they could fall in no nobler cause, they determined at the hazard of their lives to be honorably avenged, and to leave the rest. They resigned to hope their unknown chance of happiness; but in the face of death they resolved to rely upon themselves alone. And when the moment came they were minded to resist and suffer, rather than to fly and save their lives; they ran away from the word of dishonor, but on the battlefield their feet stood fast, and in an instant, at the height of their fortune, they passed away from the scene, not of their fear, but of their glory.

43.   "Such was the end of these men; they were worthy of Athens, and the living need not desire to have a more heroic spirit, although they may pray for a less fatal issue. The value of such a spirit is not to be expressed in words. Any one can discourse to you forever about the advantage of a brave defence which you know already. But instead of listening to him I would have you day by day fix your eyes upon the greatness of Athens, until you become filled with the love of her; and when you are impressed by the spectacle of her glory, reflect that this empire has been acquired by men who knew their duty and had the courage to do it, who in the hour of conflict had the fear of dishonor always present to them, and who, if ever they failed in an enterprise, would not allow their virtues to be lost to their country, but freely gave their lives to her as the fairest offering which they could present at her feast. The sacrifice which they collectively made was individually repaid to them; for they received again each one for himself a praise which grows not old, and the noblest of all sepulchres—I speak not of that in which their remains are laid, but of that in which their glory survives, and is proclaimed always and on every fitting occasion both in word and deed. For the whole earth is the sepulchre of famous men; not only are they commemorated by columns and inscriptions in their own country, but in foreign lands there dwells also an unwritten memorial of them, graven not on stone but in the hearts of men. Make them your examples, and, esteeming courage to be freedom and freedom to be happiness, do not weigh too nicely the perils of war. The unfortunate who has no hope of a change for the better has less reason to throw away his life than the prosperous who, if he survives, is always liable to a change for the worse, and to whom any accidental fall makes the most serious difference. To a man of spirit, cowardice and disaster coming together are far more bitter than death, striking him unperceived at a time when he is full of courage and animated by the general hope.

44.   "Wherefore I do not now commiserate the parents of the dead who stand here; I would rather comfort them. You know that your life has been passed amid manifold vicissitudes; and that they may be deemed fortunate who have gained most honor, whether an honorable death like theirs, or an honorable sorrow like yours, and whose days have been so ordered that the term of their happiness is likewise the term of their life. I know how hard it is to make you feel this, when the good fortune of others will too often remind you of the gladness which once lightened your hearts. And sorrow is felt at the want of those blessings, not which a man never knew, but which were a part of his life before they were taken from him. Some of you are of an age at which they may hope to have other children, and they ought to bear their sorrow better; not only will the children who may hereafter be born make them forget their own lost ones, but the city will be doubly a gainer. She will not be left desolate, and she will be safer. For a man's counsel cannot have equal weight or worth, when he alone has no children to risk in the general danger. To those of you who have passed their prime, I say: 'Congratulate yourselves that you have been happy during the greater part

of your days; remember that your life of sorrow will not last long, and be comforted by the glory of those who are gone. For the love of honor alone is ever young, and not riches, as some say, but honor is the delight of men when they are old and useless.'

45.   "To you who are the sons and brothers of the departed, I see that the struggle to emulate them will be an arduous one. For all men praise the dead, and, however preeminent your virtue may be, hardly will you be thought, I do not say to equal, but even to approach them. The living have their rivals and detractors, but when a man is out of the way, the honor and goodwill which he receives is unalloyed. And, if I am to speak of womanly virtues to those of you who will henceforth be widows, let me sum them up in one short admonition: To a woman not to show more weakness than is natural to her sex is a great glory, and not to be talked about for good or for evil among men.

46.   "I have paid the required tribute, in obedience to the law, making use of such fitting words as I had. The tribute of deeds has been paid in part; for the dead have been honorably interred, and it remains only that their children should be maintained at the public charge until they are grown up; this is the solid prize with which, as with a garland, Athens crowns her sons living and dead, after a struggle like theirs. For where the rewards of virtue are greatest, there the noblest citizens are enlisted in the service of the state. And now, when you have duly lamented, every one his own dead, you may depart."

. . .

Book III

. . .

82.   For not long afterwards[3] nearly the whole Hellenic world was in commotion; in every city the chiefs of the democracy and of the oligarchy were struggling, the one to bring in the Athenians, the other the Lacedaemonians. Now, in time of peace, men would have had no excuse for introducing either, and no desire to do so, but when they were at war and both sides could easily obtain allies to the hurt of their enemies and the advantage of themselves, the dissatisfied party was only too ready to invoke foreign aid. And revolution brought upon the cities of Hellas many terrible calamities, such as have been and always will be while human nature remains the same, but which are more or less aggravated and differ in character with every new combination of circumstances. In peace and prosperity both states and

---

[3][In 427 B.C., or four years after Pericles' Funeral Oration.—*Ed.*]

individuals are actuated by high motives, because they do not fall under the dominion of imperious necessities; but war which takes away the comfortable provision of daily life is a hard master, and tends to assimilate men's characters to their conditions.

When troubles had once begun in the cities, those who followed carried the revolutionary spirit further and further, and determined to outdo the report of all who had preceded them by the ingenuity of their enterprises and the atrocity of their revenges. The meaning of words had no longer the same relation to things, but was changed by them as they thought proper. Reckless daring was held to be loyal courage; prudent delay was the excuse of a coward; moderation was the disguise of unmanly weakness; to know everything was to do nothing. Frantic energy was the true quality of man. A conspirator who wanted to be safe was a recreant in disguise. The lover of violence was always trusted, and his opponent suspected. He who succeeded in a plot was deemed knowing, but a still greater master in craft was he who detected one. On the other hand, he who plotted from the first to have nothing to do with plots was a breaker up of parties and a poltroon who was afraid of the enemy. In a word, he who could outstrip another in a bad action was applauded, and so was he who encouraged to evil one who had no idea of it. The tie of party was stronger than the tie of blood, because a partisan was more ready to dare without asking why. (For party associations are not based upon established law, nor do they seek the public good; they are formed in defiance of the laws and from self-interest.) The seal of good faith was not divine law, but fellowship in crime. If any enemy when he was in the ascendant offered fair words, the opposite party received them, not in a generous spirit, but by a jealous watchfulness of his actions. Revenge was dearer than self-preservation. Any agreements sworn to by either party, when they could do nothing else, were binding as long as both were powerless. But he who on a favorable opportunity first took courage and struck at his enemy when he saw him off his guard, had greater pleasure in a perfidious than he would have had in an open act of revenge; he congratulated himself that he had taken the safer course, and also that he had over-reached his enemy and gained the prize of superior ability. In general, the dishonest more easily gain credit for cleverness than the simple for goodness; men take a pride in the one, but are ashamed of the other.

The cause of all these evils was the love of power originating in avarice and ambition, and the party-spirit which is engendered by them when men were fairly embarked in a contest. For the leaders on either side used specious names, the one party professing to uphold the constitutional equality of the many, the other the wisdom of an aristocracy, while they made the public interests, to which in name they were devoted, in reality their prize. Striving in every way to overcome each other, they committed the most monstrous crimes; yet even these were surpassed by the magnitude of their revenges which they pursued to the very utmost, neither party observing any definite limits either of justice or public expediency, but both alike making the caprice of the moment their law. Either by the help of an unrighteous sentence, or grasping power with the strong hand, they were eager to satiate the impatience of party-spirit. Neither faction cared for religion; but any fair pretence which succeeded in effecting some odious purpose was greatly lauded. And the citizens who were of neither party fell a prey to both; either they were disliked because they held aloof, or men were jealous of their surviving.

83. Thus revolution gave birth to every form of wickedness in Hellas. The simplicity which is so large an element in a noble nature was laughed to scorn and disappeared. An attitude of perfidious antagonism everywhere prevailed; for there was no word binding enough, nor oath terrible enough to reconcile enemies. Each man was strong only in the conviction that nothing was secure; he must look to his own safety, and could not afford to trust others.

· · ·

Book V

· · ·

84. In the ensuing summer, Alcibiades sailed to Argos with twenty ships, and seized any of the Argives who were still suspected to be of the Lacedaemonian faction, three hundred in number; and the Athenians deposited them in the subject islands near at hand. The Athenians next made an expedition against the island of Melos[4] with thirty ships of their own, six Chian, and two Lesbian, twelve hundred hoplites and three hundred archers besides twenty mounted archers of their own, and about fifteen hundred hoplites furnished by their allies in the islands. The Melians are colonists of the Lacedaemonians who would not submit to Athens like the other islanders. At first they were neutral and took no part. But when the Athenians tried to coerce them by ravaging their lands they were driven into open hostilities. The generals, Cleomedes the son of Lycomedes and Tisias the son of Tisimachus, encamped with the Athenian forces on the island. But before they did the country any harm they sent envoys to negotiate with the Melians. Instead of bringing these envoys before the people, the Melians desired them to explain their errand to the magistrates and to the chief men. They spoke as follows—

85. "Since we are not allowed to speak to the people, lest, forsooth, they should be deceived by seductive and unanswerable arguments which they would hear set forth in a single uninterrupted oration (for we are per-

---

[4][In 416 B.C.—*Ed.*]

fectly aware that this is what you mean in bringing us before a select few), you who are sitting here may as well make assurance yet surer. Let us have no set speeches at all, but do you reply to each several statement of which you disapprove, and criticise it at once. Say first of all how you like this mode of proceedings."

86.   The Melian representatives answered:—"The quiet interchange of explanations is a reasonable thing, and we do not object to that. But your warlike movements, which are present not only to our fears but to our eyes, seem to belie your words. We see that, although you may reason with us, you mean to be our judges; and that at the end of the discussion if the justice of our cause prevail and we therefore refuse to yield, we may expect war; if we are convinced by you, slavery."

87.   ATHENIAN: Nay, but if you are only going to argue from fancies about the future, or if you meet us with any other purpose than that of looking your circumstances in the face and saving your city, we have done; but if this is your intention we will proceed.

88.   MELIAN: It is an excusable and natural thing that men in our position should have much to say and should indulge in many fancies. But we admit that this conference has met to consider the question of our preservation; and therefore let the argument proceed in the manner which you propose.

89.   ATHENIAN: Well, then, we Athenians will use no fine words; we will not go out of our way to prove at length that we have a right to rule, because we overthrew the Persians; or that we attack you now because we are suffering any injury at your hands. We should not convince you if we did; nor must you expect to convince us by arguing that, although a colony of the Lacedaemonians, you have taken no part in their expeditions, or that you have never done us any wrong. But you and we should say what we really think, and aim only at what is possible, for we both alike know that into the discussion of human affairs, the question of justice only enters where the pressure of necessity is equal, and that the powerful exact what they can, and the weak grant what they must.

90.   MELIAN: Well, then, since you set aside justice and invite us to speak of expediency, in our judgment it is certainly expedient that you should respect a principle which is for the common good; and that to every man when in peril a reasonable claim should be accounted a claim of right, and any plea which he is disposed to urge, even if failing of the point a little, should help his cause. Your interest in this principle is quite as great as ours, inasmuch as you, if you fall, will incur the heaviest vengeance, and will be the most terrible example to mankind.

91.   ATHENIAN: The fall of our empire, if it should fall, is not an event to which we look forward with dismay; for ruling states such as Lacedaemon are not cruel to their vanquished enemies. And we are fighting not so much against the Lacedaemonians as against our own subjects who may some day rise up and overcome their former masters. But this is a danger which you

may leave to us. And we will now endeavor to show that we have come in the interests of our empire, and that in what we are about to say we are only seeking the preservation of your city. For we want to make you ours with the least trouble to ourselves, and it is for the interests of us both that you should not be destroyed.

92.   MELIAN: It may be your interest to be our masters, but how can it be ours to be your slaves?

93.   ATHENIAN: To you the gain will be that by submission you will avert the worst; and we shall be all the richer for your preservation.

94.   MELIAN: But must we be your enemies? Will you not receive us as friends if we are neutral and remain at peace with you?

95.   ATHENIAN: No, your enmity is not half so mischievous to us as your friendship; for the one is in the eyes of our subjects an argument of our power, the other of our weakness.

96.   MELIAN: But are your subjects really unable to distinguish between states in which you have no concern, and those which are chiefly your own colonies, and in some cases have revolted and been subdued by you?

97.   ATHENIAN: Why, they do not doubt that both of them have a good deal to say for themselves on the score of justice, but they think that states like yours are left free because they are able to defend themselves, and that we do not attack them because we dare not. So that your subjection will give us an increase of security, as well as an extension of empire. For we are masters of the sea, and you who are islanders, and insignificant islanders too, must not be allowed to escape us.

98.   MELIAN: But do you not recognise another danger? For once more, since you drive us from the plea of justice and press upon us your doctrine of expediency, we must show you what is for our interest, and, if it be for yours also, may hope to convince you:—Will you not be making enemies of all who are now neutrals? When they see how you are treating us they will expect you some day to turn against them; and if so, are you not strengthening the enemies whom you already have, and bringing upon you others who, if they could help, would never dream of being your enemies at all?

99.   ATHENIAN: We do not consider our really dangerous enemies to be any of the peoples inhabiting the mainland who, secure in their freedom, may defer indefinitely any measures of precaution which they take against us, but islanders who, like you, happen to be under no control, and all who may be already irritated by the necessity of submission to our empire—these are our real enemies, for they are the most reckless and most likely to bring themselves as well as us into a danger which they cannot but foresee.

100.   MELIAN: Surely then, if you and your subjects will brave all this risk, you to preserve your empire and they to be quit of it, how base and cowardly it would be in us, who retain our freedom, not to do and suffer anything rather than be your slaves.

101.   ATHENIAN: Not so, if you calmly reflect: for you are not fighting against equals to whom you cannot yield without disgrace, but you are tak-

ing counsel whether or not you shall resist an overwhelming force. The question is not one of honor but of prudence.

102.   MELIAN: But we know that the fortune of war is sometimes impartial, and not always on the side of numbers. If we yield now all is over; but if we fight there is yet a hope that we may stand upright.

103.   ATHENIAN: Hope is a good comforter in the hour of danger, and when men have something else to depend upon, although hurtful, she is not ruinous. But when her spendthrift nature has induced them to stake their all, they see her as she is in the moment of their fall, and not till then. While the knowledge of her might enable them to beware of her, she never fails. You are weak and a single turn of the scale might be your ruin. Do not you be thus deluded; avoid the error of which so many are guilty, who, although they might still be saved if they would take the natural means, when visible grounds of confidence forsake them, have recourse to the invisible, to prophecies and oracles and the like, which ruin men by the hopes which they inspire in them.

104.   MELIAN: We know only too well how hard the struggle must be against your power, and against fortune, if she does not mean to be impartial. Nevertheless we do not despair of fortune, for we hope to stand as high as you in the favor of heaven, because we are righteous, and you against whom we contend are unrighteous; and we are satisfied that our deficiency in power will be compensated by the aid of our allies the Lacedaemonians; they cannot refuse to help us, if only because we are their kinsmen, and for the sake of their own honor. And therefore our confidence is not so utterly blind as you suppose.

105.   ATHENIAN: As for the Gods, we expect to have quite as much of their favor as you: for we are not doing or claiming anything which goes beyond common opinion about divine or men's desires about human things. For of the Gods we believe, and of men we know, that by a law of their nature wherever they can rule they will. This law was not made by us, and we are not the first who have acted upon it; we did but inherit it, and shall bequeath it to all time, and we know that you and all mankind, if you were as strong as we are, would do as we do. So much for the Gods; we have told you why we expect to stand as high in their good opinion as you. And then as to the Lacedaemonians—when you imagine that out of very shame they will assist you, we admire the simplicity of your idea, but we do not envy you the folly of it. The Lacedaemonians are exceedingly virtuous among themselves, and according to their national standard of morality. But in respect of their dealings with others, although many things might be said, a word is enough to describe them—of all men whom we know they are the most notorious for identifying what is pleasant with what is honorable, and what is expedient with what is just. But how inconsistent is such a character with your present blind hope of deliverance!

106.   MELIAN: That is the very reason why we trust them; they will look to their interest, and therefore will not be willing to betray the Melians, who

are their own colonists, lest they should be distrusted by their friends in Hellas and play into the hands of their enemies.

107.   ATHENIAN: But do you not see the path of expediency is safe, whereas justice and honor involve danger in practice, and such dangers the Lacedaemonians seldom care to face?

108.   MELIAN: On the other hand we think that whatever perils there may be, they will be ready to face them for our sakes, and will consider danger less dangerous where we are concerned. For if they need our aid we are close at hand, and they can better trust our loyal feeling because we are their kinsmen.

109.   ATHENIAN: Yes, but what encourages men who are invited to join in a conflict is clearly not the goodwill of those who summon them to their side, but a decided superiority in real power. To this no men look more keenly than the Lacedaemonians; so little confidence have they in their own resources that they only attack their neighbors when they have numerous allies, and therefore they are not likely to find their way by themselves to an island, when we are masters of the sea.

110.   MELIAN: But they may send their allies; the Cretan sea is a large place; and the masters of the sea will have more difficulty in overtaking vessels which want to escape than the pursued in escaping. If the attempt should fail, they may invade Attica itself, and find their way to allies of yours whom Brasidas did not reach; and then you will have to fight, not for the conquest of a land in which you have no concern, but nearer home, for the preservation of your confederacy and of your own territory.

111.   ATHENIAN: Help may come from Lacedaemon to you as it has come to others, and should you ever have actual experience of it, then you will know that never once have the Athenians retired from a siege through fear of a foe elsewhere. You told us that the safety of your city would be your first care, but we remark that, in this long discussion, not a word has been uttered by you which would give a reasonable man expectation of deliverance. Your strongest grounds are hopes deferred, and what power you have is not to be compared with that which is already arrayed against you. Unless after we have withdrawn you mean to come, as even now you may, to a wiser conclusion, you are showing a great want of sence. For surely you cannot dream of flying to that false sence of honor which has been the ruin of so many when danger and dishonor were staring them in the face. Many men with their eyes still open to the consequences have found the word "honor" too much for them, and have suffered a mere name to lure them on, until it has drawn down upon them real and irretrievable calamities; through their own folly they have incurred a worse dishonor than fortune would have inflicted upon them. If you are wise you will not run this risk; you ought to see that there can be no disgrace in yielding to a great city which invites you to become her ally on reasonable terms, keeping your own land, and merely paying tribute, and that you will certainly gain no honor if, having to choose

between two alternatives, safety and war, you obstinately prefer the worse. To maintain our rights against equals, to be politic with superiors, and to be moderate towards inferiors is the path of safety. Reflect once more when we have withdrawn, and say to yourselves over and over again that you are deliberating about your one and only country, which may be saved or may be destroyed by a single decision.

112.   The Athenians left the conference: the Melians, after consulting among themselves, resolved to persevere in their refusal, and made answer as follows:—"Men of Athens, our resolution is unchanged; and we will not in a moment surrender that liberty which our city, founded seven hundred years ago, still enjoys; we will trust to the good-fortune which by the favor of the Gods has hitherto preserved us, and for human help to the Lacedaemonians, and endeavor to save ourselves. We are ready however to be your friends, and the enemies neither of you nor of the Lacedaemonians, and we ask you to leave our country when you have made such a peace as may appear to be in the interest of both parties."

113.   Such was the answer of the Melians; the Athenians, as they quitted the conference, spoke as follows:—"Well, we must say, judging from the decision at which you have arrived, that you are the only men who deem the future to be more certain than the present, and regard things unseen as already realized in your fond anticipation, and that the more you cast yourselves upon the Lacedaemonians and fortune, and hope, and trust them, the more complete will be your ruin."

114.   The Athenian envoys returned to the army, and the generals, when they found that the Melians would not yield, immediately commenced hostilities. They surrounded the town of Melos with a wall, dividing the work among the several contingents. They then left troops of their own and of the allies to keep guard both by land and by sea, and retired with the greater part of their army; the remainder carried on the blockade.

116.   . . .The place was now closely invested, and there was treachery among the citizens themselves. So the Melians were induced to surrender at discretion. The Athenians thereupon put to death all who were of military age, and made slaves of the women and children. They then colonised the island, sending thither five hundred settlers of their own.

Xenophon

Born in Athens in the twilight years of the Athenian Empire, Xenophon (c. 444 B.C.–c. 357 B.C.) was a student of Socrates and a soldier of fortune. The author of numerous works, both philosophical and historical, Xenophon was an acute observer of his times, keen to explore the relationship between Greek notions of morality and government and the realities of early fourth-century life. Like many young men of his generation, he came to see Sparta as the great hope for a rebirth of Greek ascendancy, a position that eventually led to his exile from Athens.

His travels as a soldier placed him in a unique position to compare and contrast governments and societies throughout the Greek and Persian worlds. In 401 B.C., Xenophon joined a Greek regiment recruited by Prince Cyrus of Persia. Cyrus believed that with the help of the Greeks he could seize the throne occupied by his older brother King Artaxerxes. He might have succeeded if it were not for his untimely death in the battle of Cunaxa (401 B.C.). In the passage included here, Xenophon wrote what amounted to a eulogy for Cyrus. As you read, pay particular attention to the connections Xenophon made between Cyrus' character and his policies. What did he admire most about Cyrus? What made him "most like a king" and "most deserving of an empire"?

Consider the following questions as you study the text below.

1. What role did physical strength and courage play in Xenophon's idea of a perfect king? From Xenophon's perspective, could one be a great king without being a great warrior?

2. Which qualities in his subjects did Cyrus reward? Which did he punish? What connections did Xenophon see between Cyrus' character and his administration of justice?

The Character of Cyrus

This then, was the end of Cyrus. Of all the Persians who lived after Cyrus the Great, he was the most like a king and the most deserving of an empire, as is admitted by everyone who is known to have been personally

From Xenophon, *The Persian Expedition*, trans. Rex Warner (Harmondsworth, Middlesex: Penguin Books, 1952). Reprinted with permission of Penguin Books.

acquainted with him. In his early life, when he was still a child being brought up with his brother, and the other children, he was regarded as the best of them all in every way. All the children of Persian nobles are brought up at the Court, and there a child can pick up many lessons in good behaviour while having no chance of seeing or hearing anything bad. The boys see and hear some people being honoured by the King and others being dismissed in disgrace, and so from their childhood they learn how to command and how to obey. Here, at the Court, Cyrus was considered, first, to be the best-behaved of his contemporaries and more willing even than his inferiors to listen to those older than himself; and then he was remarkable for his fondness for horses and being able to manage them extremely well. In the soldierly arts also of archery and javelin-throwing they judged him to be most eager to learn and most willing to practise them. When he got to the age for hunting, he was most enthusiastic about it, and only too ready to take risks in his encounters with wild animals. There was one occasion when a she-bear charged at him and he, showing no fear, got to grips with the animal and was pulled off his horse. The scars from the wounds he got then were still visible on his body, but he killed the animal in the end, and as for the first man who came to help him Cyrus made people think him very lucky indeed.

When he was sent down to the coast by his father as satrap of Lydia and Great Phrygia and Cappadocia, and had been declared Commander-in-Chief of all who are bound to muster in the plain of Castolus, the first thing he did was to make it clear that in any league or agreement or undertaking that he made he attached the utmost importance to keeping his word. The cities which were in his command trusted him and so did the men. And the enemies he had were confident that once Cyrus had signed a treaty with them nothing would happen to them contrary to the terms of the treaty. Consequently when he was at war with Tissaphernes all the cities, with the exception of the Milesians, chose to follow him rather than Tissaphernes. The Milesians were afraid of him because he refused to give up the cause of the exiled government. Indeed, he made it clear by his actions, and said openly that, once he had become their friend, he would never give them up, not even if their numbers became fewer and their prospects worse than they were.

If anyone did him a good or an evil turn, he evidently aimed at going one better. Some people used to refer to an habitual prayer of his, that he might live long enough to be able to repay with interest both those who had helped him and those who had injured him. It was quite natural then that he was the one man in our times to whom so many people were eager to hand over their money, their cities and their own persons.

No one, however, could say that he allowed criminals and evil-doers to mock his authority. On the contrary, his punishments were exceptionally severe, and along the more frequented roads one often saw people who had been blinded or had had their feet or hands cut off. The result was that in

Cyrus's provinces anyone, whether Greek or native, who was doing no harm could travel without fear wherever he liked and could take with him whatever he wanted.

Of course it is well known that he treated with exceptional distinction all those who showed ability for war. In his first war, which was against the Pisidians and Mysians, he marched into their country himself and made those whom he saw willing to risk their lives governors over the territory which he conquered; and afterwards he gave them other honours and rewards, making it clear that the brave were going to be the most prosperous while the cowards only deserved to be their slaves. Consequently there was never any lack of people who were willing to risk their lives when they thought that Cyrus would get to know of it.

As for justice, he made it his supreme aim to see that those who really wanted to live in accordance with its standards became richer than those who wanted to profit by transgressing them. It followed from this that not only were his affairs in general conducted justly, but he enjoyed the services of an army that really was an army. Generals and captains who crossed the sea to take service under him as mercenaries knew that to do Cyrus good service paid better than any monthly wage. Indeed, whenever anyone carried out effectively a job which he had assigned, he never allowed his good work to go unrewarded. Consequently it was said that Cyrus got the best officers for any kind of job.

When he saw that a man was a capable administrator, acting on just principles, improving the land under his control and making it bring in profit, he never took his post away from him, but always gave him additional responsibility. The result was that his administrators did their work cheerfully and made money confidently. Cyrus was the last person whom they kept in the dark about their possessions, since he showed no envy for those who became rich openly, but, on the contrary, tried to make use of the wealth of people who attempted to conceal what they had.

Everyone agrees that he was absolutely remarkable for doing services to those whom he made friends of and knew to be true to him and considered able to help him in doing whatever job was on hand. He thought that the reason why he needed friends was to have people to help him, and he applied exactly the same principle to others, trying to be of the utmost service to his friends whenever he knew that any of them wanted anything. I suppose that he received more presents than any other single individual, and this for a variety of reasons. But more than anyone else he shared them with his friends, always considering what each individual was like and what, to his knowledge, he needed most. When people sent him fine things to wear, either armour or beautiful dresses, they say that the remark he made about these was that he could not possibly wear all this finery on his own body, but he thought the finest thing for a man was that his friends should be well turned out. There is, no doubt, nothing surprising in the fact that he surpassed his friends in doing them great services, since he had the greater power to do so. What seems to me more admirable than this is the fact that he outdid them in ordinary consideration and in the anxiety to give pleasure. Often, when he had had a particularly good wine, he used to send jars half full of it to his friends with the message: 'Cyrus has not for a long time come across a better wine than this; so he has sent some to you and wants you to finish it up to-day with those whom you love best.' Often too he used to send helpings of goose and halves of loaves and such things, telling the bearer to say when he presented them: 'Cyrus enjoyed thus; so he wants you to taste it too.' When there was a scarcity of fodder,—though he himself, because of the number of his servants and his own wise provision, was able to get hold of it,—he used to send round to his friends and tell them to give the fodder he sent to the horses they rode themselves, so that horses which carried his friends should not go hungry.

Whenever he went on an official journey, and was likely to be seen by great numbers of people, he used to call his friends to him and engage them in serious conversation, so that he might show what men he honoured. My own opinion, therefore, based on what I have heard, is that there has never been anyone, Greek or foreigner, more generally beloved. And an additional proof of this is in the fact that, although Cyrus was a subject, no one deserted him and went over to the King,—except that Orontas tried to do so; but in his case he soon found that the man whom he thought reliable was more of a friend to Cyrus than to him. On the other hand there were many who left the King and came over to Cyrus, when war broke out between the two, and these also were people who had been particularly favoured by the King; but they came to the conclusion that if they did well under Cyrus their services would be better rewarded than they would be by the King. What happened at the time of his death is also a strong proof not only of his own courage but of his ability to pick out accurately people who were reliable, devoted and steadfast. For when he died every one of his friends and table-companions died fighting for him, except Ariaeus, who had been posted on the left wing in command of the cavalry. When Ariaeus heard that Cyrus had fallen, he and the whole army which he led took to flight.

The Last Days of Socrates

Although Socrates (c. 470–399 B.C.) was an influential philosopher and teacher, he wrote nothing. So we must rely on secondary accounts for information about his life and beliefs. Such accounts, particularly the writings of his most famous disciple, Plato, make it possible to reconstruct the broad outlines of his career. Socrates was born in Athens, the son of a stonecutter. Instead of following his father's trade, he began early in life to frequent the Athenian *agora* (marketplace), where he listened to the intellectuals of the city argue questions of politics, art, morality, and philosophy.

Before long, he had acquired a reputation for wisdom and had gathered about himself a group of young disciples who were intrigued by the unusual manner in which he taught. Unlike the sophists ("wise men"), the professional teachers of the day who were willing to teach anyone anything for a suitable fee, Socrates professed himself to be ignorant. Instead of attempting to teach, he wandered about Athens seeking wisdom by asking questions of everyone he met, including the city's leading politicians, generals, artists, and philosophers. As might be expected, under Socrates' questioning many of the self-styled sages proved to be without wisdom. Although Socrates' unflinching quest for wisdom and truth won him many loyal followers, it inevitably aroused the enmity of those whose ignorance he unmasked. Through their influence in Athens, his enemies succeeded in having him brought to trial and condemned to death. But they were unable to silence him, for his words live on in the dialogues of Plato.

Although he professed to have no wisdom of his own, Socrates did have a positive philosophy. The basic premise of this philosophy was the doctrine that *virtue is knowledge*, or that the good life is the life of wisdom. To gain knowledge and hence virtue, he believed, education is necessary. But knowledge is not something that can be poured into an individual from the outside. Rather, it lies deep within each person and needs only to be drawn out. Socrates' method for bringing this inborn knowledge to the surface was to ask a series of questions, a technique known as the *dialectic method.*

The selections that follow are an account of the last days of Socrates written by Plato some time after the events described. Socrates had been hauled into court by a group of accusers who charged him with being an atheist and a corrupter of youth. In Plato's *Apology*, Socrates is represented as replying to the charges with a general defense of his way of life. In the *Crito*, Plato pictures Socrates waiting in prison for his execution and arguing with a friend (who has arranged for his escape) about whether he would be justified in running away, even though he has been unjustly convicted. The extract from the *Phaedo* records Socrates' death. These selections give us a fresh and living portrait of Socrates the man, a fairly comprehensive account of his philosophy, and a glimpse of the social and legal structure of the Athens of his day.

Consider the following questions as you study the text below.

1. Why might Socrates have been so irritating to a portion of the Athenian population? What were the key arguments in Socrates' self-defense?

2. Why did Socrates refuse to escape from prison when given a chance to do so? What light does this shed on his notion of the responsibility of the individual to his or her community?

The Apology

SCENE: The Court of Justice

I cannot tell what impression my accusers have made upon you, Athenians: for my own part, I know that they nearly made me forget who I was, so plausible were they; and yet they have scarcely uttered one single word of truth. But of all their many falsehoods, the one which astonished me most, was when they said that I was a clever speaker, and that you must be careful not to let me mislead you. I thought that it was most impudent of them not to be ashamed to talk in that way; for as soon as I opened my mouth the lie will be exposed, and I shall prove that I am not a clever speaker in any way at all: unless, indeed, by a clever speaker they mean a man who speaks the truth. If that is their meaning, I agree with them that I am a much greater orator than they. My accusers, then I repeat, have said little or nothing that is true: but from me you shall hear the whole truth. Certainly you will not hear an elaborate speech, Athenians, drest up, like theirs, with words and phrases. I will say to you what I have to say, without preparation, and in the words which come first, for I believe that my cause is just; so let none of you expect anything else. Indeed, my friends, it would hardly be seemly for me, at my age, to come before you like a young man with his specious falsehoods. But there is one thing, Athenians, which I do most earnestly beg and entreat of you. Do not be surprised and do not interrupt, if in my defence I speak in the same way that I am accustomed to speak in the market-place, at the tables of the money-changers, where many of you have heard me, and elsewhere. The truth is this: I am more than seventy years old, and this is the first time that I have ever come before a Court of Law; so your manner of speech here is

Trans. F. J. Church.

quite strange to me. If I had been really a stranger, you would have forgiven me for speaking in the language and the fashion of my native country: and so now I ask you to grant me what I think I have a right to claim. Never mind the style of my speech—it may be better or it may be worse—give your whole attention to the question, Is what I say just, or is it not? That is what makes a good judge, as speaking the truth makes a good advocate.

I have to defend myself, Athenians, first against the old false charges of my old accusers, and then against the later ones of my present accusers. For many men have been accusing me to you, and for very many years, who have not uttered a word of truth: and I fear them more than I fear Anytus and his companions, formidable as they are. But, my friends, those others are still more formidable; for they got hold of most of you when you were children, and they have been more persistent in accusing me with lies, and in trying to persuade you that there is one Socrates, a wise man, who speculates about the heavens, and who examines into all things that are beneath the earth, and who can "make the worse appear the better reason." These men, Athenians, who spread abroad this report, are the accusers whom I fear; for their hearers think that persons who pursue such inquiries never believe in the gods. And then they are many, and their attacks have been going on for a long time; and they spoke to you when you were at the age most readily to believe them: for you were all young, and many of you were children: and there was no one to answer them when they attacked me. And the most unreasonable thing of all is that commonly I do not even know their names: I cannot tell you who they are, except in the case of the comic poets. But all the rest who have been trying to prejudice you against me, from motives of spite and jealousy, and sometimes, it may be, from conviction, are the enemies whom it is hardest to meet. For I cannot call any one of them forward in Court, to cross-examine him: I have, as it were, simply to fight with shadows in my defence, and to put questions which there is no one to answer. I ask you, therefore, to believe that, as I say, I have been attacked by two classes of accusers—first by Meletus and his friends, and then by those older ones of whom I have spoken. And, with your leave, I will defend myself first against my old enemies; for you heard their accusations first, and they were much more persistent than my present accusers are.

Well, I must make my defence, Athenians, and try in the short time allowed me to remove the prejudice which you have had against me for a long time. I hope that I may manage to do this, if it be good for you and for me, and that my defence may be successful, but I am quite aware of the nature of my task, and I know that it is a difficult one. Be the issue, however, as God wills, I must obey the law, and make my defence.

Let us begin again, then, and see what is the charge which has given rise to the prejudice against me, which was what Meletus relied on when he drew his indictment. What is the calumny which my enemies have been spreading about me? I must assume that they are formally accusing me, and read their indictment. It would run somewhat in this fashion: "Socrates is an evil-doer, who meddles with inquiries into things beneath the earth, and in heaven, and who 'makes the worse appear the better reason,' and who teaches others these same things." That is what they say: and in the Comedy of Aristophanes you yourselves saw a man called Socrates swinging round in a basket, and saying that he walked the air, and talking a great deal of nonsense about matters of which I understand nothing, either more or less. I do not mean to disparage that kind of knowledge, if there is any man who possesses it. I trust Meletus may never be able to prosecute me for that. But, the truth is, Athenians, I have nothing to do with these matters, and almost all of you are yourselves my witnesses of this. I beg all of you who have heard me converse, and they are many, to inform your neighbors and tell them if any of you ever heard me conversing about such matters, either more or less. That will show you that the other common stories about me are as false as this one.

But, the fact is, that not one of these stories is true; and if you have heard that I undertake to educate men, and exact money from them for so doing, that is not true either; though I think that it would be a fine thing to be able to educate men, as Gorgias of Leontini, and Prodicus of Ceos, and Hippias of Elis do. For each of them, my friends, can go into any city, and persuade the young men to leave the society of their fellow-citizens, with any of whom they might associate for nothing, and to be only too glad to be allowed to pay money for the privilege of associating with themselves. And I believe that there is another wise man from Paros residing in Athens at this moment. I happened to meet Callias, the son of Hipponicus, a man who has spent more money on the Sophists than every one else put together. So I said to him—he has two sons—"Callias, if your two sons had been foals, or calves, we could have hired a trainer for them who would have made them perfect in the excellence which belongs to their nature. He would have been either a groom or a farmer. But whom do you intend to take to train them, seeing that they are men? Who understands the excellence which belongs to men and to citizens? I suppose that you must have thought of this, because of your sons. Is there such a person," said I, "or not?" "Certainly there is," he replied. "Who is he," said I, "and where does he come from, and what is his fee?" "His name is Evenus, Socrates," he replied. "He comes from Paros, and his fee is five minae." Then I thought that Evenus was a fortunate person if he really understood this art and could teach so cleverly. If I had possessed knowledge of that kind, I should have given myself airs and prided myself on it. But, Athenians, the truth is that I do not possess it.

Perhaps some of you may reply: "But, Socrates, what is this pursuit of yours? Whence come these calumnies against you? You must have become engaged in some pursuit out of the common. All these stories and reports of you would never have gone about, if you had not been in some way different from other men. So tell us what your pursuits are, that we may not give our verdict in the dark." I think that that is a fair question, and I will try to explain to you what it is that has raised these calumnies against me, and given me this name. Listen, then: some of you perhaps will think that I am jesting, but I assure you that I will tell you the whole truth. I have gained this name, Athenians, simply by reason of a certain wisdom. But by what kind of wisdom? It is by just that wisdom which is, I believe, possible to men. In that, it may be, I am really wise. But the men of whom I was speaking just now must be wise in a wisdom which is greater than human wisdom, or in some way which I cannot describe, for certainly I know nothing of it myself, and if any man says that I do, he lies and wants to slander me. Do not interrupt me, Athenians, even if you think that I am speaking arrogantly. What I am going to say is not my own: I will tell you who says it, and he is worthy of your credit. I will bring the god of Delphi to be the witness of the fact of my wisdom and of its nature. You remember Chaerephon. From youth upwards he was my comrade; and he went into exile with the people,[1] and with the people he returned. And you remember, too, Chaerephon's character; how vehement he was in carrying through whatever he took in hand. Once he went to Delphi and ventured to put this question to the oracle,—I entreat you again, my friends, not to cry out,—he asked if there was any man who was wiser than I: and the priestess answered that there was no man. Chaerephon himself is dead, but his brother here will confirm what I say.

Now see why I tell you this. I am going to explain to you the origin of my unpopularity. When I heard of the oracle I began to reflect: What can God mean by this dark saying? I know very well that I am not wise, even in the smallest degree. Then what can he mean by saying that I am the wisest of men? It cannot be that he is speaking falsely, for he is a god and cannot lie. And for a long time I was at a loss to understand his meaning: then, very reluctantly, I turned to seek for it in this manner. I went to a man who was reputed to be wise, thinking that there, if anywhere, I should prove the answer wrong, and meaning to point out to the oracle its mistake, and to say, "You said that I was the wisest of men, but this man is wiser than I am." So I examined the man—I need not tell you his name, he was a politician—but this was the result, Athenians. When I conversed with him I came to see that, though a great many persons, and most of all he himself, thought that he was wise, yet he was not wise. And then I tried to prove to him that he was not wise, though he fancied that he was: and by so doing I made him, and many of the bystanders, my enemies. So when I went away, I thought to myself, "I am wiser than this man: neither of us probably knows anything that is really good, but he thinks he has knowledge, when he has not, while I, having no knowledge, do not think that I have. I seem at any rate, to be a little wiser than he is on this point: I do not think that I know what I do not know." Next I went to another man who was reputed to be still wiser than

---

[1][At the time of the oligarchy of the Thirty, 404 B.C.—*Trans.*]

the last, with exactly the same result. And there again I made him, and many other men, my enemies.

Then I went on to one man after another, seeing that I was making enemies every day, which caused me much unhappiness and anxiety: still I thought that I must set God's command above everything. So I had to go to every man who seemed to possess any knowledge, and search for the meaning of the oracle: and, Athenians, I must tell you the truth; verily, by the dog of Egypt, this was the result of the search which I made at God's bidding. I found that the men, whose reputation for wisdom stood highest, were nearly the most lacking in it; while others, who were looked down on as common people, were much better fitted to learn. Now, I must describe to you the wanderings which I undertook, like a series of Heraclean labours, to make full proof of the oracle. After the politicians, I went to the poets, tragic, dithyrambic, and others, thinking that there I should find myself manifestly more ignorant than they. So I took up the poems on which I thought that they had spent most pains, and asked them what they meant, hoping at the same time to learn something from them. I am ashamed to tell you the truth, my friends, but I must say it. Almost any one of the bystanders could have talked about the works of these poets better than the poets themselves. So I soon found that it is not by wisdom that the poets create their works, but by a certain natural power and by inspiration, like soothsayers and prophets, who say many fine things, but who understand nothing of what they say. The poets seemed to me to be in a similar case. And at the same time I perceived that, because of their poetry, they thought that they were the wisest of men in other matters too, which they were not. So I went away again, thinking that I had the same advantage over the poets that I had over the politicians.

Finally, I went to the artizans, for I knew very well that I possessed no knowledge at all, worth speaking of, and I was sure that I should find that they knew many fine things. And in that I was not mistaken. They knew what I did not know, and so far they were wiser than I. But, Athenians, it seemed to me that the skilled artizans made the same mistake as the poets. Each of them believed himself to be extremely wise in matters of the greatest importance, because he was skilful in his own art: and this mistake of theirs threw their real wisdom into the shade. So I asked myself, on behalf of the oracle, whether I would choose to remain as I was, without either their wisdom or their ignorance, or to possess both, as they did. And I made answer to myself and to the oracle that it was better for me to remain as I was.

By reason of this examination, Athenians, I have made many enemies of a very fierce and bitter kind, who have spread abroad a great number of calumnies about me, and people say that I am "a wise man." For the bystanders always think that I am wise myself in any matter wherein I convict another man of ignorance. But, my friends, I believe that only God is really wise: and that by this oracle he meant that men's wisdom is worth little or nothing. I do not think that he meant that Socrates was wise. He only made use of my name, and took me as an example, as though he would say to men, "He among you is the wisest, who, like Socrates, knows that in very truth his wisdom is worth nothing at all." And therefore I still go about testing and examining every man whom I think wise, whether he be a citizen or a stranger, as God has commanded me; and whenever I find that he is not wise, I point out to him on the part of God that he is not wise. And I am so busy in this pursuit that I have never had leisure to take any part worth mentioning in public matters, or to look after my private affairs. I am in very great poverty by reason of my service to God.

And besides this, the young men who follow me about, who are the sons of wealthy persons and have a great deal of spare time, take a natural pleasure in hearing men cross-examined: and they often imitate me among themselves: then they try their hands at cross-examining other people. And I imagine, they find a great abundance of men who think that they know a great deal, when in fact they know little or nothing. And then the persons who are cross-examined get angry with me instead of with themselves, and say that Socrates is an abominable fellow who corrupts young men. And when they are asked, "Why, what does he do? what does he teach?" they do not know what to say; but, not to seem at a loss, they repeat the stock charges against all philosophers, and allege that he investigates things in the air and under the earth, and that he teaches people to disbelieve in the gods, and "to make the worse appear the better reason." For, I fancy, they would not like to confess the truth, which is that they are shown up as ignorant pretenders to knowledge that they do not possess. And so they have been filling your ears with their bitter calumnies for a long time, for they are zealous and numerous and bitter against me; and they are well disciplined and plausible in speech. On these grounds Meletus and Anytus and Lycon have attacked me. Meletus is indignant with me on the part of the poets, and Anytus on the part of the artizans and politicians, and Lycon on the part of the orators. And so, as I said at the beginning, I shall be surprised if I am able, in the short time allowed me for my defence, to remove from your minds this prejudice which has grown so strong. What I have told you, Athenians, is the truth: I neither conceal, nor do I suppress anything, small or great. And yet I know that it is just this plainness of speech which makes me enemies. But that is only a proof that my words are true, and that the prejudice against me, and the causes of it, are what I have said. And whether you look for them now or hereafter, you will find that they are so.

[*Socrates then cross-examines and discredits his chief accuser—Ed.*]

Perhaps some one will say: "Are you not ashamed, Socrates, of following pursuits which are very likely now to cause your death?" I should answer him with justice, and say: My friend, if you think that a man of any worth at all ought to reckon the chances of life and death when he acts, or that he ought to think of anything but whether he is acting rightly or wrongly, and as a good or a bad man would act, you are grievously mistaken. According to you, the demigods who died at Troy would be men of no great worth, and among them the son of Thetis, who thought nothing of danger when the alternative was disgrace. For when his mother, a goddess, addressed him, as he was burning to slay Hector, I suppose in this fashion, "My son, if thou avengest the death of thy comrade Patroclus, and slayest Hector, thou wilt die thyself, for 'fate awaits thee straightway after Hector's death'"; he heard what she said, but he scorned danger and death; he feared much more to live a coward, and not to avenge his friend. "Let me punish the evil-doer and straightway die," he said, "that I may not remain here by the beaked ships, a scorn of men, encumbering the earth." Do you suppose that he thought of danger or of death? For this, Athenians, I believe to be the truth. Wherever a man's post is, whether he has chosen it of his own will, or whether he has been placed at it by his commander, there it is his duty to remain and face the danger, without thinking of death, or of any other thing, except dishonour.

When the generals whom you chose to command me, Athenians, placed me at my post at Potidaea, and at Amphipolis, and at Delium, I remained where they placed me, and ran the risk of death, like other men: and it would be very strange conduct on my part if I were to desert my post now from fear of death or of any other thing, when God has commanded me, as I am persuaded that he has done, to spend my life searching for wisdom, and in examining myself and others. That would indeed be a very strange thing: and then certainly I might with justice be brought to trial for not believing in the gods: for I should be disobeying the oracle, and fearing death, and thinking myself wise, when I was not wise. For to fear death, my friends, is only to think ourselves wise, without being wise: for it is to think that we know what we do not know. For anything that men can tell, death may be the greatest good that can happen to them: but they fear it as if they knew quite well that it was the greatest of evils. And what is this but that shameful ignorance of thinking that we know what we do not know? In this manner too, my friends, perhaps I am different from the mass of mankind: and if I were to claim to be at all wiser than others, it would be because I do not think that I have any clear knowledge about the other world, when, in fact, I have none. But I do know very well that it is evil and base to do wrong, and to disobey my superior, whether he be man or god. And I will never do what I know to be evil, and shrink in fear from what, for all that I can tell, may be a good. And so, even if you acquit me now, and do not listen to Anytus' argument that, if I am to be acquitted, I ought never to have been brought to trial at all; and that, as it is, you are bound to put me to death, because, as he said, if I escape, all your children will forthwith be utterly corrupted by practising what Socrates teaches; if you were therefore to say to me, "Socrates, this time we will not listen to Anytus: we will let you go; but on this condition, that you cease from carrying on this search of yours, and from philosophy; if you are found following those pursuits again, you shall die": I say, if you offered to let me go on these terms, I should reply:—"Athenians, I hold you in the highest regard and love; but I will obey God rather than you: and as long as I have breath and strength I will not cease from philosophy, and from exhorting you, and declaring the truth to everyone of you whom I meet, saying, as I am wont, 'My excellent friend, you are a citizen of Athens, a city which is very great and very famous for wisdom and power of mind; are you not ashamed of caring so much for the making of money, and for reputation, and for honour? Will you not think or care about wisdom, and truth, and the perfection of your soul?'" And if he disputes my words, and says that he does care about these things, I shall not forthwith release him and go away: I shall question him and cross-examine him and test him: and if I think that he has not virtue, though he says that he has, I shall reproach him for setting the lower value on the most important things, and a higher value on those that are of less account. This I shall do to every one whom I meet, young or old, citizen or stranger: but more especially to the citizens, for they are more nearly akin to me. For, know well, God has commanded me to do so. And I think that no better piece of fortune has ever befallen you in Athens than my service to God. For I spend my whole life in going about and persuading you all to give your first and chiefest care to the perfection of your souls, and not till you have done that to think of your bodies, or your wealth; and telling you that virtue does not come from wealth, but that wealth, and every other good thing which men have, whether in public, or in private, comes from virtue. If then I corrupt the youth by this teaching, the mischief is great: but if any man says that I teach anything else, he speaks falsely. And therefore, Athenians, I say, either listen to Anytus, or do not listen to him: either acquit me, or do not acquit me: but be sure that I shall not alter my way of life; no, not if I have to die for it many times.

Do not interrupt me, Athenians. Remember the request which I made to you, and listen to my words. I think that it will profit you to hear them. I am going to say something more to you, at which you may be inclined to cry out: but do not do that. Be sure that if you put me to death, who am what I have told you that I am, you will do yourselves more harm than me. Meletus and Anytus can do me no harm: that is impossible: for I am sure that God will not allow a good man to be injured by a bad one. They may indeed kill me, or drive me into exile, or deprive me of my civil rights; and perhaps Meletus and others think those things great evils. But I do not think so: I think that it is a much greater evil to do what he is doing now, and to try to put a man to death unjustly. And now, Athenians, I am not arguing in my own defence at all, as you might expect me to do: I am trying to persuade you not to sin against God, by condemning me, and rejecting his gift to you. For if you put me to death, you will not easily find another man to fill my place. God has sent me to attack the city, as if it were a great and noble horse, to use a quaint simile, which was rather sluggish from its size, and which needed to be aroused by a gadfly: and I think that I am the gadfly that God has sent to the city to attack it; for I never cease from settling upon you, as it were, at every point, and rousing, and exhorting, and reproaching each man of you all day long. You will not easily find any one else, my friends, to fill my place: and if you take my advice, you will spare my life. You are vexed, as drowsy persons are, when they are awakened, and of course, if you listen to Anytus, you could easily kill me with a single blow, and then sleep on undisturbed for the rest of your lives, unless God were to care for you enough to send another man to arouse you. And you may easily see that it is God who has given me to your city: a mere human impulse would never have led me to neglect all my own interests, or to endure seeing my private affairs neglected now for so many years, while it made me busy myself unceasingly in your interests, and go to each man of you by himself, like a father, or an elder brother, trying to persuade him to care for virtue. There would have been a reason for it, if I had gained any advantage by this conduct, or if I had been paid for my exhortations; but you see yourselves that my accusers, though they accuse me of everything else without blushing, have not had the effrontery to say that I ever either extracted or demanded payment. They could bring no evidence of that. And I think that I have sufficient evidence of the truth of what I say in my poverty.

Perhaps it may seem strange to you that, though I am so busy in going about in private with my counsel, yet I do not venture to come forward in the assembly, and take part in the public councils. You have often heard me speak of my reason for this, and in many places: it is that I have a certain divine sign from God, which is the divinity that Meletus has caricatured in his indictment. I have had it from childhood: it is a kind of voice, which whenever I hear it, always turns me back from something which I was going to do, but never urges me to act. It is this which forbids me to take part in politics. And I think that it does well to forbid me. For, Athenians, it is quite certain that if I had attempted to take part in politics, I should have perished at once and long ago, without doing any good either to you or to myself. And do not be vexed with me for telling the truth. There is no man who will preserve his life for long, either in Athens or elsewhere, if he firmly opposes the wishes of the people, and tries to prevent the commission of much injustice and illegality in the State. He who would really fight for justice, must do so as a private man, not in public, if he means to preserve his life, even for a short time.

I will prove to you that this is so by very strong evidence, not by mere words, but by what you value highly, actions. Listen then to what has happened to me, that you may know that there is no man who could make me consent to do wrong from the fear of death; but that I would perish at once rather than give way. What I am going to tell you may be a commonplace in the Courts of Law; nevertheless it is true. The only office that I ever held in the State, Athenians, was that of Senator. When you wished to try the ten generals, who did not rescue their men after the battle of Arginusae, in a body, which was illegal, as you all came to think afterwards, the tribe Antiochis, to which I belong, held the presidency. On that occasion I alone of all the presidents opposed your illegal action, and gave my vote against you. The speakers were ready to suspend me and arrest me; and you were clamouring

against me, and crying out to me to submit. But I thought that I ought to face
the danger out in the cause of law and justice, rather than join with you in
your unjust proposal, from fear of imprisonment or death. That was before
the destruction of the democracy. When the oligarchy came, the Thirty sent
for me, with four others, to the Council-Chamber and ordered us to bring
over Leon the Salaminian from Salamis, that they might put him to death.
They were in the habit of frequently giving similar orders to many others,
wishing to implicate as many men as possible in their crimes. But then I again
proved, not by mere words, but by my actions, that, if I may use a vulgar expression, I do not care a straw for death; but that I do care very much indeed
about not doing anything against the laws of God or man. That government
with all its power did not terrify me into doing anything wrong, but when we
left the Council-Chamber, the other four went over to Salamis, and brought
Leon across to Athens; and I went away home: and if the rule of the Thirty
had not been destroyed soon afterwards, I should very likely have been put
to death for what I did then. Many of you will be my witnesses in this matter.

Now do you think that I should have remained alive all these years, if I
had taken part in public affairs, and had always maintained the cause of justice like an honest man, and had held it a paramount duty, as it is, to do so?
Certainly not, Athenians, nor any other man either. But throughout my
whole life, both in private, and in public, whenever I have had to take part in
public affairs, you will find that I have never yielded a single point in a question of right and wrong to any man; no, not to those whom my enemies falsely assert to have been my pupils. But I was never any man's teacher. I have
never withheld myself from any one, young or old, who was anxious to hear
me converse while I was about my mission; neither do I converse for payment, and refuse to converse without payment: I am ready to ask questions
of rich and poor alike, and if any man wishes to answer me, and then listen
to what I have to say, he may. And I cannot justly be charged with causing
these men to turn out good or bad citizens: for I never either taught, or professed to teach any of them any knowledge whatever. And if any man asserts
that he ever learnt or heard any thing from me in private, which every one
else did not hear as well as he, be sure that he does not speak the truth.

Why is it, then, that people delight in spending so much time in my company? You have heard why, Athenians. I told you the whole truth when I said
that they delight in hearing me examine persons who think that they are wise
when they are not wise. It is certainly very amusing to listen to that. And, I say,
God has commanded me to examine men in oracles, and in dreams, and in
every way in which the divine will was ever declared to man. This is the truth,
Athenians, and if it were not the truth, it would be easily refuted. For if it were
really the case that I have already corrupted some of the young men, and I am
now corrupting others, surely some of them, finding as they grew older that I
had given them evil counsel in their youth, would have come forward to-day
to accuse me and take their revenge. Or if they were unwilling to do so themselves, surely their kinsmen, their fathers, or brothers, or other relatives,

would, if I had done them any harm, have remembered it, and taken their revenge. Certainly I see many of them in Court. Here is Crito, of my own deme and of my own age, the father of Critobulus; here is Lysanias of Sphettus, the father of Aeschinus: here is also Antiphon of Cephisus, the father of Epigenes. Then here are others, whose brothers have spent their time in my company; Nicostratus, the son of Theozotides, and brother of Theodotus—and Theodotus is dead, so he at least cannot entreat his brother to be silent: here is Paralus, the son of Demodocus, and the brother of Theages: here is Adeimantus, the son of Ariston, whose brother is Plato here: and Aeantodorus, whose brother is Aristodorus. And I can name many others to you, some of whom Meletus ought to have called as witnesses in the course of his own speech: but if he forgot to call them then, let him call them now—I will stand aside while he does so—and tell us if he has any such evidence. No, on the contrary, my friends, you will find all these men ready to support me, the corrupter, the injurer of their kindred, as Meletus and Anytus call me. Those of them who have been already corrupted might perhaps have some reason for supporting me: but what reason can their relatives, who are grown up, and who are uncorrupted, have, except the reason of truth and justice, that they know very well that Meletus is a liar, and that I am speaking the truth?

Well, my friends, this, together it may be with other things of the same nature, is pretty much what I have to say in my defence. There may be some one among you who will be vexed when he remembers how, even in a less important trial than this, he prayed and entreated the judges to acquit him with many tears, and brought forward his children and many of his friends and relatives in Court, in order to appeal to your feelings; and then finds that I shall do none of these things, though I am in what he would think the supreme danger. Perhaps he will harden himself against me when he notices this: it may make him angry, and he may give his vote in anger. If it is so with any of you—I do not suppose that it is, but in case it should be so—I think that I should answer him reasonably if I said: "My friend, I have kinsmen too, for in the words of Homer, 'I am not born of sticks and stones,' but of woman"; and so, Athenians, I have kinsmen, and I have three sons, one of them a lad, and the other two still children. Yet I will not bring any of them forward before you, and implore you to acquit me. And why will I do none of these things? It is not from arrogance, Athenians, nor because I hold you cheap: whether or not I can face death bravely is another question: but for my own credit, and for your credit, and for the credit of our city, I do not think it well, at my age, and with my name, to do anything of that kind. Rightly or wrongly, men have made up their minds that in some way Socrates is different from the mass of mankind. And it will be a shameful thing if those of you who are thought to excel in wisdom, or in bravery, or in any other virtue, are going to act in this fashion. I have often seen men with a reputation behaving in a strange way at their trial, as if they thought it a terrible fate to be killed, and as though they expected to live for ever, if you did not put them to death. Such men seem to me to bring discredit on the city: for any stranger would suppose that the best and most eminent Athenians, who are selected by their fellow-citizens to hold office, and for other honours, are no better than women. Those of you, Athenians, who have any reputation at all, ought not to do these things: and you ought not to allow us to do them: you should show that you will be much more merciless to men who make the city ridiculous by these pitiful pieces of acting, than to men who remain quiet.

But apart from the question of credit, my friends, I do not think that it is right to entreat the judge to acquit us, or to escape condemnation in that way. It is our duty to convince his mind by reason. He does not sit to give away justice to his friends, but to pronounce judgment: and he has sworn not to favour any man whom he would like to favour, but to decide questions according to law. And therefore we ought not teach you to forswear yourselves; and you ought not to allow yourselves to be taught, for then neither you nor we would be acting righteously. Therefore, Athenians, do not require me to do these things, for I believe them to be neither good nor just nor holy; and, more especially do not ask me to do them today, when Meletus is prosecuting me for impiety. For were I to be successful, and to prevail on you by my prayers to break your oaths, I should be clearly teaching you to believe that there are no gods; and I should be simply accusing myself by my defence of not believing in them. But, Athenians, that is very far from the truth. I do believe in the gods as no one of my accusers believes in them: and to you and to God I commit my cause to be decided as is best for you and for me.

[*He is found guilty by 281 votes to 220, and in a second vote is condemned to death—Ed.*]

You have not gained very much time, Athenians, and, as the price of it, you will have an evil name from all who wish to revile the city, and they will cast in your teeth that you put Socrates, a wise man, to death. For they will certainly call me wise, whether I am wise or not, when they want to reproach you. If you would have waited for a little while, your wishes would have been fulfilled in the course of nature; for you see that I am an old man, far advanced in years, and near to death. I am speaking not to all of you, only to those who have voted for my death. And now I am speaking to them still. Perhaps, my friends, you think that I have been defeated because I was wanting in the arguments by which I could have persuaded you to acquit me, if, that is, I had thought it right to do or to say anything to escape punishment. It is not so. I have been defeated because I was wanting, not in arguments, but in overboldness and effrontery: because I would not plead before you as you would have liked to hear me plead, or appeal to you with weeping and wailing, or say and do many other things, which I maintain are unworthy of me, but which you have been accustomed to from other men. But when I was defending myself, I thought that I ought not to do anything unmanly because of the danger which I ran, and I have not changed my mind now. I would very much rather defend myself as I did, and die, than as you would have had me do, and live. Both in a law suit, and in war, there are some things which neither I nor any other man may do in order to escape from death. In battle a man often sees that he may at least escape from death by throwing down his arms and falling on his knees before the pursuer to beg for his life. And there are many other ways of avoiding death in every danger, if a man will not scruple to say and to do anything. But, my friends, I think that it is a much harder thing to escape from wickedness than from death; for wickedness is swifter than death. And now I, who am old and slow, have been overtaken by the slower pursuer: and my accusers, who are clever and swift, have been overtaken by the swifter pursuer, which is wickedness. And now I shall go hence, sentenced by you to death; and they will go hence, sentenced by truth to receive the penalty of wickedness and evil. And I abide by this award as well as they. Perhaps it was right for these things to be so: and I think that they are fairly measured.

And now I wish to prophesy to you, Athenians who have condemned me. For I am going to die, and that is the time when men have most prophetic power. And I prophesy to you who have sentenced me to death, that a far severer punishment than you have inflicted on me, will surely overtake you as soon as I am dead. You have done this thing, thinking that you will be relieved from having to give an account of your lives. But I say that the result will be very different from that. There will be more men who will call you to account, whom I have held back, and whom you did not see. And they will be harder masters to you than I have been, for they will be younger, and you will be more angry with them. For if you think that you will restrain men from reproaching you for your evil lives by putting them to death, you are very much mistaken. That way of escape is hardly possible, and it is not a good one. It is much better, and much easier, not to silence reproaches, but to make yourselves as perfect as you can. This is my parting prophecy to you who have condemned me.

With you who have acquitted me I should like to converse touching this thing that has come to pass, while the authorities are busy, and before I go to the place where I have to die. So, I pray you, remain with me until I go hence: there is no reason why we should not converse with each other while it is possible. I wish to explain to you, as my friends, the meaning of what has befallen me. A wonderful thing has happened to me, judges—for you I am right in calling judges. The prophetic sign, which I am wont to receive from the divine voice, has been constantly with me all through my life till now, opposing me in quite small matters if I were not going to act rightly. And now you yourselves see what has happened to me; a thing which might be thought, and which is sometimes actually reckoned, the supreme evil. But the sign of God did not withstand me when I was leaving my house in the morning, nor when I was coming up hither to the Court, nor at any point in my speech, when I was going to say anything: though at other times it has often stopped me in the very act of speaking. But now, in this matter, it has never once withstood me, either in my words or my actions. I will tell you what I believe to be the reason of that. This thing that has come upon me must be a good: and those of us who think that death is an evil must needs be mistaken. I have a clear proof that that is so; for my accustomed sign would certainly have opposed me, if I had not been going to fare well.

And if we reflect in another way we shall see that we may well hope that death is a good. For the state of death is one of two things: either the dead man wholly ceases to be, and loses all sensation; or, according to the common belief, it is a change and migration of the soul unto another place. And if death is the absence of all sensation, and like the sleep of one whose slumbers are unbroken by any dreams, it will be a wonderful gain. For if a man had to select that night in which he slept so soundly that he did not even see any dreams, and had to compare with it all the other nights and days of his life, and then had to say how many days and nights in his life he had spent better and more pleasantly than this night, I think that a private person, nay, even the great King himself, would find them easy to count, compared with the others. If that is the nature of death, I for one count it a gain. For then it appears that eternity is nothing more than a single night. But if death is a journey to another place, and the common belief be true, that there are all who have died, what good could be greater than this, my judges? Would a journey not be worth taking, at the end of which, in the other world, we should be released from the self-styled judges who are here, and should find the true judges, who are said to sit in judgment below, such as Minos, and Rhadamanthus, and Aeacus, and Triptolemus, and the other demigods who were just in their lives? Or what would you not give to converse with Orpheus and Musaeus and Hesiod and Homer? I am willing to die many times, if this be true. And for my own part I should have a wonderful interest in meeting there Palamedes, and Ajax the son of Telamon, and the other men of old who have died through an unjust judgment, and in comparing my experiences with theirs. That I think would be no small pleasure. And, above all, I could spend my time in examining those who are there, as I examine men here, and in finding out which of them is wise, and which of them thinks himself wise, when he is not wise. What would we not give, my judges, to be able to examine the leader of the great expedition against Troy, or Odysseus, or Sisyphus, or countless other men and women whom we could name? It would be an infinite happiness to converse with them, and to live with them, and to examine them. Assuredly there they do not put men to death for doing that. For besides the other ways in which they are happier than we are, they are immortal, at least if the common belief be true.

And you too, judges, must face death with a good courage, and believe this as a truth, that no evil can happen to a good man, either in life, or after death. His fortunes are not neglected by the gods; and what has come to me to-day has not come by chance. I am persuaded that it was better for me to die now, and to be released from trouble: and that was the reason why the sign never turned me back. And so I am hardly angry with my accusers, or with those who have condemned me to die. Yet it was not with this mind that they accused me and condemned me, but meaning to do me an injury. So far I may find fault with them.

Yet I have one request to make of them. When my sons grow up, visit them with punishment, my friends, and vex them in the same way that I have vexed you, if they seem to you to care for riches, or for any other thing, before virtue: and if they think that they are something, when they are nothing at all, reproach them, as I have reproached you, for not caring for what they should, and for thinking that they are great men when in fact they are worthless. And if you will do this, I myself and my sons will have received our deserts at your hands.

But now the time has come, and we must go hence; I to die, and you to live. Whether life or death is better is known to God, and to God only.

Crito

SCENE: The Prison of Socrates

SOCRATES: Why have you come at this hour, Crito? Is it not still early?

CRITO: Yes, very early.

SOCRATES: About what time is it?

CRITO: It is just day-break.

SOCRATES: I wonder that the jailor was willing to let you in.

CRITO: He knows me now, Socrates, I come here so often; and besides, I have done him a service.

SOCRATES: Have you been here long?

CRITO: Yes; some time.

SOCRATES: Then why did you sit down without speaking? Why did you not wake me at once?

CRITO: Indeed, Socrates, I wish that I myself were not so sleepless and sorrowful. But I have been wondering to see how sweetly you sleep. And I purposely did not wake you, for I was anxious not to disturb your repose. Often before, all through your life, I have thought that your temper was a happy one; and I think so more than ever now, when I see how easily and calmly you bear the calamity that has come to you.

SOCRATES: Nay, Crito, it would be absurd if at my age I were angry at having to die.

CRITO: Other men as old are overtaken by similar calamities, Socrates; but their age does not save them from being angry with their fate.

SOCRATES: That is so: but tell me, why are you here so early?

CRITO: I am the bearer of bitter news, Socrates: not bitter, it seems, to you; but to me, and to all your friends, both bitter and grievous: and to none of them, I think, is it more grievous than to me.

SOCRATES: What is it? Has the ship come from Delos, at the arrival of which I am to die?

CRITO: No, it has not actually arrived: but I think that it will be here to-day, from the news which certain persons have brought from Sunium, who

Trans. F. J. Church.

left it there. It is clear from their news that it will be here to-day; and then, Socrates, to-morrow your life will have to end.

SOCRATES: Well, Crito, may it end fortunately. Be it so, if so the gods will. But I do not think that the ship will be here to-day.

CRITO: Why do you suppose not?

SOCRATES: I will tell you. I am to die on the day after the ship arrives, am I not?

CRITO: That is what the authorities say.

SOCRATES: Then I do not think that it will come to-day, but to-morrow. I judge from a certain dream which I saw a little while ago in the night: so it seems to be fortunate that you did not wake me.

CRITO: And what was this dream?

SOCRATES: A fair and comely woman, clad in white garments, seemed to come to me, and call me and say, "O Socrates—
The third day hence shall thou fair Phthia reach."

CRITO: What a strange dream, Socrates!

SOCRATES: But its meaning is clear; at least to me, Crito.

CRITO: Yes, too clear, it seems. But, O my good Socrates, I beseech you for the last time to listen to me and save yourself. For to me your death will be more than a single disaster: not only shall I lose a friend the like of whom I shall never find again, but many persons, who do not know you and me well, will think that I might have saved you if I had been willing to spend money, but that I neglected to do so. And what character could be more disgraceful than the character of caring more for money than for one's friends? The world will never believe that we were anxious to save you, but that you yourself refused to escape.

SOCRATES: But, my excellent Crito, why should we care so much about the opinion of the world? The best men, of whose opinion it is worth our while to think, will believe that we acted as we really did.

CRITO: But you see, Socrates, that it is necessary to care about the opinion of the world too. This very thing that has happened to you proves that the multitude can do a man not the least, but almost the greatest harm, if he be falsely accused to them.

SOCRATES: I wish that the multitude were able to do a man the greatest harm, Crito, for then they would be able to do him the greatest good too. That would have been well. But, as it is, they can do neither. They cannot make a man either wise or foolish: they act wholly at random.

CRITO: Well, be it so. But tell me this, Socrates. You surely are not anxious about me and your other friends, and afraid lest, if you escape, the informers should say that we stole you away, and get us into trouble, and involve us in a great deal of expense, or perhaps in the loss of all of our property, and, it may be, bring some other punishment upon us besides? If you have any fear of that kind, dismiss it. For of course we are bound to run those risks, and still greater risks than those if necessary, in saving you. So do not, I beseech you, refuse to listen to me.

SOCRATES: I am anxious about that, Crito, and about much besides.

CRITO: Then have no fear on that score. There are men who, for no very large
sum, are ready to bring you out of prison into safety. And then, you
know, these informers are cheaply bought, and there would be no need
to spend much upon them. My fortune is at your service, and I think that
it is sufficient: and if you have any feeling about making use of my
money, there are strangers in Athens, whom you know, ready to use
theirs, and one of them, Simmias of Thebes, has actually brought enough
for this very purpose. And Cebes and many others are ready too. And
therefore, I repeat, do not shrink from saving yourself on that ground.
And do not let what you said in the Court, that if you went into exile you
would not know what to do with yourself, stand in your way; for there
are many places for you to go to, where you will be welcomed. If you
choose to go to Thessaly, I have friends there who will make much of
you, and shelter you from any annoyance from the people of Thessaly.

    And besides, Socrates, I think that you will be doing what is wrong,
if you abandon your life when you might preserve it. You are simply
playing the game of your enemies; it is exactly the game of those who
wanted to destroy you. And what is more, to me you seem to be abandoning your children too: you will leave them to take their chance in life,
as far as you are concerned, when you might bring them up and educate
them. Most likely their fate will be the usual fate of children who are left
orphans. But you ought not to beget children unless you mean to take the
trouble of bringing them up and educating them. It seems to me that you
are choosing the easy way, and not the way of a good and brave man, as
you ought, when you have been talking all your life long of the value that
you set upon virtue. For my part, I feel ashamed both for you, and for us
who are your friends. Men will think that the whole of this thing which
has happened to you—your appearance in court to take your trial, when
you need not have appeared at all; the very way in which the trial was
conducted; and then lastly this, for the crowning absurdity of the whole
affair, is due to our cowardice. It will look as if we had shirked the danger
out of miserable cowardice; for we did not save you, and you did not
save yourself, when it was quite possible to do so, if we had been good
for anything at all. Take care, Socrates, lest these things be not evil only,
but also dishonourable to you and to us. Consider then; or rather the time
for consideration is past; we must resolve; and there is only one plan possible. Everything must be done to-night. If we delay any longer, we are
lost. O Socrates, I implore you not to refuse to listen to me.

SOCRATES: My dear Crito, if your anxiety to save me be right, it is most valuable: but if it be not right, its greatness makes it all the more dangerous.
We must consider then whether we are to do as you say, or not; for I am
still what I always have been, a man who will listen to no voice but the
voice of the reasoning which on consideration I find to be truest. I cannot cast aside my former arguments because this misfortune has come
to me. They seem to me to be as true as ever they were, and I hold

exactly the same ones in honour and esteem as I used to: and if we have no better reasoning to substitute for them, I certainly shall not agree to your proposal, not even though the power of the multitude should scare us with fresh terrors, as children are scared with hobgoblins, and inflict upon us new fines, and imprisonments, and deaths. How then shall we most fitly examine the question? Shall we go back first to what you say about the opinions of men, and ask if we used to be right in thinking that we ought to pay attention to some opinions, and not to others? Used we to be right in saying so before I was condemned to die, and has it now become apparent that we were talking at random, and arguing for the sake of argument, and that it was really nothing but play and nonsense? I am anxious, Crito, to examine our former reasoning with your help, and to see whether my present position will appear to me to have affected its truth in any way, or not; and whether we are to set it aside, or to yield assent to it. Those of us who thought at all seriously, used always to say, I think, exactly what I said just now, namely, that we ought to esteem some of the opinions which men form highly, and not others. Tell me, Crito, if you please, do you not think that they were right? For you, humanly speaking, will not have to die to-morrow, and your judgment will not be biased by that circumstance. Consider then: do you not think it reasonable to say that we should not esteem all the opinions of men, but only some, nor the opinions of all men, but only of some men? What do you think? Is not this true?

CRITO: It is.

SOCRATES: And we should esteem the good opinions, and not the worthless ones?

CRITO: Yes.

SOCRATES: But the good opinions are those of the wise, and the worthless ones those of the foolish?

CRITO: Of course.

SOCRATES: And what used we to say about this? Does a man who is in training, and who is in earnest about it, attend to the praise and blame and opinion of all men, or of the one man only who is a doctor or a trainer?

CRITO: He attends only to the opinion of the one man.

SOCRATES: Then he ought to fear the blame and welcome the praise of this one man, not of the many?

CRITO: Clearly.

SOCRATES: Then he must act and exercise, and eat and drink in whatever way the one man who is his master, and who understands the matter, bids him; not as others bid him?

CRITO: That is so.

SOCRATES: Good. But if he disobeys this one man, and disregards his opinion and his praise, and esteems instead what the many, who understand nothing of the matter, say, will he not suffer for it?

CRITO: Of course he will.

SOCRATES: And how will he suffer? In what direction, and in what part of
        himself?

CRITO: Of course in his body. That is disabled.

SOCRATES: You are right. And, Crito, to be brief, is it not the same, in every-
        thing? And, therefore, in questions of right and wrong, and of the base
        and the honourable, and of good and evil, which we are now consider-
        ing, ought we to follow the opinion of the many and fear that, or the
        opinion of the one man who understands these matters (if we can find
        him), and feel more shame and fear before him than before all other
        men? For if we do not follow him, we shall cripple and maim that part
        of us which, we used to say, is improved by right and disabled by
        wrong. Or is this not so?

CRITO: No, Socrates, I agree with you.

SOCRATES: Now, if, by listening to the opinions of those who do not under-
        stand, we disable that part of us which is improved by health and crip-
        pled by disease, is our life worth living, when it is crippled? It is the
        body, is it not?

CRITO: Yes.

SOCRATES: Is life worth living with the body crippled and in a bad state?

CRITO: No, certainly not.

SOCRATES: Then is life worth living when that part of us which is maimed
        by wrong and benefited by right is crippled? Or do we consider that
        part of us, whatever it is, which has to do with right and wrong to be of
        less consequence than our body?

CRITO: No, certainly not.

SOCRATES: But more valuable?

CRITO: Yes, much more so.

SOCRATES: Then, my excellent friend, we must not think so much of what
        the many will say of us; we must think of what the one man, who un-
        derstands right and wrong, and of what Truth herself will say of us.
        And so you are mistaken to begin with, when you invite us to regard
        the opinion of the multitude concerning the right and the honourable
        and the good, and their opposites. But, it may be said, the multitude
        can put us to death?

CRITO: Yes, that is evident. That may be said, Socrates.

SOCRATES: True. But, my excellent friend, to me it appears that the conclu-
        sion which we have just reached, is the same as our conclusion of for-
        mer times. Now consider whether we still hold to the belief, that we
        should set the highest value, not on living, but on living well?

CRITO: Yes, we do.

SOCRATES: And living well and honourably and rightly mean the same
        thing: do we hold to that or not?

CRITO: We do.

SOCRATES: Then, starting from these premises, we have to consider whether it
        is right or not right for me to try to escape from prison, without the

consent of the Athenians. If we find that it is right, we will try: if not, we will let it alone. I am afraid that considerations of expense, and of reputation, and of bringing up my children, of which you talk, Crito, are only the reflections of our friends, the many, who lightly put men to death, and who would, if they could, as lightly bring them to life again, without a thought. But reason, which is our guide, shows us that we can have nothing to consider but the question which I asked just now: namely, shall we be doing right if we give money and thanks to the men who are to aid me in escaping, and if we ourselves take our respective parts in my escape? Or shall we in truth be doing wrong, if we do all this? And if we find that we should be doing wrong, then we must not take any account either of death, or of any other evil that may be the consequence of remaining quietly here, but only of doing wrong.

CRITO: I think that you are right, Socrates. But what are we to do?

SOCRATES: Let us consider that together, my good sir, and if you can contradict anything that I say, do so, and I will be convinced: but if you cannot, do not go on repeating to me any longer, my dear friend, that I should escape without the consent of the Athenians. I am very anxious to act with your approval: I do not want you to think me mistaken. But now tell me if you agree with the doctrine from which I start, and try to answer my questions as you think best.

CRITO: I will try.

SOCRATES: Ought we never to do wrong intentionally at all; or may we do wrong in some ways, and not in others? Or, as we have often agreed in former times, is it never either good or honourable to do wrong? Have all our former conclusions been forgotten in these few days? Old men as we were, Crito, did we not see, in days gone by, when we were gravely conversing with each other, that we were no better than children? Or is not what we used to say most assuredly the truth, whether the world agrees with us or not? Is not wrong-doing an evil and a shame to the wrongdoer in every case, whether we incur a heavier or a lighter punishment than death as the consequence of doing right? Do we believe that?

CRITO: We do.

SOCRATES: Then we ought never to do wrong at all?

CRITO: Certainly not.

SOCRATES: Neither, if we ought never to do wrong at all, ought we to repay wrong with wrong, as the world thinks we may?

CRITO: Clearly not.

SOCRATES: Well then, Crito, ought we to do evil to any one?

CRITO: Certainly I think not, Socrates.

SOCRATES: And is it right to repay evil with evil, as the world thinks, or not right?

CRITO: Certainly it is not right.

SOCRATES: For there is no difference, is there, between doing evil to a man, and wronging him?

CRITO: True.

SOCRATES: Then we ought not to repay wrong with wrong or do harm to any man, no matter what we may have suffered from him. And in conceding this, Crito, be careful that you do not concede more than you mean. For I know that only a few men hold, or ever will hold this opinion. And so those who hold it, and those who do not, have no common ground of argument; they can of necessity only look with contempt on each other's belief. Do you therefore consider very carefully whether you agree with me and share my opinion. Are we to start in our inquiry from the doctrine that it is never right either to do wrong, or to repay wrong with wrong, or to avenge ourselves on any man who harms us, by harming him in return? Or do you disagree with me and dissent from my principle? I myself have believed in it for a long time, and I believe in it still. But if you differ in any way, explain to me how. If you still hold to our former opinion, listen to my next point.

CRITO: Yes, I hold to it, and I agree with you. Go on.

SOCRATES: Then, my next point, or rather my next question, is this: Ought a man to perform his just agreements, or may he shuffle out of them?

CRITO: He ought to perform them.

SOCRATES: Then consider. If I escape without the State's consent, shall I be injuring those whom I ought least to injure, or not? Shall I be abiding by my just agreements or not?

CRITO: I cannot answer your question, Socrates. I do not understand it.

SOCRATES: Consider it in this way. Suppose the laws and the commonwealth were to come and appear to me as I was preparing to run away (if that is the right phrase to describe my escape) and were to ask, "Tell us, Socrates, what have you in your mind to do? What do you mean by trying to escape, but to destroy us, the laws, and the whole city, so far as in you lies? Do you think that a state can exist and not be overthrown, in which the decisions of law are of no force, and are disregarded and set at nought by private individuals?" How shall we answer questions like that, Crito? Much might be said, especially by an orator, in defence of the law which makes judicial decisions supreme. Shall I reply, "But the state has injured me: it has decided my cause wrongly." Shall we say that?

CRITO: Certainly we will, Socrates.

SOCRATES: And suppose the laws were to reply, "Was that our agreement? or was it that you would submit to whatever judgments the state should pronounce?" And if we were to wonder at their words, perhaps they would say, "Socrates, wonder not at our words, but answer us; you yourself are accustomed to ask questions and to answer them. What complaint have you against us and the city, that you are trying to destroy us? Are we not, first, your parents? Through us your father took your mother and begat you. Tell us, have you any fault to find with those of us that are the laws of marriage?" "I have none," I should reply. "Or have you any fault to find with those of us that regulate the nurture and education of the child, which you, like others, received? Did not we do well in bidding your father educate you in music and gymnastic?" "You did," I should say. "Well then, since you were brought into the world and nurtured and educated by us, how, in the first place, can you deny that you are our child and our slave, as your fathers were before you? And if this be so, do you think that your rights are on a level with ours? Do you think that you have a right to retaliate upon us if we should try to do anything to you? You had not the same rights that your father had, or that your master would have had, if you had been a slave. You had no right to retaliate upon them if they ill-treated you, or to answer them if they reviled you, or to strike them back if they struck you, or to repay them evil with evil in any way. And do you think that you may retaliate on your country and its laws? If we try to destroy you, because we think it right, will you in return do all that you can to destroy us, the laws, and your country, and say that in so doing you are doing right, you, the man, who in truth thinks so much of virtue? Or are you too wise to see that your country is worthier, and more august, and more sacred, and holier and held in higher honour both by the gods and by all men of understanding, than your father and your mother and all your other ancestors; and that it is your bounden duty to reverence it, and to submit to it, and to approach it more humbly than you would approach your father, when it is angry with you; and either to do whatever it bids you to do or to persuade it to excuse you; and to obey in silence if it orders you to endure stripes or imprisonment, or if it send you to battle to be wounded or to die? That is what is your duty. You must not give way, nor retreat, nor desert your post. In war, and in the court of justice, and everywhere, you must do whatever your city and your country bid you do, or you must convince them that their commands are unjust. But it is against the law of God to use violence to your father or to your mother; and much more so is it against the law of God to use violence to your country." What answer shall we make, Crito? Shall we say that the laws speak truly, or not?

CRITO: I think that they do.

SOCRATES: "Then consider, Socrates," perhaps they would say, "if we are right in saying that by attempting to escape you are attempting to injure us. We brought you into the world, we nurtured you, we educated you, we gave you and every other citizen a share of all the good things we could. Yet we proclaim that if any man of the Athenians is dissatisfied with us, he may take his goods and go away whithersoever he pleases: we give that permission to every man who chooses to avail himself of it, so soon as he has reached man's estate, and sees us, the laws, and the administration of our city. No one of us stands in his way or forbids him to take his goods and go wherever he likes, whether it be to an Athenian colony, or to any foreign country, if he is dissatisfied with us and with the city. But we say that every man of you who remains here, seeing how we administer justice, and how we govern the city in other matters, has agreed, by the very fact of remaining here, to do whatsoever we bid him. And, we say, he who disobeys us, does a threefold wrong: he disobeys us who are his parents, and he disobeys us who fostered him, and he disobeys us after he has agreed to obey us, without persuading us that we are wrong. Yet we did not bid him sternly to do whatever we told him. We offered him an alternative; we gave him his choice, either to obey us, or to convince us that we were wrong: but he does neither.

"These are the charges, Socrates, to which we say that you will expose yourself, if you do what you intend; and that not less, but more than other Athenians." And if I were to ask, "And why?" they might retort with justice that I have bound myself by the agreement with them more than other Athenians. They would say, "Socrates, we have very strong evidence that you were satisfied with us and with the city. You would not have been content to stay at home in it more than other Athenians, unless you had been satisfied with it more than they. You never went away from Athens to the festivals, save once to the Isthmian games, nor elsewhere except on military service; you never made other journeys like other men; you had no desire to see other cities or other laws; you were contented with us and our city. So strongly did you prefer us, and agree to be governed by us: and what is more, you begat children in this city, you found it so pleasant. And besides, if you had wished, you might at your trial have offered to go into exile. At that time you could have done with the State's consent, what you are trying now to do without it. But then you gloried in being willing to die. You said that you preferred death to exile. And now you are not ashamed of those words; you do not respect us the laws, for you are trying to destroy us: and you are acting just as a miserable slave would act, trying to run away, and breaking the covenant and agreement which you made to submit to our government. First, therefore, answer this question. Are we right, or are we wrong, in saying that you have agreed not in mere words, but in reality to live under our government?" What are we to say, Crito? Must we not admit that it is true?

CRITO: We must, Socrates.

SOCRATES: Then they would say, "Are you not breaking your covenants and agreements with us? And you were not led to make them by force or by fraud: you had not to make up your mind in a hurry. You had seventy years in which you might have gone away, if you had been dissatisfied with us, or if the agreement had seemed to you unjust. But you preferred neither Lacedaemon nor Crete, though you are fond of saying that they are well governed, nor any other state, either of the Hellenes, or the Barbarians. You went away from Athens less than the lame and the blind and the cripple. Clearly you, far more than other Athenians, were satisfied with the city, and also with us who are its laws: for who would be satisfied with a city which had no laws? And now will not you abide by your agreement? If you take our advice, you will, Socrates: then you will not make yourself ridiculous by going away from Athens.

"For consider: what good will you do yourself or your friends by thus transgressing, and breaking your agreement? It is tolerably certain that they, on their part, will at least run the risk of exile, and of losing their civil rights, or of forfeiting their property. For yourself, you might go to one of the neighbouring cities, to Thebes or to Megara for instance—for both of them are well governed—but, Socrates, you will come as an enemy to these commonwealths; and all who care for their city will look askance at you, and think that you are a subverter of law. And you will confirm the judges in their opinion, and make it seem that their verdict was a just one. For a man who is a subverter of law, may well be supposed to be a corrupter of the young and thoughtless. Then will you avoid well-governed states and civilised men? Will life be worth having, if you do? Or will you consort with such men, and converse without shame—about what, Socrates? About the things which you talk of here? Will you tell them that virtue, and justice, and institutions, and law are the most precious things that men can have? And do you not think that that will be a shameful thing in Socrates? You ought to think so. But you will leave these places; you will go to the friends of Crito in Thessaly: for there there is most disorder and license: and very likely, they will be delighted to hear of the ludicrous way in which you escaped from prison, dressed up in peasant's clothes, or in some other disguise which people put on when they are running away, and with your appearance altered. But will no one say how you, an old man, with probably only a few more years to live, clung so greedily to life that you dared to transgress the highest laws? Perhaps not, if you do not displease them. But if you do, Socrates, you will hear much that will make you blush. You will pass your life as the flatterer and the slave of all men; and what will you be doing but feasting in Thessaly? It will be as if you had made a journey to Thessaly for an entertainment. And where will be all our old sayings about justice and virtue then? But you wish to live for the sake of your children? You want to bring them up and educate them? What? Will you take them with you to Thessaly, and bring them up and educate them there? Will you make them strangers to their own country, that you may bestow this benefit on them too? Or supposing that you leave them in Athens, will they be brought up and educated better if you are alive, though you are not with them? Yes; your friends will take care of them. Will your friends take care of them if you make a journey to Thessaly, and not if you make a journey to Hades? You ought not to think that, at least if those who call themselves your friends are good for anything at all.

"No, Socrates, be advised by us who have fostered you. Think neither of children, nor of life, nor of any other thing before justice, that when you come to the other world you may be able to make your defence before the rulers who sit in judgment there. It is clear that neither you nor any of your friends will be happier, or juster, or holier in this life, if you do this thing, nor will you be happier after you are dead. Now you will go away wronged, not by us, the laws, but by men. But if you repay evil with evil, and wrong with wrong in this shameful way, and break your agreements and covenants with us, and injure those whom you should least injure, yourself, and your friends, and your country, and us, and so escape, then we shall be angry with you while you live, and when you die our brethren, the laws in Hades, will not receive you kindly; for they will know that on earth you did all that you could to destroy us. Listen then to us, and let not Crito persuade you to do as he says."

Know well, my dear friend Crito, that this is what I seem to hear, as the worshippers of Cybele seem, in their frenzy, to hear the music of flutes: and the sound of these words rings loudly in my ears, and drowns all other words. And I feel sure that if you try to change my mind you will speak in vain; nevertheless, if you think that you will succeed, say on.

CRITO: I can say no more, Socrates.

SOCRATES: Then let it be, Crito: and let us do as I say, seeing that God so directs us.

Phaedo

SCENE: The Prison of Socrates

. . .

When he had finished speaking Crito said, "Be it so, Socrates. But have you any commands for your friends or for me about your children, or about other things? How shall we serve you best?"

"Simply by doing what I always tell you, Crito. Take care of your own selves, and you will serve me and mine and yourselves in all that you do, even though you make no promises now. But if you are careless of your own selves, and will not follow the path of life which we have pointed out in our discussions both today and at other times, all your promises now, however profuse and earnest they are, will be of no avail."

"We will do our best," said Crito. "But how shall we bury you?"

"As you please," he answered; "only you must catch me first, and not let me escape you." And then he looked at us with a smile and said, "My friends, I cannot convince Crito that I am the Socrates who has been conversing with you, and arranging his arguments in order. He thinks that I am the

Trans. F. J. Church.

body which he will presently see a corpse, and he asks how he is to bury me. All the arguments which I have used to prove that I shall not remain with you after I have drunk the poison, but that I shall go away to the happiness of the blessed, with which I tried to comfort you and myself, have been thrown away on him. Do you therefore be my sureties to him, as he was my surety at the trial, but in a different way. He was surety for me then that I would remain; but you must be my sureties to him that I shall go away when I am dead, and not remain with you: then he will feel my death less; and when he sees my body being burnt or buried, he will not be grieved because he thinks that I am suffering dreadful things: and at my funeral he will not say that it is Socrates whom he is laying out, or bearing to the grave, or burying." "For, dear Crito," he continued, "you must know that to use words wrongly is not only a fault in itself; it also creates evil in the soul. You must be of good cheer, and say that you are burying my body: and you must bury it as you please, and as you think right."

With these words he rose and went into another room to bathe himself: Crito went with him and told us to wait. So we waited, talking of the argument, and discussing it, and then again dwelling on the greatness of the calamity which had fallen upon us: it seemed as if we were going to lose a father, and to be orphans for the rest of our life. When he had bathed, and his children had been brought to him,—he had two sons quite little, and one grown up,—and the women of his family were come, he spoke with them in Crito's presence, and gave them his last commands; then he sent the women and children away, and returned to us. By that time it was near the hour of sunset, for he had been a long while within. When he came back to us from the bath he sat down, but not much was said after that. Presently the servant of the Eleven came and stood before him and said, "I know that I shall not find you unreasonable like other men, Socrates. They are angry with me and curse me when I bid them drink the poison because the authorities make me do it. But I have found you all along the noblest and gentlest and best man that has ever come here; and now I am sure that you will not be angry with me, but with those who you know are to blame. And so farewell, and try to bear what must be as lightly as you can; you know why I have come." With that he turned away weeping, and went out.

Socrates looked up at him, and replied, "Farewell: I will do as you say." Then he turned to us and said, "How courteous the man is! And the whole time that I have been here, he has constantly come in to see me, and sometimes he has talked to me, and has been the best of men; and now, how generously he weeps for me! Come, Crito, let us obey him: let the poison be brought if it is ready; and if it is not ready, let it be prepared."

Crito replied, "Nay, Socrates, I think that the sun is still upon the hills; it has not set. Besides, I know that other men take the poison quite late, and eat and drink heartily, and even enjoy the company of their chosen friends, after the announcement has been made. So do not hurry; there is still time."

Socrates replied, "And those whom you speak of, Crito, naturally do so; for they think that they will be gainers by so doing. And I naturally shall not do so; for I think that I should gain nothing by drinking the poison a little later, but my own contempt for so greedily saving up a life which is already spent. So do not refuse to do as I say."

Then Crito made a sign to his slave who was standing by; and the slave went out, and after some delay returned with the man who was to give the poison, carrying it prepared in a cup. When Socrates saw him, he asked, "You understand these things, my good sir, what have I to do?"

"You have only to drink this," he replied, "and to walk about until your legs feel heavy, and then lie down; and it will act of itself." With that he handed the cup to Socrates, who took it quite cheerfully, without trembling, and without any change of colour or of feature, and looked up at the man with that fixed glance of his, and asked, "What say you to making a libation from this draught? May I, or not?" "We only prepare so much as we think sufficient, Socrates," he answered. "I understand," said Socrates. "But I suppose that I may, and must, pray to the gods that my journey hence may be prosperous: that is my prayer; be it so." With these words he put the cup to his lips and drank the poison quite calmly and cheerfully. Till then most of us had been able to control our grief fairly well; but when we saw him drinking, and then the poison finished, we could do so no longer: my tears came fast in spite of myself, and I covered my face and wept for myself: it was not for him, but at my own misfortune at losing such a friend. Even before that Crito had been unable to restrain his tears, and had gone away; and Apollodorus, who had never once ceased weeping the whole time, burst into a loud cry, and made us one and all break down by his sobbing and grief, except only Socrates himself. "What are you doing, my friends?" he exclaimed. "I sent away the women chiefly in order that they might not offend in this way; for I have heard that a man should die in silence. So calm yourselves and bear up." When we heard that we were ashamed, and we ceased from weeping. But he walked about, until he said that his legs were getting heavy, and then he lay down on his back, as he was told. And the man who gave the poison began to examine his feet and legs, from time to time: then he pressed his foot hard, and asked if there was any feeling in it; and Socrates said, "No": and then his legs, and so higher and higher, and showed us that he was cold and stiff. And Socrates felt himself, and said that when it came to his heart, he should be gone. He was already growing cold about the groin, when he uncovered his face, which had been covered, and spoke for the last time. "Crito," he said, "I owe a cock to Asclepius: do not forget to repay it." "It shall be done," replied Crito. "Is there anything else that you wish?" He made no answer to this question; but after a short interval there was a movement, and the man uncovered him, and his eyes were fixed. Then Crito closed his mouth and his eyes.

Such was the end of our friend, a man, I think, who was the wisest and justest, and the best man that I have ever known.

Plato

The son of a wealthy and noble family—on his mother's side he was descended from the great law-giver, Solon—Plato (427–347 B.C.) was preparing for a career in politics when the trial and execution of Socrates changed the course of his life. He abandoned his political career and turned to philosophy, opening a school on the outskirts of Athens dedicated to the Socratic search for wisdom. Plato's school, known as the Academy, was the first university in the history of the West. It continued operating for over nine hundred years, from 387 B.C. until it was closed by an edict of the Roman emperor Justinian in A.D. 529.

Unlike Socrates, Plato was a writer as well as a teacher. His writings are in the form of dialogues, with Socrates as the principal speaker. In the selection that follows, the Allegory of the Cave (perhaps the most famous passage in all his works), Plato describes symbolically the predicament in which human beings find themselves and proposes a way of salvation. In addition, the Allegory presents, in brief form, most of Plato's main philosophical theories: his belief that the world revealed by our senses is not the real world but only a poor copy of it, and that the real world can be apprehended only intellectually; his idea that knowledge cannot be transferred from teacher to student, but rather that education consists in directing students' minds toward what is real and important and allowing them to apprehend it for themselves; his faith that the universe ultimately is good; his conviction that enlightened individuals have an obligation to the rest of society, and that a good society must be one in which the truly wise are the rulers. Woven into these themes is a defense of the life of Socrates and a condemnation of Athenian society for having executed him.

The Allegory is from Book VII of Plato's best-known work, *The Republic*, which represents a conversation between Socrates and some friends on the nature of justice, and which includes Plato's plan for an ideal state ruled by philosophers.

Consider the following questions as you study the text below.

1. How did Plato define "the Good"? What must a person do in order to see things as they really are?

2. According to Plato, what was the purpose of government? What kind of government was best suited to achieving this purpose? In Plato's view, why did most governments fail in this regard?

The Republic

[The Allegory of the Cave]

Next, said I [Socrates], here is a parable to illustrate the degrees in which our nature may be enlightened or unenlightened. Imagine the condition of men living in a sort of cavernous chamber underground, with an entrance open to the light and a long passage all down the cave. Here they have been from childhood, chained by the leg and also by the neck, so that they cannot move and can see only what is in front of them, because the chains will not let them turn their heads. At some distance higher up is the light of a fire burning behind them; and between the prisoners and the fire is a track with a parapet built along it, like the screen at a puppet-show, which hides the performers while they show their puppets over the top.

I see, said he [Glaucon].

Now behind this parapet imagine persons carrying along various artificial objects, including figures of men and animals in wood or stone or other materials, which project above the parapet. Naturally, some of these persons will be talking, others silent.

It is a strange picture, he said, and a strange sort of prisoners.

Like ourselves, I replied; for in the first place prisoners so confined would have seen nothing of themselves or of one another, except the shadows thrown by the fire-light on the wall of the Cave facing them, would they?

Not if all their lives they had been prevented from moving their heads.

And they would have seen as little of the objects carried past.

Of course.

Now, if they could talk to one another, would they not suppose that their words referred only to those passing shadows which they saw?

Necessarily.

And suppose their prison had an echo from the wall facing them? When one of the people crossing behind them spoke, they could only suppose that the sound came from the shadow passing before their eyes.

No doubt.

In every way, then, such prisoners would recognize as reality nothing but the shadows of those artificial objects.

Inevitably.

Now consider what would happen if their release from the chains and the healing of their unwisdom should come about in this way. Suppose one of them set free and forced suddenly to stand up, turn his head, and walk

The Republic of Plato, trans. F. M. Cornford (Oxford: The Clarendon Press, 1941), pp. 227–35. Reprinted by permission of Oxford University Press.

with eyes lifted to the light; all these movements would be painful, and he would be too dazzled to make out the objects whose shadows he had been used to see. What do you think he would say, if someone told him that what he had formerly seen was meaningless illusion, but now, being somewhat nearer to reality and turned towards more real objects, he was getting a truer view? Suppose further that he were shown the various objects being carried by and were made to say, in reply to questions, what each of them was. Would he not be perplexed and believe the objects now shown him to be not so real as what he formerly saw?

Yes, not nearly so real.

And if he were forced to look at the fire-light itself, would not his eyes ache, so that he would try to escape and turn back to the things which he could see distinctly, convinced that they really were clearer than these other objects now being shown to him?

Yes.

And suppose someone were to drag him away forcibly up the steep and rugged ascent and not let him go until he had hauled him out into the sunlight, would he not suffer pain and vexation at such treatment, and, when he had come out into the light, find his eyes so full of its radiance that he could not see a single one of the things that he was now told were real?

Certainly he would not see them all at once.

He would need, then, to grow accustomed before he could see things in that upper world. At first it would be easiest to make out shadows, and then the images of men and things reflected in water, and later on the things them-selves. After that, it would be easier to watch the heavenly bodies and the sky itself by night, looking at the light of the moon and stars rather than the Sun and the Sun's light in the day-time.

Yes, surely.

Last of all, he would be able to look at the Sun and contemplate its na-ture, not as it appears when reflected in water or any alien medium, but as it is in itself in its own domain.

No doubt.

And now he would begin to draw the conclusion that it is the Sun that produces the seasons and the course of the year and controls everything in the visible world, and moreover is in a way the cause of all that he and his companions used to see.

Clearly he would come at last to that conclusion.

Then if he called to mind his fellow prisoners and what passed for wis-dom in his former dwelling-place, he would surely think himself happy in the change and be sorry for them. They may have had a practice of honour-ing and commending one another, with prizes for the man who had the keen-est eye for the passing shadows and the best memory for the order in which they followed or accompanied one another, so that he could make a good guess as to which was going to come next. Would our released prisoner be likely to covet those prizes or to envy the men exalted to honour and power in the Cave? Would he not feel like Homer's Achilles, that he would far sooner "be on earth as a hired servant in the house of a landless man" or endure anything rather than go back to his old beliefs and live in the old way?

Yes, he would prefer any fate to such a life.

Now imagine what would happen if he went down again to take his former seat in the Cave. Coming suddenly out of the sunlight, his eyes would be filled with darkness. He might be required once more to deliver his opinion on those shadows, in competition with the prisoners who had never been released, while his eyesight was still dim and unsteady; and it might take some time to become used to the darkness. They would laugh at him and say that he had gone up only to come back with his sight ruined; it was worth no one's while even to attempt the ascent. If they could lay hands on the man who was trying to set them free and lead them up, they would kill him.

Yes, they would.

Every feature in this parable, my dear Glaucon, is meant to fit our earlier analysis. The prison dwelling corresponds to the region revealed to us through the sense of sight, and the fire-light within it to the power of the Sun. The ascent to see the things in the upper world you may take as standing for the upward journey of the soul into the region of the intelligible; then you will be in possession of what I surmise, since that is what you wish to be told. Heaven knows whether it is true; but this, at any rate, is how it appears to me. In the world of knowledge, the last thing to be perceived and only with great difficulty is the essential Form of Goodness. Once it is perceived, the conclusion must follow that, for all things, this is the cause of whatever is right and good; in the visible world it gives birth to light and to the lord of light, while it is itself sovereign in the intelligible world and the parent of intelligence and truth. Without having had a vision of this Form no one can act with wisdom, either in his own life or in matters of state.

So far as I can understand, I share your belief.

Then you may also agree that it is no wonder if those who have reached this height are reluctant to manage the affairs of men. Their souls long to spend all their time in that upper world—naturally enough, if here once more our parable holds true. Nor, again, is it at all strange that one who comes from the contemplation of divine things to the miseries of human life should appear awkward and ridiculous when, with eyes still dazed and not yet accustomed to the darkness, he is compelled, in a law-court or elsewhere, to dispute about the shadows of justice or the images that cast those shadows, and to wrangle over the notions of what is right in the minds of men who have never beheld Justice itself.

It is not at all strange.

No; a sensible man will remember that the eyes may be confused in two ways—by a change from light to darkness or from darkness to light; and he will recognize that the same thing happens to the soul. When he sees it troubled and unable to discern anything clearly, instead of laughing thoughtlessly, he will ask whether, coming from a brighter existence, its unaccustomed vision is obscured by the darkness, in which case he will think its condition enviable and its life a happy one; or whether, emerging from the depths of ignorance, it is dazzled by excess of light. If so, he will rather feel sorry for it; or, if he were inclined to laugh, that would be less ridiculous than to laugh at the soul which has come down from the light.

That is a fair statement.

If this is true, then, we must conclude that education is not what it is said to be by some, who profess to put knowledge into a soul which does not possess it, as if they could put sight into blind eyes. On the contrary, our own account signifies that the soul of every man does possess the power of learning the truth and the organ to see with; and that, just as one might have to turn the whole body round in order that the eye should see light instead of darkness, so that entire soul must be turned away from this changing world, until its eye can bear to contemplate reality and that supreme splendour which we have called the Good. Hence there may well be an art whose aim would be to effect this very thing, the conversion of the soul, in the readiest way; not to put the power of sight into the soul's eye, which already has it, but to ensure that, instead of looking in the wrong direction, it is turned the way it ought to be.

Yes, it may well be so.

It looks, then, as though wisdom were different from those ordinary virtues, as they are called, which are not far removed from bodily qualities, in that they can be produced by habituation and exercise in a soul which has not possessed them from the first. Wisdom, it seems, is certainly the virtue of some diviner faculty, which never loses its power, though its use for good or harm depends on the direction towards which it is turned. You must have noticed in dishonest men with a reputation for sagacity the shrewd glance of a narrow intelligence piercing the objects to which it is directed. There is nothing wrong with their power of vision, but it has been forced into the service of evil, so that the keener its sight, the more harm it works.

Quite true.

And yet if the growth of a nature like this had been pruned from earliest childhood, cleared of those clinging overgrowths which come of gluttony and all luxurious pleasure and, like leaden weights charged with affinity to this mortal world, hang upon the soul, bending its vision downwards; if, freed from these, the soul were turned round towards true reality, then this same power in these very men would see the truth as keenly as the objects it is turned to now.

Yes, very likely.

Is it not also likely, or indeed certain after what has been said, that a state can never be properly governed either by the uneducated who know nothing of truth or by men who are allowed to spend all their days in the pursuit of culture? The ignorant have no single mark before their eyes at which they must aim in all the conduct of their own lives and of affairs of state; and the others will not engage in action if they can help it, dreaming that, while still alive, they have been translated to the Islands of the Blest.

Quite true.

It is for us, then, as founders of a commonwealth, to bring compulsion to bear on the noblest natures. They must be made to climb the ascent to the vision of Goodness, which we called the highest object of knowledge; and, when they have looked upon it long enough, they must not be allowed, as they now are, to remain on the heights, refusing to come down again to the prisoners or to take any part in their labours and rewards, however much or little these may be worth.

Shall we not be doing them an injustice, if we force on them a worse life than they might have?

You have forgotten again, my friend, that the law is not concerned to make any one class specially happy, but to ensure the welfare of the commonwealth as a whole. By persuasion or constraint it will unite the citizens in harmony, making them share whatever benefits each class can contribute to the common good; and its purpose in forming men of that spirit was not that each should be left to go his own way, but that they should be instrumental in binding the community into one.

True, I had forgotten.

You will see, then, Glaucon, that there will be no real injustice in compelling our philosophers to watch over and care for the other citizens. We can fairly tell them that their compeers in other states may quite reasonably refuse to collaborate: there they have sprung up, like a self-sown plant, in despite of their country's institutions; no one has fostered their growth, and they cannot be expected to show gratitude for a care they have never received. "But," we shall say, "it is not so with you. We have brought you into existence for your country's sake as well as for your own, to be like leaders and king-bees in a hive; you have been better and more thoroughly educated than those others and hence you are more capable of playing your part both as men of thought and as men of action. You must go down, then, each in his turn, to live with the rest and let your eyes grow accustomed to the darkness. You will then see a thousand times better than those who live there always; you will recognize every image for what it is and know what it represents, because you have seen justice, beauty, and goodness in their reality; and so you and we shall find life in our commonwealth no mere dream, as it is in most existing states, where men live fighting one another about shadows and quarrelling for power, as if that were a great prize; whereas in truth government can be at its best and free from dissension only where the destined rulers are least desirous of holding office."

Quite true.

Then will our pupils refuse to listen and to take their turns at sharing in the work of the community, though they may live together for most of their time in a purer air?

No; it is a fair demand, and they are fair-minded men. No doubt, unlike any ruler of the present day, they will think of holding power as an unavoidable necessity.

Yes, my friend; for the truth is that you can have a well-governed society only if you can discover for your future rulers a better way of life than being in office; then only will power be in the hands of men who are rich, not in gold, but in wealth that brings happiness, a good and wise life. All goes wrong when, starved for lack of anything good in their own lives, men turn to public affairs hoping to snatch from thence the happiness they hunger for. They set about fighting for power, and this internecine conflict ruins them and their country. The life of true philosophy is the only one that looks down upon offices of state; and access to power must be confined to men who are not in love with it; otherwise rivals will start fighting. So whom else can you compel to undertake the guardianship of the commonwealth, if not those who, besides understanding best the principles of government, enjoy a nobler life than the politician's and look for rewards of a different kind?

There is indeed no other choice.

Aristotle on Government

Aristotle (384–322 B.C.) was a native of Macedonia. At the age of eighteen he journeyed to Athens and enrolled as a student in the Academy, where he remained for twenty years until the death of Plato. He then moved to Asia Minor to become political adviser to the ruler of a small kingdom. There he married the king's niece. It is said that he spent his honeymoon gathering seashells for use in scientific studies. From Asia Minor he was called back to his native Macedonia to serve as tutor to Alexander (later "the Great"), who was then a boy of twelve. When Alexander set out to conquer the world, Aristotle returned to Athens and established a school of his own, the Lyceum, as a rival to the Academy. For the next eleven years he divided his time among teaching, public lecturing, and writing. His philosophical system is known as the *peripatetic* (or "walking") philosophy, a title derived from his habit of pacing back and forth as he lectured. At the death of Alexander in 323 B.C., Aristotle, because of his former association with the conqueror, found himself unpopular in Athens. Fearing the anger of the mob and remembering the fate of Socrates, he fled the city, not wishing, as he put it, "to give the Athenians a second chance of sinning against philosophy." He died in exile the following year.

Aristotle was a remarkably productive and versatile thinker. His extant works include major treatises on physics, astronomy, zoology, biology, botany, psychology, logic, ethics, metaphysics, political theory, constitutional history, rhetoric, and the theory of art.

The following selection is from one of Aristotle's major works, *The Politics*. His views in *The Politics* on the social nature of humanity, the purpose of government, and the most desirable kind of society have formed the basis, along with Plato's *Republic*, for almost all subsequent political theory in the West.

Consider the following questions as you study the text below.

1. What did Aristotle mean when he said that "every polis exists by nature"? Why, in his view, was a person without a polis less than a true person?

2. What arguments did Aristotle advance in support of his assertion that government by the middle class is superior to other forms of government? What advantages did he assign to such a government?

Aristotle: The Politics

1252a1   Observation tells us that every state is an association, and that every association is formed with a view to some good purpose. I say 'good', because in all their actions all men do in fact aim at what they think good. Clearly then, as all associations aim at some good, that association which is the most sovereign among them all and embraces all others will aim highest, i.e. at the most sovereign of all goods. This is the association which we call the state, the association which is 'political'.

1252a7   It is an error to suppose, as some do, that the roles of a statesman, of a king, of a household-manager and of a master of slaves are the same, on the ground that they differ not in kind but only in point of numbers of persons—that a master of slaves, for example, has to do with a few people, a household-manager with more, and a statesman or king with more still, as if there were no differences between a large household and a small state. They also reckon that when one person is in personal control over the rest he has the role of a king, whereas when he takes his turn at ruling and at being ruled according to the principles of the science concerned, he is a statesman. But these assertions are false.

1252a17   This will be quite evident if we examine the matter according to our established method. We have to analyse other composite things till they can be subdivided no further, because we have reached the smallest parts of the wholes; so let us in the same way examine the component parts of the state and we shall see better how these too differ from each other, and whether we can acquire any systematic knowledge about the several roles mentioned.

The State Exists by Nature

The Two 'Pairs'

1252a24   We shall, I think, in this as in other subjects, get the best view of the matter if we look at the natural growth of things from the beginning. The first point is that those which are incapable of existing without each other must be united as a pair. For example, (a) the union of male and female is essential for reproduction; and this is not a matter of *choice*, but is due to the *natural* urge, which exists in the other animals too and in plants, to propagate one's kind. Equally essential is (b) the combination of the natural ruler and ruled, for the purpose of preservation. For the element that can use its intelligence to look ahead is by nature ruler and by nature master, while that which

Aristotle: The Politics, Trans. T. A. Sinclair (London: Penguin Books, 1962), pp. 54–60, 187–98, 265–8.

has the bodily strength to do the actual work is by nature a slave, one of those who are ruled. Thus there is a common interest uniting master and slave.

Formation of the Household

1252a34   Nature, then, has distinguished between female and slave: she recognizes different functions and lavishly provides different tools, not an all-purpose tool like the Delphic knife; for every instrument will be made best if it serves not many purposes but one. But non-Greeks assign to female and slave exactly the same status. This is because they have nothing which is by nature fitted to rule; their association consists of a male slave and a female slave. So, as the poets say, 'It is proper that Greeks should rule non-Greeks', the implication being that non-Greek and slave are by nature identical.

1252b9   Thus it was out of the association formed by men with these two, women and slaves, that a household was first formed; and the poet Hesiod was right when he wrote, 'Get first a house and a wife and an ox to draw the plough.' (The ox is the poor man's slave.) This association of persons, established according to nature for the satisfaction of daily needs, is the household, the members of which Charondas calls 'bread-fellows', and Epimenides the Cretan 'stable-companions'.

Formation of the Village

1252b15   The next stage is the village, the first association of a number of houses for the satisfaction of something *more* than daily needs. It comes into being through the processes of nature in the fullest sense, as offshoots of a household are set up by sons and grandsons. The members of such a village are therefore called by some 'homogalactic'. This is why states were at first ruled by kings, as are foreign nations to this day: they were formed from constituents which were themselves under kingly rule. For every household is ruled by its senior member, as by a king, and the offshoots too, because of their blood relationship, are ruled in the same way. This kind of rule is mentioned in Homer: 'Each man has power of law over children and wives.' He is referring to scattered settlements, which were common in primitive times. For this reason the gods too are said to be governed by a king—namely because men themselves were originally ruled by kings and some are so still. Just as men imagine gods in human shape, so they imagine their way of life to be like that of men.

Formation of the State

1252b27   The final association, formed of several villages, is the state. For all practical purposes the process is now complete; self-sufficiency has been reached, and while the state came about as a means of securing life itself, it continues in being to secure the *good* life. Therefore every state exists by nature, as the earlier associations too were natural.

This association is the end of those others, and nature is itself an end; for whatever is the end-product of the coming into existence of any object, that is what we call its nature—of a man, for instance, or a horse or a household. Moreover the aim and the end is perfection; and self-sufficiency is both end and perfection.

The State and the Individual

1253a1   It follows that the state belongs to the class of objects which exist by nature, and that man is by nature a political animal. Any one who by his nature and not simply by ill-luck has no state is either too bad or too good, either subhuman or superhuman—he is like the war-mad man condemned in Homer's words as 'having no family, no law, no home'; for he who is such by nature is mad on war: he is a non-cooperator like an isolated piece in a game of draughts.

1253a7   But obviously man is a political animal in a sense in which a bee is not, or any other gregarious animal. Nature, as we say, does nothing without some purpose; and she has endowed man alone among the animals with the power of speech. Speech is something different from voice, which is possessed by other animals also and used by them to express pain or pleasure; for their nature does indeed enable them not only to feel pleasure and pain but to communicate these feelings to each other. Speech, on the other hand serves to indicate what is useful and what is harmful, and so also what is just and what is unjust. For the real difference between man and other animals is that humans alone have perception of good and evil, just and unjust, etc. It is the sharing of a common view in *these* matters that makes a household and a state.

Correct and Deviated Constitutions Distinguished

1278b6   Having settled these questions, we must proceed to our next and ask whether we are to posit only one constitution or more than one; and if more than one, what they are and how many, and what the differences are between them. The 'constitution' of a state is the organization of the offices, and in particular of the one that is sovereign over all the others. Now in every case the citizen-body of a state is sovereign; the citizen-body *is* the constitution. Thus in democracies the people are sovereign, in oligarchies the few. That, we say, is what makes the one constitution differ from the other; and the same criterion can be applied to the others also.

1278b15   We ought at the outset to state the purpose for which the state has come to be, as well as the number of kinds of authority controlling men and their life as members of an association. At the beginning of this work, when we drew a distinction between household-management and mastership, we also stated that by nature man is a political animal. Hence men have a desire for life together, even when they have no need to seek each other's help. Nevertheless, common interest too is a factor in bringing them together, in so far as it contributes to the good life of each. The *good* life is indeed their chief end, both communally and individually; but they form and continue to maintain a political association for the sake of life itself. Perhaps we may say that there is an element of good even in mere living, provided that life is not excessively beset with troubles. Certainly most men, in their desire to keep alive, are prepared to face a great deal of suffering, as if finding in life itself a certain well-being and a natural sweetness.

1278b30   But to return to authority: it is not difficult to distinguish its recognized styles (I often speak about their definition in my public lectures). First, although the natural slave and the natural master really have the same interest, rule of master over slave is exercised primarily for the benefit of the master and only incidentally for the benefit of the slave, because if the slave deteriorates the master's rule over him is inevitably impaired.

1278b37   Then there is the authority of a man over his wife, his children, and his whole household, to which we give the name 'household-management'. This is exercised either for the benefit of those subject to the authority, or for some benefit common to both parties. In itself it is for the benefit of the subjects, as we see by the analogy of the other skills, such as that of a doctor or of an athlete's trainer, who would only incidentally be concerned with their own interests. (For of course there is nothing to prevent a trainer on occasion being himself a member of the team in training, as the man who steers the ship is always one of the members of the ship's company. The trainer or pilot looks to the good of those under his authority, but when he himself is one of them he gets the same benefit out of it incidentally as they do, in that the pilot is a member of the ship's company, and the trainer becomes one of those in training, while yet remaining their trainer.)

1279a8   That is why, whenever authority in the *state* is constituted on a basis of equality and similarly between citizens, they expect to take turns in exercising it. This principle is very old but in earlier times it was applied in a natural and proper manner: men expected each to take a turn at public service, and during tenure of office to look after the interests of someone else, who then did the same for him. But nowadays there is more to be gained out of public affairs and offices, so men want to be in office continuously. They could hardly be more zealous in their place-hunting if they were ill and their recovery depended on securing office.

1279a16   It is clear then that those constitutions which aim at the common good are right, as being in accord with absolute justice; while those which aim only at the good of the rulers are wrong. They are all deviations from the right constitutions. They are like the rule of master over slave, whereas the state is an association of free men.

Classification of Correct and Deviated Constitutions

1279a22   Having drawn these distinctions we must next consider what constitutions there are and how many. We begin with those that are correct, since when these have been defined it will be easy to see the deviations. As we have seen, 'constitution' and 'citizen-body' mean the same thing, and the citizen-body is the sovereign power in states. Sovereignty necessarily resides either in one man, or in a few, or in the many. Whenever the one, the few, or the many rule with a view to the common good, these constitutions must be correct; but if they look to the private advantage, be it of the one or the few or the mass, they are deviations. For either we must say that those who do not participate are not citizens, or they must share in the benefit.

1279a32   The usual names for right constitutions are as follows: (a) Monarchy aiming at the common interest: kingship. (b) Rule of more than one man but only a few: aristocracy (so called either because the *best* men rule or because it aims at what is *best* for the state and all its members). (c) Political control exercised by the mass of the populace in the common interest: polity. This is the name common to all constitutions. It is reasonable to use this term, because, while it is possible for one man or a few to be outstanding in point of virtue, it is difficult for a larger number to reach a high standard in all forms of virtue—with the conspicuous exception of military virtue, which is found in a great many people. And that is why in this constitution the defensive element is the most sovereign body, and those who share in the constitution are those who bear arms.

1279b4   The corresponding deviations are: from kingship, tyranny; from aristocracy, oligarchy; from polity, democracy. For tyranny is monarchy for the benefit of the monarch, oligarchy for the benefit of the men of means, democracy for the benefit of the men without means. None of the three aims to be of profit to the common interest.

An Economic Classification of Constitutions

1279b11   We must however go into a little more detail about what each of these constitutions is. Certain difficulties are involved, which one whose aim is strictly practical might be allowed to pass over; but a man who examines each subject from a philosophical standpoint cannot neglect them: he has to omit nothing, and state the truth about each topic.

1279b16   Tyranny, as has been said, is a monarchy which is exercised like a mastership over the association which is the state; oligarchy occurs when the sovereign power of the constitution is in the hands of those with possessions, democracy when it is in the hands of those who have no stock of possessions and are without means. The first difficulty concerns definitions. Suppose the majority to be well-off, and to be sovereign in the state; then we have a democracy, since the mass of the people is sovereign. So too, if it is somewhere the case that those who do not own property, while fewer in number than those who do, are more powerful and in sovereign control of the constitution, then that is called an oligarchy, since the few are sovereign. It looks therefore as if there were something wrong with our way of defining constitutions.

1279b26   Even if we try to include both criteria of nomenclature, combining wealth with fewness of numbers in the one case (calling it oligarchy when those who are both wealthy and few hold office), lack of wealth with large numbers in the other (calling it democracy when those who are both poor and numerous hold office)—even then we are only raising a fresh difficulty. For if there is not in fact any other constitution than those with which we have been dealing, what names can we give to the two just mentioned, one in which the wealthy are more numerous, and one in which the poor are less numerous, each category being in its own case in sovereign control of the constitution? The argument seems to show that it is a matter of accident whether those who are sovereign be few or many (few in oligarchies, many in democracies): it just happens that way because everywhere the rich are few and the poor are many. So in fact the grounds of difference have been given wrongly: what really differentiates oligarchy and democracy is wealth or the lack of it. It inevitably follows that where men rule because of the possession of wealth, whether their number be large or small, that is oligarchy, and when the poor rule, that is democracy. But, as we have said, in actual fact the former are few, the latter many. Few are wealthy, but all share freedom alike: and these are the grounds of their respective claims to the constitution.

The Just Distribution
of Political Power

1280a7   First we must grasp what definitions of oligarchy and democracy men put forward, and in particular what is the oligarchic and what is the democratic view of justice. For all adhere to a justice of some kind, but they do not proceed beyond a certain point, and are not referring to the whole of justice in the sovereign sense when they speak of it. Thus it is thought that justice is equality; and so it is, but not for all persons, only for those that are equal. Inequality also is thought to be just; and so it is, but not for all, only for the unequal. We make bad mistakes if we neglect this 'for whom' when we are deciding what is just. The reason is that we are making judgements about ourselves, and people are generally bad judges where their own interests are involved. So, as justice is relative to people, and applies in the same ratio to the things and to the persons (as pointed out in my *Ethics*), these disputants, while agreeing as to equality of the thing, disagree about the persons for whom, and this chiefly for the reason already stated, that they are judging their own case, and therefore badly.

1280a21   There is also this further reason, namely that both parties are talking about justice in a *limited* sense, and so imagine themselves to be talking about justice unqualifiedly. Thus it is an error when men unequal in one respect, e.g. money, suppose themselves unequal in all, just as it is an error when men equal in one respect, e.g. in being free, suppose themselves equal in every respect. To argue thus is to neglect the decisive point. If persons originally come together and form an association for the sake of property, then they share in the state in proportion to their ownership of property. This is the apparent strength of the oligarchs' view that it is *not* just that out of a sum of a hundred minae he that contributed only one should receive equal shares with him who found the remaining ninety-nine; and that this applies equally to the original sum and to any profits subsequently made. But a state's purpose is not merely to provide a living but to make a life that is good. Otherwise it might be made up of slaves or animals other than man, and that is impossible, because slaves and animals do not participate in happiness, nor in a life that involves choice.

1280a34   A state's purpose is also to provide something more than a military pact of protection against injustice, or to facilitate mutual acquaintance and the exchange of goods, for in that case Tyrrhenians and Carthaginians, and all others with commercial treaties with each other, would be taken as citizens of a single state. Certainly they have import agreements, treaties to prevent injustice, and written documents governing their military alliance. But in the first place each has its separate officials: there are none in common to which they are both equally subject for these purposes. Secondly, neither side is concerned with the *quality* of the other, or with preventing the behaviour of any person covered by the agreements from being unjust or wicked, but only with the prevention of injustice as between each other. But all who are anxious to ensure government under good laws make it their business to have an eye to the virtue and vice of the citizens. It thus becomes evident that that which is genuinely and not just nominally called a state must concern itself with virtue. Otherwise the association is a mere military alliance, differing only in location and restricted territorial extent from an alliance whose parties are at a distance from each other; and under such conditions law becomes a mere agreement, or, as Lycophron the sophist put it, 'a mutual guarantor of justice', but quite unable to make citizens good and just.

1280b12   That this is true will be clear from some further illustrations. Suppose you merge the territories into one, making the walls of Corinth and Megara contiguous: that still does not make a single state of them, nor would it even if they established rights of marriage between the two, though this is one of the ties peculiarly characteristic of states. Or again, suppose you had 10,000 people living apart from each other, but near enough not to become dissociated: carpenter, farmer, shoemakers and suchlike are there, and furthermore they have laws prohibiting injustice in their transactions with each other; yet, so long as their association does not go beyond such things as commercial exchange and military alliance, that is still not a state. And why not? you may ask. The reason is certainly not that the association is loosely knit. For even if they actually moved close together, and maintained an association such as I have described, with each man still treating his own household like, a state, and if they mutually supported each other, as in a defensive alliance, against injustice only, even then that would not be considered a state, not at any rate in the strict sense, since the nature of their intercourse is the same whether they move close together or stay apart.

1280b29 It is clear therefore that the state is not an association of people dwelling in the same place, established to prevent its members from committing injustice against each other, and to promote transactions. Certainly all these features must be present if there is to be a state; but even the presence of every one of them does not make a state *ipso facto*. The state is an association intended to enable its members, in their households and the kinships, to live *well*; its purpose is a perfect and self-sufficient life. However, this will not be attained unless they occupy one and the same territory and intermarry. It is indeed on that account that we find in states connections between relatives by marriage, brotherhoods, sacrifices to the gods, and the various civilized pursuits of a life lived together. All these activities are the product of affection, for it is our affection for others that causes us to choose to live together; thus they all contribute towards that good life which is the purpose of the state; and a state is an association of kinships and villages which aims at a perfect and self-sufficient life—and that, we hold, means living happily and nobly.

1281a2 So we must lay it down that the association which is a state exists not for the purpose of living together but for the sake of noble actions. Those who contribute most to this kind of association are for that very reason entitled to a larger share in the state than those who, though they may be equal or even superior in free birth and in family, are inferior in the virtue that belongs to a citizen. Similarly they are entitled to a larger share than those who are superior in riches but inferior in virtue.

All this makes it clear that all those who dispute abut constitutions are using the term 'justice' in a limited sense.

The Merits of the Middle Constitution

1295a25 What is the best constitution and what is the best life for the majority of states and the majority of men? We have in mind men whose virtue does not rise above that of ordinary people, and whose education does not depend on the luck either of their natural ability or of their resources; and who have not an ideally perfect constitution, but, first, away of living in which as many as possible can join and, second, a constitution within the compass of the greatest number of states. The 'aristocracies', as they are called, that we have just been discussing do not fall within the competence of most states, but some of them do approximate closely to what we call polity (hence we ought to speak of both constitutions as though they were one and the same).

1295a34   The decision on all these points rests on the same set of elementary principles. If we were right when in our *Ethics* we stated that virtue is a mean, and that the happy life is a life without hindrance in its accordance with virtue, then the best life must be the middle life, consisting in a mean which is open to men of every kind to attain. And the same principles must be applicable to the virtue or badness of constitutions and states. For the constitution of a state is in a sense the way it lives.

1295b1   In all states there are three state-sections: the very well-off, the very badly off, and thirdly those in between. Since therefore it is agreed that moderation and a middle position are best, it is clear that, in the matter of the goods of fortune also, to own a middling amount is best of all. This condition is most easily obedient to reason, and following reason is just what is difficult both for the exceedingly rich, handsome, strong and well-born, and for their opposites, the extremely poor, the weak, and those grossly deprived of honour. The former incline more to arrogance and crime on a large scale, the latter are more than averagely prone to wicked ways and petty crime. The unjust deeds of the one class are due to an arrogant spirit, the unjust deeds of the other to wickedness. Add the fact that it is among the members of the middle section that you find least reluctance to hold office as well as least eagerness to do so; and both these attitudes, eagerness and reluctance, are detrimental to states.

1295b13   There are other drawbacks about the two extremes. Those who have a superabundance of good fortune, strength, riches, friends, and so forth, neither wish to submit to rule nor understand how to do so; and this is engrained in them from childhood at home: even at school they are so full of *la dolce vita* that they have never grown used to being ruled. Those on the other hand who are greatly deficient in these qualities are too subservient. So they do not know how to rule, but only how to be ruled as a slave is; while the others do not know how to be ruled in any way at all, and can command only like a master ruling over slaves. The result is a state not of free men but of slaves and masters, the former full of envy, the latter of contempt. Nothing could be farther removed from friendship or from partnership in a state. Sharing is a token of friendship; one does not want to share even a journey with one's enemies. The state aims to consist as far as possible of those who are like and equal, a condition found chiefly among the middle people. And so the best-run constitution is certain to be found in this state, whose composition is, we maintain, the natural one for a state to have.

1295b28   It is the middle citizens in a state who are the most secure: they neither covet, like the poor, the possessions of others, nor do others covet theirs as the poor covet those of the rich. So they live without risk, not scheming and not being schemed against. Phocylides' prayer was therefore justified when he wrote, 'Those in the middle have many advantages; that is where I wish to be in the state.'

1295b34   It is clear then both that the best partnership in a state is the one which operates through the middle people, and also that those states in which the middle element is large, and stronger if possible than the other two together, or at any rate stronger than either of them alone, have every chance of having a well-run constitution. For the addition of its weight to either side will turn the balance and prevent excess at the opposing extremes. For this reason it is a most happy state of affairs when those who take part in the constitution have a middling, adequate amount of property; since where one set of people possess a great deal and the other nothing, the result is either extreme democracy or unmixed oligarchy, or a tyranny due to the excesses of either. For tyranny often emerges from an over-enthusiastic democracy or from an oligarchy, but much more rarely from intermediate constitutions or from those close to them. The reason for this we will speak of later when we deal with changes in constitutions.

1296a7   The superiority of the middle constitution is clear also from the fact that it alone is free from factions. Where the middle element is large, there least of all arise factions and divisions among the citizens. And big states are freer from faction, for this same reason, namely that their middle element is large. In small states it is easy for the whole body of citizens to become divided into two, which leaves no middle at all, and nearly everybody either rich or poor. Democracies too are safer than oligarchies in this respect and longer-lasting thanks to their middle people, who are more numerous and take a larger share of honours in democracies than in oligarchies. For when in their absence the unpropertied preponderate in numbers, trouble arises and they soon come to grief. An indication of the truth of what we have been saying is to be found in the fact that the best lawgivers have come from the middle citizens—Solon, for example, whose middle position is revealed in his poems, and Lycurgus, who was not a king, and Charondas and most of the rest.

Aristotle on Education

In the previous selection from the *Politics*, Aristotle outlined the basis of political associations, described the possible types of constitutions, and made an argument for the superiority of government by the middle class. Using his customary technique, he began at the beginning, with assumptions about the fundamental and *natural* principles of social interaction, and then methodically built his larger vision of political associations upon the foundation of those assumptions. At the heart of his discussion was the belief that a true state is one that makes "the encouragement of goodness its end."

In "The Care of Infancy," Aristotle turns from the macro to the micro, from the state as a whole to the development of the individual. As in his discussion of the state, he begins at the beginning, in this case with the proper care of infants and young children. Moreover, his discussion of early education is built on a belief that the purpose of education is the encouragement of goodness in individuals. Thus, in Aristotle's view, true education helps produce individuals who are capable of making constructive contributions to the creation and maintenance of a true state. As you read the selection, pay close attention to Aristotle's assumptions. Who was responsible for the education of children? What role should the state play in education? Was he writing about the education of all children, rich and poor, male and female?

Consider the following questions as you study the text below.

1. In Aristotle's opinion, are good individuals born or made? Is goodness a question of nature or nurture?

2. Is Aristotle most concerned with the physical, intellectual, or moral development of the child? What connections might he have made between these three types of development?

The Care of Infancy

Once the children are born, it must be understood that the character of their diet makes a great difference to their bodily strength. From careful observation of the lower animals and of peoples which devote themselves to

Trans. John Burnet.

138

the creation of a war-like condition, we find that a diet consisting mainly of milk is best adapted to their bodies, and one without much wine on account of the diseases it produces. Further, it is good for them to make all the movements that it is possible for them to make at that age. To prevent their tender limbs becoming deformed, some peoples even at the present day have recourse to certain mechanical appliances to make their children's bodies straight. It is a good thing too to accustom them to cold from early childhood: it is most serviceable from the point of view of health and as a preparation for military service. This is the reason of the custom which prevails among many of the barbarians, either of dipping children after birth into a cold stream or of covering them only with a light wrapper as the Celts do. It is better to practise from the very beginning every habit that can be produced by training,—though the habituation should be a gradual process,—and the bodily condition of children is admirably adapted by its natural warmth for training in the endurance of cold.

This, then, with some other things of a similar character is the sort of treatment that it is desirable to apply to the first stage of life. As to the next stage, up to the fifth year, it is too soon to put the child to any sort of lessons or compulsory exercises. That might interfere with its growth. It must, however, get motion enough to counteract sluggishness of body, and this must be provided by certain occupations, above all by play. As to the games, they must not be vulgar, and they must neither be too fatiguing nor too slack and soft.

The character of the stories, true or fictitious, which are to be told to children of this age, must receive the best attention of the officers called Inspectors of Children.

All these things should pave the way for the occupations of later life, so most of their games should be imitations of what they will have to do in earnest later on. The attempt made in the *Laws* to put down children's shouts and crying by prohibition is a complete mistake; they are good for the growth. In fact, they are a sort of gymnastic for their bodies; it is holding the breath that gives people strength in gymnastic exercises, and children get the same advantage by shouting.

The Inspectors of Children must exercise a general supervision over the way they pass their time, and see especially that they are as little as possible in the company of servants. Children at this age, and up to the age of seven, have necessarily to be brought up at home, and it is only reasonable to expect that, even at that time of life, they will catch the taint of lowness from what they see and hear. Indecency, above all, the legislator must utterly banish from the city. From carelessness in the use of indecent language it is but a short step to indecent acts. From the young, however, it is especially necessary to remove all indecency, so that they may neither see nor hear anything of the sort. If anyone is found saying or doing any of these forbidden things, and if he is a free man but not yet old enough to be entitled to a place at the common meals, he is to be punished by degradation and whipping; if he is above that age, by degradations unworthy of a free man, to punish him for behaving like a slave. And, since we are banishing language of this kind, we must clearly do the same with the sight of improper pictures and plays. The magistrate must see to it that there is no statue or picture representing anything indecent, except in the temples of those gods in whose worship scurrility is recognised by use and wont; and in this case the law allows men to perform divine worship on behalf of themselves, their children, and their wives. As to the young, we must pass a law that they are not to be spectators of Iambi or Comedy till they reach the age when they are entitled to a place at the public tables and to take strong drink, and then their education will have given them immunity from the bad effects of such things.

Well, for the present, we have only discussed these matters in a cursory way; later on we must pause and determine the point more clearly by discussing all the difficulties involved both in their exclusion from such spectacles and in their admission to them. On the present occasion we have only touched on the subject so far as was necessary for our purpose. There was a saying of Theodoros the tragic actor that put the point very well. He never allowed anyone, not even one of the poorer actors, to create a part before him, holding that audiences are won over by what they hear first. So we must make everything that is bad seem strange to the young, and above all everything that involves depravity or malice.

When the first five years are past, for the next two years up to the age of seven, they should begin to look on at the lessons they will have to learn at that age. For there are two stages of life in accordance with which education must be divided, one from the seventh year till puberty, and the other from puberty till the twenty-first. Those who divide the ages of man by periods of seven years are not, speaking broadly, far wrong; but it is better to keep to the divisions which nature has made, the aim of all art and all education being just to supplement the deficiencies of nature.

Roman roads and monuments offer a lasting testimony to Roman engineering prowess. The Arch of Titus, pictured here, stands on a road in Rome.

ROME

According to legend Rome was founded in the year 753 B.C. The twins, Romulus and Remus, whose father was the god, Mars, and their mother a mortal, having been abandoned to die, were nursed by a she-wolf and raised by a shepherd. After Remus was killed in a quarrel, Romulus founded a settlement on the banks of the Tiber River, naming it after himself. So began the career of the "Eternal City" on its seven hills, which remains to this day one of the world's great metropolises. Putting legend aside, we can say that Latium, the area of Italy in which Rome is situated, was inhabited early in the first millenium B.C., with the Latins living mainly in fortified hill towns among which Rome gradually came to the fore. From a small community often under attack from hostile neighbors Rome slowly expanded its influence and power until eventually it came to dominate and control the entire Mediterranean world. The history of ancient Rome, extending until the fifth century A.D. when it went into a final decline under the onslaught of nomadic peoples on its frontiers, covers a period of over one thousand years.

This long history can be divided into several periods, which reflect both changes within Roman society itself and the position of Rome in the world. In its earliest times the city was ruled by kings, but by the end of the sixth century B.C. the last of these was deposed, and the republic, which was to form the Roman constitution for the next period, established. The word *republic* itself reveals the conception of society and government it embodied. It is a combination of the Latin words *res publica*, which mean simply "public thing." The government or, perhaps better, the organization of society was thought to be a public matter, something that the citizens of Rome shared in common. So one might draw the conclusion that during the period of the republic, Rome was a democracy. It is true, as Polybius illustrates in his *Histories*, that the political organization, with its balance of powers, bears a suggestive resemblance to our own. However, it must also be recognized that Roman society was organized according to a rigid class system, with the members of the population being either patricians, who were possessed of wealth and privilege, or plebeians, who lived in a degraded situation and did the work.

Rome remained a republic, both in form and spirit, for around four hundred years. But around 100 B.C. the republican structure began to break down. There followed nearly a century of turbulence, as successive "strong men" arose and grappled with each other for power. The period, often referred to as "the Roman revolution," was a time when near-anarchy alternated with military dictatorship, as the institutions of the republic disintegrated. Leaders—the Gracchi brothers, Marius, Sulla, Pompey, and others—rose to power and fell. Finally, the state was taken in hand by one of the most gifted and celebrated figures in Western history, Julius Caesar. After a brilliant military career, Caesar assumed control of affairs, initiating a wide range of social and political reforms. But he never lived to bring these to fruition, being assassinated in 44 B.C. by a group of senators in an episode made forever famous by Shakespeare.

The Roman revolution came to an end in 31 B.C. when the grand-nephew of Julius Caesar, Octavian, defeated Mark Antony at the naval battle of Actium, off the coast of Greece. Returning to Rome, and later acquiring the name Augustus, Octavian became the first in a long line of Roman emperors. The new Augustus, was, however, too shrewd to assume the title of emperor. Instead he referred to himself as *princeps*, which meant simply "first citizen of Rome." At the same time he retained the outward structure and institutions of the republic so that, to the ordinary Roman, it would be far from apparent that the locus of effective political power was being concentrated in the capable hands of Augustus.

So began imperial Rome. Augustus was succeeded (in A.D. 14) by Tiberius, who was followed by a series of emperors who, with certain notable exceptions such as Nero, ruled well for nearly two hundred years. The last of these so-called "good emperors" was the Stoic philosopher, Marcus Aurelius, who died in A.D. 180. From that time on, although on occasion effective emperors arose, the line of successsion began slowly to degenerate and, with it, the fortunes of Rome. The decline of Rome was not an event that occurred abruptly but rather something that continued over several centuries. By the end of the fifth century A.D. the career of ancient Rome, and, with it, classical civilization, had come effectively to an end.

LOOKING AHEAD

As you learn about Roman civilization, consider the following questions.

1. Compare and contrast the Roman Empire with the Near Eastern empires that preceded it. What made it possible for the Romans to dominate the Mediterranean?

2. What did it mean to be a citizen of the Roman Empire? How did one become a citizen?

Polybius

It is easy to misunderstand what Polybius meant when he wrote that he was going to interrupt his history of Rome to enter on a disquisition "on the Roman constitution." We may immediately think that he will go on to describe some document comparable to our own Constitution, but this is far from his intent. What Polybius meant by "constitution" is the organization of the Roman people themselves, and particularly of their political powers and relationships. His ultimate aim was to explain the success of the Roman social and political system, and, especially, to account for Rome's quick and phenomenal rise to domination of "nearly the whole world." To do this he chose as his crucial date the very time of one of Rome's greatest military defeats, at the hands of the Carthaginians in 216 B.C.

Although his exact dates are not known, Polybius was probably born around 200 B.C. He was a Greek from the Peloponnesus. How such a person should come to write the history of Rome is of special interest. As a young man Polybius became a political leader of the Achaean League in southern Greece. Their Roman masters, convinced that the Greeks were plotting to throw off Roman rule, in 168 B.C. arrested one thousand members of the League, including Polybius, and transported them to Italy as hostages. There Polybius remained in exile for the next sixteen years. Far from his homeland and with his career destroyed, Polybius devoted his time to study. Fortunately, he was sent to Rome where he had ready access to records and documents, so he took that government as the subject of his scholarship. The result was the *Histories*. Polybius was finally set free in 151 B.C. and returned to Greece, where he again became active in political and diplomatic affairs.

Consider the following questions as you study the text below.

1. According to Polybius, what role did "the people" play in Roman government? When he referred to the people, who exactly did he mean? Who was not included in this group?

2. What differences did Polybius note between Roman and Carthaginian government? In his view, what was the most important difference between the two governments? Why?

Histories

Book VI

1.   I am aware that some will be at a loss to account for my interrupting the course of my narrative for the sake of entering upon the following disquisition on the Roman constitution. But I think that I have already in many passages made it fully evident that this particular branch of my work was one of the necessities imposed on me by the nature of my original design; and I pointed this out with special clearness in the preface which explained the scope of my history. I there stated that the feature of my work which was at once the best in itself, and the most instructive to the students of it, was that it would enable them to know and fully realise in what manner, and under what kind of constitution, it came about that nearly the whole world fell under the power of Rome in somewhat less than fifty-three years—an event certainly without precedent. This being my settled purpose, I could see no more fitting period than the present for making a pause, and examining the truth of the remarks about to be made on this constitution. In private life if you wish to satisfy yourself as to the badness or goodness of particular persons, you would not, if you wish to get a genuine test, examine their conduct at a time of uneventful repose, but in the hour of brilliant success or conspicuous reverse. For the true test of a perfect man is the power of bearing with spirit and dignity violent changes of fortune. An examination of a constitution should be conducted in the same way: and therefore being unable to find in our day a more rapid or more signal change than that which has happened to Rome, I reserve my disquisition on its constitution for this place. . . .

What is really educational and beneficial to students of history is the clear view of the causes of events, and the consequent power of choosing the better policy in a particular case. Now in every practical undertaking by a state we must regard as the most powerful agent for success or failure the form of its constitution; for from this as from a fountainhead all conceptions and plans of action not only proceed, but attain their consummation.

11.   . . . I will now endeavour to describe [the constitution] of Rome at the period of their disastrous defeat at Cannae [in 216 B.C.]. . . .

As for the Roman constitution, it had three elements, each of them possessing sovereign powers: and their respective share of power in the whole state had been regulated with such a scrupulous regard to equality and equilibrium, that no one could say for certain, not even a native, whether the constitution as a whole were an aristocracy or democracy or despotism. And no

The Histories of Polybius, trans. Evelyn S. Shuckburgh.

wonder: for if we confine our observation to the power of the Consuls we should be inclined to regard it as despotic; if on that of the Senate, as aristocratic; and if finally one looks at the power possessed by the people it would seem a clear case of democracy. What the exact powers of these several parts were, and still, with slight modifications, are, I will now state.

12.   The Consuls, before leading out the legions, remain in Rome and are supreme masters of the administration. All other magistrates, except the Tribunes, are under them and take their orders. They introduce foreign ambassadors to the Senate; bring matters requiring deliberation before it; and see to the execution of its decrees. If, again, there are any matters of state which require the authorisation of the people, it is their business to see to them, to summon the popular meetings, to bring the proposals before them, and to carry out the decrees of the majority. In the preparations for war, also, and in a word in the entire administration of a campaign, they have all but absolute power. It is competent to them to impose on the allies such levies as they think good, to appoint the Military Tribunes, to make up the roll for soldiers and select those that are suitable. Besides they have absolute power of inflicting punishment on all who are under their command while on active service: and they have authority to expend as much of the public money as they choose, being accompanied by a quaestor who is entirely at their orders. A survey of these powers would in fact justify our describing the constitution as despotic,—a clear case of royal government. Nor will it affect the truth of my description, if any of the institutions I have described are changed in our time, or in that of our posterity: and the same remarks apply to what follows.

13.   The Senate has first of all the control of the treasury, and regulates the receipts and disbursements alike. For the Quaestors cannot issue any public money for the various departments of the state without a decree of the Senate, except for the service of the Consuls. The Senate controls also what is by far the largest and most important expenditure, that, namely, which is made by the censors every lustrum for the repair or construction of public buildings; this money cannot be obtained by the censors except by the grant of the Senate. Similarly all crimes committed in Italy requiring a public investigation, such as treason, conspiracy, poisoning, or wilful murder, are in the hands of the Senate. Besides, if any individual or state among the Italian allies requires a controversy to be settled, a penalty to be assessed, help or protection to be afforded,—all this is the province of the Senate. Or again, outside Italy, if it is necessary to send an embassy to reconcile warring communities, or to remind them of their duty, or sometimes to impose requisitions upon them, or to receive their submission, or finally to proclaim war against them,—this too is the business of the Senate. In like manner the reception to be given foreign ambassadors in Rome, and the answers to be returned to them, are decided by the Senate. With such business the people have nothing to do. Consequently, if one were staying at Rome when the

Consuls were not in town, one would imagine the constitution to be a complete aristocracy: and this has been the idea entertained by many Greeks, and by many kings as well, from the fact that nearly all the business they had to do with Rome was settled by the Senate.

14.   After this one would naturally be inclined to ask what part is left for the people in the constitution, when the Senate has these various functions, especially the control of the receipts and expenditure of the exchequer; and when the Consuls, again, have absolute power over the details of military preparation, and an absolute authority in the field? There is, however, a part left the people, and it is a most important one. For the people is the sole fountain of honour and of punishment; and it is by these two things and these alone that dynasties and constitutions and, in a word, human society are held together: for where the distinction between them is not sharply drawn both in theory and practice, there no undertaking can be properly administered,—as indeed we might expect when good and bad are held in exactly the same honour. The people then is the only court to decide matters of life and death; and even in cases where the penalty is money, if the sum to be assessed is sufficiently serious, and especially when the accused have held the higher magistracies. And in regard to this arrangement there is one point deserving especial commendation and record. Men who are on trial for their lives at Rome, while sentence is in process of being voted,—if even only one of the tribes whose votes are needed to ratify the sentence has not voted,— have the privilege at Rome of openly departing and condemning themselves to a voluntary exile. Such men are safe at Naples or Praeneste or at Tibur, and at other towns with which this arrangement has been duly ratified on oath.

Again, it is the people who bestow offices on the deserving, which are the most honourable rewards of virtue. It has also the absolute power of passing or repealing laws; and, most important of all, it is the people who deliberate on the question of peace and war. And when provisional terms are made for alliance, suspension of hostilities, or treaties, it is the people who ratify them or the reverse.

These considerations again would lead one to say that the chief power in the state was the people's, and that the constitution was a democracy.

15.   Such, then, is the distribution of power between the several parts of the state. I must now show how each of these several parts can, when they choose, oppose or support each other.

The Consul, then, when he has started on an expedition with the powers I have described, is to all appearance absolute in the administration of the business in hand; still he has need of the support both of people and Senate, and, without them, is quite unable to bring the matter to a successful conclusion. For it is plain that he must have supplies sent to his legions from time to time; but without a decree of the Senate they can be supplied neither with corn, nor clothes, nor pay, so that all the plans of a commander must be futile, if the Senate is resolved either to shrink from danger or hamper his plans. And again, whether a Consul shall bring any undertaking to a conclusion or no depends entirely on the Senate: for it has absolute authority at the end of a year to send another Consul to supersede him, or to continue the existing one in his command. Again, even to the successes of the generals, the Senate has the power to add distinction and glory, and on the other hand to obscure their merits and lower their credit. For these high achievements are brought in tangible form before the eyes of the citizens by what are called "triumphs." But in these triumphs the commanders cannot celebrate with proper pomp, or in some cases celebrate at all, unless the Senate concurs and grants the necessary money. As for the people, the Consuls are pre-eminently obliged to court their favour, however distant from home may be the field of their operations; for it is the people, as I have said before, that ratifies, or refuses to ratify, terms of peace and treaties; but most of all because when laying down their office they have to give account of their administration before it. Therefore in no case is it safe for the Consuls to neglect either the Senate or the goodwill of the people.

16.   As for the Senate, which possesses the immense power I have described, in the first place it is obliged in public affairs to take the multitude into account, and respect the wishes of the people; and it cannot put into execution the penalty for offences against the republic, which are punishable with death, unless the people first ratifies its decrees. Similarly even in matters which directly affect the senators,—for instance, in the case of a law depriving senators of certain dignities and offices, or even actually cutting down their property,—even in such cases the people has the sole power of passing or rejecting the law. But most important of all is the fact that, if the Tribunes interpose their veto, the Senate not only is unable to pass a decree, but cannot even hold a meeting at all, whether formal or informal. Now, the Tribunes are always bound to carry out the decree of the people, and above all things to have regard for their wishes: therefore, for all these reasons the Senate stands in awe of the multitude, and cannot neglect the feelings of the people.

17.   In like manner the people on its part is far from being independent of the Senate, and is bound to take its wishes into account both collectively and individually. For contracts, too numerous to count, are given out by the censors in all parts of Italy, for the repairs or construction of public buildings; there is also the collection of revenue, from many rivers, harbours, gardens, mines, and land—every thing, in a word, that comes under the control of the Roman government: and in all these the people at large are engaged; so that there is scarcely a man, so to speak, who is not interested either as a contractor or as being employed in the works. For some purchase the contracts from the censors for themselves; and others go partners with them; while others again go security for these contractors, or actually pledge their property to the treasury for them. Now over all these transactions the Senate has absolute control. It can grant an extension of time; and in case of unforeseen accident can relieve the contractors from a portion of their

obligation, or release them from it altogether, if they are absolutely unable to fill it. And there are many details in which the Senate can inflict great hardships, or, on the other hand, grant great indulgences to the contractors: for in every case the appeal is to it. But the most important point of all is that the judges are taken from its members in the majority of trials, whether public or private, in which the charges are heavy. Consequently, all citizens are much at its mercy; and being alarmed at the uncertainty as to when they may need its aid, are cautious about resisting or actively opposing its will. And for a similar reason men do not rashly resist the wishes of the Consuls, because one and all may become subject to their absolute authority on a campaign.

18.   The result of this power of the several estates for mutual help or harm is a union sufficiently firm for all emergencies, and a constitution than which it is impossible to find a better. For whenever any danger from without compels them to unite and work together, the strength which is developed by the State is so extraordinary, that everything required is unfailingly carried out by the eager rivalry shown by all classes to devote their whole minds to the needs of the hour, and to secure that any determination come to should not fail for want of promptitude; while each individual works, privately and publicly alike, for the accomplishment of the business in hand. Accordingly, the peculiar constitution of the State makes it irresistible, and certain of obtaining whatever it determines to attempt. Nay, even when these external alarms are past, and the people are enjoying their good fortune and the fruits of their victories, and, as usually happens, growing corrupted by flattery and idleness, show a tendency to violence and arrogance,—it is in these circumstances, more than ever, that the constitution is seen to possess within itself the power of correcting abuses. For when any one of the three classes becomes puffed up, and manifests an inclination to be contentious and unduly encroaching, the mutual interdependency of all the three, and the possibility of the pretentions of any one being checked and thwarted by the others, must plainly check this tendency: and so the proper equilibrium is maintained by the impulsiveness of the one part being checked by its fear of the other.

THE ROMAN REPUBLIC COMPARED WITH OTHERS

51.   Now the Carthaginian constitution seems to me originally to have been well contrived in these most distinctively important particulars. For they had kings, and the Gerusia had the powers of an aristocracy, and the multitude were supreme in such things as affected them; and on the whole the adjustment of its several parts was very like that of Rome and Sparta. But about the period of its entering on the Hannibalian war the political state of Carthage was on the decline, that of Rome improving. For whereas there is in every body, or polity, or business a natural stage of growth, zenith, and

decay; and whereas everything in them is best at the zenith; we may thereby judge of the difference between these two constitutions as they existed at that period. For exactly so far as the strength and prosperity of Carthage preceded that of Rome in point of time, by so much was Carthage then past its prime, while Rome was exactly at its zenith, as far as its political constitution was concerned. In Carthage therefore the influence of the people in the policy of the state had already risen to be supreme, while at Rome the Senate was at the height of its power: and so, as in the one measures were deliberated upon by the many, in the other by the best men, the policy of the Romans in all public undertakings proved the stronger; on which account, though they met with capital disasters, by force of prudent counsels they finally conquered the Carthaginians in the war.

52.   If we look however at separate details, for instance at the provisions for carrying on a war, we shall find that whereas for a naval expedition the Carthaginians are the better trained and prepared,—as it is only natural with a people with whom it has been hereditary for many generations to practise this craft, and to follow the seaman's trade above all nations in the world,—yet, in regard to military service on land, the Romans train themselves to a much higher pitch than the Carthaginians. The former bestow their whole attention upon this department: whereas the Carthaginians wholly neglect their infantry, though they do take some slight interest in the cavalry. The reason of this is that they employ foreign mercenaries, the Romans native and citizen levies. It is in this point that the latter policy is preferable to the former. They have their hopes of freedom ever resting on the courage of mercenary troops: the Romans on the valour of their own citizens and the aid of their allies. The result is that even if the Romans have suffered a defeat at first, they renew the war with undiminished forces, which the Carthaginians cannot do. For, as the Romans are fighting for country and children, it is impossible for them to relax the fury of their struggle; but they persist with obstinate resolution until they have overcome their enemies. What has happened in regard to their navy is an instance in point. In skill the Romans are much behind the Carthaginians, as I have already said; yet the upshot of the whole naval war has been a decided triumph for the Romans, owing to the valour of their men. For although nautical science contributes largely to success in sea-fights, still it is the courage of the marines that turns the scale most decisively in favour of victory. The fact is that Italians as a nation are by nature superior to Phoenicians and Libyans both in physical strength and courage; but still their habits also do much to inspire the youth with enthusiasm for such exploits. One example will be sufficient of the pains taken by the Roman state to turn out men ready to endure anything to win a reputation in their country for valour.

53.   Whenever one of their illustrious men dies, in the course of his funeral, the body with all its paraphernalia is carried into the forum to the Rostra, as a raised platform there is called, and sometimes is propped upright

upon it so as to be conspicuous, or, more rarely, is laid upon it. Then with all the people standing round, his son, if he has left one of full age and he is there, or, failing him, one of his relations, mounts the Rostra and delivers a speech concerning the virtues of the deceased, and the successful exploits performed by him in his lifetime. By these means the people are reminded of what has been done, and made to see it with their own eyes,—not only such as were engaged in the actual transactions but those also who were not;— and their sympathies are so deeply moved, that the loss appears not to be confined to the actual mourners, but to be a public one affecting the whole people. After the burial and all the usual ceremonies have been performed, they place the likeness of the deceased in the most conspicuous spot in his house, surmounted by a wooden canopy or shrine. This likeness consists of a mask made to represent the deceased with extraordinary fidelity both in shape and colour. These likenesses they display at public sacrifices adorned with much care. And when any illustrious member of the family dies, they carry these masks to the funeral, putting them on men whom they thought as like the originals as possible in height and other personal peculiarities. And these substitutes assume clothes according to the rank of the person represented; if he was a consul or praetor, a toga with purple stripes; if a censor, whole purple; if he had also celebrated a triumph or performed any exploit of that kind, a toga embroidered with gold. These representatives also ride themselves in chariots, while the fasces and axes, and all the other customary insignia of the particular offices, lead the way, according to the dignity of the rank in the state enjoyed by the deceased in his lifetime; and on arriving at the Rostra they all take their seats on ivory chairs in their order. There could not easily be a more inspiring spectacle than this for a young man of noble ambitions and virtuous aspirations. For can we conceive any one to be unmoved at the sight of all the likenesses collected together of the men who have earned glory, all as it were living and breathing? Or what could be a more glorious spectacle?

54. Besides, the speaker over the body about to be buried, after having finished the panegyric of this particular person, starts upon the others whose representatives are present, beginning with the most ancient, and recounts the successes and achievements of each. By this means the glorious memory of brave men is continually renewed; the fame of those who have performed any noble deed is never allowed to die; and the renown of those who have done good service to their country becomes a matter of common knowledge to the multitude, and part of the heritage of posterity. But the chief benefit of the ceremony is that it inspires young men to shrink from no exertion for the general welfare, in the hope of obtaining the glory which awaits the brave. And what I say is confirmed by this fact. Many Romans have volunteered to decide a whole battle by single combat; not a few have deliberately accepted certain death, some in time of war to secure the safety of the rest, some in time of peace to preserve the safety of the commonwealth.

There have also been instances of men in office putting their own sons to death, in defiance of every custom and law, because they rated the interests of their country higher than those of natural ties even with their nearest and dearest. There are many stories of this kind, related of many men in Roman history; but one will be enough for our present purpose; and I will give the name as an instance to prove the truth of my words.

55.   The story goes that Horatius Cocles, while fighting with two enemies at the head of the bridge over the Tiber, which is the entrance to the city on the north, seeing a large body of men advancing to support his enemies, and fearing that they would force their way into the city, turned round, and shouted to those behind him to hasten back to the other side and break down the bridge. They obeyed him: and whilst they were breaking the bridge, he remained at his post receiving numerous wounds, and checked the progress of the enemy: his opponents being panic stricken, not so much by his strength as by the audacity with which he held his ground. When the bridge had been broken down, the attack of the enemy was stopped; and Cocles then threw himself into the river with his armour on and deliberately sacrificed his life, because he valued the safety of his country and his own future reputation more highly than his present life, and the years of existence that remained to him. Such is the enthusiasm and emulation for noble deeds that are engendered among the Romans by their customs.

56.   Again the Roman customs and principles regarding money transactions are better than those of the Carthaginians. In the view of the latter nothing is disgraceful that makes for gain; with the former nothing is more disgraceful than to receive bribes and to make profit by improper means. For they regard wealth obtained from unlawful transactions to be as much a subject of reproach, as a fair profit from the most unquestioned source is of commendation. A proof of the fact is this. The Carthaginians obtain office by open bribery, but among the Romans the penalty for it is death. With such a radical difference, therefore, between the rewards offered to virtue among the two people, it is natural that the ways adopted for obtaining them should be different also.

But the most important difference for the better which the Roman commonwealth appears to me to display is in their religious beliefs. For I conceive that what in other nations is looked upon as a reproach, I mean a scrupulous fear of the gods, is the very thing which keeps the Roman Commonwealth together. To such an extraordinary height is this carried among them, both in private and public business, that nothing could exceed it. Many people might think this unaccountable; but in my opinion their object is to use it as a check upon the common people. If it were possible to form a state wholly of philosophers, such a custom would perhaps be unnecessary. But seeing that every multitude is fickle, and full of lawless desires, unreasoning anger, and violent passion, the only resource is to keep them in check by mysterious terrors and scenic effects of this sort. Wherefore, to my mind, the ancients were not acting without purpose or at random, when they brought in among the vulgar those opinions about the gods, and the belief in the punishments in Hades: much rather do I think that men nowadays are acting rashly and foolishly in rejecting them. This is the reason why, apart from anything else, Greek statesmen, if entrusted with a single talent, though protected by ten checking-clerks, as many seals, and twice as many witnesses, yet cannot be induced to keep faith: whereas among the Romans, in their magistracies and embassies, men have the handling of a great amount of money, and yet from pure respect to their oath keep their faith intact. And, again, in other nations it is a rare thing to find a man who keeps his hands out of the public purse, and is entirely pure in such matters: but among the Romans it is a rare thing to detect a man in the act of committing such a crime.

Plutarch

Born in the small Greek town of Chaironeia, Plutarch (c. A.D. 45–125) was the author of over two hundred works, of which about half survive. He wrote on a wide variety of subjects, including essays on moral, philosophical, religious and scientific issues. He is most famous, however, for his biographies of famous Greeks and Romans. Plutarch's *Lives* were not mere hagiography, simple celebrations of the virtues of great men. Instead, Plutarch explored the lives of his subjects in detail, focusing on the critical events that he believed revealed the true character of the actors involved.

The example of Plutarch's work included here comes from Plutarch's life of Marcus Licinius Crassus (d. 53 B.C.), a man famous for his unbounded ambition and avarice. It describes Crassus' rivalry with the Roman general Pompey (146–48 B.C) and his participation in the suppression of the slave revolt led by the gladiator Spartacus. Between 73 and 71 B.C., Spartacus and his followers won battle after battle against the Roman forces sent to put down the uprising. The revolt came to an end when an army led by Crassus succeeded where others had failed. As you read Plutarch's description of the revolt, pay particular attention to the ways in which Roman politics shaped the Senate's response to Spartacus.

Consider the following questions as you study the text below.

1. How did Plutarch characterize Spartacus? Did he believe the revolt was in any way justified? How did Plutarch explain Spartacus' initial success?

2. What was the relationship between Crassus and Pompey? Why was Pompey rewarded with a major triumph for his victories in Spain, while Crassus received no triumph at all for his victory over Spartacus? What light does this shed on the nature of Roman politics in the last decades of the Republic?

The Insurrection of the Gladiators

The insurrection of the gladiators and their devastation of Italy, which is generally called the war of Spartacus, had its origin as follows. A certain Lentulus Batiatus had a school of gladiators at Capua, most of whom were Gauls and Thracians. Through no misconduct of theirs, but owing to the

From *Plutarch's Lives*, Vol. III, trans. William Heinemann.

injustice of their owner, they were kept in close confinement and reserved for gladiatorial combats. Two hundred of these planned to make their escape, and when information was laid against them, those who got wind of it and succeeded in getting away, seventy-eight in number, seized cleavers and spits from some kitchen and sallied out. On the road they fell in with waggons conveying gladiators' weapons to another city; these they plundered and armed themselves. Then they took up a strong position and elected three leaders. The first of these was Spartacus, a Thracian of Nomadic stock, possessed not only of great courage and strength, but also in sagacity and culture superior to his fortune, and more Hellenic than Thracian. It is said that when he was first brought to Rome to be sold, a serpent was seen coiled about his face as he slept, and his wife, who was of the same tribe as Spartacus, a prophetess, and subject to visitations of the Dionysiac frenzy, declared it the sign of a great and formidable power which would attend him to a fortunate issue. This woman shared in his escape and was then living with him.

To begin with, the gladiators repulsed the soldiers who came against them from Capua, and getting hold of many arms of real warfare, they gladly took these in exchange for their own, casting away their gladiatorial weapons as dishonourable and barbarous. Then Clodius the praetor was sent out from Rome against them with three thousand soldiers, and laid siege to them on a hill which had but one ascent. and that a narrow and difficult one, which Clodius closely watched; everywhere else there were smooth and precipitous cliffs. But the top of the hill was covered with a wild vine of abundant growth, from which the besieged cut off the serviceable branches, and wove these into strong ladders of such strength and length that when they were fastened at the top they reached along the face of the cliff to the plain below. On these they descended. safely, all but one man, who remained above to attend to the arms. When the rest had got down, he began to drop the arms, and after he had thrown them all down, got away himself also last of all in safety. Of all this the Romans were ignorant, and therefore their enemy surrounded them, threw them into consternation by the suddenness of the attack, put them to flight, and took their camp. They were also joined by many of the herdsmen and shepherds of the region, sturdy men and swift of foot, some of whom they armed fully, and employed others as scouts and light infantry.

In the second place, Publius Varinus, the praetor, was sent out against them, whose lieutenant, a certain Furius, with two thousand soldiers, they first engaged and routed; then Spartacus narrowly watched the movements of Cossinius, who had been sent out with a large force to advise and assist Varinus in the command, and came near seizing him as he was bathing near Salinae. Cossinius barely escaped with much difficulty, and Spartacus at once seized his baggage, pressed hard upon him in pursuit, and took his camp with great slaughter. Cossinius also fell. By defeating the praetor himself in many battles, and finally capturing his lictors and the very horse he rode, Spartacus was soon great and formidable; but he took a proper view of the situation, and since he could not expect to overcome the Roman power, began to lead his army toward the Alps, thinking it necessary for them to cross the mountains and go to their respective homes, some to Thrace, and some to Gaul. But his men were now strong in numbers and full of confidence, and would not list to him, but went ravaging over Italy.

It was now no longer the indignity and disgrace of the revolt that harassed the senate, but they were constrained by their fear and peril to send both consuls into the field, as they would to a war of the utmost difficulty and magnitude. Gellius, one of the consuls, fell suddenly upon the Germans, who were so insolent and bold as to separate themselves from the main body of Spartacus, and cut them all to pieces; but when Lentulus, the other consul, had surrounded the enemy with large forces, Spartacus rushed upon them, joined battle, defeated the legates of Lentulus, and seized all their baggage. Then, as he was forcing his way towards the Alps, he was met by Cassius, the governor of Cisalpine Gaul, with an army of ten thousand men, and in the battle that ensued, Cassius was defeated, lost many men, and escaped himself with difficulty.

On learning of this, the Senate angrily ordered the consuls to keep quiet, and chose Crassus to conduct the war, and many of the nobles were induced by his reputation and their friendship for him to serve under him. Crassus himself, accordingly, took position on the borders of Picenum, expecting to receive the attack of Spartacus, who was hastening thither; and he sent, Mummius, his legate, with two legions, by a circuitous route, with orders to follow the enemy, but not to join battle nor even skirmish with them. Mummius, however, at the first promising opportunity, gave battle and was defeated; many of his men were slain, and many of them threw away their arms and fled for their lives. Crassus gave Mummius himself a rough reception, and when he armed his soldiers anew, made them give pledges that they would keep their arms. Five hundred of them, moreover, who had shown the greatest cowardice and been first to fly, he divided into fifty decades, and put to death one from each decade, on whom the lot fell, thus reviving, after the lapse of many years, an ancient mode of punishing the soldiers. For disgrace also attaches to this manner of death, and many horrible and repulsive features attend the punishment, which the whole army witnesses.

When he had thus disciplined his men, he led them against the enemy. But Spartacus avoided him, and retired through Lucania to the sea. At the Straits, he chanced upon some Cilician pirate craft, and determined to seize Sicily. By throwing two thousand men into the island, he thought to kindle anew the servile war there, which had not long been extinguished, and needed only a little additional fuel. But the Cilicians, after coming to terms with him and receiving his gifts, deceived him and sailed away. So Spartacus marched back again from the sea and established his army in the peninsula of Rhegium. Crassus now came up, and observing that the nature of the place suggested what must be done, he determined to build a wall across the isthmus, thereby at once keeping his soldiers from idleness, and his enemies from provisions. Now the task was a huge one and difficult, but he accomplished and finished it, contrary to all expectation, in a short time, running a ditch from sea to sea through the neck of land three hundred furlongs in length and fifteen feet in width and depth alike. Above the ditch he also built a wall of astonishing height and strength. All this work Spartacus neglected and despised at first; but soon his provisions began to fail, and when he wanted to sally forth from the peninsula, he saw that he was walled in, and that there was nothing more to be had there. He therefore waited for a snowy night and a wintry storm, when he filled up a small portion of the ditch with earth and timber and the boughs of trees, and so threw a third part of his force across.

Crassus was now in fear lest some impulse to march upon Rome should seize Spartacus, but took heart when he saw that many of the gladiator's men had seceded after a quarrel with him, and were encamped by themselves on a Lucanian lake. This lake, they say, changes from time to time in the character of its water, becoming sweet, and then again bitter and undrinkable. Upon this detachment Crassus fell, and drove them away from the lake, but he was robbed of the slaughter and pursuit of the fugitives by the sudden appearance of Spartacus, who checked their flight.

Before this Crassus had written to the Senate that they must summon Lucullus from Thrace and Pompey from Spain, but he was sorry now that he had done so, and was eager to bring the war to an end before those generals came. He knew that the success would be ascribed to the one who came up with assistance, and not to himself. Accordingly, in the first place, he determined to attack those of the enemy who had seceded from the rest and were campaigning on their own account (they were commanded by Caius Canicius and Castus), and with this in view, sent out six thousand men to preoccupy a certain eminence, bidding them keep their attempt a secret. And they did try to elude observation by covering up their helmets, but they were seen by two women who were sacrificing for the enemy, and would have been in peril of their lives had not Crassus quickly made his appearance and given battle, the most stubbornly contested of all; for although he slew twelve thousand three hundred men in it, he found only two who were wounded in the back. The rest all died standing in the ranks and fighting the Romans.

After the defeat of this detachment, Spartacus retired to the mountains of Petelia, followed closely by Quintus, one of the officers of Crassus, and by Scrophas, the quaestor, who hung upon the enemy's rear. But when Spartacus faced about, there was a great rout of the Romans, and they barely managed to drag the quaestor, who had been wounded, away into safety. This success was the ruin of Spartacus, for it filled his slaves with over-confidence. They would no longer consent to avoid battle, and would not even obey their leaders, but surrounded them as soon as they began to march, with arms in their hands, and forced them to lead back through Lucania against the Romans, the very thing which Crassus also most desired. For

Pompey's approach was already announced, and there were not a few who publicly proclaimed that the victory in this war belonged to him; he had only to come and fight and put an end to the war. Crassus, therefore, pressed on to finish the struggle himself, and having encamped near the enemy, began to dig a trench. Into this the slaves leaped and began to fight with those who were working there, and since fresh men from both sides kept coming up to help their comrades, Spartacus saw the necessity that was upon him, and drew up his whole army in order of battle.

In the first place, when his horse was brought to him, he drew his sword, and saying that if he won the day he would have many fine horses of the enemy's, but if he lost it he did not want any, he slew his horse. Then pushing his way towards Crassus himself through many flying weapons and wounded men, he did not indeed reach him, but slew two centurions who fell upon him together. Finally, after his companions had taken to flight, he stood alone, surrounded by a multitude of foes, and was still defending himself when he was cut down. But although Crassus had been fortunate, had shown most excellent generalship, and had exposed his person to danger, nevertheless, his success did not fail to enhance the reputation of Pompey. For the fugitives from the battle encountered that general and were cut to pieces, so that he could write to the senate that in open battle, indeed, Crassus had conquered the slaves, but that he himself had extirpated the war. Pompey, accordingly, for his victories over Sertorius and in Spain, celebrated a splendid triumph; but Crassus, for all his self-approval, did not venture to ask for the major triumph, and it was thought ignoble and mean in him to celebrate even the minor triumph on foot, called the ovation, for a servile war. How the minor triumph differs from the major, and why it is named as it is, has been told in my life of Marcellus.

After this, Pompey was at once asked to stand for the consulship, and Crassus, although he had hopes of becoming his colleague, did not hesitate to ask Pompey's assistance. Pompey received his request gladly (for he was desirous of having Crassus, in some way or other, always in debt to him for some favour), and eagerly promoted his candidature, and finally said in a speech to the assembly that he should be no less grateful to them for the colleague than for the office which he desired. However, when once they had assumed office, they did not remain on this friendly basis, but differed on almost every measure, quarrelled with one another about everything, and by their contentiousness rendered their consulship barren politically and without achievement, except that Crassus made a great sacrifice in honour of Hercules, feasted the people at ten thousand tables, and made them an allowance of grain for three months. And when at last their term of office was closing, and they were addressing the assembly, a certain man, not a noble, but a Roman knight, rustic and rude in his way of life, Onatius Aurelius, mounted the rostra and recounted to the audience a vision that had come to him in his sleep.

Suetonius

Julius Caesar is generally acknowledged to be one of the great figures in Western history. But is this reputation justified? In what did his greatness lie? One thing certainly can be said: he was one of the most successful military men of all times. More than that, he was an extraordinarily popular political leader. As a conqueror he dramatically expanded the Roman Empire. As a statesman he enacted a series of laws that substantially benefitted the soldiers and ordinary citizens but he did so often at the expense of the liberties the people had enjoyed under the Republic. In any event, Caesar held power for only two years after his return to Rome from his military adventures in Western Europe and the Near East before being assassinated by his political enemies. So the question remains, unanswered: Had he lived, what further might Caesar have accomplished?

We know a good deal about the life and character of Caesar, thanks mainly to the writings of two gifted biographers—Plutarch and Suetonius—both of whom lived about a hundred years after the death of their subject. Little is known about Suetonius, from whom the following selection is taken, except that he was at one time secretary to the emperor Hadrian. The biography, which is part of a larger work, *Lives of the Caesars*, is by no means adulatory; indeed, the author often seems intent on destroying the reputation of Caesar. On the other hand, he is generous in his estimate of Caesar's strengths. Above all the entire piece gives a vivid picture of the political intrigues, turbulence, and violence of the years of the decline and collapse of republican Rome.

Consider the following questions as you study the text below.

1. What was the relationship between Caesar's military success and political power? Did Caesar fight for Rome or for himself?

2. What steps did Caesar take to gain the support of the people of Rome? What connections, if any, did Suetonius make between Caesar's public acts and policies and his private life?

The Lives of the Caesars

Book I

THE DEIFIED JULIUS

. . .

Backed by his father-in-law and son-in-law, out of all the numerous provinces [Caesar] made the Gauls his choice, as the most likely to enrich him and furnish suitable material for triumphs. At first, it is true, by the bill of Vatinius he received only Cisalpine Gaul* with the addition of Illyricum; but presently he was assigned Gallia Comata as well by the senate, since the members feared that even if they should refuse it, the people would give him this also. Transported with joy at this success, he could not keep from boasting a few days later before a crowded house, that having gained his heart's desire to the grief and lamentation of his opponents, he would therefore from that time mount on their heads; and when someone insultingly remarked that that would be no easy matter for any woman, he replied in the same vein that Semiramis too had been queen in Syria and the Amazons in days of old had held sway over a great part of Asia.

When at the close of his consulship the praetors Gaius Memmius and Lucius Domitius moved an inquiry into his conduct the previous year, Caesar laid the matter before the senate; and when they failed to take it up, and three days had been wasted in fruitless wrangling, went off to his province. Whereupon his quaestor was at once arraigned on several counts, as a preliminary to his own impeachment. Presently he himself too was prosecuted by Lucius Antistius, tribune of the commons, and it was only by appealing to the whole college that he contrived not to be brought to trial, on the ground that he was absent on public service. Then to secure himself for the future, he took great pains always to put the magistrates for the year under personal obligation, and not to aid any candidates or suffer any to be elected, save as guaranteed to defend him in his absence. And he did not hesitate in some cases to exact an oath to keep this pledge or even a written contract.

When however Lucius Domitius, candidate for the consulship, openly threatened to effect as consul what he had been unable to do as praetor, and to take his armies from him, Caesar compelled Pompeius and Crassus to come to Luca, a city in his province, where he prevailed on them to stand for a second consulship, to defeat Domitius; and he also succeeded through their

*[Roughly northern Italy—*Ed.*]

Trans J. C. Rolfe.

influence in having his term as governor of Gaul made five years longer. Encouraged by this, he added to the legions which he had received from the state others at his own cost, one actually composed of men of Transalpine Gaul and bearing a Gallic name too (for it was called Alauda), which he trained in the Roman tactics and equipped with Roman arms; and later on he gave every man of it citizenship. After that he did not let slip any pretext for war, however unjust and dangerous it might be, picking quarrels as well with allied as with hostile and barbarous nations; so that once the senate decreed that a commission be sent to inquire into the condition of the Gallic provinces, and some even recommended that Caesar be handed over to the enemy. But as his enterprises prospered, thanksgivings were appointed in his honour oftener and for longer periods than for anyone before his time.

During the nine years of his command this is in substance what he did. All that part of Gaul which is bounded by the Pyrenees, the Alps and the Cevennes, and by the Rhine and Rhone rivers, a circuit of some thirty-two hundred miles, with the exception of some allied states which had rendered him good service, he reduced to the form of a province; and imposed upon it a yearly tribute of forty million sesterces. He was the first Roman to build a bridge and attack the Germans beyond the Rhine, and he inflicted heavy losses upon them. He invaded the Britons too, a people unknown before, vanquished them, and exacted moneys and hostages. Amid all these successes he met with adverse fortune but three times in all: in Britain, where his fleet narrowly escaped destruction in a violent storm; in Gaul, when one of his legions was routed at Gergovia; and on the borders of Germany, when his lieutenants Titurius and Aurunculeius were ambushed and slain.

Within this same space of time he lost first his mother, then his daughter, and soon afterwards his grandchild. Meanwhile, as the community was aghast at the murder of Publius Clodius, the senate had voted that only one consul should be chosen, and expressly named Gnaeus Pompeius. When the tribunes planned to make him Pompey's colleague, Caesar urged them rather to propose to the people that he be permitted to stand for a second consulship without coming to Rome, when the term of his governorship drew near its end, to prevent his being forced for the sake of the office to leave his province prematurely and without finishing the war. On the granting of this, aiming still higher and flushed with hope, he neglected nothing in the way of lavish expenditure or of favours to anyone, either in his public capacity or privately. He began a forum with the proceeds of his spoils, the ground for which cost more than a hundred million sesterces. He announced a combat of gladiators and a feast for the people in memory of his daughter, a thing quite without precedent. To raise the expectation of these events to the highest possible pitch, he had the material for the banquet prepared in part by his own household, although he had let contracts to the markets as well. He gave orders too that whenever famous gladiators fought without winning the favour of the people, they should be rescued by force and kept for him. He had the novices trained, not in a gladiatorial school by professionals, but in private houses by Roman knights and even by senators who were skilled in arms, earnestly beseeching them, as is shown by his own letters, to give the recruits individual attention and personally direct their exercises. He doubled the pay of the legions for all time. Whenever grain was plentiful, he distributed it to them without stint or measure, and now and then gave each man a slave from among the captives.

Moreover, to retain his relationship and friendship with Pompey, Caesar offered him his sister's granddaughter Octavia in marriage, although she was already the wife of Gaius Marcellus, and asked for the hand of Pompey's daughter, who was promised to Faustus Sulla. When he had put all Pompey's friends under obligation, as well as the great part of the senate, through loans made without interest or at a low rate, he lavished gifts on men of all other classes, both those whom he invited to accept his bounty and those who applied to him unasked, including even freedmen and slaves who were special favourites of their masters or patrons. In short, he was the sole and ever ready help of all who were in legal difficulties or in debt and of young spendthrifts, excepting only those whose burden of guilt or of poverty was so heavy, or who were so given up to riotous living, that even he could not save them; and to these he declared in the plainest terms that what they needed was a civil war.

He took no less pains to win the devotion of princes and provinces all over the world, offering prisoners to some by the thousand as a gift, and sending auxiliary troops to the aid of others whenever they wished, and as often as they wished, without the sanction of the senate or people, besides adorning the principal cities of Asia and Greece with magnificent public works, as well as those of Italy and the provinces of Gaul and Spain. At last, when all were thunderstruck at his actions and wondered what their purpose could be, the consul Marcus Claudius Marcellus, after first making proclamation that he purposed to bring before the senate a matter of the highest public moment, proposed that a successor to Caesar be appointed before the end of his term, on the ground that the war was ended, peace was established, and the victorious army ought to be disbanded; also that no account be taken of Caesar at the elections, unless he were present, since Pompey's subsequent action had not annulled the decree of the people. And it was true that when Pompey proposed a bill touching the privileges of officials, in the clause where he debarred absentees from candidacy for office he forgot to make a special exception in Caesar's case, and did not correct the oversight until the law had been inscribed on a tablet of bronze and deposited in the treasury. Not content with depriving Caesar of his provinces and his privilege, Marcellus also moved that the colonists whom Caesar had settled in Novum Comum by the bill of Vatinius should lose their citizenship, on the ground that it had been given from political motives and was not authorized by the law.

Greatly troubled by these measures, and thinking, as they say he was often heard to remark, that now that he was the leading man of the state, it was harder to push him down from the first place to the second than it would be from the second to the lowest, Caesar stoutly resisted Marcellus, partly through vetoes of the tribunes and partly through the other consul, Servius Sulpicius. When next year Gaius Marcellus, who had succeeded his cousin Marcus as consul, tried the same thing, Caesar by a heavy bribe secured the support of the other consul, Aemilius Paulus, and of Gaius Curio, the most reckless of the tribunes. But seeing that everything was being pushed most persistently, and that even the consuls-elect were among the opposition, he sent a written appeal to the senate, not to take from him the privilege which the people had granted, or else to compel the others in command of armies to resign also; feeling sure, it was thought, that he could more readily muster his veterans as soon as he wished, than Pompey his newly levied troops. He further proposed a compromise to his opponents, that after giving up eight legions and Transalpine Gaul, he be allowed to keep two legions and Cisalpine Gaul, or at least one legion and Illyricum, until he was elected consul.

But when the senate declined to interfere, and his opponents declared that they would accept no compromise in a matter affecting the public welfare, he crossed to Hither Gaul, and after holding all the assizes, halted at Ravenna, intending to resort to war if the senate took any drastic action against the tribunes of the commons who interposed vetoes in his behalf. Now this was his excuse for the civil war, but it is believed that he had other motives. Gnaeus Pompeius used to declare that since Caesar's own means were not sufficient to complete the works which he had planned, nor to do all that he had led the people to expect on his return, he desired a state of general unrest and turmoil. Others say that he dreaded the necessity of rendering an account for what he had done in his first consulship contrary to the auspices and the laws, and regardless of vetoes; for Marcus Cato often declared, and took oath too, that he would impeach Caesar the moment he had disbanded his army. It was openly said too that if he was out of office on his return, he would be obliged, like Milo, to make his defence in a court hedged about by armed men. The latter opinion is the more credible one in view of the assertion of Asinius Pollio, that when Caesar at the battle of Pharsalus saw his enemies slain or in flight, he said, word for word: "They would have it so. Even I, Gaius Caesar, after so many great deeds, should have been found guilty, if I had not turned to my army for help." Some think that habit had given him a love of power, and that weighing the strength of his adversaries against his own, he grasped the opportunity of usurping the depotism which had been his heart's desire from early youth. Cicero too was seemingly of this opinion, when he wrote in the third book of his *De Officiis* that Caesar ever had upon his lips these lines of Euripides, of which Cicero himself adds a version:—

If wrong may e'er be right, for a throne's sake
Were wrong most right:—be God in all else feared.

Accordingly, when word came that the veto of the tribunes had been set aside and they themselves had left the city, he at once sent on a few cohorts with all secrecy, and then, to disarm suspicion, concealed his purpose by appearing at a public show, inspecting the plans of a gladiatorial school which he intended building, and joining as usual in a banquet with a large company. It was not until after sunset that he set out very privily with a small company, taking the mules from a bakeshop hard by and harnessing them to a carriage; and when his lights went out and he lost his way, he was astray for some time, but at last found a guide at dawn and got back to the road on foot by narrow by-paths. Then, overtaking his cohorts at the river Rubicon, which was the boundary of his province, he paused for a while, and realising what a step he was taking, he turned to those about him and said: "Even yet we may draw back; but once cross yon little bridge, and the whole issue is with the sword."

As he stood in doubt, this sign was given him. On a sudden there appeared hard by a being of wondrous stature and beauty, who sat and played upon a reed; and when not only the shepherds flocked to hear him, but many of the soldiers left their posts, and among them some of the trumpeters, the apparition snatched a trumpet from one of them, rushed to the river, and sounding the war-note with mighty blast, strode to the opposite bank. Then Caesar cried: "Take we the course which the signs of the gods and the false dealing of our foes point out. The die is cast," said he.

Accordingly, crossing with his army, and welcoming the tribunes of the commons, who had come to him after being driven from Rome, he harangued the soldiers with tears, and rending his robe from his breast besought their faithful service. It is even thought that he promised every man a knight's estate, but that came of a misunderstanding; for since he often pointed to the finger of his left hand as he addressed them and urged them on, declaring that to satisfy all those who helped him to defend his honour he would gladly tear his very ring from his hand, those on the edge of the assembly, who could see him better than they could hear his words, assumed that he said what his gesture seemed to mean; and so the report went about that he had promised them the right of the ring and four hundred thousand sesterces as well.

The sum total of his movements after that is, in their order, as follows: He overran Umbria, Picenum, and Etruria, took prisoner Lucius Domitius, who had been irregularly named his successor, and was holding Corfinium with a garrison, let him go free, and then proceeded along the Adriatic to Brundisium, where Pompey and the consuls had taken refuge, intending to cross the sea as soon as might be. After vainly trying by every kind of hindrance to prevent their sailing, he marched off to Rome, and after calling the senate together to discuss public business, went to attack Pompey's strongest forces, which were in Spain under command of three of his lieutenants—Marcus Petreius, Lucius Afranius, and Marcus Varro—saying to his friends before he left, "I go to meet an army without a leader, and I shall return to meet a leader without an army." And in fact, though his advance was delayed by the siege of Massilia, which had shut its gates against him, and by extreme scarcity of supplies, he nevertheless quickly gained a complete victory.

Returning thence to Rome, he crossed into Macedonia, and after blockading Pompey for almost four months behind mighty ramparts, finally routed him in the battle at Pharsalus, followed him in his flight to Alexandria, and when he learned that his rival had been slain, made war on King Ptolemy, whom he perceived to be plotting against his own safety as well; a war in truth of great difficulty, convenient neither in time nor place, but carried on during the winter season, within the walls of a well-provisioned and crafty foeman, while Caesar himself was without supplies of any kind and ill-prepared. Victor in spite of all, he turned over the rule of Egypt to Cleopatra and her young brother, fearing that if he made a province of it, it might one day under a headstrong governor be a source of revolution. From Alexandria he crossed to Syria, and from there went to Pontus, spurred on by the news that Pharnaces, son of Mithridates the Great, had taken advantage of the situation to make war, and was already flushed with numerous successes; but Caesar vanquished him in a single battle within five days after his arrival and four hours after getting sight of him, often remarking on Pompey's good luck in gaining his principal fame as a general by victories over such feeble foemen. Then he overcame Scipio and Juba, who were patching up the remnants of their party in Africa, and the sons of Pompey in Spain.

In all the civil wars he suffered not a single disaster except through his lieutenants, of whom Gaius Curio perished in Africa, Gaius Antonius fell into the hands of the enemy in Illyricum, Publius Dolabella lost a fleet also off Illyricum, and Gnaeus Domitius Calvinus an army in Pontus. Personally he always fought with the utmost success, and the issue was never even in doubt save twice: once at Dyrrachium, where he was put to flight, and said of Pompey, who failed to follow up his success, that he did not know how to use a victory; again in Spain, in the final struggle, when, believing the battle lost, he actually thought of suicide.

Having ended the wars, he celebrated five triumphs, four in a single month, but at intervals of a few days, after vanquishing Scipio; and another on defeating Pompey's sons. The first and most splendid was the Gallic triumph, the next the Alexandrian, then the Pontic, after that the African, and finally the Spanish, each differing from the rest in its equipment and display of spoils. As he rode through the Velabrum on the day of his Gallic triumph, the axle of his chariot broke, and he was all but thrown out; and he mounted the Capitol by torchlight, with forty elephants bearing lamps on his right and his left. In his

Pontic triumph he displayed among the show-pieces of the procession an inscription of but three words, "I came, I saw, I conquered," not indicating the
events of the war, as the others did, but the speed with which it was finished.

To each and every foot-soldier of his veteran legions he gave
twenty-four thousand sesterces by way of booty, over and above the two
thousand apiece which he had paid them at the beginning of the civil strife.
He also assigned them lands, but not side by side, to avoid dispossessing
any of the former owners. To every man of the people, besides ten pecks of
grain and the same number of pounds of oil, he distributed the three hundred sesterces which he had promised at first, and one hundred apiece to
boot because of the delay. He also remitted a year's rent in Rome to tenants
who paid two thousand sesterces or less, and in Italy up to five hundred sesterces. He added a banquet and a dole of meat, and after his Spanish victory
two dinners; for deeming that the former of these had not been served with
a liberality creditable to his generosity, he gave another five days later on a
most lavish scale.

He gave entertainments of divers kinds: a combat of gladiators and also
stage-plays in every ward all over the city, performed too by actors of all languages, as well as races in the circus, athletic contests, and a sham sea-fight.
In the gladiatorial contest in the Forum Furius Leptinus, a man of praetorian
stock, and Quintus Calpenus, a former senator and pleader at the bar, fought
to a finish. A Pyrrhic dance was performed by the sons of the princes of Asia
and Bithynia. During the plays Decimus Laberius, a Roman Knight, acted a
farce of his own composition, and having been presented with five hundred
thousand sesterces and a gold ring, passed from the stage through the or-
chestra and took his place in the fourteen rows. For the races the circus was
lengthened at either end and a broad canal was dug all about it; then young
men of the highest rank drove four-horse and two-horse chariots and rode
pairs of horses, vaulting from one to the other. The game called Troy was performed by two troops, of younger and of older boys. Combats with wild
beasts were presented on five successive days, and last of all there was a battle between two opposing armies, in which five hundred foot-soldiers, twenty elephants, and thirty horsemen engaged on each side. To make room for
this, the goals were taken down and in their place two camps were pitched
over against each other. The athletic competitions lasted for three days in a
temporary stadium built for the purpose in the region of the Campus Mar-
tius. For the naval battle a pool was dug in the lesser Codeta and there was a
contest of ships of two, three, and four banks of oars, belonging to the Tyrian
and Egyptian fleets, manned by a large force of fighting men. Such a throng
flocked to all these shows from every quarter, that many strangers had to
lodge in tents pitched in the streets or along the roads, and the press was
often such that many were crushed to death, including two senators.

Then turning his attention to the reorganisation of the state, he reformed
the calendar, which the negligence of the pontiffs had long since so disordered,

through their privilege of adding months or days at pleasure, that the harvest festivals did not come in summer nor those of the vintage in the autumn; and he adjusted the year to the sun's course by making it consist of three hundred and sixty-five days, abolishing the intercalary month, and adding one day every fourth year. Furthermore, that the correct reckoning of seasons might begin with the next Kalends of January, he inserted two other months between those of November and December; hence the year in which these arrangements were made was one of fifteen months, including the intercalary month, which belonged to that year according to the former custom.

He filled the vacancies in the senate, enrolled additional patricians, and increased the number of praetors, aediles, and quaestors, as well as of the minor officials; he reinstated those who had been degraded by official action of the censors or found guilty of bribery by verdict of the jurors. He shared the elections with the people on this basis: that except in the case of the consulship, half of the magistrates should be appointed by the people's choice, while the rest should be those whom he had personally nominated. And these he announced in brief notes like the following, circulated in each tribe: "Caesar the Dictator to this or that tribe. I commend to you so and so, to hold their positions by your votes." He admitted to office even the sons of those who had been proscribed. He limited the right of serving as jurors to two classes, the equestrian and senatorial orders, disqualifying the third class, the tribunes of the treasury.

He made the enumeration of the people neither in the usual manner nor place, but from street to street aided by the owners of blocks of houses, and reduced the number of those who received grain at public expense from three hundred and twenty thousand to one hundred and fifty thousand. And to prevent the calling of additional meetings at any future time for purposes of enrollment, he provided that the places of such as died should be filled each year by the praetors from those who were not on the list.

Moreover, to keep up the population of the city, depleted as it was by the assignment of eighty thousand citizens to colonies across the sea, he made a law that no citizen older than twenty or younger than forty, who was not detained by service in the army, should be absent from Italy for more than three successive years; that no senator's son should go abroad except as the companion of a magistrate or on his staff; and that those who made a business of grazing should have among their herdsmen at least one-third who were men of free birth. He conferred citizenship on all who practised medicine at Rome, and on all teachers of the liberal arts, to make them more desirous of living in the city and to induce others to resort to it.

As to debts, he disappointed those who looked for their cancellation, which was often agitated, but finally decreed that the debtors should satisfy their creditors according to a valuation of their possessions at the price which they had paid for them before the civil war, deducting from the principal whatever interest had been paid in cash or pledged through bankers;

an arrangement which wiped out about a fourth part of their indebtedness. He dissolved all guilds, except those of ancient foundation. He increased the penalties for crimes; and inasmuch as the rich involved themselves in guilt with less hesitation because they merely suffered exile, without any loss of property, he punished murderers of freemen by the confiscation of all their goods, as Cicero writes, and others by the loss of one-half.

He administered justice with the utmost conscientiousness and strictness. Those convicted of extortion he even dismissed from the senatorial order. He annulled the marriage of an ex-praetor, who had married a woman the very day after her divorce, although there was no suspicion of adultery. He imposed duties on foreign wares. He denied the use of litters and the wearing of scarlet robes or pearls to all except to those of a designated position and age, and on set days. In particular he enforced the law against extravagance, setting watchmen in various parts of the market, to seize and bring to him dainties which were exposed for sale in violation of the law; and sometimes he sent his lictors and soldiers to take from a dining-room any articles which had escaped the vigilance of his watchmen, even after they had been served.

In particular, for the adornment and convenience of the city, also for the protection and extension of the Empire, he formed more projects and more extensive ones every day: first of all, to rear a temple to Mars, greater than any in existence, filling up and levelling the pool in which he had exhibited the sea-fight, and to build a theatre of vast size, sloping down from the Tarpeian rock; to reduce the civil code to fixed limits, and of the vast and prolix mass of statutes to include only the best and most essential in a limited number of volumes; to open to the public the greatest possible libraries of Greek and Latin books, assigning to Marcus Varro the charge of procuring and classifying them; to drain the Pomptine marshes; to let out the water from Lake Fucinus; to make a highway from the Adriatic across the summit of the Apennines as far as the Tiber; to cut a canal through the Isthmus; to check the Dacians, who had poured into Pontus and Thrace; then to make war on the Parthians by way of Lesser Armenia, but not to risk a battle with them until he had first tested their mettle.

All these enterprises and plans were cut short by his death. But before I speak of that, it will not be amiss to describe briefly his personal appearance, his dress, his mode of life, and his character, as well as his conduct in civil and military life.

He is said to have been tall of stature, with a fair complexion, shapely limbs, a somewhat full face, and keen black eyes; sound of health, except that towards the end he was subject to sudden fainting fits and to nightmare as well. He was twice attacked by the falling sickness during his campaigns. He was somewhat over-nice in the care of his person, being not only carefully trimmed and shaved, but even having superfluous hair plucked out, as some have charged; while his baldness was a disfigurement which troubled him greatly, since he found that it was often the subject of the gibes of his detractors. Because of it he used to comb forward his scanty locks from the crown of his head, and of all the honours voted him by the senate people there was none which he received or made use of more gladly than the privilege of wearing a laurel wreath at all times. They say, too, that he was remarkable in his dress; that he wore a senator's tunic with fringed sleeves reaching to the wrist, and always had a girdle over it, though rather a loose one; and this, they say, was the occasion of Sulla's *mot*, when he often warned the nobles to keep an eye on the ill-girt boy.

That he was unbridled and extravagant in his intrigues is the general opinion, and that he seduced many illustrious women, among them Postumia, wife of Servius Sulpicius, Lollia, wife of Aulus Gabinius, Tertulla, wife of Marcus Crassus, and even Gnaeus Pompey's wife Mucia. At all events there is no doubt that Pompey was taken to task by the elder and the younger Curio, as well as by many others, because through a desire for power he had afterwards married the daughter of a man on whose account he divorced a wife who had borne him three children, and whom he had often referred to with a groan as an Aegisthus. But beyond all others Caesar loved Servilla, the mother of Marcus Brutus, for whom in his first consulship he bought a pearl costing six million sesterces. During the civil war, too, besides other presents, he knocked down some fine estates to her in a public auction at a nominal price, and when some expressed their surprise at the low figure, Cicero wittily remarked: "It's a better bargain than you think, for there is a third off." And in fact it was thought that Servilla was prostituting her own daughter Tertia to Caesar.

That he did not refrain from intrigues in the provinces is shown in particular by this couplet, which was also shouted by the soldiers in his Gallic triumph:—

> Men of Rome, keep close your consorts, here's a bald adulterer.
> Gold in Gaul you spent in dalliance, which you borrowed here in Rome.

He had love affairs with queens too, including Eunoe that Moor, wife of Bogudes, on whom, as well as on her husband, he bestowed many splendid presents, as Naso writes; but above all with Cleopatra, with whom he often feasted until daybreak, and he would have gone through Egypt with her in her state-barge almost to Aethiopia, had not his soldiers refused to follow him. Finally he called her to Rome and did not let her leave until he had ladened her with high honours and rich gifts, and he allowed her to give his name to the child which she bore. In fact, according to certain Greek writers, this child was very like Caesar in looks and carriage. Mark Anthony declared to the senate that Caesar had really acknowledged the boy, and that Gaius Matius, Gaius Oppius, and other friends of Caesar knew this. Of these Gaius Oppius, as if admitting that the situation required apology and defence, published a book, to prove that the child whom Cleopatra fathered on

Caesar was not his. Helvius Cinna, tribune of the commons, admitted to several that he had a bill drawn up in due form, which Caesar had ordered him to propose to the people in his absence, making it lawful for Caesar to marry what wives he wished, "for the purpose of begetting children." But to remove all doubt that he had an evil reputation for shameless vice and for adultery, I have only to add that the elder Curio in one of his speeches calls him "every woman's man and every man's woman."

That he drank very little wine not even his enemies denied. There is a saying of Marcus Cato that Caesar was the only man who undertook to overthrow the state when sober. Even in the matter of food Gaius Oppius tells us that he was so indifferent, that once when his host served stale oil instead of fresh, and the other guests would have none of it, Caesar partook even more plentifully than usual, not to seem to charge his host with carelessness or lack of manners.

Neither when in command of armies nor as a magistrate at Rome did he show a scrupulous integrity; for as certain men have declared in their memoirs, when he was proconsul in Spain, he not only begged money from the allies, to help pay his debts, but also attacked and sacked some towns of the Lusitanians although they did not refuse his terms and opened their gates to him on his arrival. In Gaul he pillaged shrines and temples of the gods filled with offerings, and oftener sacked towns for the sake of plunder than for any fault. In consequence he had more gold than he knew what to do with, and offered it for sale throughout Italy and the provinces at the rate of three thousand sesterces the pound. In his first consulship he stole three thousand pounds of gold from the Capitol, replacing it with the same weight of gilded bronze. He made alliances and thrones a matter of barter, for he extorted from Ptolemy alone in his own name and that of Pompey nearly six thousand talents, while later on he met the heavy expenses of the civil wars and of his triumphs and entertainments by the most barefaced pillage and sacrilege.

In eloquence and in the art of war he either equalled or surpassed the fame of their most eminent representatives. After his accusation of Dolabella, he was without question numbered with the leading advocates. At all events when Cicero reviews the orators in his *Brutus*, he says that he does not see to whom Caesar ought to yield the palm, declaring that his style is elegant as well as transparent, even grand and in a sense noble. Again in a letter to Cornelius Nepos he writes thus of Caesar: "Come now, what orator would you rank above him of those who have devoted themselves to nothing else? Who has cleverer or more frequent epigrams? Who is either more picturesque or more choice in diction?" He appears, at least in his youth, to have imitated the manner of Caesar Strabo, from whose speech entitled "For the Sardinians" he actually transferred some passages word for word to a trial address of his own. He is said to have delivered himself in a high-pitched voice with impassioned action and gestures, which were not without grace. He left several speeches, including some which are attributed to him on insufficient evidence. Augustus had good reason to think that the speech "For Quintus Metellus" was rather taken down by shorthand writers who could not keep pace with his delivery, than published by Caesar himself; for in some copies I find that even the title is not "For Metellus," but, "Which He Wrote for Metellus," although the discourse purports to be from Caesar's lips, defending Metellus and himself against the charges of their common detractors. Augustus also questions the authenticity of the address "To His Soldiers in Spain," although there are two sections of it, one purporting to have been spoken at the first battle, the other at the second, when Asinius Pollio writes that because of the sudden onslaught of the enemy he actually did not have time to make an harangue.

He left memoirs too of his deeds in the Gallic war and in the civil strife with Pompey; for the author of the Alexandrian, African, and Spanish Wars is unknown; some think it was Oppius, others Hirtius, who also supplied the final book of the Gallic War, which Caesar left unwritten. With regard to Caesar's memoirs Cicero, also in the *Brutus* speaks in the following terms: "He wrote memoirs which deserve the highest praise; they are naked in their simplicity, straightforward yet graceful, stripped of all rhetorical adornment, as of a garment; but while his purpose was to supply material to others, on which those who wished to write history might draw, he haply gratified silly folk, who will try to use the curling-irons on his narrative, but he has kept men of any sense from touching the subject." Of these same memoirs Hirtius uses this emphatic language: "They are so highly rated in the judgment of all men, that he seems to have deprived writers of an opportunity, rather than given them one; yet our admiration for this feat is greater than that of others; for they know how well and faultlessly he wrote, while we know besides how easily and rapidly he finished his task." Asinius Pollio thinks that they were put together somewhat carelessly and without strict regard for truth; since in many cases Caesar was too ready to believe the accounts which others gave of their actions, and gave a perverted account of his own, either designedly or perhaps from forgetfulness; and he thinks that he intended to rewrite and revise them. He left besides a work in two volumes "On Analogy," the same number of "Speeches Criticising Cato," in addition to a poem, entitled "The Journey." He wrote the first of these works while crossing the Alps and returning to his army from Hither Gaul, where he had held the assizes; the second about the time of the battle of Munda, and the third in the course of a twenty-four days' journey from Rome to Farther Spain. Some letters of his to the senate are also preserved, and he seems to have been the first to reduce such documents to pages and the form of a notebook, whereas previously consuls and generals sent their reports written right across the sheet. There are also letters of his to Cicero, as well as to his intimates on private affairs, and in the latter, if he had anything confidential to say, he wrote it in cipher, that is, by so changing the order of the letters of the alphabet, that not a word could be made out. If anyone wishes to decipher these, and get at their meaning, he must substitute the fourth letter of the alphabet, namely D, for A, and so with the others. We also have mention of certain writings of his boyhood and early youth, such as the "Praises of Hercules," a tragedy "Oedipus," and a "Collection of Apophthegms"; but Augustus forbade the publication of all these minor works in a very brief and frank letter sent to Pompeius Macer, whom he had selected to set his libraries in order.

He was highly skilled in arms and horsemanship, and of incredible powers of endurance. On the march he headed his army, sometimes on horseback, but oftener on foot, bareheaded both in the heat of the sun and in the rain. He covered great distances with incredible speed, making a hundred miles a day in a hired carriage and with little baggage, swimming the rivers which barred his path or crossing them on inflated skins, and very often arriving before the messengers sent to announce his coming.

In the conduct of his campaigns it is a question whether he was more cautious or more daring, for he never led his army where ambuscades were possible without carefully reconnoitering the country, and he did not cross to Britain without making personal inquiries about the harbours, the course, and the approach to the island. But on the other hand, when news came that his camp in Germany was beleaguered, he made his way to his men through the enemies' pickets, disguised as a Gaul. He crossed from Brundisium to Dyrrachium in winter time, running the blockade of the enemy's fleets; and when the troops which he had ordered to follow him delayed to do so, and he had sent to fetch them many times in vain, at last in secret and alone he boarded a small boat at night with his head muffled up; and he did not reveal who he was, or suffer the helmsman to give way to the gale blowing in their teeth, until he was all but overwhelmed by the waves.

No regard for religion ever turned him from any undertaking, or even delayed him. Though the victim escaped as he was offering sacrifice, he did not put off his expedition against Scipio and Juba. Even when he had a fall as he disembarked, he gave the omen a favourable turn by crying: "I hold thee fast, Africa." Furthermore, to make the prophecies ridiculous which declared that the stock of the Scipios was fated to be fortunate and invincible in that province, he kept with him in camp a contemptible fellow belonging to the Cornelian family, to whom the nickname Salvito had been given as a reproach for his manner of life.

Marcus Aurelius

The nephew and adopted son of the emperor Antoninus Pius, Marcus (121–180) ascended to the purple on the death of Antoninus in the year 161. He is often referred to as the last of the "good emperors." Unfortunately, much of his reign was spent far from Rome on military campaigns along the borders of the empire in the Danube valley. During his campaigning on the frontier Marcus wrote his *Meditations* at night in his tent. Unlike Cicero, who embodied his Stoic philosophy in writings concerned with statecraft and law, Marcus devoted his attention to the universal but personal problems of human life and fate. The *Meditations*, which contain most of the major themes of the Stoic philosophy, were probably not meant for publication but were rather simply a written soliloquy that Marcus held with himself, summing up his thoughts of each day.

The selection that follows contains a sampling of the daily thoughts of Marcus. In reading it, do not forget that the author of these meditations was the emperor of Rome, the most powerful political figure in the Western world.

Consider the following questions as you study the text below.

1. What were the main themes of Marcus' advice to his readers? In his view, what were the really important things in life?

2. What was Marcus' attitude toward the pursuit of fame? Was he in step with general Roman opinion on this subject?

Meditations

Book II

1. Begin the morning by saying to yourself, "I shall meet with the busy-body, the ungrateful, arrogant, deceitful, envious, unsocial." All of these things happen to them by reason of their ignorance of what is good and evil. But I who have seen the nature of the good that it is beautiful, and of the bad that it is ugly, and the nature of him who does wrong, that it is akin to me, not only of the same blood or seed, but that it participates in the same intelligence

Marcus Aurelius Antoninus, *Meditations*, trans George Long. Minor changes have been made in the spelling and punctuation of the translation.

and the same portion of the divinity, I can neither be injured by any of them, for no one can fix on me what is ugly, nor can I be angry with my kinsman, nor hate him. For we are made for cooperation, like feet, like hands, like eyelids, like the rows of the upper and lower teeth. To act against one another then is contrary to nature; and it is acting against one another to be vexed and to turn away.

2.   Whatever this is that I am, it is a little flesh and breath, and the ruling part. Throw away your books; no longer distract yourself; it is not allowed. But as if you were now dying, despise the flesh; it is blood and bones and a network, a contexture of nerves, veins, and arteries. See the breath also, what kind of a thing it is, air, and not always the same, but every moment sent out and again sucked in. The third then is the ruling part. Consider thus: You are an old man; no longer let this be a slave, no longer be pulled by the strings like a puppet to unsocial movements, no longer be either dissatisfied with your present lot, or shrink from the future.

3.   All that is from the gods is full of providence. That which is from fortune is not separated from nature or without an interweaving and involution with the things which are ordered by providence. From thence all things flow; and there is besides necessity, and that which is for the advantage of the whole universe, of which you are a part. But that is good for every part of nature which the nature of the whole brings, and what serves to maintain this nature. Now the universe is preserved, as by the changes of the elements so by the changes of things compounded of the elements. Let these principles be enough for you, let them always be fixed opinions. But cast away the thirst after books, that you may not die murmuring, but cheerfully, truly, and from your heart thankful to the gods.

4.   Remember how long you have been putting off these things, and how often you have received an opportunity from the gods, and yet do not use it. You must now at last perceive of what universe you are a part, and of what administrator of the universe your existence is an efflux, and that a limit of time is fixed for you, which if you do not use for clearing away the clouds from your mind, it will go and you will go, and it will never return.

5.   Every moment think steadily as a Roman and a man to do what you have in hand with perfect and simple dignity, and a feeling of affection, and freedom, and justice; and to give yourself relief from all other thoughts. And you will give yourself relief, if you do every act of your life as if it were the last, laying aside all carelessness and passionate aversion from the commands of reason, and all hypocrisy, and self-love, and discontent with the portion which has been given to you. You see how few the things are, the which if a man lays hold of, he is able to live a life which flows in quiet, and is like the existence of the gods; for the gods on their part will require nothing more from him who observes these things.

·   ·   ·

7. Do the things external which fall upon you distract you? Give yourself time to learn something new and good, and cease to be whirled around. But then you must also avoid being carried about the other way. For those too are triflers who have wearied themselves in life by their activity, and yet have no object to which to direct every movement and, in a word, all their thoughts.

8. Though not observing what is in the mind of another a man has seldom been seen to be unhappy; but those who do not observe the movements of their own minds must of necessity be unhappy.

9. This you must always bear in mind, what is the nature of the whole, and what is my nature, and how this is related to that, and what kind of a part it is of what kind of a whole; and that there is no one who hinders you from always doing and saying the things which are according to the nature of that of which you are a part.

.   .   .

11. Since it is possible that you may depart from life this very moment, regulate every act and thought accordingly. But to go away from among men, if there are gods, is not a thing to be afraid of, for the gods will not involve you in evil; but if indeed they do not exist, or if they have no concern about human affairs, what is it to me to live in a universe devoid of gods or devoid of providence? But in truth they do exist, and they do care for human things, and they have put all the means in man's power to enable him not to fall into real evils. And as to the rest, if there was anything evil, they would have provided for this also, that it should be altogether in a man's power not to fall into it. Now that which does not make a man worse, how can it make a man's life worse? But neither through ignorance, nor having the knowledge, but not the power to guard against or correct these things, is it possible that the nature of the universe has overlooked them; nor is it possible that it has made so great a mistake, either through want of power or want of skill, that good and evil should happen indiscriminately to the good and the bad. But death certainly, and life, honor and dishonor, pain and pleasure, all these things equally happen to good men and bad, being things which make us neither better nor worse. Therefore they are neither good nor evil.

12. How quickly all things disappear, in the universe the bodies themselves, but in time the remembrance of them; what is the nature of all sensible things, and particularly those which attract with the bait of pleasure, or terrify by pain, or are noised abroad by vapory fame; how worthless and contemptible, and sordid, and perishable, and dead they are—all this it is the part of the intellectual faculty to observe. To observe too who these are whose opinions and voices give reputation; what death is, and the fact that, if a man looks at it in itself, and by the abstractive power of reflection

resolves into their parts all the things which present themselves to the imagination in it, he will then consider it to be nothing else than an operation of nature; and if anyone is afraid of an operation of nature, he is a child. This, however, is not only an operation of nature, but it is also a thing which conduces to the purposes of nature. To observe too how man comes near to the deity, and by what part of him, and when this part of man is so disposed.

.   .   .

14.   Though you should be going to live three thousand years, and as many times ten thousand years, still remember that no man loses any other life than this which he now lives, nor lives any other than this which he now loses. The longest and shortest are thus brought to the same. For the present is the same to all, though that which perishes is not the same; and so that which is lost appears to be a mere moment. For a man cannot lose either the past or the future; for what a man has not, how can anyone take this from him? These two things then you must bear in mind; the one, that all things from eternity are of like forms and come round in a circle, and that it makes no difference whether a man shall see the same things during a hundred years or two hundred, or an infinite time; and the second, that the longest liver and he who will die soonest lose just the same. For the present is the only thing of which a man can be deprived, if it is true that this is the only thing which he has, and that a man cannot lose a thing if he has it not.

.   .   .

16.   The soul of man does violence to itself, first of all, when it becomes an abscess and, as it were, a tumor on the universe, so far as it can. For to be vexed at anything which happens is a separation of ourselves from nature, in some part of which the natures of all other things are contained. In the next place, the soul does violence to itself when it turns away from any man, or even moves towards him with the intention of injuring, such as are the souls of those who are angry. In the third place, the soul does violence to itself when it is overpowered by pleasure or by pain. Fourthly, when it plays a part, and does or says anything insincerely and untruly. Fifthly, when it allows any act of its own and any movement to be without an aim, and does anything thoughtlessly and without considering what it is, it being right that even the smallest things be done with reference to an end; and the end of rational animals is to follow the reason and the law of the most ancient city and polity.
17.   Of human life the time is a point, and the substance is in a flux, and the perception dull, and the composition of the whole body subject to putrefaction, and the soul a whirl, and fortune hard to divine, and fame a thing devoid of judgment. And, to say all in a word, everything which

belongs to the body is a stream, and what belongs to the soul is a dream and vapor, and life is a warfare and a stranger's sojourn, and after-fame is oblivion. What then is that which is able to conduct a man? One thing and only one—philosophy. But this consists in keeping the spirit within a man free from violence and unharmed, superior to pains and pleasures, doing nothing without a purpose, nor yet falsely and with hypocrisy, not feeling the need of another man's doing or not doing anything; and besides, accepting all that happens and all that is allotted, as coming from thence, wherever it is, from whence he himself came; and, finally, waiting for death with a cheerful mind, as being nothing else than a dissolution of the elements of which every living being is compounded. But if there is no harm to the elements themselves in each continually changing into another, why should a man have any apprehension about the change and dissolution of all the elements? For it is according to nature, and nothing is evil which is according to nature.

Book IV

3.   Men seek retreats for themselves, houses in the country, seashores, and mountains; and you too are wont to desire such things very much. But this is altogether a mark of the most common sort of men, for it is in your power whenever you shall choose to retire into yourself. For nowhere either with more quiet or more freedom from trouble does a man retire than into his own soul, particularly when he has within him such thoughts that by looking into them he is immediately in perfect tranquility; and I affirm that tranquillity is nothing else than the good ordering of the mind. Constantly then give to yourself this retreat, and renew yourself; and let your principles be brief and fundamental, which, as soon as you shall recur to them, will be sufficient to cleanse the soul completely, and to send you back free from all discontent with the things to which you return. For with what are you discontented? With the badness of men? Recall to your mind this conclusion, that rational animals exist for one another, and that to endure is a part of justice, and that men do wrong involuntarily; and consider how many already, after mutual enmity, suspicion, hatred, and fighting, have been stretched dead, reduced to ashes; and be quiet at last. But perhaps you are dissatisfied with that which is assigned to you out of the universe. Recall to your recollection this alternative; either there is providence or atoms; or remember the arguments by which it has been proved that the world is a kind of political community. But perhaps corporeal things will fasten upon you. Consider then further that the mind mingles not with the breath, whether moving quietly or violently, when it has once drawn itself apart and discovered its own power, and think also of all that you have heard and assented to about pain and pleasure. But perhaps the desire of the thing called fame will torment you. See how soon everything is forgotten, and look at the chaos of infinite time on each side of the present, and the emptiness of applause, and the changeableness and

want of judgment in those who pretend to give praise, and the narrowness of the space without which it is circumscribed. For the whole earth is a point, and how small a nook in it is this your dwelling, and how few are there in it, and what kind of people are they who will praise you.

This then remains: Remember to retire into this little territory of your own, and above all do not distract or strain yourself, but be free and look at things as a man, as a human being, as a citizen, as a mortal. But among the things readiest to your hand to which you shall turn, let there be these, which are two. One is that things do not touch the soul, for they are external and re-main immovable; but our perturbations come only from the opinion which is within. The other is that all these things, which you see, change immediately and will no longer be; and constantly bear in mind how many of these changes you have already witnessed. The universe is transformation; life is opinion.

4.   If our intellectual part is common to us, the reason also, in respect of which we are rational beings is common to us. If this is so, common also is the reason which commands us what to do and what not to do; if this is so, there is a common law also; if this is so, we are fellow-citizens; if this is so, we are members of some political community; if this is so, the world is in a manner a state. For of what other common political community will any one say that the whole human race are members? And from thence, from the common po-litical community comes also our very intellectual faculty and reasoning fac-ulty and our capacity for law; or whence do they come? For as my earthly part is a portion given to me from certain earth, and that which is watery from another element, and that which is hot and fiery from some peculiar source (for nothing comes out of that which is nothing, as nothing also re-turns to non-existence), so also the intellectual part comes from some source.

. . .

19.   He who has a vehement desire for posthumous fame does not consider that everyone of those who remember him will himself also die very soon; then again also they who have succeeded them, until the whole remembrance shall have been extinguished as it is transmitted through men who foolishly admire and perish. But suppose that those who will remember are even immortal, and that the remembrance will be immortal, what then is this to you? And I say not what is it to the dead, but what is it to the living? What is praise, except indeed so far as it has a certain utility?

. . .

32.   Consider, for example, the times of Vespasian. You will see all these things, people marrying, bringing up children, sick, dying, warring, feasting, trafficking, cultivating the ground, flattering, obstinately arrogant, suspecting, plotting, wishing for some to die, grumbling about the present,

loving, heaping up treasure, desiring consulship, kingly power. Well then, that life of these people no longer exists at all. Again, remove to the times of Trajan. Again, all is the same. Their life too is gone. In like manner view also the other epochs of time and of whole nations, and see how many after great efforts soon fell and were resolved into the elements. But chiefly you should think of those whom you have yourself known distracting themselves about idle things, neglecting to do what was in accordance with their proper constitution, and to hold firmly to this and to be content with it. And herein it is necessary to remember that the attention given to everything has its proper value and proportion. For thus you will not be dissatisfied, if you apply yourself to smaller matters no further than is fit.

. . .

43.   Time is like a river made up of the events which happen, and a violent stream; for as soon as a thing has been seen, it is carried away and another comes in its place, and this will be carried away too.

44.   Everything which happens is as familiar and well known as the rose in spring and the fruit in summer; for such is disease, and death, and calumny, and treachery, and whatever else delights fools or vexes them.

. . .

48.   Think continually how many physicians are dead after contracting their eyebrows over the sick; and how many astrologers after predicting with great pretensions the death of others; and how many philosophers after endless discourses on death or immortality; how many heroes after killing thousands; and how many tyrants who have used their power over men's lives with terrible insolence as if they were immortal; and how many cities are entirely dead, so to speak, Helice and Pompeii and Herculaneum, and others innumerable. Add to the reckoning all whom you have known, one after another. One man after burying another has been laid out dead, and another buries him; and all this in a short time. To conclude, always observe how ephemeral and worthless human things are, and what was yesterday a little mucus tomorrow will be a mummy or ashes. Pass then through this little space of time conformably to nature, and end your journey in content, just as an olive falls off when it is ripe, blessing nature who produced it, and thanking the tree on which it grew.

Book VI

13.   When we have meat before us and such eatables, we receive the impression that this is the dead body of a fish, and this is the dead body of a bird or of a pig; and again, that this Falernian is only a little grape juice, and

this purple robe some sheep's wool dyed with the blood of a shellfish. Such then are these impressions, and they reach the things themselves and penetrate them, and so we see what kind of things they are. Just in the same way ought we to act all through life, and where there are things which appear most worthy of our approbation we ought to lay them bare and look at their worthlessness and strip them of all the words by which they are exalted. For outward show is a wonderful perverter of the reason and when you are most sure that you are employed about things worth your pains, it is then that it cheats you most.

. . .

16.   Neither is transpiration, as in plants, a thing to be valued, nor respiration, as in domesticated animals and wild beasts, nor the receiving of impressions by the appearances of things, nor being moved by desires as puppets by strings, nor assembling in herds, nor being nourished by food; for this is just like the act of separating and parting with the useless part of our food. What then is worth being valued? To be received with clapping of hands? No. Neither must we value the clapping of tongues, for the praise which comes from the many is a clapping of tongues. Suppose then that you have given up this worthless thing called fame, what remains that is worth valuing? This, in my opinion—to move yourself and restrain yourself in conformity to your proper constitution, to which end both all employments and arts lead. For every art aims at this, that the thing which has been made should be adapted to the work for which it has been made; and both the vine-planter who looks after the vine, and the horse-breaker, and he who trains the dog, seek this end. But the education and the teaching of youth aim at something. In this then is the value of the education and the teaching. And if this is well, you will not seek anything else. Will you not cease to value many other things too? Then you will be neither free, nor sufficient for your own happiness, nor without passion. For of necessity you must be envious, jealous, and suspicious of those who can take away those things, and plot against those who have that which you value. Of necessity a man must be altogether in a state of perturbation who wants any of these things; and besides, he must often find fault with the gods. But to reverence and honor your own mind will make you content with yourself, and in harmony with society, and in agreement with the gods, that is, praising all that they give and have ordered.

. . .

30.   Take care that you are not made into a Caesar, that you are not dyed with this dye; for such things happen. Keep yourself then simple, good, pure, serious, free from affectation, a friend of justice, a worshipper of

the gods, kind, affectionate, strenuous in all proper acts. Strive to continue to be such as philosophy wished to make you. Reverence the gods, and help men. Life is short. There is only one fruit of this life, a pious disposition and social acts. Do everything as a disciple of Antoninus.[1] Remember his constancy in every act which was conformable to reason, and his evenness in all things, and his piety, and the serenity of his countenance, and his sweetness, and his disregard of empty fame, and his efforts to understand things; and how he would never let anything pass without having first most carefully examined it and clearly understood it; and how he bore with those who blamed him unjustly without blaming them in return; how he did nothing in a hurry; and how he listened not to calumnies, and how exact an examiner of manner and actions he was; and not given to reproach people, nor timid, nor suspicious, nor a sophist; and with how little he was satisfied, such as lodging, bed, dress, food, servants; and how laborious and patient; and how he was able on account of his sparing diet to hold out to the evening, not even requiring to relieve himself by any evacuations except at the usual hour; and his firmness and uniformity in his friendship; and how he tolerated freedom of speech in those who opposed his opinions; and the pleasure that he had when any man showed him anything better; and how religious he was without superstition. Imitate all this that you may have as good a conscience, when your last hour comes, as he had.

.   .   .

44.   If the gods have determined about me and about the things which must happen to me, they have determined well, for it is not easy even to imagine a duty without forethought; and as to doing me harm, why should they have any desire towards that? For what advantage would result to them from this or to the whole, which is the special object of their providence? But if they have not determined about me individually, they have certainly determined about the whole at least, and the things which happen by way of sequence in this general arrangement I ought to accept with pleasure and to be content with them. But if they determine about nothing—which it is wicked to believe, or if we do believe it, let us neither sacrifice nor pray nor swear by them nor do anything else which we do as if the gods were present and lived with us—but if however the gods determine about none of the things which concern us, I am able to determine about myself, and I can inquire about that which is useful; and that is useful to every man which is comformable to his own constitution and nature. But my nature is rational and social, and my city and country, so far as I am Antoninus, is Rome, but so far as I am a man, it is the world. The things then which are useful to these cities are alone useful to me.

[1] [Uncle of Marcus Aurelius and Roman emperor, 138–161—*Ed.*]

Juvenal

The typical present-day picture of ancient Rome is one of awesome grandeur. Although the monuments—like the Colosseum, the Forum, and the triumphal arches—have been damaged by the ravages of time, they still convey a sense of the Imperial City. But Rome, as it really existed, was much more than these monuments; it was the great urban metropolis of the Western world. And it is about Rome, the metropolis, that Juvenal writes in his Third Satire. From his description of life in urban Rome during the early empire it is abundantly clear that Juvenal envied his friend, Umbricius, who decided to abandon the city to settle in a quiet village in the country.

Was Rome actually as dirty and debauched as Juvenal describes it? Certainly his was not the only negative voice; other contemporary writers, such as Tacitus, have given us similar critical appraisals. But two points can help us to keep a proper perspective. First, Juvenal was a satirist. Not only is it apparent from the Third Satire that he detested Rome but also that he found joy in depicting its shortcomings in picturesque and lurid detail. So we must use some judgment in evaluating the accuracy of his description. Second, Rome was a big city, and anyone who has lived in a modern big city can recognize that many of the things Juvenal talks about could, if translated into contemporary terms, be said about any of our great metropolitan centers. But that does not mean that they lack all redeeming qualities. So, too, of ancient Rome.

Very little is known of the life of Juvenal. He was born Decimus Junius Juvenalis, probably around A.D. 55. He obviously knew the city of Rome very well and presumably lived in or near it most of his life. There is a story, which cannot be verified, that he was exiled, perhaps by the emperor Domitian, and spent a number of years in Egypt. He may also have served in the Roman army. He probably died sometime around the year 140 but the exact date is unknown.

Altogether we have sixteen satires that Juvenal wrote on a wide range of topics, including a long one entitled "Against Women." Although the translation of the Third Satire, as given in the following selection, is somewhat free, it conveys very well the flavor of Juvenal's verse.

Consider the following questions as you study the text below.

1. According to Juvenal, what are the biggest problems with the Rome of his day? How did he explain them?

2. What qualities did Juvenal associate with Greece? What did he mean when he described Rome as "Greekized"? What Roman virtues were, by implication, absent from Juvenal's "Greekized Rome"?

The Third Satire

Against the City of Rome

Troubled because my old friend is going, I still must commend him
For his decision to settle down in the ghost town of Cumae,
Giving the Sibyl one citizen more. That's the gateway to Baiae
There, a pleasant shore, a delightful retreat. I'd prefer
Even a barren rock in that bay to the brawl of Subura.
Where have we ever seen a place so dismal and lonely
We'd not be better off there, than afraid, as we are here, of fires,
Roofs caving in, and the thousand risks of this terrible city
Where the poets recite all through the dog days of August?

While they are loading his goods on one little four-wheeled wagon,
Here he waits, by the old archways which the aqueducts moisten.
This is where Numa, by night, came to visit his goddess.
That once holy grove, its sacred spring, and its temple,
Now are let out to the Jews, if they have some straw and a basket.
Every tree, these days, has to pay rent to the people.
Kick the Muses out; the forest is swarming with beggars.
So we go down to Egeria's vale, with its modern improvements.
How much more close the presence would be, were there lawns by the
    water.
Turf to the curve of the pool, not this unnatural marble!
Umbricius has much on his mind. "Since there's no place in the city,"
He says, "For an honest man, and no reward for his labors,
Since I have less today than yesterday, since by tomorrow
That will have dwindled still more, I have made my decision. I'm going
To the place where, I've heard, Daedalus put off his wings,
While my white hair is still new, my old age in the prime of its straightness,
While my fate spinner still has yarn on her spool, while I'm able
Still to support myself on two good legs, without crutches.
Rome, good-bye! Let the rest stay in the town if they want to,

The Satires of Juvenal, trans. Rolfe Humphries (Bloomington: Indiana University Press, 1958), pp. 33–45. Courtesy of Indiana University Press.

Fellows like A, B, and C, who make black white at their pleasure,
Finding it easy to grab contracts for rivers and harbors,
Putting up temples, or cleaning out sewers, or hauling off corpses,
Or, if it comes to that, auctioning slaves in the market.
Once they used to be hornblowers, working the carneys;
Every wide place in the road knew their puffed-out cheeks and their
　　squealing.
Now they give shows of their own. Thumbs up! Thumbs down! And the
　　killers
Spare or slay, and then go back to concessions for private privies.
Nothing they won't take on. Why not?—since the kindness of Fortune
(Fortune is out for laughs) has exalted them out of the gutter.
"What should I do in Rome? I am no good at lying.
If a book's bad, I can't praise it, or go around ordering copies.
I don't know the stars; I can't hire out as assassin
When some young man wants his father knocked off for a price; I have
　　never
Studied the guts of frogs, and plenty of others know better
How to convey to a bride the gifts of the first man she cheats with.
I am no lookout for thieves, so I cannot expect a commission
On some governor's staff. I'm a useless corpse, or a cripple.
Who has a pull these days, except your yes men and stooges
With blackmail in their hearts, yet smart enough to keep silent?
No honest man feels in debt to those he admits to his secrets,
But your Verres must love the man who can tattle on Verres
Any old time that he wants. Never let the gold of the Tagus,
Rolling under its shade, become so important, so precious
You have to lie awake, take bribes that you'll have to surrender,
Tossing in gloom, a threat to your mighty patron forever.

"Now let me speak of the race that our rich men dote on most fondly.
These I avoid like the plague, let's have no coyness about it.
Citizens, I can't stand a Greekized Rome. Yet what portion
Of the dregs of our town comes from Achaia only?
Into the Tiber pours the silt, the mud of Orontes,
Bringing its babble and brawl, its dissonant harps and its timbrels,
Bringing also the tarts who display their wares at the Circus.
Here's the place, if your taste is for hatwearing whores, brightly colored!
What have they come to now, the simple souls from the country
Romulus used to know? They put on the *trechedipna*
(That might be called, in our tongue, their running-to-dinner outfit),
Pin on their *niketeria* (medals), and smell *ceromatic*
(Attar of wrestler). They come, trooping from Samos and Tralles,
Adros, wherever that is, Azusa and Cucamonga,

Bound for the Esquiline or the hill we have named for the vineyard,
Termites, into great halls where they hope, some day, to be tyrants.
Desperate nerve, quick wit, as ready in speech as Isaeus,
Also a lot more long-winded. Look over there! See that fellow?
What do you take him for? He can be anybody he chooses,
Doctor of science or letters, a vet or a chiropractor,
Orator, painter, masseur, palmologist, tightrope walker.
If he is hungry enough, your little Greek stops at nothing.
Tell him to fly to the moon, and he runs right off for his space ship.
Who flew first? Some Moor, some Turk, some Croat, or some Slovene?
Not on your life, but a man from the very center of Athens.

"Should I not run away from these purple-wearing freeloaders?
Must I wait while they sign their names? Must their couches always be
    softer?
Stowaways that's how they got here, in the plums and figs from
    Damascus.
I was here long before they were: my boyhood drank in the sky
Over the Aventine hill; I was nourished by Sabine olives.
Agh, what lackeys they are, what sycophants! See how they flatter
Some ignoramus's talk, or the looks of some horrible eyesore,
Saying some Ichabod Crane's long neck reminds them of muscles
Hercules strained when he lifted Antaeus aloft on his shoulders,
Praising some cackling voice that really sounds like a rooster's
When he's pecking a hen. We can praise the same objects that they do,
Only, they are believed. Does an actor do any better
Mimicking Thais, Alcestis, Doris without any clothes on?
It seems that a woman speaks, not a mask; the illusion is perfect
Down to the absence of bulge and the little cleft under the belly.
Yet they win no praise at home, for all of their talent.
Why?—Because Greece is a stage, and every Greek is an actor.
Laugh, and he splits his sides; weep, and his tears flow in torrents
Though he's not sad; if you ask for a little more fire in the winter
He will put on his big coat; if you say ' I'm hot,' he starts sweating.
We are not equals at all; he always has the advantage,
Able, by night or day, to assume, from another's expression,
This or that look, prepared to throw up his hands, to cheer loudly
If his friend gives a good loud belch or doesn't piss crooked,
Or if a gurgle comes from his golden cup when inverted
Straight up over his nose—a good deep swig, and no heeltaps!

"Furthermore, nothing is safe from his lust, neither matron nor virgin,
Nor her affianced spouse, or the boy too young for the razor.
If he can't get at these, he would just as soon lay his friend's grandma.

(Anything, so he'll get in to knowing the family secrets!)
Since I'm discussing the Greeks, let's turn to their schools and professors,
The crimes of the hood and gown. Old Dr. Egnatius, informant,
Brought about the death of Barea, his friend and his pupil,
Born on that riverbank where the pinion of Pegasus landed.
No room here, none at all, for any respectable Roman
Where a Protogenes rules, or a Diphilus, or a Hermarchus,
Never sharing their friends—a racial characteristic!
Hands off! He puts a drop of his own, or his countryside's poison
Into his patron's ear, an ear which is only too willing
And I am kicked out of the house, and all my years of long service
Count for nothing. Nowhere does the loss of a client mean less.
"Let's not flatter ourselves. What's the use of our service?
What does a poor man gain by hurrying out in the nighttime,
All dressed up before dawn, when the praetor nags at his troopers
Bidding them hurry along to convey his respects to the ladies,
Barren, of course, like Albina, before any others can get there?
Sons of men freeborn give right of way to rich man's
Slave; a crack, once or twice, at Calvina or Catiena
Costs an officer's pay, but if you like the face of some floozy
You hardly have money enough to make her climb down from her high
        chair.
Put on the stand, at Rome, a man with a record unblemished,
No more a perjurer than Numa was, or Metellus,
What will they question? His wealth, right away, and possibly, later,
(Only possibly, though) touch on his reputation.
'How many slaves does he feed? What's the extent of his acres?
How big are his platters? How many? What of his goblets and wine
        bowls?'
His word is as good as his bond—if he has enough bonds in his strongbox.
But a poor man's oath, even if sworn on all altars
All the way from here to the farthest Dodecanese island,
Has no standing in court. What has he to fear from the lightnings
Of the outraged gods? He has nothing to lose; they'll ignore him.

"If you're poor, you're a joke, on each and every occasion.
What a laugh, if your cloak is dirty or torn, if your toga
Seems a little bit soiled, if your shoe has a crack in the leather,
Or if more than one patch attests to more than one mending!
Poverty's greatest curse, much worse than the fact of it, is that
It makes men objects of mirth, ridiculed, humbled, embarrassed.
'Out of the front-row seats!' they cry when you're out of money,
Yield your place to the sons of some pimp, the spawn of some cathouse,
Some slick auctioneer's brat, or the louts some trainer has fathered

Or the well-groomed boys whose sire is a gladiator.
Such is the law of the place, decreed by the nitwitted Otho:
All the best seats are reserved for the classes who have the most money.
Who can marry a girl if he has less money than she does?
What poor man is an heir, or can hope to be? Which of them ever
Rates a political job, even the meanest and lowest?
Long before now, all poor Roman descendants of Romans
Ought to have marched out of town in one determined migration.
Men do not easily rise whose poverty hinders their merit.
Here it is harder than anywhere else: the lodgings are hovels,
Rents out of sight; your slaves take plenty to fill up their bellies
While you make do with a snack. You're ashamed of your earthenware
    dishes—
Ah, but that wouldn't be true if you lived content in the country,
Wearing a dark-blue cape, and the hood thrown back on your shoulders.

"In a great part of this land of Italy, might as well face it,
No one puts on a toga unless he is dead. On festival days
Where the theater rises, cut from green turf, and with the great pomp
Old familiar plays are staged again, and a baby,
Safe in his mother's lap, is scared of the grotesque mask,
There you see all dressed alike, the balcony and the front rows,
Even His Honor content with a tunic of simple white.
Here, beyond our means, we have to be smart, and too often
Get our effects with too much, an elaborate wardrobe, on credit!
This is a common vice; we must keep up with the neighbors,
Poor as we are. I tell you, everything here costs you something.
How much to give Cossus the time of day, or receive from Veiento
One quick glance, with his mouth buttoned up for fear he might greet
    you?
One shaves his beard, another cuts off the locks of his boy friend,
Offerings fill the house, but these, you find, you will pay for.
Put this in your pipe and smoke it—we have to pay tribute
Giving the slaves a bribe for the prospect of bribing their masters.

"Who, in Praeneste's cool, or the wooded Volsinian uplands,
Who, on Tivoli's heights, or a small town like Gabii, say,
Fears the collapse of his house? But Rome is supported on pipestems,
Matchsticks; it's cheaper, so, for the landlord to shore up his ruins,
Patch up the old cracked walls, and notify all the tenants
They can sleep secure, though the beams are in ruins above them.
No, the place to live is out there, where no cry of *Fire*
Sounds the alarm of the night, with a neighbor yelling for water,
Moving his chattels and goods, and the whole third story is smoking.

This you'll never know: for if the ground floor is scared first,
You are the last to burn, up where the eaves of the attic
Keep off the rain, and the doves are brooding over their nest eggs.
Codrus owned one bed, too small for a midget to sleep on.
Six little jugs he had, and a tankard adorning his sideboard,
Under whose marble (clay), a bust or a statue of Chiron,
Busted, lay on its side; an old locker held Greek books
Whose divinest lines were gnawed by the mice, those vandals.
Codrus had nothing, no doubt, and yet he succeeded, poor fellow,
Losing that nothing, his all. And this is the very last straw—
No one will help him out with a meal or lodging or shelter.
Stripped to the bone, begging for crusts, he still receives nothing.

"Yet if Asturicus' mansion burns down, what a frenzy of sorrow!
Mothers dishevel themselves, the leaders dress up in black,
Courts are adjourned. We groan at the fall of the city, we hate
The fire, and the fire still burns, and while it is burning,
Somebody rushes up to replace the loss of the marble,
Some one chips in toward a building fund, another gives statues,
Naked and shining white, some masterpiece of Euphranor
Or Polyclitus' chef d'oeuvre; and here's a fellow with bronzes
Sacred to Asian gods. Books, chests, a bust of Minerva,
A bushel of siver coins. *To him that hath shall be given!*
This Persian, childless, of course, the richest man in the smart set,
Now has better things, and more, than before the disaster.
How can we help but think he started the fire on purpose?

"Tear yourself from the games, and get a place in the country!
One little Latian town, like Sora, say, or Frusino,
Offers a choice of homes, at a price you pay here, in one year,
Renting some hole in the wall. Nice houses, too, with a garden,
Springs bubbling up from the grass, no need for a windlass or
      bucket,
Plenty to water your flowers, if they need it, without any trouble.
Live there, fond of your hoe, an independent producer,
Willing and able to feed a hundred good vegetarians.
Isn't it something, to feel, wherever you are, how far off,
You are a monarch? At least, lord of a single lizard.

"Here in town the sick die from insomnia mostly.
Undigested food, on a stomach burning with ulcers,
Brings on listlessness, but who can sleep in a flophouse?
Who but the rich can afford sleep and a garden apartment?
That's the source of infection. The wheels creak by on the narrow

Streets of the wards, the drivers squabble and brawl when they're
    stopped,
More than enough to frustrate the drowsiest son of a sea cow.
When his business calls, the crowd makes way, as the rich man,
Carried high in his car, rides over them, reading or writing,
Even taking a snooze, perhaps, for the motion's composing.
Still, he gets where he wants before we do; for all of our hurry
Traffic gets in our way, in front, around and behind us.
Somebody gives me a shove with an elbow, or two-by-two-four scantling.
One clunks my head with a beam, another cracks down with a beer keg.
Mud is thick on my shins, I am trampled by somebody's big feet.
Now what?—a soldier grinds his hobnails into my toes.

"Don't you see the mob rushing along to the handout?
There are a hundred guests, each one with his kitchen servant.
Even Samson himself could hardly carry those burdens,
Pots and pans some poor little slave tries to keep on his head, while he
    hurries
Hoping to keep the fire alive by the wind of his running.
Tunics, new-darned, and ripped to shreds; there's the flash of a fir beam
Huge on some great dray, and another carries a pine tree,
Nodding above our heads and threatening death to the people.
What will be left of the mob, if that cart of Ligurian marble
Breaks its axle down and dumps its load on these swarms?
Who will identify limbs or bones? The poor man's cadaver,
Crushed, disappears like his breath. And meanwhile, at home, his
    household
Washes the dishes, and puffs up the fire, with all kinds of a clatter
Over the smeared flesh-scrapers, the flasks of oil, and the towels.
So the boys rush around, while their late master is sitting,
Newly come to the bank of the Styx, afraid of the filthy
Ferryman there, since he has no fare, not even a copper
In his dead mouth to pay for the ride through that muddy whirlpool.

"Look at other things, the various dangers of nighttime.
How high it is to the cornice that breaks, and a chunk beats my brains out,
Or some slob heaves a jar, broken or cracked, from a window.
Bang! It comes down with a crash and proves its weight on the sidewalk.
You are a thoughtless fool, unmindful of sudden disaster,
If you don't make your will before you go out to have dinner.
There are as many deaths in the night as there are open windows
Where you pass by; if you're wise, you will pray, in your wretched
    devotions,
People may be content with no more than emptying slop jars.

"There your hell-raising drunk, who has had the bad luck to kill no one,
Tosses in restless rage, like Achilles mourning Patroclus,
Turns from his face to his back, can't sleep, for only a fracas
Gives him the proper sedation. But any of these young hoodlums,
All steamed up on wine, watches his step when the crimson
Cloak goes by, a lord, with a long, long line of attendants,
Torches and brazen lamps, warning him, *Keep your distance!*
Me, however, whose torch is the moon, or the feeblest candle
Fed by a sputtering wick, he absolutely despises.
Here is how it all starts, the fight, if you think it is fighting
When he throws all the punches, and all I do is absorb them.
He stops. He tells me to stop. I stop. I have to obey him.
What can you do when he's mad and bigger and stronger than you are?
'Where do you come from?' he cries, 'you wino, you bean-bloated
      bastard?
Off what shoemaker's dish have you fed on chopped leeks and boiled
      lamb-lip?
What? No answer? Speak up, or take a swift kick in the rear.
Tell me where you hang out—in some praying-house with the Jew-boys?'
If you try to talk back, or sneak away without speaking,
All the same thing: you're assaulted, and then put under a bail bond
For committing assault. This is a poor man's freedom.
Beaten, cut up by fists, he begs and implores his assailant,
Please, for a chance to go home with a few teeth left in his mouth.

"This is not all you must fear. Shut up your house or your store,
Bolts and padlocks and bars will never keep out all the burglars,
Or a holdup man will do you in with a switch blade.
If the guards are strong over Pontine marshes and pinewoods
Near Volturno, the scum of the swamps and the filth of the forest
Swirl into Rome, the great sewer, their sanctuary, their haven.
Furnaces blast and anvils groan with the chains we are forging:
What other use have we for iron and steel? There is danger
We will have little left for hoes and mattocks and ploughshares.
Happy the men of old, those primitive generations
Under the tribunes and kings, when Rome had only one jailhouse!
"There is more I could say, I could give you more of my reasons,
But the sun slants down, my oxen seem to be calling,
My man with the whip is impatient, I must be on my way.
So long! Don't forget me. Whenever you come to Aquino
Seeking relief from Rome, send for me. I'll come over
From my bay to your hills, hiking along in my thick boots
Toward your chilly fields. What's more, I promise to listen
If your satirical verse esteems me worthy the honor."

The New Testament

The selection from the New Testament that follows contains excerpts illustrating the teachings of Jesus and the early history and theological doctrines of his followers. From the Gospel of St. Matthew comes the Sermon on the Mount, the most complete and one of the most beautiful statements of the religious views of Jesus. The selection from Romans contains a statement of Christian doctrine by the apostle Paul (Saul of Tarsus), one of the most influential of all Christian theologians. It was Paul who began the task of developing the teachings of Jesus into an organized and consistent body of theological doctrine.

The cornerstone of Paul's doctrine is the theory of original sin, with its related concepts of predestination, election, and grace. Originated by Paul, elaborated by St. Augustine in the fifth century, and reiterated by the Protestant reformer John Calvin in the sixteenth century, the doctrine of original sin is of fundamental importance in the history of Christian theology. The New Testament selections have been taken from the King James Version of the Bible, with slight alterations in form.

Consider the following questions as you study the text below.

1. What light does the passage from Matthew shed on Jesus' social and ethical vision? Which social and political groups in Judaea might have found his message most appealing? Which groups might have felt most threatened by it?

2. What did Paul mean when he said that "man is justified by faith without the deeds of the law"? In Paul's view, what, if anything, can an individual do to ensure his or her salvation?

The Gospel According to Matthew

And seeing the multitudes, he went up into a mountain: And when he was set, his disciples came unto him: And he opened his mouth, and taught them, saying, "Blessed are the poor in spirit: for theirs is the kingdom of heaven. Blessed are they that mourn: for they shall be comforted. Blessed are the meek: for they shall inherit the earth. Blessed are they which do hunger and thirst after righteousness: for they shall be filled. Blessed are the merciful:

Chapters 5, 6, 7.

for they shall obtain mercy. Blessed are the pure in heart: for they shall see God. Blessed are the peacemakers: for they shall be called the children of God. Blessed are they which are persecuted for righteousness' sake: for theirs is the kingdom of heaven. Blessed are ye, when men shall revile you, and persecute you, and shall say all manner of evil against you falsely, for my sake. Rejoice, and be exceeding glad: for great is your reward in heaven: for so persecuted they the prophets which were before you.

"Ye are the salt of the earth: but if the salt have lost his savour, wherewith shall it be salted? It is thenceforth good for nothing, but to be cast out, and to be trodden under foot of men. You are the light of the world. A city that is set on a hill cannot be hid. Neither do men light a candle, and put it under a bushel, but on a candlestick; and it giveth light unto all that are in the house. Let your light so shine before men, that they may see your good works, and glorify your Father which is in heaven.

"Think not that I am come to destroy the law, or the prophets: I am not come to destroy, but to fulfil. For verily I say unto you, till heaven and earth pass, one jot or one tittle shall in no wise pass from the law, till all be fulfilled. Whosoever therefore shall break one of these least commandments, and shall teach men so, he shall be called the least in the kingdom of heaven: but whosoever shall do and teach them, the same shall be called great in the kingdom of heaven. For I say unto you, that except your righteousness shall exceed the righteousness of the scribes and Pharisees, ye shall in no case enter into the kingdom of heaven.

"Ye have heard that it was said by them of old time, thou shalt not kill; and whosoever shall kill shall be in danger of the judgment. But I say unto you, That whosoever is angry with his brother without a cause shall be in danger of the judgment: and whosoever shall say to his brother, 'Ra-ca,' shall be in danger of the council: but whosoever shall say, 'Thou fool,' shall be in danger of hell fire. Therefore if thou bring thy gift to the altar, and there rememberest that thy brother hath ought against thee; leave there thy gift before the altar, and go thy way; first be reconciled to thy brother, and then come and offer thy gift. Agree with thine adversary quickly, whiles though art in the way with him; lest at any time the adversary deliver thee to the judge, and the judge deliver thee to the officer, and thou be cast into prison. Verily I say unto thee, Thou shalt by no means come out thence, till thou hast paid the uttermost farthing.

"Ye have heard that it was said by them of old time, Thou shalt not commit adultery. But I say unto you, That whosoever looketh on a woman to lust after her hath committed adultery with her already in his heart. And if thy right eye offend thee, pluck it out, and cast it from thee: for it is profitable for thee that one of thy members should perish, and not that thy whole body should be cast into hell. And if thy right hand offend thee, cut it off, and cast it from thee: for it is profitable for thee that one of thy members should perish, and not that thy whole body should be cast into hell. It hath been said,

Whoever shall put away his wife, let him give her a writing of divorcement. But I say unto you, That whosoever shall put away his wife, saving for the cause of fornication, causeth her to commit adultery: and whosoever shall marry her that is divorced committeth adultery.

"Again, ye have heard that it hath been said by them of old time, Thou shalt not forswear thyself, but shalt perform unto the Lord thine oaths. But I say unto you, Swear not at all; neither by heaven; for it is God's throne: nor by the earth; for it is his footstool: neither by Jerusalem; for it is the city of the great King. Neither shalt thou swear by thy head, because thou canst not make one hair white or black. But let your communication be, Yea, yea; Nay, nay: for whatsoever is more than these cometh of evil.

"Ye have heard that it hath been said, An eye for an eye, and a tooth for a tooth. But I say unto you, That ye resist not evil: but whosoever shall smite thee on thy right cheek, turn to him the other also. And if any man will sue thee at the law, and take away thy coat, let him have thy cloke also. And whosoever shall compel thee to go a mile, go with him twain. Give to him that asketh thee, and from him that would borrow of thee turn not thou away.

"Ye have heard that it hath been said, Thou shalt love thy neighbor, and hate thine enemy. But I say unto you, Love your enemies, bless them that curse you, do good to them that hate you, and pray for them which despitefully use you, and persecute you; that ye may be the children of your Father which is in heaven: for he maketh his sun to rise on the evil and on the good, and sendeth rain on the just and on the unjust. For if ye love them which love you, what reward have ye? Do not even the publicans the same? And if ye salute your brethren only, what do ye more than others? Do not even the publicans so? Be ye therefore perfect, even as your Father which is in heaven is perfect.

"Take heed that ye do not your alms before men, to be seen of them: otherwise ye have no reward of your Father which is in heaven. Therefore when thou doest thine alms do not sound a trumpet before thee, as the hypocrites do in the synagogues and in the streets, that they may have glory of men. Verily I say unto you, they have their reward. But when thou doest alms, let not thy left hand know what thy right hand doeth: that thine alms may be in secret: and thy Father which seeth in secret himself shall reward thee openly.

"And when thou prayest, thou shalt not be as the hypocrites are: for they love to pray standing in the synagogues and in the corners of the street, that they may be seen of men. Verily I say unto you, They have their reward. But thou, when thou prayest, enter into thy closet, and when thou hast shut thy door, pray to thy Father which is in secret: and thy Father which seeth in secret shall reward thee openly. But when ye pray, use not vain repetitions, as the heathen do: for they think that they shall be heard for their much speaking. Be not ye therefore like unto them: for your Father knoweth what things ye have need of, before ye ask him. After this manner therefore pray ye: Our Father which art in heaven, hallowed be thy name. Thy kingdom come. Thy will be done in earth, as it is in heaven. Give us this day our daily bread. And forgive us our debts, as we forgive our debtors. And lead us not into temptation, but deliver us from evil: For thine is the kingdom, and the power, and the glory, for ever. A-men.

"For if ye forgive men their trespasses, your heavenly Father will also forgive you: But if ye forgive not men their trespasses, neither will your father forgive your trespasses.

"Moreover when ye fast, be not, as the hypocrites, of a sad countenance: for they disfigure their faces, that they may appear unto men to fast. Verily I say unto you, They have their reward. But thou, when thou fastest, anoint thine head, and wash thy face; that thou appear not unto men to fast, but unto thy Father which is in secret: and thy Father, which seeth in secret, shall reward thee openly.

"Lay not up for yourselves, treasures upon earth, where moth and rust doth corrupt, and where thieves break through and steal. But lay up for yourselves treasures in heaven, where neither moth nor rust doth corrupt, and where thieves do not break through nor steal: For where your treasure is, there will your heart be also. The light of the body is the eye: if therefore thine eye be single thy whole body shall be full of light. But if thine eye be evil, thy whole body shall be full of darkness. If therefore the light that is in thee be darkness, how great is that darkness!

"No man can serve two masters: for either he will hate the one, and love the other; or else he will hold to the one, and despise the other. Ye cannot serve God and mammon. Therefore I say unto you, Take no thought for your life, what ye shall eat, or what ye shall drink; nor yet for your body, what ye shall put on. Is not the life more than meat, and the body than raiment? Behold the fowls of the air: for they sow not, neither do they reap, nor gather into barns; yet your heavenly Father feedeth them. Are ye not much better than they? Which of you by taking thought can add one cubit unto his stature? And why take ye thought for raiment? Consider the lilies of the field, how they grow; they toil not, neither do they spin: And yet I say unto you, That even Solomon in all his glory was not arrayed like one of these. Wherefore, if God so clothe the grass of the field, which today is, and tomorrow is cast into the oven, shall he not much more clothe you, O ye of little faith? Therefore take no thought, saying, What shall we eat? or, What shall we drink? or Wherewithal shall we be clothed? (For after all these things do the Gentiles seek:) for your heavenly Father knoweth that ye have need of all these things. But seek ye first the kingdom of God, and his righteousness; and all these things shall be added unto you. Take therefore no thought for the morow: for the morrow shall take thought for the things of itself. Sufficient unto the day is the evil thereof.

"Judge not, that ye be not judged. For with what judgment ye judge, ye shall be judged: and with what measure ye mete, it shall be measured to you again. And why beholdest thou the mote that is in thy brother's eye, but considerest not the beam that is in thine own eye? Or how wilt thou say to thy brother, Let me pull out the mote out of thine eye; and, behold, a beam is in thine own eye? Thou hypocrite, first cast out the beam out of thine own eye; and then shalt thou see clearly to cast out the mote out of thy brother's eye.

"Give not that which is holy unto the dogs, neither cast ye your pearls before swine, lest they trample them under their feet, and turn again and rend you.

"Ask, and it shall be given you; seek, and ye shall find; knock, and it shall be opened unto you: For every one that asketh receiveth; and he that seeketh findeth; and to him that knocketh it shall be opened. Or what man is there of you, whom if his son ask bread, will he give him a stone? Or if he ask a fish, will he give him a serpent? If ye then, being evil, know how to give good gifts unto your children, how much more shall your Father which is in heaven give good things to them that ask him? Therefore all things whatsoever ye would that men should do to you, do ye even so to them: for this is the law and the prophets.

"Enter ye in the strait gate: for wide is the gate, and broad is the way, that leadeth to destruction, and many there be which go in thereat: Because strait is the gate, and narrow is the way, which leadeth unto life, and few there be that find it.

"Beware of false prophets, which come to you in sheep's clothing, but inwardly they are ravening wolves. Ye shall know them by their fruits. Do men gather grapes of thorns, or figs of thistles? Even so every good tree bringeth forth good fruit; but a corrupt tree bringeth forth evil fruit. A good tree cannot bring forth evil fruit, neither can a corrupt tree bring forth good fruit. Every tree that bringeth not forth good fruit is hewn down, and cast into the fire. Wherefore by their fruits ye shall know them.

"Not every one that saith unto me, Lord, Lord, shall enter into the kingdom of heaven; but he that doeth the will of my Father which is in heaven. Many will say to me in that day, Lord, Lord, have we not prophesied in thy name? And in thy name have cast out devils? And in thy name done many wonderful works? And then will I profess unto them, I never knew you; depart from me, ye that work iniquity.

"Therefore whosoever heareth these sayings of mine, and doeth them I will liken him unto a wise man, which built his house upon a rock: And the rain descended, and the floods came, and the winds blew, and beat upon that house and it fell not: for it was founded upon a rock. And every one that heareth these sayings of mine, and doeth them not, shall be likened unto a foolish man, which built his house upon the sand: And the rain descended, and the floods came, and the winds blew, and beat upon that house; and it fell: and great was the fall of it." And it came to pass, when Jesus had ended these sayings, the people were astonished at his doctrine: For he taught them as one having authority, and not as the scribes.

The Epistle of Paul the Apostle to the Romans

. . .

As it is written, There is none righteous, no, not one: There is none that understandeth, there is none that seeketh after God. They are all gone out of the way, they are together become unprofitable; there is none that doeth good, no, not one. Their throat is an open sepulchre; with their tongues they have used deceit; the poison of asps is under their lips: Whose mouth is full of cursing and bitterness: Their feet are swift to shed blood: Destruction and misery are in their ways: And the way of peace have they not known: There is no fear of God before their eyes.

Now we know that what things soever the law saith, it saith to them who are under the law: that every mouth may be stopped, and all the world may become guilty before God. Therefore by the deeds of the law there shall no flesh be justified in his sight: for by the law is the knowledge of sin. But now the righteousness of God without the law is manifested, being witnessed by the law and the prophets; even the righteousness of God which is by faith of Jesus Christ unto all and upon all them that believe: for there is no difference. For all have sinned, and come short of the glory of God; being justified freely by his grace through the redemption that is in Christ Jesus: Whom God hath set forth to be a propitiation through faith in his blood, to declare his righteousness for the remission of sins that are past, through the forbearance of God; to declare, I say, at this time his righteousness: that he might be just, and the justifier of him which believeth in Jesus. Where is boasting then? It is excluded. By what law? or works? Nay: but by the law of faith. Therefore we conclude that a man is justified by faith without the deeds of the law. Is he the God of the Jews only? Is he not also of the Gentiles? Yes, of the Gentiles also: Seeing it is one God, which shall justify the circumcision by faith, and uncircumcision through faith. Do we then make void the law through faith? God forbid: yea, we establish the law.

. . .

Therefore being justified by faith, we have peace with God through our Lord Jesus Christ: By whom also we have access by faith into this grace wherein we stand, and rejoice in hope of the glory of God. And not only so, but we glory in tribulations also: knowing that tribulation worketh patience; and patience, experience; and experience, hope: And hope maketh not

Chapters 3:10–31; 5; 6; 9:8–21.

ashamed; because the love of God is shed abroad in our hearts by the Holy Ghost which is given unto us. For when we were yet without strength, in due time Christ died for the ungodly. For scarcely for a righteous man will one die: yet peradventure for a good man some would even dare to die. But God commandeth his love toward us, in that, while we were yet sinners, Christ died for us. Much more then, being now justified by his blood, we shall be saved from wrath through him. For if, when we were enemies, we were reconciled to God by the death of his Son, much more, being reconciled, we shall be saved by his life. And not only so, but we also joy in God through our Lord Jesus Christ, by whom we have now received the atonement.

Wherefore, as by one man sin entered into the world, and death by sin; and so death passed upon all men, for that all have sinned. For until the law sin was in the world: but sin is not imputed when there is no law. Nevertheless death reigned from Adam to Moses, even over them that had not sinned after the similitude of Adam's transgression, who is the figure of him that was to come. But not as the offence, so also is the free gift. For if through the offence of one many be dead, much more the grace of God, and the gift by grace, which is by one man, Jesus Christ, hath abounded unto many. And not as it was by one that sinned, so is the gift: for the judgment was by one to condemnation, but the free gift is of many offences unto justification. For if by one man's offence death reigned by one; much more they which receive abundance of grace and of the gift of righteousness shall reign in life by one, Jesus Christ. Therefore as by the offence of one judgment came upon all men to condemnation; even so, by the righteousness of one the free gift came upon all men unto justification of life. For as by one man's disobedience many were made sinners, so by the obedience of one shall many be made righteous. Moreover the law entered, that the offence might abound. But where sin abounded, grace did much more abound: That as sin hath reigned unto death, even so might grace reign through righteousness unto eternal life by Jesus Christ our Lord.

What shall we say then? Shall we continue in sin, that grace may abound? God forbid. How shall we, that are dead to sin, live any longer therein? Know ye not, that so many of us as were baptized into Jesus Christ were baptized into his death? Therefore we are buried with him by baptism into death: that like as Christ was raised up from the dead by the glory of the Father, even so we also should walk in newness of life. For if we have been planted together in the likeness of his death, we shall be also in the likeness of his resurrection: Knowing this, that our old man is crucified with him, that the body of sin might be destroyed, that henceforth we should not serve sin. For he that is dead is freed from sin. Now if we be dead with Christ, we believe that we shall also live with him: Knowing that Christ being raised from the dead dieth no more; death hath no more dominion over him. For in that he died, he died unto sin once: but in that he liveth, he liveth unto God. Likewise reckon ye also yourselves to be dead indeed unto sin, but alive unto God through Jesus Christ our Lord.

Let not sin therefore reign in your mortal body, that ye should obey it in the lusts thereof. Neither yield ye your members as instruments of unrighteousness unto sin: But yield yourselves unto God, as those that are alive from the dead, and your members as instruments of righteousness unto God. For sin shall not have dominion over you: for ye are not under the law, but under grace. What then? Shall we sin, because we are not under the law, but under grace? God forbid. Know ye not, that to whom ye yield yourselves servants to obey, his servants ye are to whom ye obey; whether of sin unto death, or of obedience unto righteousness? But God be thanked, that ye were the servants of sin, but ye have obeyed from the heart that form of doctrine which was delivered you. Being then made free from sin, ye became the servants of righteousness.

I speak after the manner of men because of the infirmity of your flesh: for as ye have yielded your members servants to uncleanness and to iniquity unto iniquity; even so now yield your members servants to righteousness unto holiness. For when ye were the servant of sin, ye were free from righteousness. What fruit had ye then in those things whereof ye are now ashamed? For the end of those things is death. But now being made free from sin, and become servants of God, ye have your fruit unto holiness, and the end everlasting life. For the wages of sin is death; but the gift of God is eternal life through Jesus Christ our Lord.

.   .   .

They which are the children of the flesh, these are not the children of God: but the children of the promise are counted for the seed. For this is the word of promise. At this time will I come, and Sarah shall have a son. And not only this; but when Rebecca also had conceived by one, even by our father Isaac; (for the children being not yet born, neither having done any good or evil, that the purpose of God according to election might stand, not of works, but of him that calleth): it was said unto her, The elder shall serve the younger. As it is written, Jacob have I loved, but Esau have I hated. What shall we say then? Is there unrighteousness with God? God forbid. For he saith to Moses, I will have mercy on whom I will have mercy, and I will have compassion on whom I will have compassion. So then it is not of him that willeth, nor of him that runneth, but of God that sheweth mercy. For the scripture saith unto Pharaoh, Even for this same purpose have I raised thee up, that I might shew my power in thee, and that my name might be declared throughout all the earth. Therefore hath he mercy on whom he will have mercy, and whom he will he hardeneth. Thou wilt say then unto me, Why doth he yet find fault? For who hath resisted his will? Nay but, O man, who are thou that repliest against God? Shall the thing formed say to him that formed it, Why hast thou made me thus? Hath not the potter power over the clay, of the same lump to make one vessel unto honour, and another unto dishonour?

The devotion of considerable time, skill, and resources to the production of illuminated manuscripts speaks to the value medieval Europeans placed on learning. In this page from such a manuscript, King Arthur is depicted along with his loyal knights.

THE MIDDLE AGES

The phrase "the fall of the Roman Empire," by placing before our minds the picture of a cataclysmic collapse of the imperium, can be misleading. Rome did not "fall." Rather, it went into a long decline, over a period of several centuries, as various nomadic tribes moved into its territory (to the extent even of overrunning and sacking the city of Rome itself, for example, in 476), as the army and its generals came increasingly to dominate politics, as commerce and industry dwindled, as the burden of taxation became too heavy for the average citizen to bear, and as the once highly centralized administration disintegrated and anarchy more and more ruled. As the political power of Rome waned another kind of power gradually assumed the direction of society. This was the ecclesiastical power of the Roman Catholic church; its ascendency was to lead to its dominant position in society for the next thousand years, the period now known as the Middle Ages.

The medieval world differed sharply not only from that of Rome but from our own world as well. To grasp its nature, one must understand its two central, and closely related institutions—*feudalism* and *manorialism*. Feudalism, even though it directly involved only a small minority of the population, was the more general of the two institutions, manorialism being its agricultural and economic adjunct. Although primarily political in nature, feudalism was essentially a broad social institution, governing all of the relationships between members of the military or noble class. The feudal system was hierarchical in structure. At its top (in a given region) stood the king. Everyone below him in the feudal class was a *vassal*. Thus, for example, dukes were vassals of the king, counts were vassals of dukes, and so on, down to the level of the simple knight, who had his sword and horse, but no vassal of his own. It is important not to misunderstand the medieval concept of "vassal." A vassal, even though subordinate to another person of higher rank, was himself a member of the nobility. For example, at one point the king of England was a vassal of the pope.

The feudal relationship was that of a military hierarchy and was based on the requirements of a warrior caste. The vassal swore an oath of fealty to his lord, pledging himself as a fighting man to the support and protection of the lord. In practice, this usually meant that the vassal owed his lord a certain specified number of days of military service each year. But the vassal also had other obligations to his lord of a more general nature. He helped the lord keep the peace within his domains, advised him on political matters, and served on his courts of justice. He also owed a variety of fees to the lord, such as paying a ransom to rescue him should he be captured in battle or underwriting the marriage festivities of his children. But the feudal relationship was reciprocal; the lord had obligations to his vassals as well. Mainly these involved his leading them successfully in battle but they also, and, perhaps,

more importantly, consisted in his providing them with their means of subsistence. The noble class did not work, yet they had to eat. To assure them a
livelihood, the king, who possessed the lands in his domain, granted parcels
of these to his immediate vassals who in turn subdivided them down the hierarchical chain. These lands, which, when farmed, provided the subsistence
on which nobles could live and fight, were called manors. Thus the institution of manorialism became an integral part of the feudal system.

Farming the manorial lands in support of the nobility was the work of
peasants, who, in the predominantly agricultural society of the Middle Ages,
made up the vast bulk of the population. Separated completely by caste from
the feudal nobility, the peasants had the status of serfs. Serfdom, as it existed
in the Middle Ages, should be distinguished from slavery. The serfs were
bound to the soil. Although this was a sharp restriction on their freedom—
for they could not leave the manor on which they were born without permission of the lord—it also protected them, for the lord could not sell them
and ship them away from their homes and families like animals. The lord-
serf relationship, in some respects like that of the lord and vassal, involved
mutual obligations. Mainly the serf owed to his lord a certain number of
days of work each year on the lord's domains, as well as a percentage of each
year's crops. The lord, in turn, provided protection and a minimal livelihood
for the serf. Yet, in all, the life of the average serf in the Middle Ages was
undoubtedly brutish, hard, and poor.

Two segments of medieval society, however, fell outside of the feudal-
manorial system. First was the clergy, who formed a substantial portion of
the population. Neither feudal warriors nor tillers of the soil, the clergy, with
the pope at their head, played a major role in medieval life. They were responsible for filling the spiritual needs of a people for most of whom life
after death was believed real and, indeed, more important than life on earth.
And, in an era of endemic warfare, they strove to limit bloodshed and reduce
the destruction caused by the conflicts between the various noble factions.
As the Middle Ages advanced, the hierarchy of the Church gained increasing
economic and political power. But this brought it into conflict with various
rulers throughout Europe, who were beginning to expand and consolidate
their own domains. The Church maintained, through its "doctrine of the two
swords," that temporal rulers must subordinate themselves to its authority
and, particularly during the pontificate of Innocent III in the thirteenth century, was able to support its claim. But gradually the rising temporal rulers
gained the ascendency and the power of the Church declined.

During the latter centuries of the Middle Ages, a number of technologi-
cal improvements in farming methods, including such diverse developments
as improved harnesses for horses, a more efficient plow, and the three-field
system of crop rotation, led to increased agricultural productivity. Fewer
farm laborers could, thus, produce the necessary food. A labor surplus often
developed and the unemployed serfs began to drift into the villages that then

existed, swelling their populations. By custom, if they remained there for a year they were considered to be free. In these growing towns many became artisans, fashioning the various tools and implements needed to farm the lands of the manors, which they exchanged for food. Some artisans became merchants and traders. So town life developed. The urban dwellers were no longer a part of the feudal-manorial system and thus had to develop political organizations both to govern their increasingly complex economic relationships and to protect themselves against depradations from wandering robbers, as well as from the feudal military caste. Sometimes towns banded together to foster trade among themselves, as well as to improve their self-defense. The best-known of these was the Hanse, or Hanseatic League, which united a number of towns throughout northwestern Europe.

The growth of town life, besides stimulating industry and commerce, also quickened culture. The towns became the centers of learning. Not only were enormous cathedrals built, but, perhaps before the beginning of the thirteenth century, the first universities were founded in Italy. These, the precursors of higher education today, spread quite soon to northern Europe—to Paris, and, in England, to Oxford and Cambridge. The University of Paris became the most famous of the medieval centers of learning. Its central academic orientation, as in the other universities, was a curriculum in which the works of the pagan, Aristotle, were melded with the Christian doctrines of the Church. Called *scholasticism*, this curriculum found its most eminent exponent in an Italian Dominican monk who taught at the University of Paris in the thirteenth century—St. Thomas Aquinas.

The fourteenth century saw a decline in medieval civilization as the Church fell into disarray (particularly during the so-called "Babylonian captivity") and kings contended for power and domain. The century was, thus, one of transition, a transition hastened by a disastrous event that overwhelmed Europe during the middle years of the century, killing approximately one-fourth of the total population. This was bubonic plague, or, as it was called, the Black Death.

LOOKING AHEAD

As you learn about the Middle Ages, consider the following questions.

1. What traditions and conditions contributed to the emergence of medieval civilization?

2. How would you describe the relationship between church and state during the Middle Ages? How did secular and religious authorities support one another? When and why did they clash?

3. Is it fair to describe the Middle Ages as "an age of faith"? Why or why not?

Einhard

Charlemagne (ca. 742–814) was a remarkable man. Although only semiliterate himself, he was a patron of learning, as well as of the arts. He made his capital at Aachen (Aix-la-Chapelle) a cultural center by establishing a palace school there to train both the clergy and the sons of the nobles of his court. He appointed, as director of the school, the English teacher and scholar, Alcuin of York, who was probably the outstanding intellectual of his time. He also brought together a number of other scholars from around Europe, among them Einhard.

Einhard (ca. 770–844) was born of a wealthy family in what is now southern Germany. After studying at the Abbey of Fulda, he went to Aachen as a student of Alcuin in the palace school. He remained in Aachen for nearly forty years, becoming a close friend and advisor of Charlemagne. An individual of many talents, Einhard not only continued the tradition of his mentor, Alcuin, as a teacher but also engaged in diplomatic missions for his lord. In addition he employed his skills as an architect to design the royal palace at Aachen, much of which still stands. But his major contribution to history was his biography of Charlemagne. Even after the death of the emperor in 814, Einhard remained in Aachen, continuing his position as advisor to the next monarch, Louis the Pious. It was during these years that he wrote his famous biography. He finally left the royal household in 830 and retired to a rural location in southern Germany where he founded an abbey.

Einhard's is not a disinterested biography, for the author's admiration for Charlemagne is evident throughout. Still, it gives us an informative, if brief, description of the emperor and his times. Einhard used the classical biographer, Suetonius, for his literary model, copying his style and even reproducing the language of his *Life of Augustus*, but applying it to his own subject.

Consider the following questions as you study the text below.

1. According to Einhard, what made Charlemagne a great king? What connections did he make between Charlemagne's private and public life?

2. What role did religion play in Charlemagne's life? How would you describe his relationship with Pope Leo? Did he see himself as subservient to the pope?

The Life of Charlemagne

Prologue

After I had made up my mind to describe the life and habits and, above all, the deeds of my lord and patron, the illustrious and deservedly famous King Charles, I set about doing so as succinctly as possible. I have tried not to omit anything that has come to my notice, and at the same time not to be long-winded and offend those discerning readers who object to the very idea of a modern history. But I also wanted to keep my new work from displeasing those who disapprove even of the masterpieces of the wisest and most learned authors of antiquity. To be sure, I am fully aware that there are many men of letters who do not regard contemporary matters so far beneath their notice as to treat them with contempt and consider them fit only to sink into silence and oblivion. On the contrary, the enthusiasm for things past leads some writers to recount the famous deeds of other men as best they can, and in this way they hope to insure that their own names will be remembered by posterity.

Be this as it may, none of these possible objections can prevent me from writing on the subject, since I am convinced that no one can describe these events better than I can. For I was there when they took place and I know them as an eyewitness, so to speak. Furthermore, I am not entirely sure if they will be recorded by anyone else. And so I thought it would be better to write down what I had to say even at the risk of duplicating what others might write, rather than to allow the illustrious life of the greatest king of the age and his famous deeds, unmatched by his contemporaries, to disappear forever into forgetfulness.

Besides, there was another reason, important enough in itself, I think, to make me compose this book: namely, that Charles educated me and gave me his lifelong friendship and that of his children from the time I came to the court. In this way he attached me to his person and made me so devoted to him in life and death that I might well be called ungrateful if I were to forget everything he did for me and never say a word about his great and magnificent generosity, I, who owe him so much; indeed, that would mean allowing his life to remain unremembered and unpraised, as though he had never lived! To be sure, my abilities, feeble and inadequate

Einhard, *The Life of Charlemagne*, trans. E. S. Firchow and E. H. Zeydel (Coral Gables: University of Miami Press, 1972), pp. 31–119. Used by permission of University of Miami Press.

as they are—nonexistent even—are incapable of portraying his life as it really ought to be portrayed. Even the eloquence of a Cicero would not have been up to that.

Here, then, is the book containing the life story of a truly great man. You will marvel at his deeds, and probably also at the presumption of a barbarous Frank for imagining that he could write tastefully and elegantly in Latin. For I am not much versed in the Roman tongue. Then, too, you will perhaps be amazed at my temerity in ignoring the words of Cicero when, speaking of Latin writers, he said in the first book of his *Tusculan Disputations* that "whoever puts his thoughts in writing and can not arrange and state them clearly, and delight the reader with a pleasant style, makes a complete mockery of the writer's craft." This remark of the famous orator might have kept me from writing if I had not already made up my mind to brave the judgment of the world and take a chance with my feeble talents. I thought this would be better than to allow the memory of so great a man to perish out of petty concern for my own reputation.

1. The Merovingians

The family of the Merovingians from which the Franks customarily chose their kings is believed to have ruled until the time of King Hilderich. Hilderich was deposed, tonsured, and sent to a monastery by the command of the Roman Pope Stephen. Although the royal line apparently ended only with him, it had long before ceased to matter and possessed no more except the empty title of king. The real wealth and power of the kingdom were in the hands of the prefects of the palace, the so-called majordomos, and their word was law. The king had no choice but to sit on the throne with flowing hair and full beard, content with his title and the semblance of sovereignty. He would listen to messengers coming from all around and, as they left, give them replies as though they were his own, but in reality, they had been dictated to him or even forced on him.

Except for the empty title of king and an intermittent allowance which the prefect of the palace gave or did not give him at his pleasure, the king owned nothing but a single estate, and that was not a very lucrative one. He lived on it and had a few servants there performing the most necessary duties and making a show of obsequiousness. Wherever he had to go, he went like a farmer in a cart drawn by a span of oxen with a carter driving them. That is how he went to the palace and how he went to the meetings of his people, which took place yearly for the good of the realm. And in the same way he returned home. But the administration of the state and all internal and external business was carried out by the prefect of the palace.

2. Charles' Ancestors

When Hilderich was deposed, the office of majordomo was already hereditarily held by Pepin, the father of King Charles. For Pepin's father, Charles,[1] had in his time crushed the rebels who were trying to take over all of Franconia. He had also defeated the Saracens so badly in two great battles, when they attempted to occupy Gaul, that they had to return to Spain. One of these battles had taken place in Aquitaine near Poitiers,[2] the other on the Berre River not far from Narbonne. This same Charles had in turn received the office of majordomo from his father Pepin and had administered it extremely well. It was customary for the people to bestow such an honor only on men of noble birth and great wealth.

When Pepin, the father of King Charles, held this office, bequeathed by his grandfather and father to him and to his brother Carloman, the two of them shared it quite amicably for several years, nominally under King Hilderich. But then for some unknown reason Carloman abandoned the burdensome government of the temporal kingdom—possibly because he longed for a more contemplative life—and went into retirement in Rome. There, giving up his worldly garb, he became a monk and built a monastery on Mt. Soracte near the church of St. Sylvester. For a number of years he enjoyed his longed-for seclusion, along with a few monks who had accompanied him. But when a great many noble Franks came on pilgrimages to Rome to fulfill vows and insisted on paying homage to their former lord, it was impossible for him to get any peace, which he cherished more than anything else, and he decided to move elsewhere. When he saw that the crowds of intruders were interfering with his resolve to be alone, he left the mountain and went away to the province of Samnium, to the monastery of St. Benedict on Monte Cassino, where he spent the rest of his life in prayer.

3. Charles Becomes King

Pepin, no longer majordomo but king by authority of the Roman pontiff, ruled alone over the Franks for fifteen years or more. For nine unbroken years he fought against Waifar, duke of Aquitaine, and then, at the end of the war, he died of dropsy in Paris. His sons Charles and Carloman survived him, and on them, by the will of Providence, the succession devolved. In solemn assembly the Franks appointed them kings on condition that they share the realm equally, Charles ruling the part which had belonged to their father Pepin, Carloman the part formerly controlled by his uncle Carloman.

[1][Charles Martel—*Ed.*]
[2][in 732—*Ed.*]

Both accepted these conditions and each one took over that section of the divided kingdom which he had received according to the agreement.

But peace between the two brothers was maintained only with the greatest difficulty since many of Carloman's followers plotted to break up the partnership. A few even tried to provoke a war with their intrigues. The outcome, however, showed that there was more imagined than real danger. When Carloman died, his wife and sons fled to Italy with the most important members of their court. Without any apparent reason she spurned her brother-in-law and placed herself and her children under the protection of Desiderius, king of the Lombards. Carloman had succumbed to an illness after ruling jointly for two years, and at his death Charles was unanimously proclaimed king of the Franks.

4. Plan of This Work

Because nothing has been recorded in writing about Charles' birth,[3] infancy, or even boyhood, and because no survivor has been found who claims to know of these matters, I consider it foolish to write about them. So I have decided to skip what we know nothing about and proceed to recount and describe Charles' exploits, habits, and other facts of his life. First I want to tell of his deeds at home and abroad, then describe his habits and interests, his rulership and finally his death, omitting nothing that is worth mentioning or necessary to know.

15. Conquests

These were the wars which the mighty King Charles planned so carefully and executed so brilliantly in various parts of the world during his reign of forty-seven years. As a result the kingdom of the Franks, which was already great and powerful when Charles inherited it from his father Pepin, was almost doubled in size. Formerly, the Frankish territory had encompassed only that part of Gaul lying between the Rhine and the Loire, the ocean and the Balearic Sea, as well as that part of Germania inhabited by the so-called East Franconians and bordering on Saxony and the Danube, the Rhine and the Saale—a river separating the Thuringians from the Sorbs—and, finally, the land of the Alemanni and Bavarians.

Through the wars described above Charles conquered first Aquitaine, then Gascony and the entire Pyrenees region as far south as the Ebro River. This river originates in Navarre and flows through the most fertile plains of Spain, emptying into the Balearic Sea beneath the walls of the city of Tortosa. Charles also added to his territory all of Italy from Aosta to Lower Calabria,

[3][The conjectural date of Charlemagne's birth is April 2, 742—*Ed.*]

where the border runs between the Beneventians and the Greeks—an area extending over more than a thousand miles. Furthermore, he incorporated Saxony—no small part of Germania and considered equal in length and twice the width of Franconia—and both Upper and Lower Pannonia, as well as Dacia on the other side of the Danube, Istria, Liburnia, and Dalmatia. Only the coastal towns of the latter countries he left to the emperor of Constantinople out of friendship and in consideration of a treaty he had made with him. Finally, Charles subjugated and forced to pay tribute all of the barbarian and savage nations who inhabit Germania between the Rhine and the Vistula rivers, the ocean and the Danube. They speak almost the same language but have very different customs and habits. The most important of these tribes are the Wiltzes, Sorbs, Abodrites, and Bohemians. With these he was forced to fight, but others, by far the greater number, surrendered without a struggle.

16. Foreign Relations

Charles also increased the glory of his empire by establishing friendly relations with many kings and peoples. An example is his close friendship with King Alfons of Galicia and Asturias, who always insisted on calling himself Charles' vassal when sending him letters or ambassadors. Charles also secured the favor of the Scottish kings by his great generosity, so that they always referred to him as their master and called themselves his subjects and servants. To this day there exist letters sent by them which clearly express these feelings.

With King Harun of Persia, who ruled almost all of the Orient except India, he was on such friendly terms that Harun preferred Charles' goodwill to the friendship of all other kings and potentates on earth and considered Charles alone worthy of his respect and homage. At one time the king of the Franks sent messengers with offerings to the most Holy Sepulcher, the site of the Resurrection of our Lord and Savior. When they appeared before Harun to relay their master's wishes, the king not only permitted them to carry out their mission but also gave Charles the jurisdiction over their holy and blessed place. On their return Harun sent along his own messengers with precious gifts, garments, spices, and other riches of the Orient. A few years earlier Charles had asked him for an elephant and Harun had sent him the only one he owned.

The three emperors of Constantinople, Nicephorus, Michael, and Leo, all sought Charles' friendship and alliance and sent numerous legations to his court. Only when Charles assumed the title of emperor did they begin to distrust him out of fear that he would seize their lands. To allay these fears and make sure that there would be no occasion for further trouble, Charles at once concluded a firm treaty with them. But the Greeks and the Romans remained suspicious of Frankish power. Hence a Greek proverb: "Have a Frank as a friend, but not as a neighbor."

17. Public Works

No matter how much time and effort Charles spent on planning and carrying out campaigns to enlarge his realm and subjugate foreign nations, he still was able to begin work on a number of public projects designed to help and beautify his kingdom. Some of them he actually managed to complete. The Basilica of the Holy Mother of God in Aachen, a triumph of the arts in construction, is quite rightly considered among the most remarkable of these. So, too, the bridge spanning the Rhine at Mainz, which is a full five hundred paces long, since the river is that wide at this point.[4] The bridge was destroyed by fire and was not rebuilt because Charles died a year later. He had intended to replace the wooden structure with one of stone. He also began building two magnificent palaces, one near the city of Mainz close to his estate at Ingelheim, the other in Nymwegen on the Waal River, which flows south of the island of the Batavians. But his chief concern was for the churches. When he discovered one in any part of his kingdom that was old and ready to collapse he charged the responsible bishops and priests with restoring it. And he made sure that his instructions were carried out by having his agents check up on them.

He also set up a navy to withstand the attacks of the Norsemen and had the necessary ships built on the rivers which flow from Gaul and Germania into the North Sea. Since the Norsemen were continuously invading and devastating the Gallic and Germanic coasts, he placed guards and fortifications in all harbors and large estuaries where ships could enter. In this way he prevented the enemy from landing and looting. He did the same in the south along the shores of Narbonensis, Septimania, and Italy as far south as Rome to ward off the Moors who had just begun to take up piracy. As a consequence Italy was hardly touched during his reign except for the Etruscan town of Civita Vecchia, which was treacherously captured and plundered by the Moors. Gaul and Germania were likewise spared except for a few Frisian islands along the Germanic coast which were laid waste by Norsemen.

18. Private Life

This is how Charles enlarged and defended his empire and at the same time made it beautiful. My subject from this point on will be his intellectual abilities and his extraordinary steadfastness both in success and in adversity; and, further, whatever else concerns his private and domestic life.

After the death of his father, Charles ruled the kingdom together with his brother. Everyone was surprised that he bore the latter's animosity and envy with so much patience that he could never be provoked to anger by him. At his mother's request he married a daughter of the Lombard king

[4][2250 feet—*Ed.*]

Desiderius but repudiated her for unknown reasons after one year. Then he married Hildegard, who came from a very noble Swabian family. With her he had three sons, Charles, Pepin, and Louis, and as many daughters, Rotrud, Bertha, and Gisela. He had three more daughters, Theoderada, Hiltrud, and Rotheid, two of them with his [third] wife Fastrada, who came from Eastern Franconia and was therefore Germanic, the third by a concubine whose name I cannot recall at the moment. When Fastrada died he took Liutgard to wife, who was from Alemannia and with whom he had no children. After her death he had four concubines: Madelgard, who bore him a daughter by the name of Rothild; Gerswinda from Saxony, with whom he had another daughter called Adeltrud; Regnia, who gave him two sons, Drogo and Hugo; and Adelind, who had Theoderic.

His mother Berthrada spent her old age in great honor in his house. He always treated her with the greatest respect; only when he divorced the daughter of King Desiderius, whom he had married to please her, was there any disagreement between them. Berthrada died soon after Hildegard, but she had lived long enough to see three grandsons and three granddaughters in the house of her son. Charles buried her with highest honors in the church of St. Denis, where his father had been laid to rest.

Like his mother, he treated his only sister Gisela, who had entered a convent as a young girl, with the greatest affection. She died a few years before he did in the convent where she had spent most of her life.

19. Private Life (continued)

For the education of his children Charles made the following provisions: his sons as well as his daughters were to be instructed first in those liberal arts in which he took most interest himself. As soon as the boys were old enough they had to learn how to ride, hunt, and handle weapons in Frankish style. The girls had to get used to carding wool and to the distaff and the spindle. To prevent their becoming bored and lazy he gave orders for them to be taught to engage in these and all other virtuous activities. Of his children, only two sons and one daughter died before him: Charles, who was the oldest; Pepin, whom he had made king of Italy; and his oldest daughter Rotrud, who had been engaged to marry the emperor Constantine of Greece. Pepin was survived by one son, called Bernhard, and five daughters: Adelheid, Atula, Guntrada, Bertheid, and Theoderada. How much Charles cared for his grandchildren was proved after their father's death: he made Bernhard Pepin's successor and raised the five girls together with his own daughters. When his two sons and daughter died, Charles reacted to their deaths with much less equanimity than might have been expected of so strong-minded a man. Because of his deep-seated devotion to them he broke down in tears. Also, when he was told of the death of the Roman Pope Hadrian, who was one of his best friends, he wept as much as if he had lost a brother or a favorite son. For Charles was by nature a man who had a great gift for friendship, who made friends easily and never wavered in his loyalty to them. Those whom he loved could rely on him absolutely.

He supervised the upbringing of his sons and daughters very carefully. When he was at home he never ate his meals without them and when he went away, he always took them along. At such times his sons rode by his side and his daughters followed close behind, protected by a bodyguard of hand-picked men. Although the girls were very beautiful and he loved them dearly, it was odd that he did not permit any of them to get married either to a man of his own nation or to a foreigner. Rather, he kept all of them with him until his death, saying that he could not live without their company. And on account of this, he had to suffer a number of unpleasant experiences, however lucky he was in every other respect. But he never let on that he had heard of any suspicions regarding their chastity or any rumors about them.

20. Conspiracies Against Charles

By one of the concubines he had a son whom I have not mentioned along with the others. His name was Pepin and he had a handsome face but was hunchbacked. While his father was wintering in Bavaria during the war against the Huns, Pepin pretended to be ill and became involved with some Frankish nobles in a plot against his father. He had been lured into it by empty promises that they would make him king. But the scheme was discovered and the traitors punished. Pepin was tonsured and allowed, on his own free will, to enter the monastery of Pruem, where he spent the rest of his life as a monk.

But even before this there had been a great conspiracy in Germania against Charles. All of the guilty ones were exiled; some of them only after being blinded, but the others were not harmed physically. Only three were killed because they had drawn their swords and tried to resist being taken prisoners. After they had slaughtered a number of men, they were killed themselves since there was no other way to subdue them. It was generally felt that Queen Fastrada's cruelty was responsible for these uprisings. And in both cases the reason they were aimed at Charles was because he apparently acquiesced in his wife's cruelty and seemed to have lost a good deal of his usual kindness and easy disposition. But for the rest, he was deeply loved and respected by everyone at home and abroad during all of his life, and no one ever accused him of being unnecessarily harsh.

21. Treatment of Foreigners

Charles liked foreigners and made every effort to see that they were well received. Often there were so many of them in his palace and kingdom that they were quite rightly considered a nuisance. But, magnanimous as he was, he was never bothered by such annoyances. For he felt that he would be rewarded for his troubles if they praised his generosity and gave him a good reputation.

22. Personal Appearance

Charles had a big and powerful body and was tall but well-proportioned. That his height was seven times the length of his own feet is well known. He had a round head, his eyes were unusually large and lively, his nose a little longer than average, his gray hair attractive, and his face cheerful and friendly. Whether he was standing or sitting his appearance was always impressive and dignified. His neck was somewhat short and thick and his stomach protruded a little, but this was rendered inconspicuous by the good proportion of the rest of his body. He walked firmly and his carriage was manly, yet his voice, though clear, was not as strong as one might have expected from someone his size. His health was always excellent except during the last four years of his life, when he frequently suffered from attacks of fever. And at the end he also limped with one foot. All the same, he continued to rely on his own judgment more than on that of his physicians, whom he almost hated because they ordered him to give up his customary roast meat and eat only boiled meat instead.

According to Frankish custom, he rode and hunted a great deal. There is probably no nation on earth that can match the Franks in these skills. Charles was also fond of the steam of natural hot springs. He swam a great deal and did it so well that no one could compete with him. This was why he built the palace in Aachen and spent there the last years of his life without interruption until he died. He invited not only his sons but also his nobles and friends, sometimes even his retinue and bodyguard, to bathe with him, so that frequently there would be more than a hundred people in the baths.

23. Dress

He wore the national dress of the Franks. The trunk of his body was covered with a linen shirt, his thighs with linen pants. Over these he put a tunic trimmed at the border with silk. The legs from the knee downward were wound with leggings, fastened around the calves with laces, and on his feet he wore boots. In winter he protected his shoulders and chest with a vest made of otter skins or marten fur, and over that he wrapped a blue cloak. He always carried a sword strapped to his side, and the hilt and belt thereof were made either of gold or silver. Only on special holidays or when ambassadors from foreign nations were to be received did he sometimes carry a jewel-studded saber. He disliked foreign clothes no matter how beautiful they were, and would never allow himself to be dressed in them. Only in Rome was he seen on two occasions in a long tunic, chlamys, and Roman shoes: the first time at the entreaty of Pope Hadrian and the second by request of his successor Leo. On high festival days he wore a suit of golden cloth and boots ornamented with jewels. His cloak was fastened by a golden brooch, and on his head he carried a diadem of gold, embellished with gems. On the other days, however, his dress was not much different from that of the common people.

24. Habits

Charles was a moderate eater and drinker, especially the latter, because he abominated drunkenness in any man, particularly in himself and in his associates. But he could not easily abstain from eating and often complained that fasting was bad for his health. He rarely gave banquets and then only on special feast days for large numbers of guests. His daily dinner consisted of four courses, besides the roast which the hunters used to bring in on spits and which he loved more than any other food. During the meal he either listened to music or to someone reading aloud. Stories and the deeds of the old heroes were recited to him. He also enjoyed the books of St. Augustine, especially *The City of God*.

He was so temperate in drinking wine or other beverages that he rarely drank more than three times during a meal. After his midday meal in the summer he would eat some fruit and take another drink, then remove his clothes and shoes, just as he did at night, and rest for two to three hours. His sleep at night would usually be interrupted four or five times, and as soon as he awoke, he got up. While he was being dressed and having his shoes put on, he would invite his friends to come into the room. If the count of the palace told him of some dispute which could not be settled without his decision, he ordered the litigants brought before him at once and, just as though he were sitting in a court of justice, would hear the case and pronounce judgment. At the same time he would give instructions on what had to be transacted that day, or what his ministers were to be charged with doing.

25. Studies

Charles was a gifted speaker. He spoke fluently and expressed whatever he had to say with great clarity. Not only was he proficient in his mother tongue but he also took trouble to learn foreign languages. He spoke Latin as well as his own language, but Greek he understood better than he could speak it. At times he was so eloquent that he almost seemed verbose. He was zealous in his cultivation of the liberal arts, and respected and honored highly those who taught them. He learned grammar from the Deacon Peter of Pisa, who was then already an old man. Another deacon, Albinus, surnamed Alcuin,[5] a man of Saxon origin who came from Britain and was

[5][Alcuin of York (735–804)—*Ed.*]

the greatest scholar of his time, taught him the other subjects. Under his direction, the king spent a great deal of time and effort studying rhetoric, logic, and especially astronomy. He learned how to calculate and with great diligence and curiosity investigated the course of the stars. He also tried his hand at writing and to this end always kept writing tablets and notebooks under his pillow in bed in order to practice during spare moments. But since he had only started relatively late in life, he never became very accomplished in this art.

26. Piety

The king practiced the Christian religion, in which he had been raised since childhood, with the greatest piety and devotion. That is why he built the beautiful basilica in Aachen and decorated it with gold and silver, candelabras, lattices, and portals of solid bronze. Since he was unable to get the columns and marble for the structure from anywhere else, he had them brought from Rome and Ravenna.

As long as his health permitted, the king attended church regularly in the morning and evening and took part in the late-night hours and morning mass. He was especially concerned that everything done in church should be carried out with the greatest possible dignity. Often he admonished the sacristans to see to it that nothing unseemly or unclean was brought into the church or left there. He gave many sacred vessels of gold and silver and so many priestly vestments that when services were held not even the doorkeepers—the humblest in ecclesiastical rank—had to perform their duties in everyday clothes.

Charles also worked very hard at improving the quality of liturgical reading and chanting of the psalms. He himself was well versed in both, although he would never read in public or sing, except in a low voice and together with the congregation.

27. Generosity

Charles was especially interested in helping the poor, and his generosity was of the kind for which the Greeks use the word *eleemosyna* (alms). But his charity was not limited to his own country and kingdom, for wherever he heard of Christians living in poverty, he would send them money out of compassion for their wretched lot, even overseas, to Syria and Egypt, as well as to Africa, Jerusalem, Alexandria, and Carthage. This was also the chief reason why he cultivated friendships with kings across the seas, so that the Christians living in need under their jurisdiction would receive some aid and succor.

Of all sacred and hallowed places, he loved the Cathedral of the Holy Apostle Peter in Rome most of all. He endowed its treasure room with great quantities of gold, silver, and precious stones. He sent its pontiffs many, indeed innumerable, gifts. During his entire reign nothing seemed more important to him than to exert himself to restore the city of Rome to its old splendor and to have the Cathedral of St. Peter not only secured and defended but, through his generosity, adorned and enriched beyond all other churches. Although he favored this church so much, he only visited it four times during his reign of forty-seven years, there to fulfill his vows and offer his prayers.

28. Charles Becomes Emperor

But there were also other reasons for Charles' last visit to Rome. The Romans had forced Pope Leo, on whom they had inflicted various injuries, like tearing out his eyes and cutting out his tongue, to beg for the king's assistance. Charles therefore went to Rome to put order into the confused situation and reestablish the status of the Church. This took the whole winter. It was on this occasion that he accepted the titles of Emperor and Augustus, which at first he disliked so much that he said he would never have entered the church even on this highest of holy days[6] if he had beforehand realized the intentions of the Pope. Still, he bore with astonishing patience the envy his imperial title aroused in the indignant Eastern Roman emperors. He overcame their stubborn opposition with magnanimity—of which he unquestionably had far more than they did—and sent frequent embassies to them, always calling them his brothers in his letters.

29. Reforms

After Charles had accepted the imperial title he noticed that there were many flaws in the legal code of his people, for the Franks have two separate sets of laws differing markedly in many details. He planned to fill in the gaps, to reconcile discrepancies, and to correct what was wrongly and improperly stated. But he was unable to get very much done, except for making a very few additions and even those incomplete. Even so, he did order all the unwritten laws of the nations under his rule collected and written down. He also had the same done for the very old heathen songs which tell of the deeds and wars of former kings, so that they might be preserved for posterity. In addition, he began a grammar of his native language.

---

[6][Charlemagne was crowned Emperor on Christmas day, 800—*Ed.*]

Charles gave Frankish names to the months. Before that the Franks had used partly Latin, partly barbarian names for them. He also invited appropriate designations for the twelve winds for which there had previously been barely four words. As for the months, he called January uuintarmanoth, February hornung, March lenzinmanoth, April ostarmanoth, May uuinnemanoth, June brachmanoth, July heuuimanoth, August aranmanoth, September uuitumanoth, October uuindumemanoth, November herbistmanoth, and December heilagmanoth. To the winds he gave the following names: the east wind (subsolanus) he called ostroniuuint, the southeaster (eurus) ostsundroni, the south-southeaster (euroauster) sundostroni, the south wind (auster) sundroni, the south-southwester (austroafricus) sunduuestroni, the southwester (africus) uuestsundroni, the west wind (zephyrus) uuestroni, the northwester (chorus) uuestnordroni, the north-northwester (circius) norduuestroni, the north wind (septentrio) nordroni, the northeaster (aquilo) nordostroni, and the north-northeaster (vulturnus) ostnordroni.

30. Coronation of Louis and Charles' Death

At the end of his life, when he was already beset by illness and old age, Charles summoned Louis, the king of Aquitaine and Hildegard's only surviving son, to his presence. He invited all of the Frankish nobles to a solemn assembly, in which with their consent he appointed Louis co-regent over the entire realm and heir to the imperial title. He crowned his son himself by placing the diadem on his head and ordering that he be addressed Emperor and Augustus. His decision was received by all those present with great acclaim since it seemed to be divinely inspired for the good of the kingdom. It increased his reputation as a ruler and instilled considerable respect among foreign nations. After Charles had sent his son back to Aquitaine, he started out as usual for the hunt paying no heed to his advanced age. Thus occupied, he spent what was left of the autumn not far from Aachen and returned to the palace at approximately the beginning of November. While he was wintering there he was attacked by a high fever during the month of January and had to retire to bed. As he always did when he had a temperature, he began to diet in the belief that he could cure or at least alleviate his illness by abstaining from food. In addition to the fever he developed a pain in his side, which the Greeks call pleurisy, but he kept fasting and did not take any sustenance except for an occasional drink. On the seventh day after he had taken to bed he received the Holy Communion and died on 28 January between eight and nine o'clock in the morning. Charles was then in the seventy-second year of his life and in the forty-seventh year of his reign.

31. Burial

His body was washed and prepared for burial in the usual way, then brought to the basilica and buried amid the great lamentations of the entire population. At first there was uncertainty about where he should be laid to rest because he had never given any instructions on this point during his lifetime. Finally everyone agreed that there could be no more appropriate place than the basilica which he had built at his own expense in this city out of love for God and our Lord Jesus Christ and in honor of the Holy and Immaculate Virgin. He was interred there on the same day he died. Above his grave a gilded arch was raised with his image and an inscription reading as follows: "In this tomb lies the body of Charles, the great Christian Emperor, who gloriously increased the kingdom of the Franks and ruled successfully for forty-seven years. He died in his seventies in the seventh year of the indiction, on January 28th in the year of our Lord 814."

Life in Country and Town

One of the most difficult tasks for the historian, particularly of times long past, is to get information about the lives of common people. This is especially true of a generally unlettered society, such as medieval Europe; people who do not read or write tell few lasting tales. Nevertheless, information can be gained indirectly, mainly through records and documents whose authors belonged to the literate classes. The two selections that follow are illustrative of these. The first gives some insight into rural life, the second into life in a town. Both are from medieval France.

The *Capitulare de Villis* is a set of instructions issued on behalf of the ruling monarch, in this case probably Louis the Pious, the son of Charlemagne and king of Aquitaine (in southwestern France), in the latter part of the eighth century. In it the writer instructs the stewards on a great variety of details concerning the care of the royal lands, the people who work on them, and their produce. From the details of these instructions it is possible to learn a good deal about the daily lives of people of that time, both peasants and nobility. The general impression one gains from reading the selection is that King Louis kept full and careful control over all the agricultural and related activities occurring on his domains; whether this was in fact true we have, of course, no way of knowing.

In the *Charter of the Liberties of Lorris* we turn to medieval town life. Lorris was (and still is) a small town in north-central France, not far from Orleans. The Charter reproduced was granted to the inhabitants of Lorris by King Louis VII of France in 1155. It is, perhaps, of interest to note that most of the items concerning both the privileges and the obligations of the inhabitants of the town concerned economic matters, particularly taxes and fees that could be levied against them. The Charter is historically important because it became a model for similar charters granted to many other towns in later years.

Consider the following questions as you study the text below.

1. In the *Capitulare de Villis,* what steps did Louis the Pious take to protect the interests of his people? What role did the stewards play in the management of Louis' estate? What light does this document shed on the nature of manorialism?

2. On the basis of the *Charter of the Liberties of Lorris,* how would you describe the relationship between the people of Lorris and King Louis VII? How did this relationship differ from that between Louis the Pious and the people of his estate?

Capitulare de Villis

1.   We wish that our estates which we have instituted to serve our needs discharge their services to us entirely and to no other men.

2.   Our people shall be well taken care of and reduced to poverty by no one.

3.   Our stewards shall not presume to put our people to their own service, either to force them to work, to cut wood, or to do any other task for them. And they shall accept no gifts from them, either horse, ox, cow, pig, sheep, little pig, lamb, or anything else excepting bottles of wine or other beverage, garden produce, fruits, chickens, and eggs.

4.   If any of our people does injury to us either by stealing or by some other offense he shall make good the damage and for the remainder of the legal satisfaction he shall be punished by whipping, with the exception of homicide and arson cases which are punishable by fines. The stewards, for injuries of our people to other men, shall endeavor to secure justice according to the law. Instead of paying fines our people, as we have said, shall be whipped. Freemen who live in our domains or estates shall make good the injuries they do according to their law and the fines which they have incurred shall be paid for our use either in cattle or in equivalent value.

5.   When our stewards ought to see that our work is done—the sowing, plowing, harvesting, cutting of hay, or gathering of grapes—let each one at the proper season and in each and every place organize and oversee what is to be done that it may be done well. If a steward shall not be in his district or can not be in some place let him choose a good substitute from our people or another in high repute to direct our affairs that they may be successfully accomplished. And he shall diligently see to it that a trustworthy man is delegated to take care of this work.

6.   We wish our stewards to give a tithe of all our products to the churches on our domains and that the tithe not be given to the churches of another except to those entitled to it by ancient usage. And our churches shall not have clerics other than our own, that is, of our people or our palace.

7.   Each steward shall perform his services fully, just as it has been prescribed, and if the necessity should arise that more must be done then he shall determine whether he should increase the service or the day-work.

8.   Our stewards shall take care of our vines in their district and cultivate them well. And they shall put the wine in good vessels and carefully see to it that none is lost. And other required wine which is not from our vines they shall buy for provisioning the royal estates. And when they have bought more than is needed for this provisioning they shall inform us that

"Capitulare de Villis," in *Introduction to Contemporary Civilization in the West*, 2nd ed., ed. Contemporary Civilization Staff of Columbia College (New York: Columbia University Press, 1954), Vol. I, pp. 5–13. Courtesy of Columbia University Press.

we can let them know what is to be done with it. For they shall put the product of our vines to our use. The wine which those persons on our estates pay as rent shall be put in our cellars.

9. We wish that each steward in his district have measures of the *modius, sextarius,* the *situla* of eight *sextarii,* and the *corbus,* the same as we have in our palace.

10. Our mayors, foresters, stablemen, cellarers, deans, toll-collectors, and other officers shall do the regular and fixed labor and pay the due of pigs for their holdings and fulfill well their offices in return for the manual labor remitted them. And if any mayor holds a benefice he shall send his representative so that the manual labor and other services will be performed for him.

11. No steward shall take lodging for his own need or for his dogs from our people or from those in the forests.

12. No steward shall maintain at the expense of anyone else our hostages placed on our estates.

13. The stewards shall take good care of the stallions and not allow them to remain in one pasture too long lest they damage it. And if there should be any unsound or too old or about to die they shall inform us in good time before the season for putting them with the mares.

14. They shall take good care of our mares and separate them from the colts at the right time. And when the fillies increase in number they shall also be separated to form a new herd.

15. Our stewards shall have our foals sent to the palace in the winter at the Feast of Saint Martin.

16. We wish that our stewards fully perform in the manner established for them whatever we or the queen or our officers, the seneschal or the butler, in our name or that of the queen command. If anyone shall not do this through negligence he shall abstain from drink from the time that it is made known to him until he comes into our presence or that of the queen and seeks pardon from us. And if the steward is with the army, on guard duty, or on a mission or otherwise engaged and he commands his assistants to do something and they fail to do it, then they shall come afoot to the palace and abstain from food and drink until they have given their reasons for not doing it. Then they shall receive their sentence, a whipping or whatever we or the queen deem appropriate.

17. Each steward shall have as many men taking care of the bees for our use as he has estates in his district.

18. At our mills the stewards shall have hens and geese according to the nature of the mill or as many more as is possible.

19. In our barns on the chief estates they shall have at least 100 chickens and 30 geese and on our lesser estates at least 50 chickens and 12 geese.

20. Each steward shall have the produce [of the fowl] brought always in abundance to the manor every year and besides shall inspect it three or four or more times.

21.   Each steward shall have fish-ponds on our estates where they were before and if it is possible to enlarge them, he shall do so. Where there were none before and it is now possible to have them let them be constructed.

22.   Those who hold vines from us shall have no less than three or four circles of grapes for our use.

23.   On each of our estates the stewards shall have cow-barns, pig-sties, sheepfolds, and stables for goats, as many as possible, and never be without them. And they shall further have for performing their services cows furnished by our serfs so that our barns and teams are not in the least diminished by the services of work on our demesne. And when they are charged with furnishing food they shall have lame but healthy oxens and cows, and horses that are not mangy, and other healthy animals. They shall not on that account strip, as we have said, the cow-barns or the plough-beasts.

24.   Each steward shall be responsible that whatever ought to be supplied for our table is all good and excellent and prepared carefully and cleanly. And each steward shall have grain for two meals for each day of the service that he is charged with supplying our table. Similarly the other provisions shall be good in all respects, the flour as well as the meat.

25.   The stewards shall make known on the first of September whether or not there is pasturage for the hogs.

26.   The mayors shall not have more land in their administration than they can get about and oversee in one day.

27.   Our houses shall constantly have fire and watch service that they may be safe. And when royal envoys or legates are coming to or leaving the palace, in no wise shall they exercise the right of bed and board in our manor houses except by our special order or that of the queen. But the count in his district or those persons who have been accustomed of old to caring for envoys and legates shall continue to do so as before. And packhorses and other necessary things shall be provided in the customary fashion that they may come to the palace or depart in a fashion befitting them.

28.   We wish that every year in Lent on Palm Sunday, which is called Hosanna Sunday, our stewards carefully render according to our instructions the money arising from the products of our land after we know for the particular year what our income is.

29.   Each steward shall see to it that anyone of our people who have cases to plead shall not of necessity have to come to us so that he will not lose through negligence days on which he ought to be working. And if one of our serfs has some rights to claim outside our lands, his master shall do all that he can to secure justice for him. In case the serf shall not be able to get justice his master shall not permit him to exhaust himself in his efforts but shall see to it that the matter is made known to us by himself or by his representative.

30.   Of those things that our stewards ought to provide for our needs, we wish them to put aside all the products due us from them, and what must be placed in the wagons for the army, taking it from the homes as well as

from the herdsmen, and that they know how much they have reserved for this purpose.

31.   They shall set aside each year what they ought to give as food and maintenance to the workers entitled to it and to the women working in the women's quarters and shall give it fully at the right time and make known to us what they have done with it and where they got it.

32.   Each steward shall see to it that he always has the very best seed by purchase or otherwise.

33.   After the above things have been set aside and after the sowing and other works have been done, all that remains of all the products shall be preserved until we give word to what extent they shall be sold or stored according to our order.

34.   At all times is it to be seen to with diligence that whatever is worked upon or made with hands such as lard, smoked meat, salted meat, newly salted meat, wine, vinegar, mulberry wine, cooked wine, fermentations, mustard, cheese, butter, malt, beer, honey, wax, and flour shall be prepared or made with the greatest cleanliness.

35.   We wish that fat be made of the fat sheep and pigs. Moreover the steward shall have in each estate not less than two fattened oxen either there to be made into fat or to be sent to us.

36.   Our woods and forests shall be well taken care of and where there shall be a place for a clearing let it be cleared. Our stewards shall not allow the fields to become woods and where there ought to be woods they shall not allow anyone to cut too much or damage them. And they shall look carefully after our wild beasts in the forests and also take care of the goshawks and sparrowhawks reserved for our use. They shall collect diligently our tax for the use of our forests and if our stewards or our mayors or their men put their pigs for fattening in our forests they shall be the first to pay the tenth of them to give a good example so that thereafter the other men will pay the tenth in full.

37.   The stewards shall keep our fields and cultivated lands in good shape and care for the meadows at the right time.

38.   They shall always have sufficient fat geese and chickens for our use when they ought to provide it or send it to us.

39.   We wish that the stewards collect the chickens and the eggs which the lesser officials and the holders of *mansi* pay each year and when they are not needed that they have them sold.

40.   Each steward shall always have on our estates for the sake of adornment unusual birds, peacocks, pheasants, ducks, pigeons, partridges, and turtledoves.

41.   The buildings on our estates and the fences which enclose them shall be well taken care of and the stables and kitchens, bake-houses and presses shall be carefully ordered so that the workers in our service can perform their duties fittingly and very cleanly.

42.   Each manor shall have in the store-room counterpanes, bolsters, pillows, bedclothes, table and bench covers, vessels of brass, lead, iron, and wood, andirons, chains, pot-hooks, adzes, axes, augurs, knives, and all sorts of tools so that it will not be necessary to seek them elsewhere or to borrow them. And the stewards shall be responsible that the iron instruments sent to the army are in good condition and when they are returned that they are put back into the store-room.

43.   For our women's work-shops the stewards shall provide the materials at the right time as it has been established, that is, flax, wool, woad, vermilion dye, madder, wool-combs, teasels, soap, grease, vessels, and the other lesser things which are necessary there.

44.   Of the minor foods two-thirds shall be sent for our service each year, vegetables as well as fish, cheese, butter, honey, mustard, vinegar, millet, panic, dried and fresh herbs, radishes, and turnips; similarly wax, soap, and other lesser things. Whatever is left shall be made known to us in an inventory as we have said above. The stewards shall by no means neglect to do this as they have up to now because we wish to check by the two-thirds sent to us what that third is which remains.

45.   Each steward shall have good workmen in his district—iron-workers, goldsmiths, silversmiths, leather-workers, turners, carpenters, shield-makers, fishermen, fowlers or falconers, soap-makers, brewers who know how to make beer, cider, perry or any other beverage fit to drink, bakers who can make bread for our needs, net-makers who are skilled in making nets for hunting as well as fishing or for taking birds, and other workmen whose listing would be a lengthy matter.

46.   They shall take good care of our walled game preserves which the people call parks and always repair them in time and on no account delay so that it becomes necessary to rebuild them. They shall do the same for all the buildings.

47.   Our hunters and falconers and other servitors who attend us zealously in the palace shall receive assistance on our estates in carrying out what we or the queen have ordered by our letters when we send them on any of our affairs, or when the seneschal or butler instructs them to do anything on our authority.

48.   The wine-presses on our estates shall be well taken care of. The stewards shall see to it that no one presumes to press our grapes with his feet but that all is done cleanly and honestly.

49.   The women's quarters, that is, their houses, heated rooms, and sitting-rooms, shall be well ordered and have good fences around them and strong gates that our work may be done well.

50.   Each steward shall see to it that there are as many horses in one stable as ought to be there and as many attendants as should be with them. And those stablemen who are free and hold benefices in that district shall live off their benefices. Similarly if they are men of the domain who hold

mansi they shall live off them. Those who do not have such shall receive maintenance from the demesne.

51. Each steward shall see to it that in no manner wicked men conceal our seed under the ground or do otherwise with the result that our harvests are smaller. And likewise, concerning other misdeeds, they shall watch them so that they can do no harm.

52. We wish that our stewards render justice to our *coloni* and serfs and to the *coloni* living on our estates, to the different men fully and entirely such as they are due.

53. Each steward shall see to it that our men in their districts in no way become robbers or evil-doers.

54. Each steward shall see to it that our people work well at their tasks and do not go wandering off to markets.

55. We wish that whatever our stewards have sent, supplied, or set aside for our use they shall record in an inventory; whatever they have dispensed in another; and what is left they shall also make known to us in an inventory.

56. Each steward shall hold frequent audiences in his district, administer justice, and see to it that our peoples live uprightly.

57. If any of our serfs wishes to say anything to us about our affairs over and above his steward, the steward shall not obstruct the means of his coming to us. If the steward knows that his assistants wish to come to the palace to speak against him then he shall make known to the palace the arguments against them so that their denunciations in our ears may not engender disgust. Accordingly we wish to know whether they come from necessity or without sufficient cause.

58. When our pups are committed to the stewards to be raised, the steward shall feed them at his own expense or entrust them to his assistants, that is to the mayors and deans or to the cellarers, who shall feed them well at their own expense unless it happens that by our order or that of the queen they are to be fed on our estate at our expense. In that case the steward shall send a man for this work who will feed them well. And he shall set aside what is to be fed them so that it will not be necessary for him to go to the kennels every day.

59. Each steward when he should give service shall send every day three *librae* of wax and eight *sextaria* of soap; besides this he shall do his best to send six *librae* of wax wherever we shall be with our attendants on the Feast of Saint Andrew; he should do likewise at Mid-Lent.

60. On no account shall mayors be selected from the powerful men but from those of middling estate who are trustworthy.

61. Each steward when he should give service shall have his malt brought to the palace and at the same time have the master brewers come who are to make good beer there.

62. That we may know what and how much of everything we have, each steward every year at Christmas shall report those of our revenues

which they hold, everything differentiated clearly and orderly. That is, an accounting of the land cultivated with the oxen which our ploughmen drive and that which is cultivated by the holders of *mansi* who owe us labor-service; of the payments of pigs, the taxes, the income from judgments and fines and from the beasts taken in our forests without our permission and from the other compositions; an accounting of the mills, forests, fields, bridges, and ships; of the free men and the hundred-men who owe service for parts of our domain; of the markets, vineyards, and of those who pay us wine; of the hay, firewood, torches, planks, and other lumber; of the income from the wasteland; of the vegetables, millet, panic, wool, flax, and hemp; of the fruit of the trees, of the big and little nuts, of the graftings of various trees, of the gardens, turnips, fish-ponds, hides, skins and horns; of the honey, wax, fat, tallow, and soap; of the mulberry wine, cooked wine, mead, and vinegar; of the beer, new and old wine, new and old grain, chickens and eggs, and geese; of the fishermen, smiths, shield-makers and leather-workers; of the troughs, boxes, and cases; of the turners and saddlers; of the forges and mines, that is iron, lead, and other mines; of those paying taxes; and of the colts and fillies.

63. Of all the above mentioned things nothing that we require shall seem hard to our stewards for we wish the stewards to require them from their assistants in the same fashion without any hardship. And all things which any man shall have in his house or on his estate our stewards ought also to have on our estates.

64. Our carts which accompany the army, that is, the war-carts, shall be well-constructed, and their coverings be good, with hides on top and so sewn together that if the necessity of swimming waters should arise they can cross rivers without any water getting to the provisions inside and in this fashion our things may, as we said, get across without damage. And we wish that flour for our use be put in each cart, that is 12 *modii*, and that they put in those in which wine is sent 12 *modii* of our measure. In each cart let them have a shield, a lance, a quiver, and a bow.

65. The fish in our fish-ponds shall be sold and others put in their place so that they may always have fish in them. However, when we are not coming to our estates they shall be sold and our stewards shall dispose of them to our advantage.

66. The stewards shall report to us the number of male and female goats and their horns and skins; and they shall bring to us annually newly salted cuts of fat goats.

67. The stewards shall inform us about any vacant *mansi* or any newly acquired serfs if they have any in their district for whom they have no place.

68. We wish that each steward always have ready good barrels bound with iron which they can send to the army or to the palace and that the stewards do not make containers of leather.

69.   The stewards at all times shall report to us how many wolves each has taken and shall send the skins to us. And in the month of May they shall hunt down and destroy the whelps with poison, traps, pits, and dogs.

70.   We wish that the stewards have all sorts of plants in the garden, namely, lilies, roses, fenugreek, costmary, sage, rue, southernwood, cucumbers, pumpkins, squash, kidney-beans, cumin, rosemary, caraway, chickpeas, squill, gladiolus, dragonarum, anise, colosynth, heliotrope, spicknel, seseli, lettuce, fennel-flower, rocket, garden cress, burdock, pennyroyal, horse-parsley, parsley, celery, lovage, juniper, dill, sweet-fennel, endive, dittany, mustard, savory, water-mint, garden mint, applemint, tansy, catnip, centaury, garden-poppy, beets, hazelwort, marshmallows, tree-hibiscus, mallows, carrots, parsnip, garden-orach, amaranth, kohlrabi, cabbages, onions, chives, leeks, radishes, shallots, cibols, garlic, madder, teasel, garden beans, Moorish peas, coriander, chervil, capers, clary. And the gardener shall have house-leek growing on his house.

As for trees, we wish that they have various kinds of apple, pear, and plum trees, sorb, medlar, chestnut, peach trees of different kinds, quince, filbert, almond, mulberry, laurel, pine, fig, walnut, and cherry trees of various kinds.

Names of apple trees: *gozmaringa, geroldinga, crevedella, spirauca,* sweet ones and sour ones, and all the kind that keep, as well as those which are eaten when picked and those that are forced.

They shall have three or four kinds of pears which will keep, sweet ones, cooking, and late pears.

Charter of the Liberties of Lorris

1.   Let whoever shall have a house in the parish of Lorris pay a quit-rent of six deniers only for his house, and each acre of land which he shall have in this parish; and if he make such an acquisition, let that be the quit-rent of his house.

2.   Let no inhabitant of the parish of Lorris pay a duty of entry nor any tax for his food, and let him not pay any duty of measurement for the corn which his labor, or that of the animals which he may have shall procure him, and let him pay no duty for the wine which he shall get from his vines.

3.   Let none of them go on a [military] expedition on foot or horseback, whence he cannot return home the same day if he desire to do so.

4.   Let none of them pay toll to Étampes or Orleans, or to Milly, which is in Gâtinais, or to Melun.

Carta Franchesie Lorriaci, trans. W. Hazlitt.

5.   Let no one who has property in the parish of Lorris lose any of it for any misdeed whatsoever, unless the said misdeed be committed against us or any of our guests.

6.   Let no one going to the fairs or markets of Lorris, or in returning, be stopped or inconvenienced unless he shall have committed some misdeed that same day; and let no one on a fair or market day at Lorris, seize the bail given by his security; unless the bail be given the same day.

7.   Let forfeitures of sixty sous be reduced to five, that of five sous to twelve deniers, and the provost's fee in cases of plaint, to four deniers.

8.   Let no man of Lorris be forced to go out of it to plead before the lord king.

9.   Let no one, neither us nor any other, take any tax, offering, or exaction from the men of Lorris.

10.   Let no one sell wine at Lorris with public notice, except the king, who shall sell his wine in his cellar with that notice.

11.   We will have at Lorris, for our service and that of the queen, a credit of a full fortnight, in the articles of provisions; and if any inhabitant have received a gage from the lord king, he shall not be bound to keep it more than eight days, unless he please.

12.   If any have had a quarrel with another, but without breaking a closed house, and if it be accommodated without plaint brought before the provost, no fine shall be due, on this account, to us or to our provost; and if there has been a plaint they can still come to an agreement when they shall have paid the fine. And if any one bear plaint against another, and there has been no fine awarded against either one to the other, they shall not, on that account, owe anything to us or our provost.

13.   If any one owe an oath to another, let the latter have permission to remit it.

14.   If any men of Lorris have rashly given their pledge of a duel, and if with the consent of the provost they accommodate it before the pledges have been given, let each pay two sous and a half; and if the pledges have been given, let each pay seven sous and a half; and if the duel has been between men having the right of fighting in the list, then let the hostages of the conquered pay one hundred and twelve sous.

15.   Let no man of Lorris do forced work for us, unless it be twice a year to take our wine to Orleans, and nowhere else; and those only shall do this work who shall have horses and carts, and they shall be informed of it beforehand; and they shall receive no lodging from us. The laborers also shall bring wood for our kitchen.

16.   No one shall be detained in prison if he can furnish bail for his appearance in court.

17.   Whoever desires to sell his property may do so; and having received the price, he may leave the town, free and unmolested, if he please so to do, unless he has committed any misdeed in the town.

18.   Whoever shall have remained a year and a day in the parish of Lorris without any claim having pursued him thither, and without the right having been interdicted him, whether by us or our provost, he shall remain there free and tranquil.

19.   No one shall plead against another unless it be to recover, and ensure the observance of, what is his due.

20.   When the men of Lorris shall go to Orleans with merchandise, they shall pay, upon leaving the town, one denier for their cart, when they go not for the sake of the fair; and when they go for the sake of the fair and the market, they shall pay, upon leaving Orleans, four deniers for each cart, and on entering, two deniers.

21.   At marriages in Lorris, the public crier shall have no fee, nor he who keeps watch.

22.   No cultivator of the parish of Lorris, cultivating his land with the plow, shall give, in the time of harvest more than one hermine [six bushels] of rye to all the serjeants of Lorris.

23.   If any knight or serjeant find, in our forests, horses or other animals belonging to the men of Lorris, he must not take them to any other than to the provost of Lorris; and if any animal of the parish of Lorris be put to flight by bulls, or assailed by flies, have entered our forest, or leaped our banks, the owner of the animal shall owe no fine to the provost, if he can swear that the animal has entered in spite of his keeper. But if the animal entered with the knowledge of his keeper, the owner shall pay twelve deniers, and as much for each animal, if there be more than one.

24.   There shall be at Lorris no duty paid for using the oven.

25.   There shall be at Lorris no watch rate.

26.   All men of Lorris who shall take salt or wine to Orleans, shall pay only one denier for each cart.

27.   No men of Lorris shall owe any fine to the provost of Étampes, nor to the provost of Pithiviers nor to any in Gâtinais.

28.   None among them shall pay the entry dues in Ferrières, nor in Château-Landon, nor in Puiseaux, nor in Nibelle.

29.   Let the men of Lorris take the dead wood in the forest for their own use.

30.   Whosoever, in the market of Lorris, shall have bought or sold anything, and shall have forgotten to pay the duty, may pay it within eight days without being troubled, if he can swear that he did not withhold the right wittingly.

31.   No man of Lorris having a house or a vineyard, or a meadow, or a field, or any buildings in the domain of St. Benedict, shall be under the jurisdiction of the abbot of St. Benedict or his serjeant, unless it be with regard to the quit-rent in kind, to which he is bound; and, in that case, he shall not go out of Lorris to be judged.

32.   If any of the men of Lorris be accused of anything, and the accuser cannot prove it by witness, he shall clear himself by a single oath from the assertion of his accuser.

33.   No man of this parish shall pay any duty because of what he shall buy or sell for his use on the territory of the precincts, nor for what he shall buy on Wednesday at the market.

34.   These customs are granted to the men of Lorris, and they are common to the men who inhabit Courpalais, Chanteloup, and the bailiwick of Harpard.

35.   We order that whenever the provost shall be changed in the town, he shall swear faithfully to observe these customs; and the same shall be done by new serjeants when they shall be instituted.

Given at Orleans in the year of our Lord 1155.

Magna Carta

Magna Carta was the consequence of a dispute that had been developing over a period of years between the monarchs and the barons of England. From the time of the Norman conquest in 1066 succeeding English kings had embarked on a practice of consolidating administration and, as a result, power around the throne. Such a policy, of course, worked to the disadvantage of the barons who, in their reaction against these royal encroachments, claimed that they constituted violations of the feudal contract. Thus Magna Carta reveals much about feudal society and the customary and legal relationships between individuals and classes as these existed in the England of that time.

The dispute between king and barons intensified after the accession of King John to the throne in 1199. Much of the blame for this development lay with John himself, for he succeeded in making himself unpopular with almost every segment of his population. He alienated many of the clergy by his quarrels with Pope Innocent III; he discouraged the military class by his armed incursions into France, which led to defeat; he enraged the London merchants by imposing an ever-increasing tax burden on them; and he kept infringing on the feudal rights and privileges of the baronial class. In all of this he displayed himself as an insensitive autocrat.

The selection that follows contains about half of the Magna Carta; from it one can get a good grasp of the charter's general nature. Although it may appear from the flavor of the language employed that John is graciously granting royal favors to his subjects, it must be remembered that these concessions were forced from him by his rebellious barons.

Consider the following questions as you study the text below.

1. Whose rights are protected in the *Magna Carta*? What does the document tell us about the distribution of political power in twelfth-century England?

2. What limits did the *Magna Carta* place on the power of the king? What institutions did it establish to correct future abuses?

Magna Carta

1.   We have, in the first place, granted to God, and by this Our present Charter confirmed for Us and Our heirs forever—That the English Church shall be free and enjoy her rights in their integrity and her liberties untouched. And that We will this so to be observed appears from the fact that We of Our own free will, before the outbreak of the dissensions between Us and Our barons, granted, confirmed, and procured to be confirmed by Pope Innocent III the freedom of elections, which is considered most important and necessary to the English Church, which Charter We will both keep Ourself and will it to be kept with good faith by Our heirs forever. We have also granted to all the free men of Our kingdom, for Us and Our heirs forever, all the liberties under-written, to have and to hold to them and their heirs of Us and Our heirs.

2.   If any of Our earls, barons, or others who hold of Us in chief by knight's service shall die, and at the time of his death his heir shall be of full age and owe a relief [a form of tax], he shall have his inheritance by ancient relief; to wit, the heir or heirs of an earl of an entire earl's barony, £100; the heir or heirs of a baron of an entire barony, £100; the heir or heirs of a knight of an entire knight's fee, 100s. at the most; and he that owes less shall give less, according to the ancient custom of fees.

3.   If, however, any such heir shall be under age and in ward, he shall, when he comes of age, have his inheritance without relief or fine.

4.   The guardian of the land of any heir thus under age shall take therefrom only reasonable issues, customs, and services, without destruc-tion or waste of men or property; and if We shall have committed the ward-ship of any such land to the sheriff or any other person answerable to Us for the issues thereof, and he commit destruction or waste, We will take an amends from him, and the land shall be committed to two lawful and dis-creet men of that fee, who shall be answerable for the issues to Us or to whomsoever We shall have assigned them. And if We shall give or sell the wardship of any such land to anyone, and he commit destruction or waste upon it, he shall lose the wardship, which shall be committed to two lawful and discreet men of that fee, who shall, in like manner, be answerable unto Us as has been aforesaid.

5.   The guardian, so long as he shall have the custody of the land, shall keep up and maintain the houses, parks, fishponds, pools, mills, and other things pertaining thereto, out of the issues of the same, and shall re-store the whole to the heir when he comes of age, stocked with ploughs and tillage, according as the season may require and the issues of the land can reasonably bear.

Magna Carta, trans. A. E. Dick Howard (Charlottesville: The University Press of Virginia, 1964), pp. 33–44, 46–52. Courtesy of the Rector and Visitors of the University of Virginia.

6.   Heirs shall be married without loss of station, and the marriage shall be made known to the heir's nearest of kin before it be contracted.

7.   A widow, after the death of her husband, shall immediately and without difficulty have her marriage portion and inheritance. She shall not give anything for her marriage portion, dower, or inheritance which she and her husband held on the day of his death, and she may remain in her husband's house for forty days after his death, within which time her dower shall be assigned to her.

8.   No widow shall be compelled to marry so long as she has a mind to live without a husband, provided, however, that she give security that she will not marry without Our assent, if she holds of Us, or that of the lord of whom she holds, if she holds of another.

9.   Neither We nor Our bailiffs shall seize any land or rent for any debt solong as the debtor's chattels are sufficient to discharge the same; nor shall the debtor's sureties be distrained so long as the debtor is able to pay the debt. If the debtor fails to pay, not having the means to pay, then the sureties shall answer the debt, and, if they desire, they shall hold the debtor's lands and rents until they have received satisfaction of the debt which they have paid for him, unless the debtor can show that he has discharged his obligation to them.

10.   If anyone who has borrowed from the Jews any sum of money, great or small, dies before the debt has been paid, the heir shall pay no interest on the debt so long as he remains under age, of whomsoever he may hold. If the debt shall fall into Our hands, We will take only the principal sum named in the bond.

12.   No scutage[1] or aid shall be imposed in Our kingdom unless by common counsel thereof, except to ransom Our person, make Our eldest son a knight, and once to marry Our eldest daughter, and for these only a reasonable aid shall be levied. So shall it be with regard to aids from the City of London.

13.   The City of London shall have all her ancient liberties and free customs, both by land and water. Moreover, We will and grant that all other cities, boroughs, towns, and ports shall have all their liberties and free customs.

14.   For obtaining the common counsel of the kingdom concerning the assessment of aids (other than in the three cases aforesaid) or of scutage, We will cause to be summoned, severally by Our letters, the archbishops, bishops, abbots, earls, and great barons. We will also cause to be summoned, generally, by Our sheriffs and bailiffs, all those who hold lands directly to Us, to meet on a fixed day, but with at least forty days' notice, and at a fixed place. In all letters of such summons We will explain the cause thereof. The summons being thus made, the business shall proceed on the day appointed,

---

[1][A payment in place of a personal service—*Ed.*]

according to the advice of those who shall be present, even though not all the persons summoned have come.

15.   We will not in the future grant permission to any man to levy an aid upon his free men, except to ransom his person, make his eldest son a knight, and once to marry his eldest daughter, and on each of these occasions only a reasonable aid shall be levied.

16.   No man shall be compelled to perform more service for a knight's fee or other free tenement than is due therefrom.

17.   Common Pleas shall not follow Our Court, but shall be held in some certain place.

20.   A free man shall be amerced [fined] for a small fault only according to the measure thereof, and for a great crime according to its magnitude, saving his position; and in like manner a merchant saving his trade, and a villein [serf] saving his tillage, if they should fall under Our mercy. None of these amercements shall be imposed except by the oath of honest men of the neighborhood.

21.   Earls and barons shall be amerced only by their peers, and only in proportion to the measure of the offense.

22.   No amercement shall be imposed upon a clerk's [clergyman's] lay property, except after the manner of the other persons aforesaid, and without regard to the value of his ecclesiastical benefice.

28.   No constable or other of Our bailiffs shall take corn or other chattels of any man without immediate payment, unless the seller voluntarily consents to postponement of payment.

29.   No constable shall compel any knight to give money in lieu of castle-guard when the knight is willing to perform it in person or (if reasonable cause prevents him from performing it himself) by some other fit man. Further, if We lead or send him into military service, he shall be quit of castle-guard for the time he shall remain in service by Our command.

30.   No sheriff or other of Our bailiffs, or any other man, shall take the horses or carts of any free man for carriage without the owner's consent.

31.   Neither We nor Our bailiffs will take another man's wood for Our casles or for any other purpose without the owner's consent.

35.   There shall be one measure of wine throughout Our kingdom, and one of ale, and one measure of corn, to wit, the London quarter, and one breadth of dyed cloth, russets, and haberjets, to wit, two ells within the selvages. As with measures so shall it also be with weights.

38.   In the future no bailiff shall upon his own unsupported accusation put any man to trial without producing credible witnesses to the truth of the accusation.

39.   No free man shall be taken, imprisoned, disseised [dispossessed], outlawed, banished, or in any way destroyed, nor will We proceed against him or prosecute him, except by the lawful judgment of his peers and by the law of the land.

40.   To no one will We sell, to none will We deny or delay, right or justice.

41.   All merchants shall have safe conduct to go and come out of and into England, and to stay in and travel through England by land and water for purposes of buying and selling, free of illegal tolls, in accordance with ancient and just customs, except, in time of war, such merchants as are of a country at war with Us. If any such be found in Our dominion at the outbreak of war, they shall be attached, without injury to their persons or goods, until it be known to Us or Our Chief Justiciary how Our merchants are being treated in the country at war with Us, and if Our merchants be safe there, then theirs shall be safe with Us.

42.   In the future it shall be lawful (except for a short period in time of war, for the common benefit of the realm) for anyone to leave and return to our kingdom safely and securely by land and water, saving his fealty to Us. Excepted are those who have been imprisoned or outlawed according to the law of the land, people of the country at war with Us, and merchants, who shall be dealt with as aforesaid.

52.   If anyone has been disseised or deprived by Us, without the legal judgment of his peers, of lands, castles, liberties, or rights, We will immediately restore the same, and if any dispute shall arise thereupon, the matter shall be decided by judgment of the twenty-five barons mentioned below in the clause for securing the peace. With regard to all those things, however, of which any man was disseised or deprived, without the legal judgment of his peers, by King Henry Our Father or Our Brother King Richard, and which remain in Our hands or are held by others under Our warranty, We shall have respite during the term commonly allowed to the Crusaders, except as to those matters on which a plea had arisen, or an inquisition had been taken by Our command, prior to Our taking the Cross. Immediately after Our return from Our pilgrimmage, or if by chance We should remain behind from it, We will at once do full justice.

54.   No one shall be arrested or imprisoned upon a woman's appeal for the death of any person other than her husband.

55.   All fines unjustly and unlawfully given to Us, and all amercements levied unjustly and against the law of the land, shall be entirely remitted or the matter settled by judgment of the twenty-five barons of whom mention is made below in the clause for securing the peace, or the majority of them, together with the aforesaid Stephen, Archbishop of Canterbury, if he himself can be present, and any others whom he may wish to bring with him for the purpose; if he cannot be present, the business shall nevertheless proceed without him. If any one or more of the said twenty-five barons be interested in a suit of this kind, he or they shall be set aside, as to this particular judgment, and another or others, elected and sworn by the rest of said barons for this occasion only, be substituted in his or their stead.

60.   All the customs and liberties aforesaid, which We have granted to be enjoyed, as far as in Us lies, by Our people throughout Our kingdom, let all Our subjects, whether clerks or laymen, observe, as far as in them lies, toward their dependents.

61. Whereas We, for the honor of God and the amendment of Our realm, and in order the better to allay the discord arisen between Us and Our barons, have granted all these things aforesaid, We, willing that they be forever enjoyed wholly and in lasting strength, do give and grant to Our subjects the following security, to wit, that the barons shall elect any twenty-five barons of the kingdom at will, who shall, with their utmost power, keep, hold, and cause to be kept the peace and liberties which We have granted unto them and by this Our present Charter have confirmed, so that if We, Our Justiciary, bailiffs, or any of Our ministers offend in any respect against any man, or shall transgress any of these articles of peace or security, and the offense be brought before four of the said twenty-four barons, these four barons shall come before Us, or Our Chief Justiciary if We are out of the kingdom, declaring the offense, and shall demand speedy amends for the same. If We, or, in case of Our being out of the kingdom, Our Chief Justiciary fail to afford redress within the space of forty days from the time the case was brought before Us or, in the event of Our having been out of the kingdom, Our Chief Justiciary, the aforesaid four barons shall refer the matter to the rest of the twenty-five barons, who, together with the commonalty of the whole country, shall distrain and distress Us to the utmost of their power, to wit, by capture of Our castles, lands, and possessions and by all other possible means, until compensation be made according to their decision, saving Our person and that of Our Queen and children; as soon as redress has been had, they shall return to their former allegiance. Anyone in the kingdom may take oath that, for the accomplishment of all the aforesaid matters, he will obey the orders of the said twenty-five barons and distress Us to the utmost of his power; and We give public and free leave to everyone wishing to take such oath to do so, and to none will we deny the same. Moreover, all such of Our subjects who shall not of their own free will and accord agree to swear to the said twenty-five barons, to distrain and distress Us together with them, We will compel to do so by Our command in the manner aforesaid. If any one of the twenty-five barons shall die or leave the country or be in any way hindered from executing the said office, the rest of the said twenty-five barons shall choose another in his stead, at their discretion, who shall be sworn in like manner as the others. In all cases which are referred to the said twenty-five barons to execute, and in which a difference shall arise among them, supposing them all to be present, or in which not all who have been summoned are willing or able to appear, the verdict of the majority shall be considered as firm and binding as if the whole number should have been of one mind. The aforesaid twenty-five shall swear to keep faithfully all the aforesaid articles and, to the best of their power, to cause them to be kept by others. We will not procure, either by Ourself or any other, anything from any man whereby any of these concessions or liberties may be revoked or abated. If any such procurement be made, let it be null and void; it shall never be made use of either by Us or by any other.

62.   We have also wholly remitted and pardoned all ill-will, wrath, and malice which has arisen between Us and Our subjects, both clergy and laymen, during the disputes, to and with all men. Morover, We have fully remitted and, as far as in Us lies, wholly pardoned to and with all, clergy and laymen, all trespasses made in consequence of the said disputes from Easter in the sixteenth year of Our reign till the restoration of peace. Over and above this, We have caused to be made in their behalf letters patent by testimony of Stephen, Archbishop of Canterbury, Henry, Archbishop of Dublin, the Bishops above-mentioned, and Master Pandulph, for the security and concessions aforesaid.

63.   Wherefore We will, and firmly charge, that the English Church shall be free, and that all men in Our kingdom shall have and hold all the aforesaid liberties, rights, and concessions, well and peaceably, freely, quietly, fully, and wholly, to them and their heirs, of Us and Our heirs, in all things and places forever, as is aforesaid. It is moreover sworn, as well on Our part as on the part of the barons, that all these matters aforesaid shall be kept in good faith and without deceit. Witness the above-named and many others. Given by Our hand in the meadow which is called Runnymede, between Windsor and Staines, on the fifteenth day of June in the seventeenth year of Our reign.

Church and State

Throughout the Middle Ages, the Church and the temporal rulers of Europe waged a running battle for political supremacy. For a time, the Church seemed assured of victory. It reached the height of its power during the pontificate of Innocent III (1198–1216), who succeeded in forcing King John to surrender England to him, to be held by John in the future as a fief from the papacy. The final victory, however, went to the secular powers, who gradually effected a separation between political authority and spiritual authority, reserving the former for themselves and permitting the Church to exercise the latter.

The documents that follow reflect the Church's position at two different phases during this long struggle. The first document is concerned with a dispute between the Holy Roman Emperor, Henry IV, and Pope Gregory VII, a dispute that led to Henry's famous winter pilgrimage to Canossa to seek absolution from the pope. The document is actually a letter, written in 1081, from Gregory to the bishop of Metz, who had sought papal aid in combating the emperor. It is important because it contains Gregory's view of the position of the Church relative to the state, as well as the main arguments on which that position rested.

The second document, the papal bull *Unam Sanctam*, was written over two hundred years later (1302), during a controversy between Pope Boniface VIII and King Philip the Fair of France. Philip replied to the bull, which flatly asserts the political supremacy of the Church, by having the pope seized. Although Boniface was soon released, he died almost immediately afterward. Philip again took the initiative and managed to convert the papacy into an adjunct of the French throne. This episode marked the turning point in the political fortunes of the Church, for the popes were never able to regain the ascendancy over the secular monarchs that the papacy had enjoyed under Pope Innocent III.

Consider the following questions as you study the text below.

1. What was the basis of Pope Gregory VII's argument in favor of papal supremacy? In Gregory's judgment, did popes have power and authority to depose kings?

2. According to the Bull *Unam Sanctam*, did kings have any power, independent of that granted to them by the church? Did the church have the resources and ability to enforce the views put forth in the Bull?

The Second Letter of Gregory VII to Hermann, Bishop of Metz, March 15, 1081

GREGORY, BISHOP, servant of the servants of God, to Our well-beloved brother in Christ, Hermann, Bishop of Metz, health and the Apostolic Benediction.

We know your desire to employ yourself, and to confront dangers, in the defence of truth, and We see in your good-will, the action of Divine Providence. The ineffable grace of God and His marvellous bounty never permit His chosen ones to lapse into complete error, nor do they allow them to be altogether conquered and enslaved by sin. After the salutary trials of persecution, and the anxieties which they have experienced, the elect come forth stronger than before. Fear makes cowards shamelessly rival one another in flight; in like manner, those inspired by manly courage, strive to be in the front rank and to obtain the palm of valour and bravery. If We address this language to your charity, it is because you too wish to be in the front rank in the Christian army; that is, amongst those who, you know well, are closest to, and most worthy of, the God who gives the Victory.

You ask Us to come to your aid by Our writings and to refute the insanity of those, who maintain with their guilty tongues, that the Holy Apostolic See has not the right to excommunicate King Henry, that despiser of the Christian law, that destroyer of Churches, and of the Empire, that abettor and accomplice of heretics, and that it had not power to absolve from the oath of fidelity, which had been sworn to him. It does not seem very necessary for Us to do this, for this power is established by many authentic texts of Holy Scripture. We cannot indeed believe, that those who, for their own damnation, and with unblushing impudence oppose and fight against truth can, in their ignorance or madness, have had the audacity to use these texts as their justification. There would not, however, be anything astonishing in that, for it is the custom of the wicked to seek protection for their vices, and to defend their accomplices; it matters little to them if they ruin themselves by their lies.

To quote one proof from among many. Who does not know that saying of Our Lord and Savior Jesus Christ, in the Gospel:

> *Thou art Peter, and upon this rock I will build my church; and the gates of hell shall not prevail against it. I will give to you the keys of the Kingdom of Heaven, and whatsoever you shall bind on earth, shall be bound also in heaven, and whatsoever you shall lose upon earth, shall be loosed also in heaven. [Matthew XVI: 18, 19]*

Trans. A. H. Mathew.

Are kings an exception? Do they not form part of the flock confided to St. Peter by the Son of God? Then, We ask, who will dare to claim that he has nothing to do with the power of St. Peter, that the universal power of binding and loosing given to St. Peter, has no reference to him? No one would act in this manner, but that unhappy man, who, unwilling to bear the yoke of the Lord, would submit to that of the devil and renounce his right to belong to the fold of Christ. By this proud denial of the power divinely granted to St. Peter, he would obtain liberty, a sad liberty indeed, for the more he denied the power, the more heavily would his eternal damnation weigh upon him, on the day of judgment.

.   .   .

The blessed Pope Gregory, writing to a certain senator abbot, asserts that kings, who allow themselves to violate the decrees of the Apostolic See, ought to be deprived of their dignities. *If*, he writes,

> *any king, priest, judge, or any secular, knowing the present decree, dares to offend against it, let him lose his power and dignity, and let him declare himself guilty before God of the iniquity he has committed. If he does not restore what he has unjustly stolen, and do penance in proportion to his fault, let him be deprived of the most holy Body and Blood of our Lord and Redeemer Jesus Christ; and may the vengeance of the eternal judgment fall upon him.*

If blessed Gregory, who was the meekest of the doctors, decreed that kings, who violated the statutes, which he gave to a hospital, should not only be deposed, but excommunicated and damned for ever, who would dare to reproach us for having deposed and excommunicated Henry, the despiser of the apostolic judgments, the fierce enemy of Mother Church, the infamous despoiler and merciless scourge of the whole kingdom, and of the churches? Who, but one, who is still more unworthy than he, would dare to cast reproach upon us? We read in a letter of the blessed Peter, concerning the ordination of Clement:

> *If any one is a friend to those whom he (Clement) does not speak, through that very fact, he belongs to those who wish to destroy the Church of God; in the body he seems to be with us; but his spirit and his heart are against us.*

Such an enemy is to be dreaded more than one whose enmity is open, and apparent to all; for the former works evil under cover of false friendship and causes disunion and destruction in the Church. Remark this well, dearly beloved, the blessed Peter judges him, whose conduct is condemned by the Pope, in so severe a manner, that he even goes so far as to condemn those, who are bound to him by friendship, and even those who hold converse with him.

It is, therefore, impossible for a dignity which owes its origin to men of the world, and even to those ignorant of God, not to be in subjection to that dignity, which the Providence of the all-powerful God instituted, to bring honour to Him, and which, in His mercy, He has granted to the whole world. If the Son of this all-powerful God is undoubtedly God and Man, He is also the High Priest, the chief of all priests, and He is now seated at the right hand of the Father, where He intercedes for us without ceasing. The Son of God despised the earthly kingdoms, of which the sons of this world are so proud; it was of His own accord that He chose and embraced the priesthood of the Cross. Every one knows that the first kings and the first dukes, were men ignorant of God, who, influenced by blind cupidity, and intolerable presumption, aided, moreover, by the Demon-prince of this world, strove by the help of robbery, lies, and homicide, and almost every vice, to have dominion over their equals, that is, over other men. When these kings and dukes sought afterwards to draw the priests of the Lord into their ways, to whom can one more fitly compare them than to him who is the head of all the sons of pride, to him who tried to tempt the Sovereign of Pontiffs Himself, the Chief of Priests, the Son of the Most High, by showing Him all the kingdoms of the world and saying to Him, *I will give you all this if you fall down at my feet and adore me.* Who can doubt that the priests of Christ are the fathers and masters of kings; that they are the princes of all the faithful? Is it not an act of utter madness, when the son tries to rule the father, the disciple the master; when he wishes to reduce him to submission by imposing on him iniquitous conditions, though he knows well that this father and master has the power of binding and loosing on earth, as well as in heaven?

. . .

Moreover, on his death-bed, every Christian king who wishes to escape hell, to pass from darkness to light, to appear at the judgment-seat of God, after having received absolution for his faults, humbly implores the ministry of the priest. But who is there, I do not say, priest, but even layman, who has ever begged the help of an earthly king, when at the point of death, and filled with anxiety for the salvation of his soul? What king or emperor can, by right of his office, give holy baptism to a Christian, deliver him from the power of the devil, give him entrance among the children of God, or anoint him with the holy chrism? Who, among them, can consecrate the Body and Blood of the Lord, in other words, perform that greatest act of the Christian religion? Has the power of binding and absolving in heaven and on earth been given to any one of them? In all these things, the superiority of the sacerdotal dignity is evident. If no one among them has the power to ordain a cleric of Holy Church, still less have they the right of deposing him for any fault. In ecclesiastical orders, the authority which deposes ought to be superior to that which ordains. Bishops can consecrate other bishops, but they cannot dispose them, without the authority of the Apostolic See. Very little discernment is therefore necessary to understand the superiority of the priesthood over the royal state. If, in all that concerns their sins, kings are amenable to priests, much more must they be so, to the Roman Pontiff.

On closer examination, the title of king is much better suited to good Christians than to bad princes. The former seek the glory of God, and know how to govern themselves; the latter, preoccupied with their own interests, and not with the interests of God, are enemies to themselves and tyrants to others. The former are part of the Body of Jesus Christ; the latter of the body of the devil. The first-mentioned govern themselves, that they may reign eternally with the Supreme Emperor; the power of the second is exercised in such a way, that they will be lost for ever, with the prince of darkness, the king of all the sons of pride.

It is not surprising if bad bishops make common cause with an impious king; they receive their honours from that king in an unlawful way, hence they both love and dread him at the same time. By their consent to perform simoniacal ordinations, they, as it were, sell God at a low price. The elect are indissolubly united to their head; the reprobate, in like manner clings tenaciously round him who is the author of evil, especially when the matter at stake is to resist the good. To argue with them is of little avail, rather weep over their sad fate, that the all-powerful God may deliver them from the snares of Satan, and that He may in the end open their eyes to the truth.

.   .   .

What emperor or king ever restored the dead to life, cured lepers or gave sight to the blind? We have the Emperor Constantine, of pious memory, the Emperors Theodosius, Honorius, Charles and Louis, who loved justice, spread the Christian religion, and defended the Church; the Church praises and venerates them, yet she does not say that they had, to a striking extent, the gift of miracles. What altars or basilicas are there dedicated to a king or to an emperor; has the church ever allowed Mass to be celebrated in honour of any one of them? Kings and princes, so proud of being above other men, in this life, ought to fear all the more, lest they should be condemned to eternal fire in the life hereafter. Thus it is written: *The mighty shall be mightily tormented*. They will have to render an account of each subject under their sway. If it is no small labour for any ordinary mortal, filled with the spirit of religion, to save one single soul, that is, his own; how great is not the responsibility of princes who have the charge of thousands of souls! Holy Church punishes severely the sinner who has committed homicide; what then will happen to those who have caused death to thousands of persons for the sake of the glory of this world? It sometimes happens that, after having been the cause of death to many, they utter with their lips a *mea culpa*; but in the depths of their hearts, they rejoice at the extension of their glory and power. They are very far from wishing that they had left their great deeds undone; the fact of having sent their fellow-creatures to Tartarus, fills them with no compunction. Their repentance is worthless in the sight of God, it is not inspired by true contrition of heart, as they do not wish to give up what they have acquired by conquest, and at the cost of so much human blood. They have reason to fear; they ought often to recall to their minds what we have already said, that a very small number of saints is to be found amongst the multitude of kings who have succeeded one another, on the different thrones of the earth, since the beginning of the world. On the other hand, in one single line of Pontiffs, as for instance, the Roman Pontiffs from the time of St. Peter, more than a hundred are distinguished for eminent sanctity. What reason is there for this, unless, as has already been said, it is that kings of the earth and princes, fascinated by a vain desire of glory, subordinate their spiritual interests to the temporal interests of themselves and their kingdoms. Truly godly pontiffs, on the contrary, allow no earthly matters to come between them and the cause of God. The first-mentioned are remorseless in avenging personal affronts; but, when the offence is committed against God, they seem to lack energy to punish the offenders; the second easily forget the wrongs done to themselves, but with difficulty pardon the injuries done to God. The former, engrossed in the things of this world, set little value on spiritual things; the latter, having their thoughts constantly directed towards heaven, feel nothing but contempt for all that is of this earth.

.   .   .

In the name of the Omnipotent God, and through the authority of blessed Peter, prince of apostles, We grant you, brother Hermann, permission to fulfil the Episcopal duties in all the bishoprics of the kingdom of Lorraine in which the Bishops have been excommunicated, for having held intercourse with Henry, formerly called king. This permission will hold good so long as these Bishops remain excommunicated—that is, until they have been absolved, either by Us or by Our lawful successor.

The Bull *Unam Sanctam* of Boniface VIII

That there is one Holy Catholic and Apostolic Church we are impelled by our faith to believe and to hold—this we do firmly believe and openly confess—and outside of this there is neither salvation or remission of sins, as the bridegroom proclaims in Canticles, "My dove, my undefiled is but

"The Bull *Unam Sanctam* of Boniface VIII," in *Translations and Reprints from the Original Sources of European History*, Vol. III, No. 6 (Philadelphia: The Department of History of the University of Pennsylvania, 1912), pp. 20–23. Courtesy of the Department of History of the University of Pennsylvania.

one; she is the only one of her mother; she is the choice one of her that bare her." The Church represents one mystic body and of this body Christ is the head; of Christ, indeed, God is the head. In it is one Lord, and one faith, and one baptism. In the time of the flood, there was one ark of Noah, prefiguring the one Church, finished in one cubit, having one Noah as steersman and commander. Outside of this, all things upon the face of the earth were, as we read, destroyed. This Church we venerate and this alone, the Lord saying through his prophets, "Deliver my soul, O God, from the sword; my darling from the power of the dog." He prays thus for his soul, that is for Himself, as head, and also for the body, which He calls one, namely, the Church on account of the unity of the bridegroom, of the faith, of the sacraments, and of the charity of the Church. It is that seamless coat of the Lord, which was not rent, but fell by lot. Therefore, in this one and only Church, there is one body and one head—not two heads as if it were a monster— namely, Christ and Christ's Vicar, Peter and Peter's successor, for the Lord said to Peter himself, "Feed my sheep": *my* sheep, he said, using a general term and not designating these or those sheep, so that we must believe that all the sheep were committed to him. If, then, the Greeks, or others, shall say that they were not entrusted to Peter and his successors, they must perforce admit that they are not of Christ's sheep, as the Lord says in John, "there is one fold, and one shepherd."

In this Church and in its power are two swords, to wit, a spiritual and a temporal, and this we are taught by the words of the Gospel, for when the Apostles said, "Behold, here are two swords" (in the Church, namely, since the Apostles were speaking), the Lord did not reply that it was too many, but enough. And surely he who claims that the temporal sword is not in the power of Peter has but ill understood the word of our Lord when he said, "Put up the sword in its scabbard." Both, therefore, the spiritual and material swords, are in the power of the Church, the latter indeed to be used for the Church, the former by the Church, the one by the priest, the other by the hand of kings and soldiers, but by the will and sufferance of the priest. It is fitting, moreover, that one sword should be under the other, and the temporal authority subject to the spiritual power. For when the Apostle said "there is no power but of God and the powers that are of God are ordained," they would not be ordained unless one sword were under the other, and one, as inferior, was brought back by the other to the highest place. For, according to the Holy Dionysius, the law of divinity is to lead the lowest through the intermediate to the highest. Therefore, according to the law of the universe, things are not reduced to order directly, and upon the same footing, but the lowest through the intermediate and the inferior through the superior. It behooves us, therefore, the more freely to confess that the spiritual power excels in dignity and nobility any form whatsoever of earthly power, as spiritual interests exceed the temporal in importance. All this we see fairly from the giving of tithes, from the benediction and sanctification, from the recognition of this power and the control of the same things. For the truth bearing witness, it is for the spiritual power to establish the earthly power and judge it, if it be not good. Thus, in the case of the Church and the power of the Church, the prophecy of Jeremiah is fulfilled: "See, I have this day set thee over the nations and over the kingdoms"—and so forth. Therefore, if the earthly power shall err, it shall be judged by the spiritual power; if the lesser spiritual power err, it shall be judged by the higher. But if the supreme power err, it can be judged by God alone and not by man, the apostles bearing witness saying, the spiritual man judges all things but he himself is judged by no one. Hence this power, although given to man and exercised by man, is not human, but rather divine power, given by the divine lips to Peter, and founded on a rock for Him and his successors in Him whom he confessed, the Lord saying to Peter himself, "Whatsoever thou shalt bind," etc. Whoever, therefore, shall resist this power, ordained by God, resists the ordination of God, unless there should be two beginnings, as the Manichaean imagines. But this we judge to be false and heretical, since, by the testimony of Moses, not in the *beginnings*, but in the *beginning*, God created the heaven and the earth. We, moreover, proclaim, declare, and pronounce that it is altogether necessary to salvation for every human being to be subject to the Roman Pontiff.

Given at the Lateran the twelfth day before the Kalends of December, in our eighth year, as a perpetual memorial of this matter.

Hildegard of Bingen

The tenth child of a minor nobleman, Hildegard of Bingen (1098–1179) entered the convent at the age of eight. This in itself was not unusual. Noble families often found it easier, not to mention less expensive, to place younger daughters in convents than to find them eligible husbands. What is unusual is that Hildegard experienced spiritual visions from her early childhood on. Moreover, she was blessed with a mentor, the monk Volmar, who encouraged her to write down her thoughts and experiences. In 1147 Volmar brought Hildegard to the attention of Heinrich, archbishop of Mainz, who in turn shared her writings with Pope Eugenius. Eugenius was impressed with what he read and gave sanction for Hildegard to continue her work. Thus, at the age of forty-nine, Hildegard embarked on a public career in which she would write six full-length works, found two monasteries, and correspond with many of Europe's most important secular and religious leaders.

The two letters included here deal with a bitter conflict that occurred in the last year of Hildegard's life. Hildegard had permitted the burial in consecrated ground of a noble who had once been excommunicated. The prelates of Mainz contended that the noble had never been absolved and that his corpse must be exhumed and removed. When Hildegard refused, the prelates placed Hildegard and her community under an interdict that all but amounted to excommunication. In the first letter, Hildegard writes to the prelates at Mainz urging them to lift the interdict, a request the prelates ignored. In time, the issue came to the attention of the prelate's superior, Christian, archbishop of Mainz, who, in the second letter, agrees to lift the interdict. As you read the letters, pay particular attention to the strategies Hildegard used to influence her male audience. How did she reconcile her duty to obey her superiors with her commitment to follow her conscience?

Consider the following questions as you study the text below.

1. Why did Hildegard feel that music was so important to divine worship? How did she use musical imagery to make her case?

2. Why was Hildegard willing to defy the prelates? How would you explain Christian's decision to lift the interdict?

Hildegard to the Prelates at Mainz

By a vision, which was implanted in my soul by God the Great Artisan before I was born, I have been compelled to write these things because of the interdict by which our superiors have bound us, on account of a certain dead man buried at our monastery, a man buried without any objection, with his own priest officiating. Yet only a few days after his burial, these men ordered us to remove him from our cemetery. Seized by no small terror, as a result, I looked as usual to the True Light, and, with wakeful eyes, I saw in my spirit that if this man were disinterred in accordance with their commands, a terrible and lamentable danger would come upon us like a dark cloud before a threatening thunderstorm.

Therefore, we have not presumed to remove the body of the deceased inasmuch as he had confessed his sins, had received extreme unction and communion, and had been buried without objection. Furthermore, we have not yielded to those who advised or even commanded this course of action. Not, certainly, that we take the counsel of upright men or the orders of our superiors lightly, but we would not have it appear that, out of feminine harshness we did injustice to the sacraments of Christ, with which this man had been fortified while he was still alive. But so that we may not be totally disobedient we have, in accordance with their injunction, ceased from singing the divine praises and from participation in Mass, as had been our regular monthly custom.

As a result, my sisters and I have been greatly distressed and saddened. Weighed down by this burden, therefore, I heard these words in a vision: It is improper for you to obey human words ordering you to abandon the sacrament of the Garment of the Word of God, Who, born virginally of the Virgin Mary, is your salvation. Still, it is incumbent upon you to seek permission to participate in the sacraments from those prelates who laid the obligation of obedience upon you. For ever since Adam was driven from the bright region of paradise into the exile of this world on account of his disobedience, the conception of all people is justly tainted by that first transgression. Therefore, in accordance with God's inscrutable plan, it was necessary for a man free from all pollution to be born in human flesh, through whom all who are predestined to life might be cleansed from corruption and might be sanctified by the communion of his body so that he might remain in them and they in him for their fortification. That person, however, who is disobedient to the commands of God, as Adam was, and is completely forgetful of Him must be completely cut off from participation in

Hildegard of Bingen, *The Letters of Hildegard of Bingen*, Vol. I, trans. Joseph L. Baird and Radd K. Ehrman (New York: Oxford University Press, 1994). Reprinted by permission of Oxford University Press.

the sacrament of His body, just as he himself has turned away from Him in disobedience. And he must remain so until, purged through penitence, he is permitted by the authorities to receive the communion of the Lord's body again. In contrast, however, a person who is aware that he has incurred such a restriction not as a result of anything that he has done, either consciously or deliberately, may be present at the service of the life-giving sacrament, to be cleansed by the Lamb without sin, Who, in obedience to the Father, allowed Himself to be sacrificed on the altar of the cross that he might restore salvation to all.

In that same vision I also heard that I had erred in not going humbly and devoutly to my superiors for permission to participate in the communion, especially since we were not at fault in receiving that dead man into our cemetery. For, after all, he had been fortified by his own priest with proper Christian procedure, and, without objection from anyone, was buried in our cemetery, with all Bingen joining in the funeral procession. And so God has commanded me to report these things to you, our lords and prelates. Further, I saw in my vision also that by obeying you we have been celebrating the divine office incorrectly, for from the time of your restriction up to the present, we have ceased to sing the divine office, merely reading it instead. And I heard a voice coming from the Living Light concerning the various kinds of praises, about which David speaks in the psalm: "Praise Him with sound of trumpet: praise Him with psaltery and harp," and so forth up to this point: "Let every spirit praise the Lord" [Ps 150.3, 6]. These words use outward, visible things to teach us about inward things. Thus the material composition and the quality of these instruments instruct us how we ought to give form to the praise of the Creator and turn all the convictions of our inner being to the same. When we consider these things carefully, we recall that man needed the voice of the living Spirit, but Adam lost this divine voice through disobedience. For while he was still innocent, before his transgression, his voice blended fully with the voices of the angels in their praise of God. Angels are called spirits from that Spirit which is God, and thus they have such voices by virtue of their spiritual nature. But Adam lost that angelic voice which he had in paradise, for he fell asleep to that knowledge which he possessed before his sin, just as a person on waking up only dimly remembers what he had seen in his dreams. And so when he was deceived by the trick of the devil and rejected the will of his Creator, he became wrapped up in the darkness of inward ignorance as the just result of his iniquity.

God, however, restores the souls of the elect to that pristine blessedness by infusing them with the light of truth. And in accordance with His eternal plan, He so devised it that whenever He renews the hearts of many with the pouring out of the prophetic spirit, they might, by means of His interior illumination, regain some of the knowledge which Adam had before he was punished for his sin.

And so the holy prophets, inspired by the Spirit which they had received, were called for this purpose: not only to compose psalms and canticles (by which the hearts of listeners would be inflamed) but also to construct various kinds of musical instruments to enhance these songs of praise with melodic strains. Thereby, both through the form and quality of the instruments, as well as through the meaning of the words which accompany them, those who hear might be taught, as we said above, about inward things, since they have been admonished and aroused by outward things. In such a way, these holy prophets get beyond the music of this exile and recall to mind that divine melody of praise which Adam, in company with the angels, enjoyed in God before his fall.

Men of zeal and wisdom have imitated the holy prophets and have themselves, with human skill, invented several kinds of musical instruments, so that they might be able to sing for the delight of their souls, and they accompanied their singing with instruments played with the flexing of the fingers, recalling, in this way, Adam, who was formed by God's finger, which is the Holy Spirit. For, before he sinned, his voice had the sweetness of all musical harmony. Indeed, if he had remained in his original state, the weakness of mortal man would not have been able to endure the power and the resonance of his voice.

But when the devil, man's great deceiver, learned that man had begun to sing through God's inspiration and, therefore, was being transformed to bring back the sweetness of the songs of heaven, mankind's homeland, he was so terrified at seeing his clever machinations go to ruin that he was greatly tormented. Therefore, he devotes himself continually to thinking up and working out all kinds of wicked contrivances. Thus he never ceases from confounding confession and the sweet beauty of both divine praise and spiritual hymns, eradicating them through wicked suggestions, impure thoughts, or various distractions from the heart of man and even from the mouth of the Church itself, wherever he can, through dissension, scandal, or unjust oppression.

Therefore, you and all prelates must exercise the greatest vigilance to clear the air by full and thorough discussion of the justification for such actions before your verdict closes the mouth of any church singing praises to God or suspends it from handling or receiving the divine sacraments. And you must be especially certain that you are drawn to this action out of zeal for God's justice, rather than out of indignation, unjust emotions, or a desire for revenge, and you must always be on your guard not to be circumvented in your decisions by Satan, who drove man from celestial harmony and the delights of paradise.

Consider, too, that just as the body of Jesus Christ was born of the purity of the Virgin Mary through the operation of the Holy Spirit so, too, the canticle of praise, reflecting celestial harmony, is rooted in the Church through the Holy Spirit. The body is the vestment of the spirit, which has a living voice, and so it is proper for the body, in harmony with the soul, to use its voice to sing praises to God. Whence, in metaphor, the prophetic spirit commands us to praise God with clashing cymbals and cymbals of jubilation [cf. Ps 150.5], as well as other musical instruments which men of wisdom and zeal have invented, because all arts pertaining to things useful and necessary for mankind have been created by the breath that God sent into man's body. For this reason it is proper that God be praised in all things.

And because sometimes a person sighs and groans at the sound of singing, remembering, as it were, the nature of celestial harmony, the prophet, aware that the soul is symphonic and thoughtfully reflecting on the profound nature of the spirit, urges us in the psalm [cf. Ps 32.2, 91.4] to confess to the Lord with the harp and to sing a psalm to Him with the ten-stringed psaltery. His meaning is that the harp, which is plucked from below, relates to the discipline of the body; the psaltery, which is plucked from above, pertains to the exertion of the spirit; the ten chords, to the fulfillment of the law.

Therefore, those who, without just cause, impose silence on a church and prohibit the singing of God's praises and those who have on earth unjustly despoiled God of His honor and glory will lose their place among the chorus of angels, unless they have amended their lives through true penitence and humble restitution. Moreover, let those who hold the keys of heaven beware not to open those things which are to be kept closed nor to close those things which are to be kept open, for harsh judgment will fall upon those who rule, unleess, as the apostle says [cf. Rom 12.8], they rule with good judgment.

And I heard a voice saying thus: Who created heaven? God. Who opens heaven to the faithful? God. Who is like Him? No one. And so, O men of faith, let none of you resist Him or oppose Him, lest He fall on you in His might and you have no helper to protect you from His judgment. This time is a womanish time, because the dispensation of God's justice is weak. But the strength of God's justice is exerting itself, a female warrior battling against injustice, so that it might fall defeated.

Christian, Archbishop of Mainz, to Hildegard

Christian, archbishop of Mainz by the grace of God, to Hildegard, revered lady and beloved in Christ, and to all the brides of Christ who serve God with her, with a prayer that they might ascend from virtue unto virtue and see the God of gods in Zion [cf. Ps 83.8].

Although in the wondrous and praiseworthy power of God and the mercy of our Savior, we are woefully inadequate, nay rather completely unworthy, yet, dearest lady in Christ, having the utmost confidence in your faithful prayers that we may be made worthy, we honor with our thanks

Him from whom descends "every best gift, and every perfect gift . . . coming down from the Father of lights" [James 1.17]. For He has been pleased, and rightly so, with your soul and has illuminated it with His true and unfathomable light, and His continuing grace has been granted to your saintly devotion, to sit with Mary at the feet of the Lord [cf. Luke 10.39] and receive visions of the heavenly Jerusalem.

Dearest lady in Christ, these obvious signs of your holy life and such amazing testimonies to the truth oblige us to obey your commands and to pay especial heed to your entreaties. Thus we are rightly obliged to cast the gaze of our heart to whatever we know has been granted to your saintly prayers. And having the greatest confidence in your sanctity (next only to that we owe God), we hope, through the sacred odor of your prayers, to attain God's eternal grace. We also hope that this sinful soul of ours, made the more acceptable through your saintly intercession, will obtain the mercy of its Creator.

Hence, with regard to the tribulation and affliction which you and yours are enduring because of the suspension of the divine offices, the clearer your innocence in this matter becomes to us, the more firmly we sympathize with you. Nevertheless, the Church held that the man buried in your churchyard had incurred the sentence of excommunication while he was alive, and although some doubt remained concerning his absolution, the fact that you disregarded the outcry of the clergy and acted as if this would cause no scandal in the Church was a very dangerous act, since the statutes of the holy fathers are inviolable. You should have waited for definitive proof based on the suitable testimony of good men in the presence of the Church.

Yet we wholeheartedly sympathize with your affliction, as is only right, and therefore we have written back to the church at Mainz to this effect: we grant you the privilege of celebrating the divine offices again, on the condition that proof of the dead man's absolution has been established by the testimony of reliable men. In the meantime, saintly lady, if we have caused you annoyance in this matter, either out of guilt or ignorance, we earnestly beseech you not to withhold your compassion from one who seeks pardon. May you deign to pray the Father of mercies to present us unblemished to your sight and to the church at Mainz, for the glory of God and the honor of your church and for the salvation of our soul. May the Lord preserve your wholeness and holiness.

St. Thomas Aquinas

St. Thomas Aquinas (1225–1274), the leading philosopher and theologian of medieval scholasticism, was one of the greatest synthesizers in Western thought. The task he undertook was to reconcile the philosophy of Aristotle, rediscovered by European scholars through their contacts with the Muslims in Spain and elsewhere, with Christian theology. During a relatively short lifetime, he succeeded in combining these two disparate elements into a single comprehensive system of thought capable in principle of explaining everything in the universe that people could know. Questions have been raised about the logical consistency of the Thomistic synthesis, but, whether successful or not, it still stands as a substantial intellectual achievement.

Of noble Italian lineage, Thomas decided early in life to become a Dominican monk, much to the displeasure of his family. As a student, he was nicknamed "the dumb ox" because of his quietness and ponderous bulk. Later, as a teacher at the University of Paris, he was so popular that it was difficult to find a hall large enough to accommodate the students who flocked to his lectures. Although he based his religious beliefs ultimately on faith, Thomas did not abandon reason. Rather, as the first selection (from his *Summa Contra Gentiles*) makes clear, he held that faith and reason could never be in conflict. In the second selection, from his *Summa Theologica*, he argues that reason is capable of proving that God exists. Thomas's five arguments invite scrutiny. Do they, as he claims, establish the conclusion he draws from them, or do they fail in their task?

Consider the following questions as you study the text below.

1. According to Aquinas, what was the difference between "objects of belief" and "objects of faith"? What was the relationship between these two kinds of truth? Why were these questions so pressing in the thirteenth century?

2. For Aquinas, was the existence of God an object of belief or an object of faith? What arguments did he use to support his assertion that God existed?

Summa Contra Gentiles

Chapter III

IN WHAT WAY IT IS POSSIBLE
TO MAKE KNOWN THE DIVINE TRUTH

Since, however, not every truth is to be made known in the same way,

and it is the part of an educated man to seek for conviction in each subject, only so far as the nature of the subject allows,

as the Philosopher[1] most rightly observes as quoted by Boethius, it is necessary to show first of all in what way it is possible to make known the aforesaid truth.

Now in those things which we hold about God there is truth in two ways. For certain things that are true about God wholly surpass the capability of human reason, for instance that God is three and one: while there are certain things to which even natural reason can attain, for instance that God is, that God is one, and others like these, which even the philosophers proved demonstratively of God, being guided by the light of natural reason.

That certain divine truths wholly surpass the capability of human reason, is most clearly evident. For since the principle of all the knowledge which the reason acquires about a thing, is the understanding of that thing's essence, because according to the Philosopher's teaching the principle of a demonstration is *what a thing is*, it follows that our knowledge about a thing will be in proportion to our understanding of its essence. Wherefore, if the human intellect comprehends the essence of a particular thing, for instance a stone or a triangle, no truth about that thing will surpass the capability of human reason. But this does not happen to us in relation to God, because the human intellect is incapable by its natural power of attaining to the comprehension of His essence: since our intellect's knowledge, according to the mode of the present life, originates from the senses: so that things which are not objects of sense cannot be comprehended by the human intellect, except in so far as knowledge of them is gathered from sensibles. Now sensibles cannot lead our intellect to see in them what God is, because they are effects unequal to the power of their cause. And yet our intellect is led by sensibles to the divine knowledge so as to know about God that He is, and other such

[1][Aristotle—*Ed.*]

The "Summa Contra Gentiles" of St. Thomas Aquinas, trans. Fathers of the English Dominican Province (London: Burns & Oates, Ltd.; New York: Benziger Brothers, Inc., 1924), Vol. I, pp. 4–15. Courtesy of Benziger Brothers, Inc., and Burns & Oates, Ltd.

truths, which need to be ascribed to the first principle. Accordingly some divine truths are attainable by human reason, while others altogether surpass the power of human reason.

Again. The same is easy to see from the degrees of intellects. For if one of two men perceives a thing with his intellect with greater subtlety, the one whose intellect is of a higher degree understands many things which the other is altogether unable to grasp; as instanced in a yokel who is utterly incapable of grasping the subtleties of philosophy. Now the angelic intellect surpasses the human intellect more than the intellect of the cleverest philosopher surpasses that of the most uncultured. For an angel knows God through a more excellent effect than does man, for as much as the angel's essence, through which he is led to know God by natural knowledge, is more excellent than sensible things, even than the soul itself, by which the human intellect mounts to the knowledge of God. And the divine intellect surpasses the angelic intellect much more than the angelic surpasses the human. For the divine intellect by its capacity equals the divine essence, wherefore God perfectly understands of Himself what He is, and He knows all the things that can be understood about Him: whereas the angel knows not what God is by his natural knowledge, because the angel's essence, by which he is led to the knowledge of God, is an effect unequal to the power of its cause. Consequently an angel is unable by his natural knowledge to grasp all that God understands about Himself: nor again is human reason capable of grasping all that an angel understands by his natural power. Accordingly just as a man would show himself to be a most insane fool if he declared the assertions of a philosopher to be false because he was unable to understand them, so, and much more, a man would be exceedingly foolish, were he to suspect of falsehood the things revealed by God through the ministry of His angels, because they cannot be the object of reason's investigations.

Furthermore. The same is made abundantly clear by the deficiency which every day we experience in our knowledge of things. For we are ignorant of many of the properties of sensible things, and in many cases we are unable to discover the nature of those properties which we perceive by our senses. Much less therefore is human reason capable of investigating all the truths about the most sublime existence.

With this the saying of the Philosopher is in accord where he says that *our intellect in relation to those primary things which are most evident in nature is like the eye of a bat in relation to the sun.*

To this truth Holy Writ also bears witness. For it is written (Job xi. 7): *Peradventure thou wilt comprehend the steps of God and wilt find out the Almighty perfectly?* and (xxxvi. 26) *Behold God is great, exceeding our knowledge,* and (I Cor. xiii. 9): *We know in part.*

Therefore all that is said about God, though it cannot be investigated by reason, must not be forthwith rejected as false, as the Manicheans and many unbelievers have thought.

Chapter IV

THAT THE TRUTH ABOUT DIVINE THINGS
WHICH IS ATTAINABLE BY REASON
IS FITTINGLY PROPOSED TO MAN AS AN OBJECT OF BELIEF

While then the truth of the intelligible things of God is twofold, one to which the inquiry of reason can attain, the other which surpasses the whole range of human reason, both are fittingly proposed by God to man as an object of belief. We must first show this with regard to that truth which is attainable by the inquiry of reason, lest it appears to some, that since it can be attained by reason, it was useless to make it an object of faith by supernatural inspiration. Now three disadvantages would result if this truth were left solely to the inquiry of reason. One is that few men would have knowledge of God: because very many are hindered from gathering the fruit of diligent inquiry, which is the discovery of truth, for three reasons. Some indeed on account of an indisposition of temperament, by reason of which many are naturally indisposed to knowledge: so that no efforts of theirs would enable them to reach to the attainment of the highest degree of human knowledge, which consists in knowing God. Some are hindered by the needs of household affairs. For there must needs be among men some that devote themselves to the conduct of temporal affairs, who would be unable to devote so much time to the leisure of contemplative research as to reach the summit of human inquiry, namely the knowledge of God. And some are hindered by laziness. For in order to acquire the knowledge of God in those things which reason is able to investigate, it is necessary to have a previous knowledge of many things: since almost the entire consideration of philosophy is directed to the knowledge of God: for which reason metaphysics, which is about divine things, is the last of the parts of philosophy to be studied. Wherefore it is not possible to arrive at the inquiry about the aforesaid truth except after a most laborious study: and few are willing to take upon themselves this labour for the love of a knowledge, the natural desire for which has nevertheless been instilled into the mind of man by God.

The second disadvantage is that those who would arrive at the discovery of the aforesaid truth would scarcely succeed in doing so after a long time. First, because this truth is so profound, that it is only after long practice that the human intellect is enabled to grasp it by means of reason. Secondly, because many things are required beforehand, as stated above. Thirdly, because at the time of youth, the mind, when tossed about by the various movements of the passions, is not fit for the knowledge of so sublime a truth, whereas *calm gives prudence and knowledge*, as stated in 7 *Phys.* Hence mankind would remain in the deepest darkness of ignorance, if the path of reason were the only available way to the knowledge of God: because the knowledge of God which especially makes men perfect and good, would be acquired only by the few, and by these only after a long time.

The third disadvantage is that much falsehood is mingled with the investigations of human reason, on account of the weakness of our intellect in forming its judgments, and by reason of the admixture of phantasms. Consequently many would remain in doubt about those things even which are most truly demonstrated, through ignoring the force of the demonstration: especially when they perceive that different things are taught by the various men who are called wise. Moreover among the many demonstrated truths, there is sometimes a mixture of falsehood that is not demonstrated, but assumed for some probable or sophistical reason which at times is mistaken for a demonstration. Therefore it was necessary that definite certainty and pure truth about divine things should be offered to man by the way of faith.

Accordingly the divine clemency has made this salutary commandment, that even some things which reason is able to investigate must be held by faith: so that all may share in the knowledge of God easily, and without doubt or error.

Hence it is written (Eph. iv. 17, 18): That *henceforth you walk not as also the Gentiles walk in the vanity of their mind, having their understanding darkened*; and (Isa. liv. 13): *All thy children shall be taught of the Lord*.

Chapter V

THAT THOSE THINGS WHICH CANNOT BE INVESTIGATED BY REASON ARE FITTINGLY PROPOSED TO MAN AS AN OBJECT OF FAITH

It may appear to some that those things which cannot be investigated by reason ought not to be proposed to man as an object of faith: because divine wisdom provides for each thing according to the mode of its nature. We must therefore prove that it is necessary also for those things which surpass reason to be proposed by God to man as an object of faith.

For no man tends to do a thing by his desire and endeavour unless it be previously known to him. Wherefore since man is directed by divine providence to a higher good than human frailty can attain in the present life, as we shall show in the sequel, it was necessary for his mind to be bidden to something higher than those things to which our reason can reach in the present life, so that he might learn to aspire, and by his endeavors to tend to something surpassing the whole state of the present life. And this is especially competent to the Christian religion, which alone promises goods spiritual and eternal: for which reason it proposes many things surpassing the thought of man: whereas the old law which contained promises of temporal things, proposed few things that are above human inquiry. It was with this motive that the philosophers, in order to wean men from sensible pleasures to virtue, took care to show that there are other goods of greater account than those which appeal to the senses, the taste of which things affords much greater delight to those who devote themselves to active or contemplative virtues.

Again it is necessary for this truth to be proposed to man as an object of faith in order that he may have truer knowledge of God. For then alone do we know God truly, when we believe that He is far above all that man can possibly think of God, because the divine essence surpasses man's natural knowledge, as stated above. Hence by the fact that certain things about God are proposed to man, which surpass his reason, he is strengthened in his opinion that God is far above what he is able to think.

There results also another advantage from this, namely, the checking of presumption which is the mother of error. For some there are who presume so far on their wits that they think themselves capable of measuring the whole nature of things by their intellect, in that they esteem all things true which they see, and false which they see not. Accordingly, in order that man's mind might be freed from this presumption, and seek the truth humbly, it was necessary that certain things far surpassing his intellect should be proposed to man by God.

Yet another advantage is made apparent by the words of the Philosopher (10 *Ethic.*). For when a certain Simonides maintained that man should neglect the knowledge of God, and apply his mind to human affairs, and declared that *a man ought to relish human things, and a mortal, mortal things*: the Philosopher contradicted him, saying that *a man ought to devote himself to immortal and divine things as much as he can*. Hence he says (11 *De Anima.*) that though it is but little that we perceive of higher substances, yet that little is more loved and desired than all the knowledge we have of lower substances. He says also (2 *De Coelo et Mundo*) that when questions about the heavenly bodies can be answered by a short and probable solution, it happens that the hearer is very much rejoiced. All this shows that however imperfect the knowledge of the highest things may be, it bestows very great perfection on the soul: and consequently, although human reason is unable to grasp fully things that are above reason, it nevertheless acquires much perfection, if at least it hold things, in any way whatever, by faith.

Wherefore it is written (Eccles. iii. 25): *Many things are shown to thee above the understanding of men*, and (I Cor. ii. 10, 11): *The things . . . that are of God no man knoweth, but the Spirit of God: but to us God hath revealed them by His Spirit.*

Chapter VI

THAT IT IS NOT A MARK OF LEVITY TO ASSENT TO THE THINGS THAT ARE OF FAITH, ALTHOUGH THEY ARE ABOVE REASON

Now those who believe this truth, *of which reason affords a proof*, believe not lightly, as though *following foolish fables* (2 Pet. i. 16). For divine Wisdom Himself, Who knows all things most fully, designed to reveal to man *the secrets of God's wisdom*: and by suitable arguments proves His presence, and the truth of His doctrine and inspiration, by performing works surpassing the capability of the whole of nature, namely, the wondrous healing of the sick, the raising of the dead to life, a marvellous control over the heavenly bodies, and what excites yet more wonder, the inspiration of human minds, so that unlettered and simple persons are filled with the Holy Ghost, and in one instant are endowed with the most sublime wisdom and eloquence. And after considering these arguments, convinced by the strength of the proof, and not by the force of arms, nor by the promise of delights, but—and this is the greatest marvel of all—amidst the tyranny of persecutions, a countless crowd of not only simple but also of the wisest men, embraced the Christian faith, which inculcates things surpassing all human understanding, curbs the pleasures of the flesh, and teaches contempt of all worldly things. That the minds of mortal beings should assent to such things, is both the greatest of miracles, and the evident work of divine inspiration, seeing that they despise visible things and desire only those that are invisible. And that this happened not suddenly nor by chance, but by the disposition of God, is shown by the fact that God foretold that He would do so by the manifold oracles of the prophets, whose books we hold in veneration as bearing witness to our faith. This particular kind of proof is alluded to in the words of Heb. ii, 3, 4: *Which*, namely the salvation of mankind, *having begun to be declared by the Lord, was confirmed with us by them that heard Him, God also bearing witness by signs and wonders, and divers . . . distributions of the Holy Ghost.*

Now such a wondrous conversion of the world to the Christian faith is a most indubitable proof that such signs did take place, so that there is no need to repeat them, seeing that there is evidence of them in their result. For it would be the most wondrous sign of all if without any wondrous signs the world were persuaded by simple and lowly men to believe things so arduous, to accomplish things so difficult, and to hope for things so sublime. Although God ceases not even in our time to work miracles through His saints in confirmation of the faith.

On the other hand those who introduced the errors of the sects proceeded in contrary fashion, as instanced by Mohammed, who enticed people with the promise of carnal pleasures, to the desire of which the concupiscence of the flesh instigates. He also delivered commandments in keeping with his promises, by giving the reins to carnal pleasure, wherein it is easy for carnal men to obey: and the lessons of truth which he inculcated were only such as can be easily known to any man of average wisdom by his natural powers: yea, rather the truths which he taught were mingled by him with many fables and most false doctrines. Nor did he add any signs of supernatural agency, which alone are a fitting witness to divine inspiration, since a visible work that can be from God alone, proves the teacher of truth to be invisibly inspired: but he asserted that he was sent in the power of arms, a sign that is not lacking even to robbers and tyrants. Again, those who believed in him from the outset were not wise men practised in things divine and human, but beastlike men who dwelt in the wilds, utterly ignorant of all divine teaching; and it was by a multitude of such men and the force of arms that he impelled others to submit to his law.

Lastly, no divine oracles or prophets in a previous age bore witness to him; rather he did corrupt almost all the teaching of the Old and New Testaments by a narrative replete with fables, as one may see by a perusal of his law. Hence by a cunning device, he did not commit the reading of the Old and New Testament Books to his followers, lest he should thereby be convicted of falsehood. Thus it is evident that those who believe his words believe lightly.

Chapter VII

THAT THE TRUTH OF REASON
IS NOT IN OPPOSITION TO THE TRUTH
OF THE CHRISTIAN FAITH

Now though the aforesaid truth of the Christian faith surpasses the ability of human reason, nevertheless those things which are naturally instilled in human reason cannot be opposed to this truth. For it is clear that those things which are implanted in reason by nature, are most true, so much so that it is impossible to think them to be false. Nor is it lawful to deem false that which is held by faith, since it is so evidently confirmed by God. Seeing then that the false alone is opposed to the true, as evidently appears if we examine their definitions, it is impossible for the aforesaid truth of faith to be contrary to those principles which reason knows naturally.

Again. The same thing which the disciple's mind receives from its teacher is contained in the knowledge of the teacher, unless he teach insincerely, which it were wicked to say of God. Now the knowledge of naturally known principles is instilled into us by God, since God Himself is the author of our nature. Therefore the divine Wisdom also contains these principles. Consequently whatever is contrary to these principles, is contrary to the divine Wisdom; wherefore it cannot be from God. Therefore those things which are received by faith from divine revelation cannot be contrary to our natural knowledge.

Moreover. Our intellect is stayed by contrary arguments, so that it cannot advance to the knowledge of truth. Wherefore if conflicting knowledges were instilled into us by God, our intellect would thereby be hindered from knowing the truth. And this cannot be ascribed to God.

Furthermore. Things that are natural are unchangeable so long as nature remains. Now contrary opinions alone cannot be together in the same subject. Therefore God does not instil into man any opinion or belief contrary to natural knowledge.

Hence the Apostle says (Rom. x. 8): *Thy word is nigh thee even in thy heart and in thy mouth. This is the word of faith which we preach*. Yet because it surpasses reason some look upon it as though it were contrary thereto; which is impossible.

This is confirmed also by the authority of Augustine who says *That which truth shall make known can nowise be in opposition to the holy books whether of the Old or of the New Testament*.

From this we may evidently conclude that whatever arguments are alleged against the teachings of faith, they do not rightly proceed from the first self-evident principles instilled by nature. Wherefore they lack the force of demonstration, and are either probable or sophistical arguments, and consequently it is possible to solve them.

Summa Theologica

Third Article.

WHETHER GOD EXISTS?

The existence of God can be proved in five ways.

The first and more manifest way is the argument from motion. It is certain, and evident to our senses, that in the world some things are in motion. Now whatever is in motion is put in motion by another, for nothing can be in motion except it is in potentiality to that towards which it is in motion; whereas a thing moves inasmuch as it is in act. For motion is nothing else than the reduction of something from potentiality to actuality. But nothing can be reduced from potentiality to actuality, except by something in a state of actuality. Thus that which is actually hot, as fire, makes wood, which is potentially hot, to be actually hot, and thereby moves and changes it. Now it is not possible that the same thing should be at once in actuality and potentiality in the same respect, but only in different respects. For what is actually hot cannot simultaneously be potentially hot; but it is simultaneously potentially

Trans. Fathers of the English Dominican Province.

cold. It is therefore impossible that in the same respect and in the same way a thing should be both mover and moved, *i.e.*, that it should move itself. Therefore, whatever is in motion must be put in motion by another. If that by which it is put in motion be itself put in motion, then this also must needs be put in motion by another, and that by another again. But this cannot go on to infinity, because then there would be no first mover, and, consequently, no other mover; seeing that subsequent movers move only inasmuch as they are put in motion by the first mover; as the staff moves only because it is put in motion by the hand. Therefore it is necessary to arrive at a first mover, put in motion by no other; and this everyone understands to be God.

The second way is from the nature of the efficient cause. In the world of sense we find there is an order of efficient causes. There is no case known (neither is it, indeed, possible) in which a thing is found to be the efficient cause of itself; for so it would be prior to itself, which is impossible. Now in efficient causes it is not possible to go on to infinity, because in all efficient causes following in order, the first is the cause of the intermediate cause, and the intermediate is the cause of the ultimate cause, whether the intermediate cause be several, or one only. Now to take away the cause is to take away the effect. Therefore, if there be no first cause among efficient causes, there will be no ultimate, nor any intermediate cause. But if in efficient causes it is possible to go on to infinity, there will be no first efficient cause, neither will there be an ultimate effect, nor any intermediate efficient causes; all of which is plainly false. Therefore it is necessary to admit a first efficient cause, to which everyone gives the name of God.

The third way is taken from possibility and necessity, and runs thus. We find in nature things that are possible to be and not to be, since they are found to be generated, and to corrupt, and consequently, they are possible to be and not to be. But it is impossible for these always to exist, for that which is possible not to be at some time is not. Therefore, if everything is possible not to be, then at one time there could have been nothing in existence. Now if this were true, even now there would be nothing in existence, because that which does not exist only begins to exist by something already existing. Therefore, if at one time nothing was in existence, it would have been impossible for anything to have begun to exist; and thus even now nothing would be in existence—which is absurd. Therefore, not all beings are merely possible, but there must exist something the existence of which is necessary. But every necessary thing either has its necessity caused by another, or not. Now it is impossible to go on to infinity in necessary things which have their necessity caused by another, as has been already proved in regard to efficient causes. Therefore we cannot but postulate the existence of some being having of itself its own necessity, and not receiving it from another, but rather causing in others their necessity. This all men speak of as God.

The fourth way is taken from the gradation to be found in things. Among beings there are some more and some less good, true, noble, and the like. But 'more' and 'less' are predicated of different things, according as they resemble in their different ways something which is the maximum, as a thing is said to be hotter according as it more nearly resembles that which is hottest; so that there is something which is truest, something best, something noblest, and, consequently, something which is uttermost being; for those things that are greatest in truth are greatest in being, as it is written in *Metaph.* ii [Aristotle]. Now the maximum in any genus is the cause of all in that genus; as fire, which is the maximum of heat, is the cause of all hot things. Therefore there must also be something which is to all beings the cause of their being, goodness, and every other perfection; and this we call God.

The fifth way is taken from the governance of the world. We see that things which lack intelligence, such as natural bodies, act for an end, and this is evident from their acting always, or nearly always, in the same way, so as to obtain the best result. Hence it is plain that not fortuitously, but designedly, do they achieve their end. Now whatever lacks intelligence cannot move towards an end, unless it be directed by some being endowed with knowledge and intelligence; as the arrow is shot to its mark by the archer. Therefore some intelligent being exists by whom all natural things are directed to their end; and this being we call God.

Medieval Secular Poetry

Secular poetry, of the type illustrated by the poems included here, developed concurrently, but far from coincidentally, with the beginnings of European universities in the twelfth century. It flourished for over a century but gradually disappeared, largely as a result of ecclesiastical suppression, around the beginning of the fourteenth century. Much of this poetry was the work of a group of writers who became known as the Goliard poets, or the tribe of Golias. The origin of the name is obscure, but it could have been derived from the Old Testament Goliath, who was a Philistine giant sent to wage war against the children of Israel. The poets themselves were wandering scholars, young men who had usually done some studying at one or more of the universities. Finding themselves unwilling to endure the rigors of sustained intellectual endeavor, they had dropped out to join the ranks of academic flotsam drifting about the major medieval centers of learning. Rebels against the established clerical order, they wrote verses that were almost invariably irreverent and sometimes blatantly blasphemous. Yet the poems have a positive side as well. Almost always we find in them a glorification of nature, of life, of pleasures (particularly those of table and bed), and of the flesh in general. They were written to be enjoyed.

The following poems reveal different facets of the writers' interests and attitudes. None of the authors is known, though the first piece is generally ascribed to a man who flourished in the mid-twelfth century and referred to himself, with becoming modesty, as the archpoet of Cologne. All have been translated from their original Latin.

Consider the following questions as you study the text below.

1. For whom were these poems most likely written? Whose values and beliefs do they reflect?

2. Describe the poets' attitudes toward youth. How would you characterize their attitudes toward sin?

The Confession of Golias

Boiling in my spirit's veins With fierce indignation,
From my bitterness of soul Springs self-revelation:
Framed am I of flimsy stuff, Fit for levitation,
Like a thin leaf which the wind Scatters from its station.
While it is the wise man's part With deliberation
On a rock to base his heart's Permanent foundation,
With a running river I Find my just equation,
Which beneath the self-same sky Hath no habitation.
Carried am I like a ship Left without a sailor,
Like a bird that through the air Flies where tempests hale her;
Chains and fetters hold me not, Naught avails a jailer;
Still I find my fellows out Toper, gamester, railer.
To my mind all gravity Is a grave subjection;
Sweeter far than honey are Jokes and free affection.
All that Venus bids me do, Do I with erection,
For she ne'er in heart of man Dwelt with dull dejection.
Down the broad road do I run, As the way of youth is;
Snare myself in sin, and ne'er Think where faith and truth is,
Eager far for pleasure more Than soul's health, the sooth is,
For this flesh of mine I care, Seek not ruth where ruth is.
Prelate, most discreet of priests, Grant me absolution!
Dear's the death whereof I die, Sweet my dissolution;
For my heart is wounded by Beauty's soft suffusion;
All the girls I come not nigh, Mine are in illusion.
'Tis most arduous to make Nature's self-surrender;
Seeing girls, to blush and be Purity's defender!
We young men our longings ne'er Shall to stern law render,
Or preserve our fancies from Bodies smooth and tender.
Who, when into fire he falls, Keeps himself from burning?
Who within Pavia's walls Fame of chaste is earning?
Venus with her finger calls Youth at every turning,
Snares them with her eyes, and thralls With her amorous yearning.
If you brought Hippolitus To Pavia Sunday,
He'd not be Hippolitus On the following Monday;
Venus there keeps holiday Every day as one day;
'Mid these towers no tower dwells Venus Verecunda.
In the second place I own To the vice of gaming:
Cold indeed outside I seem, Yet my soul is flaming:

Trans. John Addington Symonds.

But when once the dice-box hath Stripped me to my shaming,
Make I songs and verses fit For the world's acclaiming.
In the third place, I will speak Of the tavern's pleasure;
For I never found nor find There the least displeasure;
Nor shall find it till I greet Angels without measure,
Singing requiems for the souls In eternal leisure.
In the public-house to die Is my resolution; Let wine to my lips be nigh
        At life's dissolution:
That will make the angels cry, With glad elocution,
"Grant this toper, God on high, Grace and absolution!"
With the cup the soul lights up, Inspirations flicker;
Nectar lifts the soul on high With its heavenly ichor;
To my lips a sounder taste Hath the tavern's liquor
Than the wine a village clerk Waters for the vicar.
Nature gives to every man Some gift serviceable;
Write I never could nor can Hungry at the table;
Fasting, any stripling to Vanquish me is able;
Hunger, thirst, I liken to Death that ends the fable.
Nature gives to every man Gifts as she is willing;
I compose my verses when Good wine I am swilling,
Wine the best for jolly guest Jolly hosts are filling;
From such wine rare fancies fine Flow like dews distilling.
Such my verse is wont to be As the wine I swallow;
No ripe thoughts enliven me While my stomach's hollow;
Hungry wits on hungry lips Like a shadow follow,
But when once I'm in my cups I can beat Apollo.
Never to my spirit yet Flew poetic vision
Until first my belly had Plentiful provision;
Let but Bacchus in the brain Take a strong position,
Then comes Phoebus flowing in With a fine precision.
There are poets, worthy men, Shrink from public places,
And in lurking-hole or den Hide their pallid faces;
There they study, sweat, and woo Pallas and the Graces,
But bring nothing forth to view Worth the girls' embraces.
Fasting, thirsting, toil the bards, Swift years flying o'er them;
Shun the strife of open life, Tumults of the forum;
They, to sing some deathless thing, Lest the world ignore them,
Die the death, expend their breath, Drowned in dull decorum.
Lo! my frailties I've betrayed, Shown you every token,
Told you what your servitors Have against me spoken;
But of those men each and all Leave their sins unspoken,
Though they play, enjoy to-day: Scorn their pledges broken.
Now within the audience-room Of this blessed prelate,
Sent to hunt out vice, and from Hearts of men expel it;

Let him rise, nor spare the bard, Cast at him a pellet:
He whose heart knows not crime's smart, Show my sin and tell it!
I have uttered openly All I knew that shamed me,
And have spued the poison forth That so long defamed me;
Of my old ways I repent, New life hath reclaimed me;
God beholds the heart—'twas man Viewed the face and blamed me.
Goodness now hath won my love, I am wroth with vices;
Made a new man in my mind, Lo, my soul arises!
Like a babe new milk I drink— Milk for me suffices,
Lest my heart should longer be Filled with vain devices.
Thou Elect of fair Cologne, Listen to my pleading!
Spurn not thou the penitent; See, his heart is bleeding!
Give me penance! what is due For my faults exceeding
I will bear with willing cheer, All thy precepts heeding.
Lo the lion, king of beasts, Spares the meek and lowly;
Toward submissive creatures he Tames his anger wholly.
Do the like, ye powers of earth, Temporal and holy!
Bitterness is more than's right When 'tis bitter solely.

Let's Away with Study

Let's away with study, Folly's sweet.
Treasure all the pleasure Of our youth:
Time enough for age To think on truth.
So short a day,
And life so quickly hasting,
And in study wasting Youth that would be gay!
'Tis our spring that slipping, Winter draweth near, Life itself we're losing,
    And this sorry cheer
Dries the blood and cheers the heart, Shrivels all delight.
Age and all its crowd of ills Terrifies our sight.
So short a day,
And life so quickly hasting,
And in study wasting Youth that would be gay!
Let us as the gods do, 'Tis the wiser part:
Leisure and love's pleasure Seek the young in heart
Follow the old fashion, Down into the street!
Down among the maidens, And the dancing feet!

Helen Waddell, *Mediaeval Latin Lyrics*, 5th ed. (London: Constable and Company, Ltd., 1948), p. 221. Courtesy of Constable and Company, Ltd.

So short a day,
And life so quickly hasting,
And in study wasting Youth that would be gay!
There for the seeing Is all loveliness,
White limbs moving Light in wantonness.
Gay go the dancers, I stand and see,
Gaze, till their glances Steal myself from me.
So short a day,
And life so quickly hasting,
And in study wasting Youth that would be gay!

Gaudeamus Igitur

Let us live, then, and be glad While young life's before us! After youthful pastime had, After old age hard and sad, Earth will slumber o'er us.

Where are they who in this world, Ere we kept, were keeping? Go ye to the gods above; Go to hell; inquire thereof: They are not; they're sleeping.

Brief is life, and brevity Briefly shall be ended: Death comes like a whirlwind strong, Bears us with his blast along; None shall be defended.

Live this university, Men that learning nourish; Live each member of the same, Long live all that bear its name; Let them ever flourish!

Live the commonwealth also, And the men that guide it! Live our town in strength and health, Founders, patrons, by whose wealth We are here provided!

Live all girls! A health to you Melting maids and beauteous! Live the wives and women too, Gentle, loving, tender, true, Good, industrious, duteous!

Perish cares that pule and pine! Perish envious blamers! Die the Devil, thine and mine! Die the starch-necked Philistine!

Scoffers and defamers!

Trans. John Addington Symonds.

Jean, Sire de Joinville

The idea of Crusades originated with Pope Urban II in 1095, and during the next two centuries thousands of European knights "took up the cross" (hence the word "Crusade") and headed for the Near East. There was even a children's Crusade in 1212, consisting of several thousand youths (mostly under twelve years of age). None reached their goal, most of the children being sold into slavery along the way.

One of the later Crusades was organized and led by the warrior-king, Louis IX of France in 1248. To mount his Crusade, Louis built a city on the southern coast of France. This city, Aigues Mortes—with its encircling stone walls and giant towers, its chapel where the crusading knights prayed, and its equestrian statue of Louis in the town square—remains today as a living museum of the Middle Ages.

Although the Crusaders finally failed in their primary, religious objective, they succeeded in other ways. Perhaps most importantly, they brought together two disparate cultures—that of Christian Western Europe and that of the Muslim Middle East. This intermingling of cultures was to have substantial effects in the years to follow, particularly on the social and economic structure of the West.

The selection that follows is taken from an account of King Louis's first Crusade, which sailed to the island of Cyprus and then on to Damietta, on the Mediterranean coast of Egypt, written by one of its participants, Jean, Sire de Joinville (1224–1319). Following his victory at Damietta, Louis moved up the Nile against Cairo but his army was defeated and he was captured and held for ransom. The selection is interesting not only for its vivid description of the Crusaders' travels and the battles they fought but as well for the glimpses it gives of feudal society and the knightly caste.

Consider the following questions as you study the text below.

1. What did Joinville choose to emphasize in his narrative? What, if anything, did Joinville tell his readers about the Saracens and their lands?

2. How did Joinville explain the disasters that befell the Crusaders after the capture of Damietta? In his opinion, could defeat have been avoided?

Memoirs

. . .

JOINVILLE LEAVES HIS CASTLE

. . .

I departed from Joinville on foot, barefoot, in my shirt—not to reenter the castle till my return; and thus I went to Blécourt, and Saint-Urbain, and to other places thereabouts where there are holy relics. And never while I went to Blécourt and Saint-Urbain would I turn my eyes towards Joinville for fear my heart should melt within me at the thought of the fair castle I was leaving behind, and my two children.

I and my companions ate that day at Fontaine-l'Archevêque before Donjeux; and the Abbot Adam of Saint-Urbain—whom God have in His grace!—gave a great quantity of fair jewels to myself and the nine knights I had with me. Thence we went to Auxonne, and thence again, with the baggage, which we had placed in boats, from Auxonne to Lyons down the river Saône; and along by the side of the boats were led the great warhorses.

At Lyons we embarked on the Rhône to go to Arles the White; and on the Rhône we found a castle called Roche-de-Glun, which the king had caused to be destroyed, because Roger, the lord of the castle, was accused of robbing pilgrims and merchants.

THE CRUSADERS EMBARK, AUGUST 1248

In the month of August we entered into our ship at the Roche-de-Marseille. On the day that we entered into our ship, they opened the door of the ship and put therein all the horses we were to take overseas; and then they reclosed the door, and caulked it well, as when a cask is sunk in water, because, when the ship is on the high seas, all the said door is under water.

When the horses were in the ship, our master mariner called to his seamen, who stood at the prow, and said: "Are you ready?" and they answered, "Aye, sir—let the clerks and priests come forward!" As soon as these had come forward, he called to them, "Sing, for God's sake!" and they all, with one voice, chanted: "*Veni Creator Spiritus.*"

Then he cried to his seamen "Unfurl the sails, for God's sake!" and they did so.

In a short space the wind filled our sails and had borne us out of sight of land, so that we saw naught save sky and water, and every day the wind

Trans. Frank T. Marzials.

carried us further from the land where we were born. And these things I tell you, that you may understand how foolhardy is that man who dares, having other's chattels in his possession, or being in mortal sin, to place himself in such peril, seeing that, when you lie down to sleep at night on shipboard, you lie down not knowing whether, in the morning, you may find yourself at the bottom of the sea.

At sea a singular marvel befell us; for we came across a mountain, quite round, before the coast of Barbary. We came across it about the hour of vespers, and sailed all night, and thought to have gone about fifty leagues; and, on the morrow, we found ourselves before the same mountain; and this same thing happened to us some two or three times. When the sailors saw this, they were all amazed, and told us we were in very great peril; for we were nigh unto the land of the Saracens of Barbary.

Then spake a certain right worthy priest, who was called the Dean of Maurupt; and he told us that never had any mischance occurred in his parish—whether lack of water, or overplus of rain, or any other mischance—but so soon as he had made three processions, on three Saturdays, God and His mother sent them deliverance. It was then a Saturday. We made the first procession round the two masts of the ship. I had myself carried in men's arms, because I was grievously sick. Never again did we see the mountain, and on the third Saturday we came to Cyprus.

SOJOURN IN CYPRUS—
EMBASSAGE FROM THE TARTARS—
JOINVILLE TAKES SERVICE WITH THE KING

When we came to Cyprus, the king was already there, and we found great quantities of the king's supplies; that is to say, the cellarage of the king, and his treasure, and his granaries. The king's cellarage was set in the middle of the fields, on the shore by the sea. There his people had stacked great barrels of wine, which they had been buying for two years before the king's arrival; and the barrels were stacked one upon the other in such sort that when you looked at them in front, the stacks seemed as if they were barns.

The wheat and the barley they had set up in heaps in the midst of the fields, and when you looked at them, it seemed as if they were mountains, for the rain, which had long been beating on the grain, had caused it to sprout, so that the outside looked like green grass. Now it happened that when they wished to take the grain into Egypt, they took away the upper crust with the green grass, and found the wheat and barley within as fresh as if newly threshed.

The king himself, as I heard tell in Syria, would very willingly have gone on to Egypt, without stopping, had it not been for his barons, who advised him to wait for such of his people as had not yet arrived.

While the king was sojourning in Cyprus, the great king of the Tartars sent envoys to him, with many good and gracious words. Among other things, he signified that he was ready to help the king to conquer the Holy Land, and to deliver Jerusalem from the hands of the Saracens.

The king received the envoys in very friendly fashion, and sent other envoys in return, who remained away two years. And the king, by his envoys, sent to the King of the Tartars a tent made like a chapel, very costly, for it was all of fair, fine scarlet cloth. The king, moreover, to see if he could draw the Tartars to our faith, caused images to be graven in the said chapel, representing the Annunciation of our Lady, and all the other points of the faith. And these things he sent by two brothers of the order of Preachers, who knew the Saracen language, and could show and teach the Tartars what they ought to believe.

The two brothers came back to the king at the time when the king's brothers were returning to France; and they found the king, who had left Acre, where his brothers had parted from him, and had come to Caesarea, which he was fortifying; nor was there at that time any truce or peace with the Saracens. How the king's envoys were received will I tell you, as they themselves told it to the king; and in what they reported you may hear much that is strange and marvellous; but I will not tell you of it now, because, in order to do so, I should have to interrupt matters already begun;—so to proceed.

I, who had not a thousand *livres* yearly in land, had undertaken, when I went oversea, to bear, beside my own charges, the charges of nine knights, and two knights-banneret; and so it happened, when I arrived in Cyprus, that I had no more left, my ship being paid for, than twelve score *livres tournois*; wherefore some of my knights apprised me that if I did not provide myself with moneys, they would leave me. But God, who never failed me yet, provided for me in such fashion that the king, who was at Nicosia, sent for me, and took me into his service, and placed eight hundred livres in my coffers; and thus I had more moneys than I required.

.   .   .

THE HOST LEAVES CYPRUS—1249

As soon as we entered into the month of March, by the king's command the king, the barons, and the other pilgrims ordered that the ships should be re-laden with wine and provisions, so as to be ready to move when the king directed. And when the king saw that all had been duly ordered, the king and queen embarked on their ships on the Friday before Pentecost (21st May 1249), and the king told his barons to follow in their ships straight to Egypt. On the Saturday the king set sail and all the others besides, which was a fair thing to look upon, for it seemed as if all the sea, so far as the eye could reach, were covered by the canvas of the ships' sails; and the number of the ships, great and small, was reckoned at eighteen hundred.

The king anchored at the head of a hillock which is called the Point of Limassol, and all the other vessels anchored round about him. The king landed on the day of Pentecost. After we had heard mass a fierce and powerful wind, coming from the Egyptian side, arose in such sort that out of two thousand eight hundred knights, whom the king was taking into Egypt, there remained no more than seven hundred whom the wind had not separated from the king's company and carried away to Acre and other strange lands; nor did they afterwards return to the king for a long while.

The day after Pentecost the wind had fallen. The king and such of us as had, according to God's will remained with him, set sail forthwith, and met the Prince of Morea, and the Duke of Burgundy, who had been sojourning in Morea. On the Thursday after Pentecost the king arrived before Damietta, and we found there, arrayed on the seashore, all the power of the soldan—a host fair to look upon, for the soldan's arms are of gold, and when the sun struck upon them they were resplendent. The noises they made with their cymbals and horns was fearful to listen to.

The king summoned his barons to take counsel what they should do. Many advised that he should wait till his people returned, seeing that no more than a third part had remained with him; but to this he would by no means agree. The reason he gave was, that to delay would put the foe in good heart, and, particularly, he said that there was no port before Damietta in which he could wait for his people, and that, therefore, any strong wind arising might drive the ships to other lands, like as the ships had been driven on the day after Pentecost.

PREPARATION FOR DISEMBARKATION IN EGYPT

It was settled that the king should land on the Friday before Trinity and do battle with the Saracens, unless they refused to stand. The king ordered my Lord John of Beaumont to assign a galley to my Lord Everard of Brienne and to myself, so as that we might land, we and our knights, because the great ships could not get close up to the shore.

As God so willed, when I returned to my ship, I found a little ship that my Lady of Beyrout, who was cousin-german to my Lord of Montbéliard and to myself, had given me, and that carried eight of my horses.

When the Friday came I and my Lord Everard went, fully armed, to the king and asked for the galley; whereupon my Lord John of Beaumont told us that we should not have it. When our people saw that they would get no galley, they let themselves drop from the great ship into the ship's boat, pell-mell, and as best they could, so that the boat began to sink. The sailors saw that the boat was sinking, little by little, and they escaped into the big ship and left my knights in the boat. I asked the master how many more people there were in the boat than the boat could hold. He told me twenty men-at-arms; and I asked him whether he could take our people to land if I relieved him of so many, and he said, "Yes." So I relieved him in such sort that in three journeys he took them to the ship that had carried my horses.

While I was conducting these people a knight belonging to my Lord Everard of Brienne, and whose name was Plonquet, thought to go down from the great ship into the boat; but the boat moved away, and he fell into the sea and was drowned.

When I came back to my ship I put into my little boat a squire whom I made a knight, and whose name was my Lord Hugh of Vaucouleurs, and two very valiant bachelors—of whom the one had the name my Lord Villain of Versey, and the other my Lord William of Dammartin—who were at bitter enmity the one against the other. Nor could any one make peace between them, because they had seized each other by the hair in Morea. And I made them forgive their grievances and embrace, for I swore to them on holy relics that we should not land in company of their enmity.

Then we set ourselves to get to land, and came alongside of the barge belonging to the king's great ship, there where the king himself was. And his people began to cry to us because we were going more quickly than they, that I should land by the ensign of St. Denis, which was being borne in another vessel before the king. But I heeded them not, and caused my people to land in front of a great body of Turks, at a place where there were full six thousand men on horseback.

So soon as these saw us land, they came toward us, hotly spurring. We, when we saw them coming, fixed the points of our shields into the sand and the handles of our lances in the sand with the points set towards them. But when they were so near that they saw the lances about to enter their bellies, they turned about and fled.

THE CRUSADERS DISEMBARK IN FRONT OF THE SARACENS

My Lord Baldwin of Rheims, a right good man, who had come to land, requested me, by his squire, to wait for him; and I let him know I should do so willingly, for that a right good man such as he ought surely to be waited for in like case of need,—whereby I had his favour all the time that he lived. With him came to us a thousand knights; and you may be assured that, when I landed, I had neither squire, no knight, no varlet that I had brought with me from my own country, and yet God never left me without such as I needed.

At our left hand landed the Count of Jaffa, who was cousin-german to the Count of Montbéliard, and of the lineage of Joinville. It was he who landed in greatest pride, for his galley came all painted, within and without, with escutcheons of his arms, which arms are *or* with a cross of gules *patée*. He had at least three hundred rowers in his galley, and for each rower there was a targe, with the count's arms thereon, and to each targe was a pennon attached with his arms wrought in gold.

While he was coming it seemed as if his galley flew, so did the rowers urge it forward with their sweeps; and it seemed as if the lightning were falling from the skies at the sound that the pennants made, and the cymbals, and the drums, and the Saracenic horns that were in his galley. So soon as the galley had been driven into the sand as far up as they could drive it, both he and his knights leapt from the galley, well armed and well equipped, and came and arrayed themselves beside us.

I had forgotten to tell you that when the Count of Jaffa landed he immediately caused his tents and pavilions to be pitched; and so soon as the Saracens saw them pitched, they all came and gathered before us, and then came on again, spurring hotly, as if to run in upon us. But when they saw that we should not fly, they shortly turned and went back again.

On the right hand, at about a long-crossbow-shot's distance, landed the galley that bore the ensign of St. Denis. And there was a Saracen who, when they had landed, came and charged in around them, either because he could not hold in his horse, or because he thought the other Saracens would follow him; but he was hacked in pieces.

ST. LOUIS TAKES POSSESSION OF DAMIETTA

When the king heard tell that the ensign of St. Denis was on shore he went across his ship with large steps; and maugre the legate who was with him would not leave from following the ensign, but leapt into the sea, which was up to his armpits. So he went, with his shield hung to his neck, and his helmet on his head, and his lance in his hand, till he came to his people who were on the shore. When he reached the land, and looked upon the Saracens, he asked what people they were, and they told him they were Saracens; and he put his lance to his shoulder, and his shield before him, and would have run in upon the Saracens if the right worthy men who were about him would have suffered it.

The Saracens sent thrice to the soldan, by carrier-pigeons, to say that the king had landed, but never received any message in return, because the soldan's sickness was upon him. Wherefore they thought that the soldan was dead, and abandoned Damietta. The king sent a knight forward to know if it was sooth that Damietta was so abandoned. The knight returned to the king and said it was sooth and that he had been in the houses of the soldan. Then the king sent for the legate and all the prelates of the host, and all chanted with a loud voice, *Te Deum laudamus*. Afterwards the king mounted his horse, and we all likewise, and we went and encamped before Damietta.

Very unadvisedly did the Turks leave Damietta, in that they did not cut the bridge of boats, for that would have been a great hindrance to us; but they wrought us very much hurt in setting fire to the bazaar, where all the merchandise is collected, and everything that is sold by weight. The damage that followed from this was as great as if—which God forbid!—some one were, tomorrow, to set fire to the Petit-Pont in Paris.

Now let us declare that God Almighty was very gracious to us when he preserved us from death and peril on our disembarkation, seeing that we landed on foot and affronted our enemies who were mounted. Great grace did our Lord also show us when He delivered Damietta into our hands, for otherwise we could only have taken it by famine, and of this we may be fully assured, for it was by famine that King John had taken it in the days of our fathers (in 1219).

MISTAKE OF ST. LOUIS—DISORDER AMONG THE CRUSADERS

Our Lord can say of us, as He said of the children of Israel—*et pro nihilo habuerunt terram desiderabilem*.[1] And what does He say afterwards? He says that they forgot God their Saviour. And so did we forget Him as I will shortly tell you.

But first I will tell you of the king who summoned his barons, the clerks, and the laymen, and asked them to help him decide how the booty taken in the city should be divided. The patriarch was the first to speak, and he spoke thus: "Sire, methinks it were well that you should keep the wheat, and the barley, and the rice, and whatever is needed to sustain life, so as to provision the city; and that you should have it cried throughout the host that all other goods are to be brought to the legate's quarters, under pain of excommunication." To this advice all the other barons assented. Now, as it fell out, all the goods brought to the legate's quarters did not amount in value to more than six thousand livres.

When this had been done, the king and the barons summoned John of Valery, the right worthy man, and spoke to him thus: "Sir of Valery," said the king, "we are agreed that the legate should hand over to you the six thousand livres, so that you may divide them as may seem best to you." "Sire," replied the right worthy man, "you do me much honour, and great thanks be yours! But, please God! that honour can I not accept, nor can I carry out your wish, for by so doing I should make null the good customs of the Holy Land, whereby, when the cities of the enemy are captured, the king takes a third of the goods found therein, and the pilgrims take two thirds. And this custom was well observed by King John when he took Damietta, and as old folks tell us, the same custom was observed by the kings of Jerusalem, who were before King John. If then it pleases you to hand over to me the two parts of the wheat, and the barley, and the rice, and the other provisions, then shall I willingly undertake to make division among the pilgrims."

The king did not decide to do this; so matters remained as they were; and many were ill-pleased that the king should set aside the good old customs.

---

[1] "They despised the pleasant land."

The king's people, who ought, by liberal dealing, to have retained the merchants, made them pay, so it was said, the highest rents they could exact for the shops in which to sell their goods; and the rumour of this got abroad to foreign lands, so that many merchants forebore to come and bring supplies to the host.

The barons, who ought to have kept what was theirs so as to spend it in fitting time and place, took to giving great feasts, and an outrageous excess of meats. The common people took to consorting with lewd women; whereby it happened, after we returned from captivity, that the king discharged a great many of his people. And when I asked him why he had done this, he told me that he had found, of a certainty, that those whom he had discharged held their ill places of assemblage at a short stone's throw from his pavilion, and that at a time when the host was in greatest distress and misery.

THE SARACENS ATTACK THE CAMP—DEATH OF WALTER OF AUTRÈCHE

Now let us go back to the matter in hand, and tell how, shortly after we had taken Damietta, all the horsemen of the soldan came before the camp, and attacked it from the land side. The king and all the horsemen armed themselves. I, being in full armour, went to speak to the king, and found him fully armed, sitting on a settle, and round him were the right worthy knights belonging to his own division, all in full armour. I asked if he desired that I and my people should issue from the camp, so that the Saracens should not fall upon our tents. When my Lord John of Beaumont heard my question, he cried to me in a very loud voice, and commanded me, in the king's name, not to leave my quarters till the king so ordered.

I have told you of the right worthy knights who were of the king's special following, for there were eight of them, all good knights who had won prizes for arms on the further or hither side of the seas, and such knights it was customary to call good knights. These are the names of the knights about the king:—my Lord Geoffry of Sargines, my Lord Matthew of Marly, my Lord Philip of Nanteuil, and my Lord Imbert of Beaujeu, Constable of France; but the last was not then present, he was outside the camp—he and the master of the crossbowmen, with most of the king's sergeants-at-arms— to guard the camp so that the Turks might not do any mischief thereto.

Now it happened that my Lord Walter Autrèche got himself armed at all points of his pavilion; and when he was mounted upon his horse, with a shield at his neck and his helmet on his head, he caused the flaps of his pavilion to be lifted, and struck spurs into his horse to ride against the Turks; and as he left his pavilion, all alone, all his men shouted with a loud voice, "Chatillon." But so it chanced that or ever he came up to the Turks he fell, and his horse flew over his body; and the horse went on, covered with his arms, to our enemies, because the Saracens were, for the most part, mounted on mares, for which reason the horse drew to the side of the Saracens.

And those who looked on told us that four Turks came by Lord Walter, who lay upon the ground, and as they went by, gave him great blows with their maces there where he lay. Then did the Constable of France and several of the king's sergeants deliver him, and they brought him back in their arms to his pavilion. When he came there he was speechless. Several of the surgeons and physicians of the host went to him, and because it did not seem to them that he was in danger of death, they had him blooded in both arms.

That night, very late, my Lord Aubert of Narcy proposed that we should go and see him, for as yet we had not seen him, and he was a man of great name and of great valour. We entered into his pavilion, and the chamberlain came to meet us, and asked us to move quietly, so as not to wake his master. We found him lying on coverlets of miniver, and went to him very softly, and found him dead. When this was told to the king, he replied that he would not willingly have a thousand such men acting contrary to his orders as this man had done.

RENEWED ATTACKS ON THE PART OF THE SARACENS—THE KING DECIDES TO AWAIT THE ARRIVAL OF THE COUNT OF POITIERS

The Saracens entered every night into the camp on foot and killed our people there where they found them sleeping, whereby it chanced that they killed the sentinel of the lord of Courtenay, and left him lying on a table, and cut off his head, and took it away with them. And this they did because the soldan gave a besant of gold for every Christian man's head.

And we were at this disadvantage because the battalions guarded the camp, each one its night, on horseback; and when the Saracens wished to enter into the camp, they waited till the noise of the horses and of the battalions had passed, and then crept into the camp behind the horses, making their way out before it was day. So the king ordered that the battalion that had been used to keep guard on horseback should keep guard on foot, whereby all the camp was in safety, because of our men who kept guard, and were spread out in such wise that one man touched the other.

After this was done, the king decided not to leave Damietta until his brother, the Count of Poitiers, had arrived with the remaining forces of France. And so that the Saracens might not charge on their horses into the midst of the camp, the king caused all the camp to be enclosed with great earthworks, and on the earthworks were set crossbowmen to watch every night, and sergeants; and such were set also at the entrance to the camp.

Usµmah Ibn-Munqidh

The Muslim warrior and courtier Usµmah Ibn-Munqidh (1095–1188) lived a life that was shaped by the Crusades. Born in the same year that Pope Urban II launched the first European assault on the Holy Land, Usµmah spent most of his life at war, fighting both European and Arab enemies. But Usµmah was more than a soldier. A nobleman, hunter, poet, and scholar, he was as famous for his writings as he was for his skill in battle.

In the excerpt from his *Memoirs* included here, Usµmah tried to provide his countrymen with some insight into the character of the European invaders by describing "some instances of their doings and their curious mentality." As you read the passage, pay close attention to the topics Usµmah focused on in his effort to get at the essential qualities of the Frankish character. What details did he think were most telling? How would you explain his decision to highlight his experiences with European medicine?

Consider the following questions as you study the text below.

1. Did Usµmah see the Franks as fully human? In his view, how did they differ from Arabs? Was it possible for Franks and Arabs to become friends? What obstacles did Usµmah see to mutual understanding between the two groups?

2. Why did Usµmah find it difficult to explain the physical courage and military skill of the Franks? Why did he see a contradiction between their skill in battle and their supposed lack of sexual jealousy?

An Appreciation of the Frankish Character

Their lack of sense.—Mysterious are the works of the Creator, the author of all things! When one comes to recount cases regarding the Franks, he cannot but glorify Allah (exalted is he!) and sanctify him, for he sees them as animals possessing the virtues of courage and fighting, but nothing else; just as animals have only the virtues of strength and carrying loads. I shall now give some instances of their doings and their curious mentality.

Usµmah Ibn-Munqidh, *An Arab-Syrian Gentleman and Warrior in the Period of the Crusades: Memoirs of Usµmah Ibn-Munqidh.* Trans. Philip K. Hitti (New York: Columbia University Press, 1929). Reprinted by permission of Columbia Univeristy Press.

In the army of King Fulk, son of Fulk, was a Frankish reverend knight who had just arrived from their land in order to make the holy pilgrimage and then return home. He was of my intimate fellowship and kept such constant company with me that he began to call me "my brother." Between us were mutual bonds of amity and friendship. When he resolved to return by sea to his homeland, he said to me:

> My brother, I am leaving for my country and I want thee to send with me thy son (my son, who was then fourteen years old, was at that time in my company) to our country, where he can see the knights and learn wisdom and chivalry. When he returns, he will be like a wise man.

Thus there fell upon my ears words which would never come out of the head of a sensible man; for even if my son were to be taken captive, his captivity could not bring him a worse misfortune than carrying him into the lands of the Franks. However, I said to the man:

> By thy life, this has exactly been my idea. But the only thing that prevented me from carrying it out was the fact that his grandmother, my mother, is so fond of him and did not this time let him come out with me until she exacted an oath from me to the effect that I would return him to her.

Thereupon he asked, "Is thy mother still alive?" "Yes," I replied. "Well," said he, "disobey her not."

Their curious medication.—A case illustrating their curious medicine is the following:

The lord of al-Munaytirah wrote to my uncle asking him to dispatch a physician to treat certain sick persons among his people. My uncle sent him a Christian physician named Thābit. Thābit was absent but ten days when he returned. So we said to him, "How quickly hast thou healed thy patients!" He said:

> They brought before me a knight in whose leg [81] an abscess had grown; and a woman afflicted with imbecility. To the knight I applied a small poultice until the abscess opened and became well; and the woman I put on diet and made her humor wet. Then a Frankish physician came to them and said, "This man knows nothing about treating them." He then said to the knight, "Which wouldst thou prefer, living with one leg or dying with two?" The latter replied, "Living with one leg." The physician said, "Bring me a strong knight and a sharp ax." A knight came with the ax. And I was standing by. Then the physician laid the leg of the patient on a block of wood and bade the knight strike his leg with the ax and chop it off at one blow. Accordingly he struck it—while I was looking on—one blow, but the leg was not severed. He dealt another blow, upon which the marrow of the leg flowed out and the patient died on the spot. He then examined the woman and said, "This is a woman in whose head there is a devil which has possessed her. Shave off her hair." Accordingly they shaved it off and the woman began once more to eat their ordinary diet—garlic and mustard. Her imbecility took a turn for

the worse. The physician then said, "The devil has penetrated through her head." He therefore took a razor, made a deep cruciform incision on it, peeled off the skin at the middle of the incision until the bone of the skull was exposed and rubbed it with salt. The woman also expired instantly. Thereupon I asked them whether my services were needed any longer, and when they replied in the negative I returned home, having learned of their medicine what I knew not before.

I have, however, witnessed a case of their medicine which was quite different from that.

The king of the Franks had for treasurer a knight named Bernard [*barnād*], who (may Allah's curse be upon him!) was one of the most accursed and wicked among the Franks. A horse kicked him in the leg, which was subsequently infected and which opened in fourteen different places. Every time one of these cuts would close in one place, another would open in another place. All this happened while I was praying for his perdition. Then came to him a Frankish physician and removed from the leg all the ointments which were on it and began to wash it with very strong vinegar. By this treatment all the cuts were healed and the man became well again. He was up again like a devil.

Another case illustrating their curious medicine is the following:

In Shayzar we had an artisan named abu-al-Fath, who had a boy whose neck was afflicted with scrofula. Every time a part of it would close, another part would open. This man happened to go to Antioch on business of his, accompanied by his son. A Frank noticed the boy and asked his father about him. Abu-al-Fath replied, "This is my son." The Frank said to him, "Wilt thou swear by thy religion that if I prescribe to thee a medicine which will cure thy boy, thou wilt charge nobody fees for prescribing it thyself? In that case, I shall prescribe to thee a medicine which will cure the boy." The man took the oath and the Frank said:

> Take uncrushed leaves of glasswort, burn them, then soak the ashes in olive oil and sharp vinegar. Treat the scrofula with them until the spot on which it is growing is eaten up. Then take burnt lead, soak it in ghee butter [*samn*] and treat him with it. That will cure him.

The father treated the boy accordingly, and the boy was cured. The sores closed and the boy returned to his normal condition of health.

I have myself treated with this medicine many who were afflicted with such disease, and the treatment was successful in removing the cause of [82] the complaint.

Newly arrived Franks are especially rough: One insists that Usāmah should pray eastward.—Everyone who is a fresh emigrant from the Frankish lands is ruder in character than those who have become acclimatized and have held long association with the Moslems. Here is an illustration of their rude character.

Whenever I visited Jerusalem I always entered the Aqṣa Mosque, beside which stood a small mosque which the Franks had converted into a church. When I used to enter the Aqṣa Mosque, which was occupied by the Templars [al-dāwiyyah], who were my friends, the Templars would evacuate the little adjoining mosque so that I might pray in it. One day I entered this mosque, repeated the first formula, "Allah is great," and stood up in the act of praying, upon which one of the Franks rushed on me, got hold of me and turned my face eastward saying, "This is the way thou shouldst pray!" A group of Templars hastened to him, seized him and repelled him from me. I resumed my prayer. The same man, while the others were otherwise busy, rushed once more on me and turned my face eastward, saying, "This is the way thou shouldst pray!" The Templars again came in to him and expelled him. They apologized to me, saying, "This is a stranger who has only recently arrived from the land of the Franks and he has never before seen anyone praying except eastward." Thereupon I said to myself, "I have had enough prayer." So I went out and have ever been surprised at the conduct of this devil of a man, at the change in the color of his face, his trembling and his sentiment at the sight of one praying towards the *qiblah*.

Another wants to show to a Moslem God as a child.—I saw one of the Franks come to al-Amīr Mu'īn-al-Dīn (may Allah's mercy rest upon his soul!) when he was in the Dome of the Rock and say to him, "Dost thou want to see God as a child?" Mu'īn-al-Dīn said, "Yes." The Frank walked ahead of us until he showed us the picture of Mary with Christ (may peace be upon him!) as an infant in her lap. He then said, "This is God as a child." But Allah is exalted far above what the infidels say about him!

Franks lack jealousy in sex affairs.—The Franks are void of all zeal and jealousy. One of them may be walking along with his wife. He meets another man who takes the wife by the hand and steps aside to converse with her while the husband is standing on one side waiting for his wife to conclude the conversation. If she lingers too long for him, he leaves her alone with the conversant and goes away.

Here is an illustration which I myself witnessed:

When I used to visit Nāblus, I always took lodging with a man named Mu'izz, whose home was a lodging house for the Moslems. The house had windows which opened to the road, and there stood opposite to it on the other side of the road a house belonging to a Frank who sold wine for the merchants. He would take some wine in a bottle and go around announcing it by shouting, "So and so, the merchant, has just opened a cask full of this wine. He who wants to buy some of it will find it in such and such a place." The Frank's pay for the announcement made would be the wine in that bottle. One day this Frank went home and found a man with his wife in the same bed. He asked him, "What could have made thee enter into my wife's room?" The man replied, "I was tired, so I went in to rest." "But how," asked he, "didst thou get into my bed?" The other replied, "I found a bed that was spread, so I slept in it." "But," said he, "my wife was sleeping together with thee!" The other replied, "Well, the bed is hers. How could I therefore have prevented her from using her own bed?" [83] "By the truth of my religion," said the husband, "if thou shouldst do it again, thou and I would have a quarrel." Such was for the Frank the entire expression of his disapproval and the limit of his jealousy.

Another illustration:

We had with us a bath-keeper named Sālim, originally an inhabitant of al-Ma'arrah, who had charge of the bath of my father (may Allah's mercy rest upon his soul!). This man related the following story:

> I once opened a bath in al-Ma'arrah in order to earn my living. To this bath there came a Frankish knight. The Franks disapprove of girding a cover around one's waist while in the bath. So this Frank stretched out his arm and pulled off my cover from my waist and threw it away. He looked and saw that I had recently shaved off my pubes. So he shouted, "Sālim!" As I drew near him he stretched his hand over my pubes and said, "Sālim, good! By the truth of my religion, do the same for me." Saying this, he lay on his back and I found that in that place the hair was like his beard. So I shaved it off. Then he passed his hand over the place and, finding it smooth, he said, "Sālim, by the truth of my religion, do the same to madame [*al-dāma*]" (*al-dāma* in their language means the lady), referring to his wife. He then said to a servant of his, "Tell madame to come here." Accordingly the servant went and brought her and made her enter the bath. She also lay on her back. The knight repeated, "Do what thou hast done to me." So I shaved all that hair while her husband was sitting looking at me. At last he thanked me and handed me the pay for my service.

Consider now this great contradiction! They have neither jealousy nor zeal but they have great courage, although courage is nothing but the product of zeal and of ambition to be above ill repute.

Here is a story analogous to the one related above:

I entered the public bath in Ṣūr [Tyre] and took my place in a secluded part. One of my servants thereupon said to me, "There is with us in the bath a woman." When I went out, I sat on one of the stone benches and behold! the woman who was in the bath had come out all dressed and was standing with her father just opposite me. But I could not be sure that she was a woman. So I said to one of my companions, "By Allah, see if this is a woman," by which I meant that he should ask about her. But he went, as I was looking at him, lifted the end of her robe and looked carefully at her. Thereupon her father turned toward me and said, "This is my daughter. Her mother is dead and she has nobody to wash her hair. So I took her in with me to the bath and washed her head." I replied, "Thou hast well done! This is something for which thou shalt be rewarded [by Allah]!"

Another curious case of medication.—A curious case relating to their medicine is the following, which was related to me by William of Bures [*kilyām dabūr*], the lord of Ṭabarayyah [Tiberias], who was one of the principal chiefs among the Franks. It happened that William had accompanied al-Amīr Mu'īn-al-Dīn (may Allah's mercy rest upon his soul!) from 'Akka to Ṭabarayyah when I was in his company too. On the way William related to us the following story in these words:

> We had in our country a highly esteemed knight who was taken ill and was on the point of death. We thereupon came to one of our great priests and said to him, "Come with us and examine so and so, the knight." "I will," he replied, and walked along with us while we were assured in ourselves that if he would only lay his hand on him the patient would recover. When the priest saw the patient, he said, "Bring me some wax." We fetched him a little wax, which he softened and shaped like the knuckles of fingers, and he stuck one in each nostril. The knight died on the spot. [84] We said to him, "He is dead." "Yes," he replied, "he was suffering great pain, so I closed up his nose that he might die and get relief."
> Let this go and let us resume the discussion regarding Harim.

A funny race between two aged women.—We shall now leave the discussion of their treatment of the orifices of the body to something else.

I found myself in Ṭabarayyah at the time the Franks were celebrating one of their feasts. The cavaliers went out to exercise with lances. With them went out two decrepit, aged women whom they stationed at one end of the race course. At the other end of the field they left a pig which they had scalded and laid on a rock. They then made the two aged women run a race while each one of them was accompanied by a detachment of horsemen urging her on. At every step they took, the women would fall down and rise again, while the spectators would laugh. Finally one of them got ahead of the other and won that pig for a prize.

Their judicial trials: A duel.—I attended one day a duel in Nāblus between two Franks. The reason for this was that certain Moslem thieves took by surprise one of the villages of Nāblus. One of the peasants of that village was charged with having acted as guide for the thieves when they fell upon the village. So he fled away. The king sent and arrested his children. The peasant thereupon came back to the king and said, "Let justice be done in my case. I challenge to a duel the man who claimed that I guided the thieves to the village." The king then said to the tenant who held the village in fief, "Bring forth someone to fight the duel with him." The tenant went to his village, where a blacksmith lived, took hold of him and ordered him to fight the duel. The tenant became thus sure of the safety of his own peasants, none of whom whom be killed and his estate ruined.

I saw this blacksmith. He was a physically strong young man, but his heart failed him. He would walk a few steps and then sit down and ask for a drink. The one who had made the challenge was an old man, but he was strong in spirit and he would rub the nail of his thumb against that of the forefinger in defiance, as if he was not worrying over the duel. Then came the viscount [al-biskund], i.e., the seignior of the town, and gave each one of the two contestants a cudgel and a shield and arranged the people in a circle around them.

The two met. The old man would press the blacksmith backward until he would get him as far as the circle, then he would come back to the middle of the arena. They went on exchanging blows until they looked like pillars smeared with blood. The contest was prolonged and the viscount began to urge them to hurry, saying, "Hurry on." The fact that the smith was given to the use of the hammer proved now of great advantage to him. The old man was worn out and the smith gave him a blow which made him fall. His cudgel fell under his back. The smith knelt down over him and tried to stick his fingers into the eyes of his adversary, but could not do it because of the great quantity of blood flowing out. Then he rose up and hit his head with the cudgel until he killed him. They then fastened a rope around the neck of the dead person, dragged him away and hanged him. The lord who brought the smith now came, gave the smith his own mantle, made him mount the horse behind him and rode off with him. This case illustrates the kind of jurisprudence [85] and legal decisions the Franks have—may Allah's curse be upon them!

Ordeal by water.—I once went in the company of al-Amīr Mu'‒n-al-Dīn (may Allah's mercy rest upon his soul!) to Jerusalem. We stopped at Nāblus. There a blind man, a Moslem, who was still young and was well dressed, presented himself before al-Amīr carrying fruits for him and asked permission to be admitted into his service in Damascus. The amīr consented. I inquired about this man and was informed that his mother had been married to a Frank whom she had killed. Her son used to practice ruses against the Frankish pilgrims and coöperate with his mother in assassinating them. They finally brought charges against him and tried his case according to the Frankish way of procedure.

They installed a huge cask and filled it with water. Across it they set a board of wood. They then bound the arms of the man charged with the act, tied a rope around his shoulders and dropped him into the cask, their idea being that in case he was innocent, he would sink in the water and they would then lift him up with the rope so that he might not die in the water; and in case he was guilty, he would not sink in the water. This man did his best to sink when they dropped him into the water, but he could not do it. So he had to submit to their sentence against him—may Allah's curse be upon them! They pierced his eyeballs with red-hot awls.

Later this same man arrived in Damascus. Al-Amīr Mu'īn-al-Dīn (may Allah's mercy rest upon his soul!) assigned him a stipend large enough to meet all his needs and said to a slave of his, "Conduct him to Burhān-al-Dīn al-Balkhi (may Allah's mercy rest upon his soul!) and ask him on my behalf to order somebody to teach this man the Koran and something of Moslem jurisprudence." Hearing that, the blind man remarked, "May triumph and victory be thine! But this was never my thought." "What didst thou think I was going to do for thee?" asked Mu'īn-al-Dīn. The blind man replied, "I thought thou wouldst give me a horse, a mule and a suit of armor and make me a knight." Mu'īn-al-Dīn then said, "I never thought that a blind man could become a knight."

A Frank domesticated in Syria abstains from eating pork.—Among the Franks are those who have become acclimatized and have associated long with the Moslems. These are much better than the recent comers from the Frankish lands. But they constitute the exception and cannot be treated as a rule.

Here is an illustration. I dispatched one of my men to Antioch on business. There was in Antioch at that time al-Ra'īs Theodoros Sophianos [*tādrus ibn-al-ṣaffī*], to whom I was bound by mutual ties of amity. His influence in Antioch was supreme. One day he said to my man, "I am invited by a friend of mine who is a Frank. Thou shouldst come with me so that thou mayest see their fashions." My man related the story in the following words:

> I went along with him and we came to the home of a knight who belonged to the old category of knights who came with the early expeditions of the Franks. He had been by that time stricken off the register and exempted from service, and possessed in Antioch an estate on the income of which he lived. The knight presented an excellent table, with food extraordinarily clean and delicious. Seeing me abstaining from food, he said, "Eat, be of good cheer! I never eat Frankish dishes, but I have Egyptian women cooks and never eat except their cooking. Besides, pork never enters my home." I ate, but guardedly, and after that we departed.
>
> As I was passing in the market place, a Frankish woman all of a sudden hung to my clothes and began to mutter words in their language, and I could not understand what she was saying. This made me immediately the center of a big crowd of Franks. I was convinced that death was at hand. But all of a sudden that same knight approached. On seeing me, he came and said to that woman, "What is the matter between thee and this Moslem?" She replied, "This is he who has killed [86] my brother Hurso ['*urs*]." This Hurso was a knight in Afāmiyah who was killed by someone of the army of Hamāh. The Christian knight shouted at her, saying, "This is a bourgeois [*burjāsi*] (i.e., a merchant) who neither fights nor attends a fight." He also yelled at the people who had assembled, and they all dispersed. Then he took me by the hand and went away. Thus the effect of that meal was my deliverance from certain death.

St. Catherine of Siena

It is relatively easy to analyze the structure of the medieval church, to describe its long struggle for political supremacy with the secular rulers of western Europe, and even to grasp the main points of its theology. But what of the central fact that lay behind all of these things—the religious beliefs and practices of ordinary Christians during the Middle Ages? What did the religious life really mean to the average person? Obviously, we can never fully answer this question. Nevertheless, we do have numerous accounts written by or about individuals that describe in detail their inner lives of faith and devotion; people such as St. Francis of Assisi, St. Bonaventure, St. Catherine of Siena, and many others. In most of these accounts we can discern a strain of mysticism, a sincere belief in one's having had a direct, personal contact with the divine. Usually this meant a form of mystical communion, in which the person's soul experienced a direct union with God. An even stronger, physical connection was experienced by St. Francis: he had imprinted on his body the stigmata, or the wounds suffered by Jesus on the cross. In the case of St. Catherine, she believed that in her mystical experiences she had direct conversations with God. As Raymond of Capua, her religious superior, describes these experiences,

> About two years before her death, such a clarity of Truth was revealed to her from Heaven that Catherine was constrained to spread it about by means of writing, asking her secretaries to stand ready to take down whatever came from her mouth as soon as they noticed that she had gone into ecstasy. Thus in a short time was composed a dialogue between a soul who asks the Lord four questions, and the Lord himself who replies to the soul.

The selection that follows contains excerpts from the beginning and end of this mystical dialogue between St. Catherine and God.

St. Catherine was born in Siena, in northern Italy, in 1347, the twenty-fourth of twenty-five children; she died in Rome in 1380 while on a mission for Pope Urban VI to try to heal schisms within the church. Although she was a mystic, she was also an able theologian, a political negotiator, and a religious administrator—in other words, a gifted woman of practical affairs. Her greatest mystical experience, her "mystical death," occurred in 1368, when for four hours she experienced mystical union with God while her body lay seemingly lifeless to those around her.

Consider the following questions as you study the text below.

1. How would you describe Catherine's relationship with God? What role did the church and clergy play in her spiritual life?

2. Why was self-discovery so important to Catherine? What did her examination of herself reveal?

The Dialogue

Prologue

IN THE NAME OF CHRIST
CRUCIFIED AND OF GENTLE MARY

A soul rises up, restless with tremendous desire for God's honor and the salvation of souls. She has for some time exercised herself in virtue and has become accustomed to dwelling in the cell of self-knowledge in order to know better God's goodness toward her, since upon knowledge follows love. And loving, she seeks to pursue truth and clothe herself in it.

But there is no way she can so savor and be enlightened by this truth as in continual humble prayer, grounded in the knowledge of herself and of God. For by such prayer the soul is united with God, following in the footsteps of Christ crucified, and through desire and affection and the union of love he makes of her another himself. So Christ seems to have meant when he said, "If you will love me and keep my word, I will show myself to you, and you will be one thing with me and I with you."[1] And we find similar words in other places from which we can see it is the truth that by love's affection the soul becomes another himself.

To make this clearer still, I remember having heard from a certain servant of God[2] that, when she was at prayer, lifted high in spirit, God would not hide from her mind's eye his love for his servants. No, he would reveal it, saying among other things, "Open your mind's eye and look within me, and you will see the dignity and beauty of my reasoning creature. But beyond

Catherine of Siena, *The Dialogue*, trans. Suzanne Noffke (Mahwah, N.J.: Paulist Press, 1980), pp. 25–27, 363–66. Used by permission of Paulist Press.

---

[1]Cf. Jn. 14:21–23.

[2]Catherine refers to herself in the third person throughout *The Dialogue*. Almost imperceptibly at this point she changes from present to past tense, a perspective she maintains in the narrative passages throughout the rest of the work.

the beauty I have given the soul by creating her in my image and likeness, look at those who are clothed in the wedding garment of charity, adorned with many true virtues: They are united with me through love. So I say, if you should ask me who they are, I would answer," said the gentle loving Word, "that they are another me; for they have lost and drowned their own will and have clothed themselves and united themselves and conformed themselves with mine."

It is true, then, that the soul is united to God through love's affection.

Now this soul's will was to know and follow truth more courageously. So she addressed four petitions to the most high and eternal Father, holding up her desire for herself first of all—for she knew that she could be of no service to her neighbors in teaching or example or prayer without first doing herself the service of attaining and possessing virtue.

Her first petition, therefore, was for herself. The second was for the reform of holy Church. The third was for the whole world in general, and in particular for the peace of Christians who are rebelling against holy Church with great disrespect and persecution. In her fourth petition she asked divine providence to supply in general and in particular for a certain case which had arisen.

This desire of hers was great and continuous. But it grew even more when First Truth[3] showed her the world's need and how storm-tossed and offensive to God it is. And she had on her mind, besides, a letter she had received from her spiritual father, a letter in which he expressed pain and unbearable sadness over the offense against God, the damnation of souls, and persecutions against holy Church. All of this stirred up the flame of her holy desire with grief for the offense but with gladness in the hope by which she waited for God to provide against such great evils.

She found herself eager for the next day's Mass—it would be Mary's day[4]—because in communion the soul seems more sweetly bound to God and better knows his truth. For then the soul is in God and God in the soul just as the fish is in the sea and the sea in the fish. So when it was morning and time for Mass she took her place with eager desire. From her deep knowledge of herself, a holy justice gave birth to hatred and displeasure against herself, ashamed as she was of her imperfection, which seemed to her to be the cause of all the evils in the world. In this knowledge and hatred and justice she washed away the stains of guilt, which it seemed to her were, and which indeed were, in her own soul, saying, "O eternal Father, I accuse myself before you, asking that you punish my sins in this life. And since I by my sins am the cause of the sufferings my neighbors must endure, I beg you in mercy to punish me for them."

. . .

---

[3][God—*Ed.*]
[4]Saturday, the day traditionally dedicated to Mary.

Conclusion

. . .

Now that soul had seen the truth and the excellence of obedience with the eye of her understanding, and had known it by the light of most holy faith; she had heard it with feeling and tasted it with anguished longing in her will as she gazed into the divine majesty. So she gave him thanks, saying:

Thanks, thanks be to you, eternal Father, that you have not despised me, your handiwork, nor turned your face from me, nor made light of these desires of mine. You, Light, have disregarded my darksomeness; you, Life, have not considered that I am death; nor you, Doctor, considered these grave weaknesses of mine. You, eternal Purity, have disregarded my wretched filthiness; you who are infinite have overlooked the fact that I am finite, and you, Wisdom, the fact that I am foolishness.

For all these and so many other endless evils and sins of mine, your wisdom, your kindness, your mercy, your infinite goodness have not despised me. No, in your light you have given me light. In your wisdom I have come to know the truth; in your mercy I have found your charity and affection for my neighbors. What has compelled you? Not my virtues, but only your charity.

Let this same love compel you to enlighten the eye of my understanding with the light of faith, so that I may know your truth, which you have revealed to me. Let my memory be great enough to hold your favors, and set my will ablaze in your charity's fire. Let that fire burst the seed of my body and bring forth blood; then with that blood, given for love of your blood, and with the key of obedience, let me unlock heaven's gate.

I heartily ask the same of you for every reasoning creature, all and each of them, and for the mystic body of holy Church. I acknowledge and do not deny that you loved me before I existed, and that you love me unspeakably much, as one gone mad over your creature.

O eternal Trinity! O Godhead! That Godhead, your divine nature, gave the price of your Son's blood its value. You, eternal Trinity, are a deep sea: The more I enter you, the more I discover, and the more I discover, the more I seek you. You are insatiable, you in whose depth the soul is sated yet remains always hungry for you, thirsty for you, eternal Trinity, longing to see you with the light in your light. Just as the deer longs for the fountain of living water, so does my soul long to escape from the prison of my darksome body and see you in truth. O how long will you hide your face from my eyes?

O eternal Trinity, fire and abyss of charity, dissolve this very day the cloud of my body! I am driven to desire, in the knowledge of yourself that you have given me in your truth, to leave behind the weight of this body of mine, and give my life for the glory and praise of your name. For by the light of understanding within your light I have tasted and seen your depth, eternal Trinity, and the beauty of your creation. Then, when I considered myself in you, I saw that I am your image. You have gifted me with power from yourself, eternal Father, and my understanding with your wisdom—such wisdom as is proper to your only-begotten Son; and the Holy Spirit, who proceeds from you and from your Son, has given me a will, and so I am able to love.

You, eternal Trinity, are the craftsman; and I your handiwork have come to know that you are in love with the beauty of what you have made, since you made of me a new creation in the blood of your Son.

O abyss! O eternal Godhead! O deep sea! What more could you have given me than the gift of your very self?

You are a fire always burning but never consuming; you are a fire consuming in your heat all the soul's selfish love; you are a fire lifting all chill and giving light. In your light you have made me know your truth: You are that light beyond all light who gives the mind's eye supernatural light in such fullness and perfection that you bring clarity even to the light of faith. In that faith I see that my soul has life, and in that light receives you who are Light.

In the light of faith I gain wisdom in the wisdom of the Word your Son, in the light of faith I am strong, constant, persevering; in the light of faith I have hope: It does not let me faint along the way. This light teaches me the way, and without this light I would be walking in the dark. This is why I asked you, eternal Father, to enlighten me with the light of most holy faith.

Truly this light is a sea, for it nourishes the soul in you, peaceful sea, eternal Trinity. Its water is not sluggish, so the soul is not afraid because she knows the truth. It distills, revealing hidden things, so that here, where the most abundant light of your faith abounds, the soul has, as it were, a guarantee of what she believes. This water is a mirror in which you, eternal Trinity, grant me knowledge; for when I look into this mirror, holding it in the hand of love, it shows me myself, as your creation, in you, and you in me through the union you have brought about of the Godhead with our humanity.

This light shows you to me, and in this light I know you, highest and infinite Good: Good above every good, joyous Good, Good beyond measure and understanding! Beauty above all beauty; Wisdom above all wisdom—indeed you are wisdom itself! You who are the angels' food are given to humans with burning love. You, garment who covers all nakedness, pasture the starving within your sweetness, for you are sweet without trace of bitterness.

O eternal Trinity, when I received with the light of most holy faith your light that you gave me, I came to know therein the way of great perfection, made smooth for me by so many wonderful explanations. Thus I may serve you in the light, not in the dark; and I may be a mirror of a good and holy life; and I may rouse myself from my wretched life in which, always through my own fault, I have served you in darkness. I did not know your truth, and so I did not love it. Why did I not know you? Because I did not see you with the glorious light of most holy faith, since the cloud of selfish love darkened the eye of my understanding. Then with your light, eternal Trinity, you dispelled the darkness.

But who could reach to your height to thank you for so immeasurable a gift, for such generous favors, for the teaching of truth that you have given me? A special grace, this, beyond the common grace you give to other creatures. You willed to bend down to my need and that of others who might see themselves mirrored here.

You responded, Lord; you yourself have given and you yourself answered and satisfied me by flooding me with a gracious light, so that with that light I may return thanks to you. Clothe, clothe me with yourself, eternal Truth, so that I may run the course of this mortal life in true obedience and in the light of most holy faith. With that light I sense my soul once again becoming drunk! Thanks be to God! Amen.

Giovanni Boccaccio

It is a commonplace that medieval civilization reached its apex in the thirteenth century and then went into decline in the fourteenth. Many explanations have been offered for this historical phenomenon, their diversity emphasizing the complexity of the causes at work. Among these certainly must be included a natural catastrophe that overwhelmed Europe in the middle years of the fourteenth century—the Black Death.

We now know what the millions of victims of the Black Death did not—that their disease was bubonic plague, a highly infectious and usually fatal illness caused by contact with infected rats or the fleas they carried. The Black Death, so named because its victims were marked with dark, purplish spots, originated in Asia and was brought to Europe by Genoese ships from the east in 1347. During the next four years it decimated the population of Europe, spreading out in all directions from Italy. Although the toll varied from locality to locality and estimates of total fatalities must be received with discretion, scholars have concluded that the plague (along with several recurrences later in the century) probably claimed the lives of some twenty-five million people, or roughly one-fourth of the population of Europe.

Only a little thought is needed to appreciate the effects on the survivors of such an overwhelming catastrophe. Some of these, as well as a vivid account of the plague, are described by Giovanni Boccaccio (1313–1375) in the Prelude to his *Decameron*, which was itself, at least in conception, a consequence of the Black Death. Boccaccio knew what he was describing, for he was in Florence himself when the Black Death struck there with devastating force in the spring of 1348.

In the *Decameron* itself, members of an imaginary group of Florentines who have fled the city tell a series of stories to pass the time during their exile.

Consider the following questions as you study the text below.

1. What explanation, if any, did Boccaccio offer for the appearance and spread of the plague? According to his report, how did people respond to the epidemic? Did he favor a particular type of response?

2. What clues does Boccaccio offer as to the social and economic consequences of the plague? Did the plague cause greater damage in the city or in the country? Why?

The Decameron

Prelude

Whenever, fairest ladies, I pause to consider how compassionate you all are by nature, I invariably become aware that the present work will seem to you to possess an irksome and ponderous opening. For it carries at its head the painful memory of the deadly havoc wrought by the recent plague, which brought so much heartache and misery to those who witnessed, or had experience of it. But I do not want you to be deterred, for this reason, from reading any further, on the assumption that you are to be subjected, as you read, to an endless torrent of tears and sobbing. You will be affected no differently by this grim beginning than walkers confronted by a steep and rugged hill, beyond which there lies a beautiful and delectable plain. The degree of pleasure they derive from the latter will correspond directly to the difficulty of the climb and the descent. And just as the end of mirth is heaviness, so sorrows are dispersed by the advent of joy.

This brief unpleasantness (I call it brief, inasmuch as it is contained within few words) is quickly followed by the sweetness and the pleasure which I have already promised you, and which, unless you were told in advance, you would not perhaps be expecting to find after such a beginning as this. Believe me, if I could decently have taken you whither I desire by some other route, rather than along a path so difficult as this, I would gladly have done so. But since it is impossible without this memoir to show the origin of the events you will read about later, I really have no alternative but to address myself to its composition.

I say, then, that the sum of thirteen hundred and forty-eight years had elapsed since the fruitful Incarnation of the Son of God, when the noble city of Florence, which for its great beauty excels all others in Italy, was visited by the deadly pestilence. Some say that it descended upon the human race through the influence of the heavenly bodies, others that it was a punishment signifying God's righteous anger at our iniquitous way of life. But whatever its cause, it had originated some years earlier in the East, where it had claimed countless lives before it unhappily spread westward, growing in strength as it swept relentlessly on from one place to the next.

In the face of its onrush, all the wisdom and ingenuity of man were unavailing. Large quantities of refuse were cleared out of the city by officials specially appointed for the purpose, all sick persons were forbidden entry, and numerous instructions were issued for safeguarding the people's health, but all to no avail. Nor were the countless petitions humbly directed to God by the pious, whether by means of formal processions or in any other guise, any less ineffectual. For in the early spring of the year we have mentioned, the plague began, in a terrifying and extraordinary manner, to make its disastrous effects apparent. It did not take the form it had assumed in the East, where if anyone bled from the nose it was an obvious portent of certain death. On the contrary, its earliest symptoms, in men and women alike, was the appearance of certain swellings in the groin or the armpit, some of which were egg-shaped whilst others were roughly the size of the common apple. Sometimes the swellings were large, sometimes not so large, and they were referred to by the populace as *gavòccioli*. From the two areas already mentioned, the deadly *gavòcciolo* would begin to spread, and within a short time it would appear at random all over the body. Later on, the symptoms of the disease changed, and many people began to find dark blotches and bruises on their arms, thighs, and other parts of the body, sometimes large and few in number, at other times tiny and closely spaced. These, to anyone unfortunate enough to contract them, were just as infallible a sign that he would die as the *gavòcciolo* had been earlier, and as indeed it still was.

Against these maladies, it seemed that all the advice of physicians and all the power of medicine were profitless and unavailing. Perhaps the nature of the illness was such that it allowed no remedy: or perhaps those people who were treating the illness (whose numbers had increased enormously because the ranks of the qualified were invaded by people, both men and women, who had never received any training in medicine), being ignorant of its causes, were not prescribing the appropriate cure. At all events, few of those who caught it ever recovered, and in more cases death occurred within three days from the appearance of the symptoms we have described, some people dying more rapidly than others, the majority without any fever or other complications.

But what made this pestilence even more severe was that whenever those suffering from it mixed with people who were still unaffected, it would rush upon these with the speed of a fire racing through dry or oily substances that happened to be placed within its reach. Nor was this the full extent of its evil, for not only did it infect healthy persons who conversed or had any dealings with the sick, making them ill or visiting an equally horrible death upon them, but it also seemed to transfer the sickness to anyone touching the clothes or other objects which had been handled or used by its victims.

It is a remarkable story that I have to relate. And were it not for the fact that I am one of many people who saw it with their own eyes, I would scarcely dare to believe it, let alone commit it to paper, even though I had heard it from a person whose word I could trust. The plague I have been describing was of so contagious a nature that very often it visibly did more than simply pass from one person to another. In other words, whenever an animal other than a human being touched anything belonging to a person who had been stricken or exterminated by the disease, it not only caught the sickness, but died from it almost at once. To all of this, as I have just said, my own eyes bore witness on more than one occasion. One day, for instance, the rags of a pauper who had died from the disease were thrown into the street, where they attracted the attention of two pigs. In their wonted fashion, the pigs first of all gave the rags a thorough mauling with their snouts after which they took them between their teeth and shook them against their cheeks. And within a short time they began to writhe as though they had been poisoned, then they both dropped dead to the ground, spread eagled upon the rags that had brought about their undoing.

These things, and many others of a similar or even worse nature, caused various fears and fantasies to take root in the minds of those who were still alive and well. And almost without exception, they took a single and very inhuman precaution, namely to avoid or run away from the sick and their belongings, by which means they all thought that their own health would be preserved.

Some people were of the opinion that a sober and abstemious mode of living considerably reduced the risk of infection. They therefore formed themselves into groups and lived in isolation from everyone else. Having withdrawn to a comfortable abode where there were no sick persons, they locked themselves in and settled down to a peaceable existence, consuming modest quantities of delicate foods and precious wines and avoiding all excesses. They refrained from speaking to outsiders, refused to receive news of the dead or the sick, and entertained themselves with music and whatever other amusements they were able to devise.

Others took the opposite view, and maintained that an infallible way of warding off this appalling evil was to drink heavily, enjoy life to the full, go round singing and merrymaking, gratify all of one's cravings whenever the opportunity offered, and shrug the whole thing off as one enormous joke. Moreover, they practised what they preached to the best of their ability, for they would visit one tavern after another, drinking all day and night to immoderate excess; or alternatively (and this was their more frequent custom), they would do their drinking in various private houses, but only in the ones where the conversation was restricted to subjects that were pleasant or entertaining. Such places were easy to find, for people behaved as though their days were numbered, and treated their belongings and their own persons with equal abandon. Hence most houses had become common property, and any passing stranger could make himself at home as naturally as though he were the rightful owner. But for all their riotous manner of living, these people always took good care to avoid any contact with the sick.

In the face of so much affliction and misery, all respect for the laws of God and man had virtually broken down and been extinguished in our city. For like everybody else, those ministers and executors of the laws who were not either dead or ill were left with so few subordinates that they were unable to discharge any of their duties. Hence everyone was free to behave as he pleased.

There were many other people who steered a middle course between the two already mentioned, neither restricting their diet to the same degree as the first group, nor indulging so freely as the second in drinking and other forms of wantonness, but simply doing no more than satisfy their appetite. Instead of incarcerating themselves, these people moved about freely, holding in their hands a posy of flowers, or fragrant herbs, or one of a wide range of spices, which they applied at frequent intervals to their nostrils, thinking it an excellent idea to fortify the brain with smells of that particular sort; for the stench of dead bodies, sickness, and medicines seemed to fill and pollute the whole of the atmosphere.

Some people, pursuing what was possibly the safer alternative, callously maintained that there was no better or more efficacious remedy against a plague than to run away from it. Swayed by this argument, and sparing no thought for anyone but themselves, large numbers of men and women abandoned their city, their homes, their relatives, their estates and their belongings, and headed for the countryside, either in Florentine territory or, better still, abroad. It was as though they imagined that the wrath of God would not unleash this plague against men for their iniquities irrespective of where they happened to be, but would only be aroused against those who found themselves within the city walls; or possibly they assumed that the whole of the population would be exterminated and that the city's last hour had come.

Of the people who held these various opinions, not all of them died. Nor, however, did they all survive. On the contrary, many of each different persuasion fell ill here, there, and everywhere, and having themselves, when they were fit and well, set an example to those who were as yet unaffected, they languished away with virtually no one to nurse them. It was not merely a question of one citizen avoiding another, and of people almost invariably neglecting their neighbours and rarely or never visiting their relatives, addressing them only from a distance; this scourge had implanted so great a terror in the hearts of men and women that brothers abandoned brothers, uncles their nephews, sisters their brothers, and in many cases wives deserted their husbands. But even worse, and almost incredible, was the fact that fathers and mothers refused to nurse and assist their own children, as though they did not belong to them.

Hence the countless numbers of people who fell ill, both male and female, were entirely dependent upon either the charity of friends (who were few and far between) or the greed of servants, who remained in short supply despite the attraction of high wages out of all proportion to the services they performed. Furthermore, these latter were men and women of coarse intellect and the majority were unused to such duties, and they did little more than hand things to the invalid when asked to do so and watch over him when he was dying. And in performing this kind of service, they frequently lost their lives as well as their earnings.

As a result of this wholesale desertion of the sick by neighbours, relatives and friends, and in view of the scarcity of servants, there grew up a practice almost never previously heard of, whereby when a woman fell ill, no matter how gracious or beautiful or gently bred she might be, she raised no objection to being attended by a male servant, whether he was young or not. Nor did she have any scruples about showing him every part of her body as freely as she would have displayed it to a woman, providing that the nature of her infirmity required her to do so; and this explains why those women who recovered were possibly less chaste in the period that followed.

Moreover a great many people died who would perhaps have survived had they received some assistance. And hence, what with the lack of appropriate means for tending the sick, and the virulence of the plague, the number of deaths reported in the city whether by day or night was so enormous that it astonished all who heard tell of it, to say nothing of the people who actually witnessed the carnage. And it was perhaps inevitable that among the citizens who survived there arose certain customs that were quite contrary to established tradition.

It had once been customary, as it is again nowadays, for the women relatives and neighbours of a dead man to assemble in his house in order to mourn in the company of the women who had been closest to him; moreover his kinsfolk would forgather in front of his house along with his neighbours and various other citizens, and there would be a contingent of priests, whose numbers varied according to the quality of the deceased; his body would be taken thence to the church in which he had wanted to be buried, being borne on the shoulders of his peers amidst the funeral pomp of candles and dirges. But as the ferocity of the plague began to mount, this practice all but disappeared entirely and was replaced by different customs. For not only did people die without having many women about them, but a great number departed this life without anyone at all to witness their going. Few indeed were those to whom the lamentations and bitter tears of their relatives were accorded; on the contrary, more often than not bereavement was the signal for laughter and witticisms and general jollification—the art of which the women, having for the most part suppressed their feminine concern for the salvation of the souls of the dead, had learned to perfection. Moreover it was rare for the bodies of the dead to be accompanied by more than ten or twelve neighbours to the church, nor were they borne on the shoulders of worthy and honest citizens, but by a kind of gravedigging fraternity, newly come into being and drawn from the lower orders of society. These people assumed the title of sexton, and demanded a fat fee for their services, which consisted in taking up the coffin and hauling it swiftly away, not to the church specified by the dead man in his will, but usually to the nearest at hand. They would be preceded by a group of four or six clerics, who between them carried one or two candles at most, and sometimes none at all. Nor did the priests go to the trouble of pronouncing solemn and lengthy funeral rites, but, with the aid of these so-called sextons, they hastily lowered the body into the nearest empty grave they could find.

As for the common people and a large proportion of the bourgeoisie, they presented a much more pathetic spectacle, for the majority of them were constrained, either by their poverty or the hope of survival, to remain in their houses. Being confined to their own parts of the city, they fell ill daily in their thousands, and since they had no one to assist them or attend to their needs, they inevitably perished almost without exception. Many dropped dead in the open streets, both by day and by night, whilst a great many others, though dying in their own houses, drew their neighbours' attention to the fact more by the smell of their rotting corpses than by any other means. And what with these, and the others who were dying all over the city, bodies were here, there, and everywhere.

Whenever people died, their neighbours nearly always followed a single, set routine, prompted as much by their fear of being contaminated by the decaying corpse as by any charitable feelings they may have entertained towards the deceased. Either on their own, or with the assistance of bearers whenever these were to be had, they extracted the bodies of the dead from their houses and left them lying outside their front doors, where anyone going about the streets, especially in the early morning, could have observed countless numbers of them. Funeral biers would then be sent for, upon which the dead were taken away, though there were some who, for the lack of biers, were carried off on plain boards. It was by no means rare for more than one of these biers to be seen with two or three bodies upon it at a time; on the contrary, many were seen to contain a husband and wife, two or three brothers and sisters; a father and son, or some other pair of close relatives. And times without number it happened that two priests would be on their way to bury someone, holding a cross before them, only to find that bearers carrying three or four additional biers would fall in behind them; so that whereas the priests had thought they had only one burial to attend to, they in fact had six or seven, and sometimes more. Even in these circumstances, however, there were no tears or candles or mourners to honour the dead; in fact, no more respect was accorded to dead people than would nowadays be shown toward dead goats. For it was quite apparent that the one thing which, in normal times, no wise man had ever learned to accept with patient resignation (even though it struck so seldom and unobtrusively), had now been brought home to the feeble-minded as well, but the scale of the calamity caused them to regard it with indifference.

Such was the multitude of corpses (of which further consignments were arriving every day and almost by the hour at each of the churches), that there was not sufficient consecrated ground for them to be buried in, especially if each was to have its own plot in accordance with long-established custom. So when all the graves were full, huge trenches were excavated in the churchyards, into which new arrivals were placed in their hundreds, stowed tier upon tier like ships' cargo, each layer of corpses being covered over with a thin layer of soil till the trench was filled to the top.

But rather than describe in elaborate detail the calamities we experienced in the city at that time, I must mention that, whilst an ill wind was blowing through Florence itself, the surrounding region was no less badly affected. In the fortified towns, conditions were similar to those in the city itself on a minor scale; but in the scattered hamlets and the countryside proper, the poor unfortunate peasants and their families had no physicians or servants whatever to assist them, and collapsed by the wayside, in their fields, and in their cottages at all hours of the day and night, dying more like animals than human beings. Like the townspeople, they too grew apathetic in their ways, disregarded their affairs, and neglected their possessions. Moreover they all behaved as though each day was to be their last, and far from making provision for the future by tilling their lands, tending their flocks, and adding to their previous labours, they tried in every way they could think of to squander the assets already in their possession. Thus it came about that oxen, asses, sheep, goats, pigs, chickens, and even dogs (for all their deep fidelity to man) were driven away and allowed to roam freely through the fields, where the crops lay abandoned and had not even been reaped, let alone gathered in. And after a whole day's feasting, many of these animals, as though possessing the power of reason, would return glutted in the evening to their own quarters, without any shepherd to guide them.

But let us leave the countryside and return to the city. What more remains to be said, except that the cruelty of heaven (and possibly, in some measure, also that of man) was so immense and so devastating that between March and July of the year in question, what with the fury of the pestilence and the fact that so many of the sick were inadequately cared for or abandoned in their hour of need because the healthy were too terrified to approach them, it is reliably thought that over a hundred thousand human lives were extinguished within the walls of the city of Florence? Yet before this lethal catastrophe fell upon the city, it is doubtful whether anyone would have guessed it contained so many inhabitants.

Ah, how great a number of splendid palaces, fine houses, and noble dwellings, once filled with retainers, with lords and with ladies, were bereft of all who had lived there, down to the tiniest child! How numerous were the famous families, the vast estates, the notable fortunes, that were seen to be left without a rightful successor! How many gallant gentlemen, fair ladies, and sprightly youths, who would have been judged hale and hearty by Galen, Hippocrates and Aesculapius (to say nothing of others), having breakfasted in the morning with their kinfolk, acquaintances and friends, supped that same evening with their ancestors in the next world!

In this page from an early printed book, the Dominican monk Johann Tetzel (mounted on a donkey) greets potential purchasers of papal indulgences. In exchange for a donation to the fund for the construction of St. Peter's basilica, contributors received a papal indulgence granting them forgiveness for their sins.

RENAISSANCE
AND REFORMATION

The word "renaissance" means rebirth. The idea of rebirth, as it developed in Renaissance Italy, had two meanings, one specific and the other general. First, the term referred to the rebirth of interest in the history and achievements of the classical world—Greece and Rome. The Italian Renaissance scholars, who referred to themselves as "humanists," believed that they were rediscovering the classical world. What they rediscovered, and what inspired them, was the classical notion that man, his works, and his life in this world are the most interesting and important subjects of human concern. The idea of humanity and the present life is encapsulated in the term "humanism," which captures the Renaissance notion of rebirth in its more general aspects.

What led to the Renaissance and why did it begin in Italy? Although its causes were undoubtedly complex, two factors can be singled out for special mention. The Christian church had its center in Rome, and by the late Middle Ages it had developed into an enormous bureaucratic institution, with the popes wielding extraordinary powers. Almost inevitably the ecclesiastical leaders devoted more attention to the management of their bureaucracy than to the spiritual needs of their people. The result was secularization at the highest levels of the Church. A number of the Renaissance popes became patrons of the arts and, with the wealth that flowed into the papal coffers in Rome from throughout Europe, subsidized such artists as Michelangelo and Raphael. A second important reason for the Italian Renaissance lay in the growth of commerce in the city-states, particularly of northern Italy. This led to the development of banks, which created great wealth for a number of banking families, an example being the Medicis of Florence, who not only fostered art but also became prominent figures in the history of early modern Europe.

From Italy the Renaissance gradually spread across the Alps into northern Europe during the fifteenth century. But there it developed in a somewhat different way. Although northern humanists devoted much of their attention to classical writings, in general they did not adopt a predominantly secular view of life, as in Italy, but developed their humanism within the context of their Christian faith. This difference is clearly evidenced in the career of Erasmus of Rotterdam, the most eminent of the northern humanists. Although Erasmus devoted much of his life to a study of the classics, his object was not primarily to emulate the ancients. Rather he viewed himself as a conciliator attempting to reconcile the classical ideal of life with his own Christian faith. It is noteworthy that one of his most important works was his translation of the New Testament from Greek into Latin.

As the Renaissance waned in the early sixteenth century it was superseded by a movement which, although in part its product, nevertheless departed markedly from it in spirit. This was the Reformation, which originated in northern Europe. Although the Reformation, as the term implies, began as a reform movement within the Church, it finally resulted in a permanent split within Western Christendom. It was, it should be added, far from the first attempt at religious reform. During the Middle Ages various reform movements had come into being but these were accommodated by the hierarchy of the Church, either by extirpation, as with the Albigensians of southern France, or by assimilation, as with the Franciscans of Italy. But the situation in the sixteenth century developed in such a way that no accommodation was to prove possible.

The Reformation, which burst upon the European scene in the figure of a German monk, Martin Luther, did not spring from nothing. In the centuries just preceding Luther, as the upper hierarchy of the Church became increasingly secular, a variety of protest movements were born and flourished. An example was a group that originated in the Netherlands around 1400, calling themselves Brothers of the Common Life. Laymen rather than clerics, the Brothers abandoned the ritual and ceremony of the Church, emphasizing instead the personal Christian virtues of piety and humility. Many of the common people responded positively to them and their movement spread by the end of the century through a wide area of northern Europe.

Luther was a product of this context of protest and reform. When Erasmus leveled the weapon of his satire against some of the more sordid practices of the clerical hierarchy, he found in Luther a sympathetic supporter. Like Erasmus, Luther began his criticisms of the clergy in an attempt to reform the Church from within. But circumstances, including both the intransigence of the hierarchy and Luther's own uncompromising character, conspired to escalate his protests into a confrontation with the ecclesiastical authorities, resulting in his excommunication and eventually in the establishment of the Lutheran church, thus institutionalizing the schism within Christianity.

Luther was particularly outraged by a variety of abuses that had gradually taken root in the Church. These included the practice of *simony*, in which offices in the Church were sold for money. A similar practice was that of *nepotism*, in which Church officials bestowed sinecures in the Church on their children and other relatives. Another egregious practice was the traffic in *indulgences*. An indulgence was a special document issued by the Church, usually in exchange for a donation, that relieved a properly confessed communicant from some of the punishments of purgatory. Although indulgences were never (in theory) sold, the line drawn was often a very thin one. Most of these objectionable practices involved money, which was gathered from the faithful throughout Europe to make its way to papal headquarters in Rome. Luther was understandably enraged by these financial depradations, writing that it was a wonder that, after them, the people "still have anything to eat." But Luther's deepest and most dangerous thrust against the established Church lay in his doctrines of "justification by faith" and "the priesthood of all believers." If one accepts these doctrines, the hierarchically structured Church, with the pope wielding spiritual authority directly from God, becomes redundant. Obviously the Church could not acquiesce in this notion; Protestantism had to be declared a heresy.

The second important figure of the Reformation was a younger contemporary of Luther, the Frenchman John Calvin. Calvin's chief contributions to Protestantism were twofold. First, he supplied the movement with a comprehensive theology. Here he was not revolutionary but conservative, for he returned, for his inspiration, to St. Paul and St. Augustine, reviving their doctrine of original sin and pressing it to its ultimate consequences with the rigor of his legal mind. Calvin's second contribution to the Protestant movement lay in the breadth of his religious appeal. Whereas the followers of Luther were largely Germans, churches and denominations (an example being Scottish Presbyterianism) based on Calvinism sprang up throughout much of Western Europe.

The response of the established Church to the reform movements of Protestantism was generally to combat and, if possible, to extirpate them. As a result the history of Western Europe in the century following Luther was punctuated by religious wars, often of an unusually bloody and violent nature. These reached their climax in the Thirty Years' War, which devastated Germany in the years from 1618 to 1648. Nevertheless, the Catholic response to Protestantism was not wholly negative and repressive. Many responsible Church leaders recognized that serious problems existed within their institution and made efforts to resolve these. Most notable of the attempts made to reform the Church from within by members of its hierarchy was the Council of Trent, which met over a number of years in the latter part of the sixteenth century in the town of Trent in northern Italy. While reaffirming the central doctrines of the Church against Protestantism, the Council condemned many of the practices that had sprung up within it.

But the most important event for Western civilization during the period of the Renaissance and Reformation occurred far from European shores. This was the arrival of Christopher Columbus, followed by a host of adventurers, explorers, and, finally, settlers in a land hitherto unknown to Europeans—the Americas. From this time, and with increasing importance, America was to become a part of the history of Western civilization.

LOOKING AHEAD

As you learn about the Renaissance and Reformation, consider the following questions.

1. Did the Renaissance and Reformation represent breaks with medieval civilization? If so, which of these two events represented the most dramatic departure from the past?

2. How would you characterize Renaissance humanism? How did humanism influence Renaissance art, literature, and politics?

3. Why did the Reformation succeed while so many religious reform movements before it had failed? What role did printing play in the spread of new religious ideas?

Pico della Mirandola

Giovanni Pico, the count of Mirandola (1463–1494), epitomized both in his life and in his writings the Renaissance ideal of manhood. Nobly born, wealthy, handsome, and brilliant, he was well embarked on a distinguished intellectual career that would probably have made him the undisputed leader of the humanistic movement in Italy when he fell victim to fever at the age of thirty.

Unwilling to limit himself, as many other humanists did, to translating and imitating the literature of classical Greece and Rome, Pico undertook the task of assimilating all the great writings of the past, whatever their source, searching out the elements of truth in each and assembling these truths into a new philosophical synthesis of his own. The *Oration on the Dignity of Man* is a part of his ambitious project. After seven years of study in various European universities, Pico arrived in Rome at the age of twenty-three and announced that he was prepared to defend in public debate against anyone a list of nine hundred theses representing the conclusions that he had derived from his studies. (He even offered to pay the travel expenses of scholars coming long distances.) The debate, scheduled for January 1487, never took place. Pope Innocent VIII, suspicious that Pico was straying from orthodoxy, appointed a commission to examine the list of theses. When the commission confirmed the pope's suspicions by labeling a number of them heretical, Innocent forced the debate to be canceled.

The nature of the *Oration*, which Pico had intended as an introductory address for the debate, is evident from its title. Apart from the intrinsic interest of the discussion itself, including Pico's many references to the most diverse literary sources, the significance of the *Oration* lies in its eloquent summation of the Renaissance interest in humans and the belief in the dignity of human life.

Consider the following questions as you study the text below.

1. How did Pico define the qualities that comprise the dignity of man? Why was he willing to place humans on a higher level than even the angels?

2. What significance do you attach to Pico's willingness to draw on a wide range of authorities in support of his position? What, for example, should we make of his concurrence with the views of Muslim scholars and of the prophet Mohammed himself?

On the Dignity of Man

Most reverend fathers: I have read in the writings of the Arabs that Azdallah the Saracen, when asked what thing on this worldly stage appeared most marvelous to him, replied that he perceived nothing more wonderful than Man. This opinion is concurred in by that famous statement of Hermes Trismegistus:

Man, Asclepius, is a great miracle.

As I pondered the sense of these sayings, I became dissatisfied with those arguments which are brought forth in profusion by many people to establish the excellence of Humanity: namely, that Man is the intermediary of all created things, slave to those above him, king to those below; that Man is the interpreter of nature, by virtue of the sharpness of his senses, the searching of his reason, and the light of his understanding; that Man is the interval between time and eternity, the copula of the universe (as the Persians say), or even its wedding, a little lower, on David's authority, than the angels. These are great things, certainly, but not of prime importance; not so great that they lay just claim to the highest admiration. For, under these conditions, why should we not give even greater admiration to the angels themselves, and to the blessed choir of Heaven?

At length, I felt that I had come to understand both why Man is the most fortunate of creatures, and thus worthy of all admiration, and what, finally, this situation is which he has received in the scheme of the universe—a position to be envied, not only by the beasts, but by the stars, by the spirits beyond the world. The answer is marvelous and incredible. How could it be otherwise? For it is on this account that Man is rightly said and believed to be a great miracle, truly a being to be admired.

Hear now, Fathers, what this solution is, and, in your courtesy, grant my discourse a friendly audience.

The Supreme Father, God the Creator, had already fashioned this worldly residence which we see about us, the majestic temple of His Godhood, after the laws of His secret wisdom. He had adorned the zone beyond the heavens with intellects; He had quickened the ethereal spheres into life with eternal souls; He had filled the foul and filthy regions of the lower world with a multitude of animals of every sort. But, His work completed, the Demiurge desired that there be someone to contemplate the reason of such a great work, to love its beauty, to wonder at its vastness. Thus, when everything had been finished (as Moses and Timaeus bear witness), He turned His thoughts last of all to bringing forth Man. But there remained no archetype on which to pattern the new creature, no treasure to bestow on the

Giovanni Pico della Mirandola, *De Hominis Dignitate*, trans. Douglass S. Parker.

new son as an inheritance, no place in all the new world where that contemplator of the universe might sit. By this time, all things were full; all things had been distributed in the highest, middle, and lowest orders. But it was not the nature of the Father's power to fail, as though exhausted, in the last act of creation; nor of His wisdom, to waver in a necessary deed through lack of a plan; nor of His beneficent love, to compel the very being who was to praise the divine generosity in other things to impugn that generosity in himself. At length the Greatest Craftsman decided that this being, to whom He could give nothing of its own, should share in everything which he had assigned to each of the other beings. Thus he received Man as a work of undefined pattern, and placing him in the center of the world, addressed him as follows:

> *I have given you, O Adam, neither a fixed location, nor an especial appearance, nor any gift peculiarly your own; therefore, you may attain and possess, as you wish and as you will, whatever location, whatever appearance, whatever gifts you yourself desire. The nature of all other things is limited and confined within laws which I have laid down. You, confined by no limits, will determine your nature for yourself by your judgment, into whose power I have consigned you. I have placed you in the middle of the world, whence you may survey the more conveniently everything which is in the world. I have made you neither heavenly nor earthly, neither mortal nor immortal; thus, as a free and sovereign craftsman, you may mold yourself whatever form you choose. You will be able to degenerate into those lower creatures, which are brutes; you will be able, by the determination of your mind, to be reborn into those higher creatures, which are divine.*

How great is the generosity of God the Father! How great and admirable is the happiness of Man, whose gift it is to have that which he wishes! Upon their birth, beasts bring with them from their mother's bag (as Lucilius says) all that they will ever possess. From the beginning of time, or soon after, the supreme spirits have been that which they will be throughout all eternity. But as Man is born, the Father has planted in him seeds of every sort, shoots of every life; those which each man cultivates will grow, and bear their fruits in him. If these are vegetable, he will become a plant; if sensual, a brute; if rational, a heavenly being; if intellectual, an angel and son of God. But if Man, not contented with any creature's lot, betakes himself into the center of his oneness, then, made one with God, in the solitary darkness of the Father he who was created above all things will excell all things.

Who would not admire this chameleon of ours? Or, rather, who would admire anything else more greatly? Asclepius of Athens does no wrong when he says of man that, in accordance with his changing aspect and his self-transforming nature, he was symbolized in the mysteries of Proteus.

Hence those metamorphoses celebrated among the Hebrews and the Pythagoreans: indeed, the most secret Hebrew theology makes transformations, now of holy Enoch into an angel of the divinity, now of other men into other divine spirits; the Pythagoreans transform evildoers into beasts, and even (if we may believe Empedocles) into plants. Imitating this, Mohammed would often say, "He who departs from the divine law becomes a beast," and rightly so. For not the bark, but the dull and insensible nature makes the plants; not the hide, but the brutish and sensual soul the beast; not the circular body, but correct reason the heavens; not separation from the body, but spiritual intelligence the angel. For should you see a man given up to his belly and creeping on the ground, you see a plant, not a man; should you see someone blinded by the empty illusions of an apparition like Calypso, enticed by titillating allurements, a slave to his senses, you see a beast, not a man; should you see a philosopher perceiving all by his correct reasoning, you would revere him—he is a being of heaven, not of earth; should you see a pure contemplator, unconscious of his body, completely withdrawn into the sanctuary of his mind, this is no earthly, no celestial being:—this is a most majestic spirit dressed in human flesh.

Is there anyone, then, who would not admire man? Not wrongly, in both the Mosaic and the Christian scriptures, he is called now by the name of "all flesh," now by the name of "every creature," since he molds, fashions, and transforms himself after the appearance of all flesh and after the nature of every creature. Therefore Evanthes the Persian, in his account of the Chaldean theology, writes that Man possesses no innate form of his own, but many extraneous and foreign ones, whence that saying of the Chaldeans that man is an animal of varied and manifold and unstable nature.

But to what end do I record this? So that, after we have been born in this condition—that of being what we wish—we shall understand that we must take especial care that it not be said against us, that we were in honor and knew it not, and became as brutes and foolish beasts. Rather, may the words of the prophet Asaph apply—"Ye are gods, and all of you are children of the most High,"—lest we, abusing the Father's most indulgent generosity, render that unfettered choice which He gave us harmful rather than beneficial. May some holy aspiration enter our hearts, so that we are not content with middling things, but pant for the highest and strain to achieve them, since we can if we will.

Let us scorn the earthly, despise the heavenly, and thus, disdaining everything which is of the world, fly to that assembly beyond the world which is nearest God, who towers over all. There, as the holy mysteries tell, Seraphim, Cherubim, and Thrones occupy the first place; let us strive to equal their dignity and glory. And, if we wish it, we shall be in no wise lower than they.

Laura Cereta

Like Hildegard of Bingen, Laura Cereta (1469–1499) was sent to a convent when she was still a young child. Unlike Hildegard, Cereta was not sent to become a nun but to begin her education. While at the convent, she received the foundation of her training in Latin, a critical step toward her future development as a writer and humanist. In many ways, her life was quite conventional. The daughter of an upper-middle-class attorney, Cereta married a Venetian merchant at the age of fifteen or sixteen. Unfortunately, her husband died after only a year and a half of marriage and Cereta was a widow before she turned eighteen. In the years after her husband's death, Cereta became part of a circle of scholars and humanists, meeting and corresponding with some of the most famous intellectuals of her day. Cereta died at the age of thirty, having established a reputation as a writer but leaving no published works.

The two letters included here were part of Cereta's *Epistolae familiares*, a collection of eighty-two letters on a wide variety of topics. In the first letter Cereta sought to defend liberal education for women. Specifically, she rejected the notion that individual examples of educated women were the exceptions that proved the rule, asserting instead that women as a class were capable of intellectual achievement. In the second letter, Cereta responded to the fear of invasion that gripped Italy in the decades after the fall of Constantinople to Turkish forces in 1453. As you read the letters, pay close attention to Cereta's use of humanist themes and strategies. Would you describe her as a typical humanist? Why or why not?

Consider the following questions as you study the text below.

1. What were Cereta's main arguments in defense of liberal education of women? Did she believe that men and women were intellectually identical, or did she see important differences in their mental characteristics? Do you consider the letter evidence that Cereta was a feminist?

2. In Cereta's view, how should Italians have responded to the threat of Turkish invasion? What arguments did she advance in support of her position? Do you think most Italians would have agreed with her? Why or why not?

In Defense of Liberal Education for Women

Your complaints are hurting my ears, for you say publicly and quite openly that you are not only surprised but pained that I am said to show this extraordinary intellect of the sort one would have thought nature would give to the most learned of men—as if you had reached the conclusion, on the facts of the case, that a similar girl had seldom been seen among the peoples of the world. You are wrong on both counts, Semproni, and now that you've abandoned the truth, you are going to spread information abroad that is clearly false

I think you should be deeply pained—no, you should actually be blushing—you who are no longer now a man full of animus but instead a stone animated by the scorn you have for the studies that make us wise, while you grow weak with the sickness of debilitating leisure. And thus in your case, it is not nature that goes astray but the mind, for which the path from the appearance of virtue to villainy is a fairly easy one. In this manner, you appear to be flattering a susceptible young girl because of the glory that has accrued to her—my—name. But the snare of flattery is seductive, for you who have always set traps for the sex that has been revered all throughout history have been ensnared yourself. And duped by your own madness, you are trying, by running back and forth, to trample me underfoot and smash me to the ground with your fists. Sly mockery is concealed here, and it is typical of the lowborn, plebeian mind to think that one can blind Medusa with a few drops of olive oil. You would have done better to have crept up on a mole than a wolf, since the former, being shrouded in darkness, would see nothing clearly, while the latter's eyes radiate light in the dark.

In case you don't know, the philosopher sees with her mind; she furnishes paths with a window of reason through which she can ascend to a state of awareness. For Providence, the knower of the future, conquers marauding evil, trampling it with feet that have eyes. I would remain silent, believe me, if you, with your long-standing hostile and envious attitude towards me, had learned to attack me alone; after all, a ray of Phoebus' can't be shamed by being surrounded by mud. But I am angry and my disgust overflows. Why should the condition of our sex be shamed by your little attacks? Because of this, a mind thirsting for revenge is set afire; because of this, a sleeping pen is wakened for insomniac writing. Because of this, redhot anger lays bare a heart and mind long muzzled by silence.

Laura Cereta, *Collected Letters of a Renaissance Feminist*, transcribed, trans. and ed. Diana Robin (Chicago: The University of Chicago Press, 1997), pp. 74–80, 139–40. Reprinted by permission of The University of Chicago Press.

My cause itself is worthy: I am impelled to show what great glory that noble lineage which I carry in my own breast has won for virtue and literature—a lineage that knowledge, the bearer of honors, has exalted in every age. For the possession of this lineage is legitimate and sure, and it has come all the way down to me from the perpetual continuance of a more enduring race.

We have read that the breast of Ethiopian Sabba, imbued with divinity, solved the prophetic riddles of the Egyptian king Solomon. The first writers believed that Amalthea, a woman erudite in the knowledge of the future, sang responses near the banks that surround the Avernus, not far from Baiae. She, who as a Sybil was worthy of the gods of this lineage, sold books full of oracles to Priscus Tarquinius. Thus the Babylonian prophetess Eriphila, looking into the future with her divine mind far removed, described the fall and the ashes of Troy, the fortunes of the Roman empire, and the mysteries of Christ, who would later be born. Nicostrata, too, the mother of Evander and very learned in prophecy as well as literature, attained such genius that she was the first to show the alphabet to the first Latins in sixteen figures. The enduring fame of Inachan Isis will flourish, for she alone of the Argive goddesses revealed to the Egyptians her own alphabet for reading. But Zenobia, an Egyptian woman of noble erudition, became so learned not only in Egyptian but also in Latin and Greek literature that she wrote the histories of barbarian and foreign peoples.

Shall we attribute illiteracy to Theban Manto, the prophesying daughter of Tiresias, and to Pyromantia, too, who was full of those Chaldaean arts when she spoke with the shades of the dead and foretold events in the future through the movements of flames, the flight of birds, and livers and entrails of animals? Where did all the great wisdom of Tritonian Pallas come from, which enabled her to educate so many Athenians in the arts, if it was not that she succeeded in unraveling the mysteries of the scriptures of Apollo, the physician, to the delight of everyone? Those little Greek women Phyliasia and Lasthenia were wonderful sources of light in the world of letters and they filled me with new life because they ridiculed the students of Plato, who frequently tied themselves in knots over the snare-filled sophistries of their arguments.

Lesbian Sappho serenaded the stony heart of her lover with tearful poems, sounds I might have thought came from Orpheus' lyre or the plectrum of Phoebus. Soon the Greek tongue of Leontium, full of the Muses, emerged, and she, who had made herself agreeable with the liveliness of her writing, dared to make a bitter attack on the divine words of Theophrastus. Nor would I omit here Proba, noted both for her exceptional tongue and her knowledge; for she wove together and composed histories of the Old Testament with fragments from Homer and Virgil.

The majesty of the Roman state deemed worthy a little Greek woman, Semiramis, for she spoke her mind about the laws in a court of law and about kings in the senate. Pregnant with virtue, Rome bore Sempronia, who, forceful in her eloquent poetry, spoke in public assemblies and filled the minds of her audiences with persuasive orations. Hortensia, the daughter of Hortensius, and also an orator, was celebrated at a public meeting with equal elegance. Her grace of speech was so great that she persuaded the triumvirs, albeit with the tears of a loyal mother, to absolve the women of Rome from having to pay the debt levied against them. Add also Cornificia, the sister of the poet Cornificius, whose devotion to literature bore such fruit that she was said to have been nurtured on the milk of the Castalian Muses and who wrote epigrams in which every phrase was graced with Heliconian flowers. I will not mention here Cicero's daughter Tulliola or Terentia or Cornelia, Roman women who reached the pinnacle of fame for their learning; and accompanying them in the shimmering light of silence will be Nicolosa of Bologna, Isotta of Verona, and Cassandra of Venice.

All history is full of such examples. My point is that your mouth has grown foul because you keep it sealed so that no arguments can come out of it that might enable you to admit that nature imparts one freedom to all human beings equally—to learn. But the question of my exceptionality remains. And here choice alone, since it is the arbiter of character, is the distinguishing factor. For some women worry about the styling: of their hair, the elegance of their clothes, and the pearls and other jewelry they wear on their fingers. Others love to say cute little things, to hide their feelings behind a mask of tranquility, to indulge in dancing, and lead pet dogs around on a leash. For all I care, other women can long for parties with carefully appointed tables, for the peace of mind of sleep, or they can yearn to deface with paint the pretty face they see reflected in their mirrors. But those women for whom the quest for the good represents a higher value restrain their young spirits and ponder better plans. They harden their bodies with sobriety and toil, they control their tongues, they carefully monitor what they hear, they ready their minds for all-night vigils, and they rouse their minds for the contemplation of probity in the case of harmful literature. For knowledge is not given as a gift but by study. For a mind free, keen, and unyielding in the face of hard work always rises to the good, and the desire for learning grows in depth and breadth.

So be it therefore. May we women, then, not be endowed by God the grantor with any giftedness or rare talent through any sanctity of our own. Nature has granted to all enough of her bounty; she opens to all the gates of choice, and through these gates, reason sends legates to the will, for it is through reason that these legates can transmit their desires. I shall make a bold summary of the matter. Yours is the authority, ours is the inborn ability. But instead of manly strength, we women are naturally endowed with cunning; instead of a sense of security, we are suspicious. Down deep we women are content with our lot. But you, enraged and maddened by the anger of the dog from whom you flee, are like someone who has been frightened by the attack of a pack of wolves. The victor does not look for the fugitive; nor does she who desires a cease-fire with the enemy conceal herself. Nor does she set up camp with courage and arms when the conditions are hopeless. Nor does it give the strong any pleasure to pursue one who is already fleeing.

Look, do you tremble from fear alone of my name? I am savage neither in mind nor hand. What is it you fear? You run away and hide in vain, for the traps that await you around every corner have been more cunningly set. Is it thus that you, a deserter, leave this city and our sight? Is it thus that, regretful of what you have done, you rely on flight as the first road to safety for yourself? May your shame then stay with you. My goodness towards men isn't always rewarded, and you may imagine in your disdain for women that I alone marvel at the felicitousness of having talent—I, who in the light of the well-deserved fame of other women, am indeed only the smallest little mouse. Therefore when you hide your envy under a bogus example, you clothe yourself with defensive words in vain.

For truth which is dear to God always emerges when falsehoods are overthrown. That road is twisted where you walk under the black gaze of an envious mind—far from human beings, from duties, and from God. Who will be surprised, do you think, Bibolo, if the lacerated and wounded heart of a girl who is filled with indignation bitterly rears itself up against your sarcasm and satire from this day on, now that your trifling arrogance has wounded her with bitter injuries? Do not think, most despicable of men, that I might believe I have fallen out of favor with Jove. I am a scholar and a pupil who has been lulled to sleep by the meager fire of a mind too humble. I have been too much burned, and my injured mind has accumulated too much passion; for tormenting itself with the defending of our sex, my mind sighs, conscious of its obligation. For all things—those deeply rooted inside us as well as those outside us—are being laid at the door of our sex.

In addition, I, who have always held virtue in high esteem and considered private things as secondary in importance, shall wear down and exhaust my pen writing against those men who are garrulous and puffed up with false pride. I shall not fail to obstruct tenaciously their treacherous snares. And I shall strive in a war of vengeance against the notorious abuse of those who fill everything with noise, since armed with such abuse, certain insane and infamous men bark and bare their teeth in vicious wrath at the republic of women, so worthy of veneration. January 13, 1488.

On the Coming of the Turks

Have you heard? The word has now spread: what was only rumored in private is now the talk of the entire city. Nor should the stories that are being bruited about be trusted altogether. The plundering fleet of the Turk has crossed over to Apulia and, alas, it is a bitter thing that, after all that has occurred, he is taking human lives. Who is so foolish that she does not fear the fate that consumes her neighbor? The savagery the tyrant showed to our ancestors is an example to those of us who survive. Do you not feel as though you hear the shouting and tumult of the invasion of Constantinople and the destruction of Chalchis and Scutari, which threw heaven and earth into disorder and silence? The bravest leaders were slain there in battle, if you remember; kings were mutilated, kingdoms overturned, captives were killed in pride and rage, and unburied bodies were thrown into the sea. The barbarian showed the vanquished no mercy; he had no respect for virgins, married women, or nuns; and he evinced no chastity and no religion. The avenging Turk gazed upon the severed heads of Christians with pleasure, he transformed all Greece into one grave and all Pergamon into a conflagration, and he, as victor, surveyed the whole world with unbridled pride.

If we treat these things that he has done as an example for ourselves, then we are pondering the very things he has in mind for us. For the Turk follows in the footsteps of his father's enmity. Indeed, inflamed, this outlaw marks us Christians, enemies of his own faith, with a sword vengeful and dripping with blood. Thus the disciple, rising again as his father's successor, pursues the peoples his father assailed. But if those clouds of bow-carrying Turks should descend on Italy, what do you think would be a sure guarantee for our defense? What will the wretched nations of peoples do, if that Thracian lion, powerful in arms, should come? Will some cities, unprepared for war, go to others for help? Already spirits weaken, and fondness for compassion withers. The comfort of a place to hide is no longer an option for us. There is no flight to friends and guardians.

The great things that have been settled can in part be consigned to the future. All of us feel pity for one another's calamities, we console those who have been defeated and show compassion to those whose cities have fallen. Nor is it possible to find one who is still able to offer any assistance. Thus we have all been led astray by hope, blinded by hate, and possessed by avarice. No one stands guard over the Christian realm; no one looks to the interests of the common good. Meanwhile our enemies grow strong; and those who artfully provoke us into war cut us down, plunder our cities, and conquer us. Think, sister, death will be one resting place for both of us. Nor should you think that there can be any home for the conquered other than the grave.

I am no Cassandra who with lamentation could foretell the destruction of Troy long before it fell. I am a more simplehearted girl who—if not present myself—can only be inoculated by previous examples of fidelity. For in the mirror of the past, events of the future can be discerned. One founder alone remains in heaven, one law, and in nature one order. We alone, turned away from god, continue to strive; we alone have become lawless and have shaken off every yoke of humanity from our savage minds. Our pardon, however, comes from heaven. Let us be aware, and let us correct the errors of our ways. Let us prepare our necks for compliance, not the knife. Let us sigh: let us show our tears to god, for the inhabitants of Nineveh washed away God's anger with their tears when they were on the point of death. For that most clement father of men took pity on his own people of Israel. He sent rolling so many helmets of the proudest troops of the Pharaoh, so many shields were seized, so many bodies floated in the blood red sea. For he knows that with dutiful hearts we receive exiles back who exercise the right to return home, if there is contrition for the wrongdoing.

Let us therefore renounce fruitless desires, let us reject all the pomp of the age. Let us, in a timely fashion, know our lord, who by his own mercy saved his more faithful servants from the depths of the ocean, the midst of fires, and the jaws of dire death. Vale. December 20, 1485.

Alessandra Strozzi

The daughter of a wealthy Florentine merchant, Alessandra Macinghi (c. 1408–1471) married Matteo Strozzi when she was fourteen and Matteo was twenty-five. As with almost all marriages involving elite families, the match was made on the basis of political and economic considerations. Florentine politics played a major role in the couple's lives. The Strozzi family belonged to a faction that opposed the Medici. When the Medici seized power in 1434, Matteo was exiled to Pesaro. Shortly after, in late 1435 or early 1436, Matteo died, most likely of the plague, leaving Alessandra a widow and mother of five at age twenty-eight.

Unlike the letters of Hildegard of Bingen and Laura Cereta, which were written in Latin and meant for a scholarly audience, Alessandra's correspondence was in the vernacular and entirely private and personal. Much of it was concerned with Alessandra's efforts to guide, protect, and advise her children. In the letter dated February 27, 1465, Alessandra gave her wayward son Lorenzo some stern advice. In the letters dated April 20 and July 26, 1465, she updated her son Filippo on her progress in finding him a wife, a project that was complicated by his status as the son of an exile. As you read the letters, try to get a sense of Alessandra's personality. How did she see herself? Was she a strong person? Was she confident in her own abilities? What was her relationship with her sons like? How involved was she in their lives?

Consider the following questions as you study the text below.

1. How did Alessandra see her role as a mother? What obligations did she have to her sons? What obligations did they have to her?

2. What qualities did Alessandra look for in a wife for her son Filippo? Did Filippo have any say in the matter?

From Alessandra to her son Lorenzo, February 27, 1453

I've done nothing about the bird-catcher's snares since I found out about them and discovered that [if you] want one of these little birds, beautiful as they are, sending it there [to Bruges] would cost at least 6 florins. And

Alessandra Strozzi, *Selected Letters of Alessandra Strozzi*, trans. Heather Gregory (Berkeley: University of California Press, 1997), pp. 67, 69, 71, 141, 143, 149, 151. Reprinted with permission of University of California Press.

because of this I haven't done anything about it. It isn't the right time to spend money on this sort of thing, because there are more important things to do with it. The Commune is ruining me as they've already imposed this new tax, announced on the 20th of this month, 32 times. They've assessed me at 5 florins, 16 soldi, [and] 10 denari, in gold, so you can work it out, how much I have to pay. So that you can do it, we'll say there are six florins for each tax. Work out the bill, if there are thirty-two [taxes], how much it is. And this has to he paid in a few months. We have to pay the tax six times for March and so on, month by month, and the payment for six taxes has already passed. So what with having to pay the Commune and starting legal proceedings against Niccolò Soderini, we have to forget about the nets. Put your mind on more important things so they really seem important to you.

Filippo was twenty-four years old on the fourth of July last year and on the 7th of next March it's twelve years since he left Florence. You were twenty on the 21st of August last year and this month it's seven years since you left Florence. Matteo is seventeen on the first day of March and on the seventh of this month it was three years since he left. Caterina will be twenty-two this May; Lesandra was eighteen last August. So now you have all the details.

To come back to what concerns you, you're old enough to behave in a different sort of way from how you have been; you've got to sort yourself out and concentrate on living properly. Up till now you've been thought of as a boy, but that's no longer the case, both because of your age and because your mistakes can't be put down to ignorance or to not knowing what you're doing. You've got the intelligence to know right from wrong, particularly when you've been told by your elders and betters. I gather you don't behave yourself as I'd like you to, and this has made very unhappy. I'm afraid you'll take a tumble one day and come out badly, because he who doesn't do his duty gets a nasty surprise. Your troubles are the worst I have, worse than all the rest. I'd been thinking of selling the farm at Antella to get rid of a lot of expense and aggravation and to help you [all] get on. Once what's owing on it has been paid it would bring in a clear eight hundred florins. Filippo has another three hundred and I'd thought of you and Filippo using the money for business ventures so you could start to accumulate some capital. [But] from all I hear you know more about throwing money away than about saving a penny, and it should be the opposite. I can see you've done us harm and brought us shame, and yourself too. I gather you've got some bad habits and lecturing you does no good at all. It looks like a bad sign to me and makes me take back all my good feelings for you. I don't know why you go your own way, knowing you're displeasing God, which matters more than anything else, and me as well, as it makes me very unhappy to hear about your failings. I leave it to you to consider the harm and shame that come from it. And you're really upsetting Jacopo; if you'd just started he could hope for better, but it's years since you started behaving so badly and he's put up with it for my sake. But if you don't mend your ways I won't be able to help any more. Let this be enough warning for you. Be wise because you need to be, and then it will be enough.

From Alessandra to her son Filippo, April 20, 1465

About finding you a wife, it seems to us and also to Tommaso Davizzi that if Francesco di Messer Guglielmino Tanagli were willing to give you his daughter, it would be a good match for all seasons, and that out of those which are available, this has the most to recommend it. I liked the da Vernia match, but from what I've heard she is clumsy and looks like a peasant. Now I will talk about it with Marco, about whether there are any others who would be better, and if there aren't, about finding out whether he [Francesco] wants to give her to you; we have only discussed it among ourselves. Francesco is well thought of and he takes part in the government, though not in the more important positions. Still, he has held offices. And if you ask "but why would he give her to an exile?" there are many reasons why he might do so. First, there's a shortage of young men of good family who have both money and abilities. Second, she has only a small dowry, I think it's a thousand florins, which is all artisan's dowry; the Manfredi gave their girl two thousand florins to marry her into the Pitti family, and she is only fifteen, whereas she [the Tanagli girl] is seventeen. So you see how it is. The third reason why I think he'll give her to us is that he has a big family and needs help to get them settled. This is the main reason why I think he'll agree. I'll find out more about it and if he doesn't want to, we'll find someone else. We will let you know.

From Alessandra to her son Filippo, July 26, 1465

It is now the 27th and Marco Parenti has come to see me. He has been talking to me about how we discussed finding you a wife a long time ago, and how we discussed the possibilities and where we thought we'd be able to go, and how it seemed to us that the best match, all other things being equal—if she had the right ideas and was beautiful, and wasn't rough or uncouth—was Francesco di Guglielmino Tanagli's daughter. We haven't heard of anything, up to the present, which would suit you better than this. And, to tell you the truth, we haven't discussed it too much, and you know the reason. However we have looked into it secretly, and we've found that there aren't any girls [whose families would marry them] to an exile, who don't have some shortcoming or other, whether [lack of] money or something else. Now the least serious drawback is the money, and when the other things we want are there we shouldn't look askance at the money, as you've said to me a number of times. So on St. Jacob's Day, as Francesco is a great friend of Marco's and trusts him greatly, having already heard several months ago that we were willing to have a look at the girl, he asked Marco about it in a fine manner and choosing his words well. He said that if he [Marco] asked for her on your behalf, when we had made up our minds, she would come to us willingly, because you're a man of substance and [his family] having always made good matches, as he had little to give her he would sooner send her away to someone of substance rather than give her to whoever he could find here, someone who would have little money, and that he wouldn't want to lower [his family's status]. He wanted Marco to go with him to his house, and he called the girl down, and he [Marco] saw her, and he [Francesco] said that if Caterina or I wanted to see her at any time he would show her to us. Marco says she looks beautiful and that she seemed suitable to him. We've been told that she has the right ideas and is capable and that she runs the household to a large extent because there are twelve children, six boys and six girls, and according to what I hear she runs it all because her mother is always pregnant and doesn't do much. Those who know the household say she manages the house and that her father has trained her to do it, and he is very well thought of and one of the best-mannered young men in Florence. So as it seems to me that we will have to wait a long time, I don't think we should put off taking this step, so let us know what we should do. And it would be good, to my way of thinking, if you asked Pandolfo [Pandolfini] about it, as he is the closest contact we have with this girl, [and ask him] to tell us all about it, and about her father's circumstances. I wouldn't tell him that we haven't discussed anything, but [say] that we have the idea, and if he would give you advice about it. And if what he says to you is favorable, like what we've heard, I would believe it, and decide to stop all this thinking, because once the decision has been made all your suffering will be over. I'm sure you will hear all about this business from Marco in much more detail than you have from me, because he discussed it and understands it better than me. Get the jewels ready and let them be beautiful, because we have found you a wife. As she is beautiful and the wife of Filippo Strozzi, she will need beautiful jewels. Just as you have honor in other things, she doesn't want to be lacking in this.

Christopher Columbus

It is easily forgotten that when Christopher Columbus (1451–1506) set sail across the "Western Ocean" with his three tiny ships on August 3, 1492, he was bound not for a new world but for "the Indies" (India, China, and the islands of East Asia). His venture was a prosaic even though a hazardous one. Despite his avowed goal of converting the people of the East to Christianity, Columbus's real reason for his voyage was less exalted: he hoped to discover a sea route that would make trade with the East—with its highly desired silks, rugs, jewelry, drugs, and spices—easier than the long and arduous caravan treks across Asia. According to Columbus's (mis)calculations, his destination could be reached by sailing some three thousand miles due west around the world. As it turned out, this was the distance to the islands of the Western hemisphere that he encountered.

Over a period of twelve years Columbus made four voyages, exploring many of the Caribbean islands and establishing several colonies. His voyages took him to the mainland of South and Central America as well. And, although he heard tales of a great ocean farther to the west, he never realized that the lands he had reached belonged not to Asia but to another continent.

The two selections that follow consist of the initial entry in a journal Columbus kept of his first voyage and a letter he wrote as he neared the end of that voyage, describing some of what he had seen and done. Of special interest is his description of the people who lived on the Caribbean islands, particularly his account of their character, style of life, and reception of the Europeans.

Consider the following questions as you study the text below.

1. How accurate were Columbus's descriptions of the New World? Do what extent did he embellish his account to meet the expectations of his audience?

2. How would you describe Columbus's attitude toward the indigenous peoples of the Americas? Did he see them as fellow human beings?

Journal and Letter

Prologue

Because, most Christian and very exalted and very excellent and very powerful Princes, King and Queen of the Spains and of the Islands of the Sea, our Lords, in this present year of 1492 after your Highnesses had made an end to the war of the Moors, who were reigning in Europe, and having finished the war in the very great city of Granada, where in this present year on the 2nd day of the month of January, I saw the Royal banners of your Highnesses placed by force of arms on the towers of the Alhambra, which is the fortress of the said City: and I saw the Moorish King come out to the gates of the City and kiss the Royal hands of your Highnesses, and the hands of the Prince, my Lord: and then in that present month, because of the information which I had given your Highnesses about the lands of India, and about a Prince who is called Great Khan, which means in our Romance language, King of Kings,—how he and his predecessors had many times sent to Rome to beg for men learned in our Holy Faith that they might be instructed therein, and that the Holy Father had never furnished them, and so, many people believing in idolatries and receiving among themselves sects of perdition, were lost:—your Highnesses, as Catholic Christians and Princes, loving the Holy Christian faith and the spreading of it, and enemies of the sect of Mahomet and of all idolatries and heresies, decided to send me, Christopher Columbus, to the said regions of India, to see the said Princes and the peoples and lands, and learn of their disposition, and of everything, and the measures which could be taken for their conversion to our Holy Faith: and you ordered that I should not go to the east by land, by which it is customary to go, but by way of the west, whence until to-day we do not know certainly that any one has gone. So that, after having banished all the Jews from all your Kingdoms and realms, in the same month of January, your Highnesses ordered me to go with a sufficient fleet to the said regions of India: and for that purpose granted me great favours and ennobled me, that from then henceforward I might entitle myself *Don* and should be High Admiral of the Ocean-Sea [*Atlantic—Ed.*] and Viceroy and perpetual Governor of all the islands and continental land which I might discover and acquire, and which from now henceforward might be discovered and acquired in the Ocean-Sea, and that my eldest son should succeed in the same manner, and thus from generation to generation for ever after: and I started from the city of Granada on Saturday, the 12th day of the month of May in the same year 1492: I came to the village of Palos, which is a sea-port, where I fitted out three vessels, very suitable for a similar undertaking: and I left the

Trans. J. B. Thacher.

said port, well supplied with a large quantity of provisions and with many seamen, on the 3rd day of the month of August in the said year on a Friday at the half hour before sunrise, and took my way to the Canary Islands of your Highnesses, which are in the said Ocean-Sea, in order to set out on my voyage from there and sail until I arrived at the Indies, and make known the message of your Highnesses to those Princes, and fulfil the commands which had thus been given me: and for this purpose, I decided to write everything I might do and see and which might take place on this voyage, very punctually from day to day, as will be seen henceforth. Also, Lords and Princes, besides describing each night what takes place during the day, and during the day, the sailings of the night, I propose to make a new chart for navigation, on which I will locate all the sea and the lands of the Ocean-Sea, in their proper places, under their winds; and further, to compose a book and show everything by means of drawing, by the latitude from the equator and by longitude from the west, and above all, it is fitting that I forget sleep, and study the navigation diligently, in order to thus fulfil these duties, which will be a great labour.

Letter

Sir:

As I know that you will have pleasure of the great victory which our Lord hath given me in my voyage, I write you this, by which you shall know that, in twenty days I passed over to the Indies with the fleet which the most illustrious King and Queen, our Lords, gave me: where I found very many islands peopled with inhabitants beyond number. And, of them all, I have taken possession for their Highnesses, with proclamation and the royal standard displayed; and I was not gainsaid. On the first which I found, I put the name San Salvador, in commemoration of His high Majesty, who marvellously hath given all this: the Indians call it Guanahani. The second I named the Island of Santa Maria de Concepcion, the third Ferrandina, the fourth Isabella, the fifth La Isla Juana [Cuba]; and so for each one a new name. When I reached Juana, I followed its coast westwardly, and found it so large that I thought it might be the mainland province of Cathay. And as I did not thus find any towns and villages on the seacoast, save small hamlets with the people whereof I could not get speech, because they all fled away forthwith, I went on farther in the same direction, thinking I should not miss of great cities or towns. And at the end of many leagues, seeing that there was no change, and that the coast was bearing me northwards, whereunto my desire was contrary since the winter was already confronting us, I formed the purpose of making from thence to the South, and as the wind also blew against me, I determined not to wait for other weather and turned back as far as a port agreed upon; from which I sent two men into the country to learn if there were a king, or any great cities. They travelled for three days, and found interminable small villages and a numberless population, but nought of ruling authority; wherefore they returned. I understood sufficiently from other Indians whom I had already taken, that this land, in its continuousness, was an island; and so I followed its coast eastwardly for a hundred and seven leagues as far as where it terminated; from which headland I saw another island to the east, ten or eight leagues distant from this, to which I at once gave the name La Spañola. And I proceeded thither, and followed the northern coast, as with La Juana, eastwardly for a hundred and seventy-eight great leagues in a direct easterly course, as with La Juana. The which, and all the others, are very large to an excessive degree, and this extremely so. In it, there are many havens on the seacoast, incomparable with any others that I know in Christendom, and plenty of rivers so good and great that it is a marvel. The lands thereof are high, and in it are very many ranges of hills, and most lofty mountains incomparably beyond the Island of Centre-frei; all most beautiful in a thousand shapes, and all accessible, and full of trees of a thousand kinds, so lofty that they seem to reach the sky. And I am assured that they never lose their foliage; as may be imagined, since I saw them as green and as beautiful as they are in Spain during May. And some of them were in flower, some in fruit, some in another stage according to their kind. And the nightingale was singing, and other birds of a thousand sorts, in the month of November, round about the way that I was going. There are palm-trees of six or eight species, wondrous to see for their beautiful variety; but so are the other trees, and fruits, and plants therein. There are wonderful pine-groves, and very large plains of verdure, and there is honey, and many kinds of birds, and many various fruits. In the earth there are many mines of metals; and there is a population of incalculable number. Spañola is a marvel; the mountains and hills, and plains and fields, and land, so beautiful and rich for planting and sowing, for breeding cattle of all sorts, for building of towns and villages. There could be no believing, without seeing, such harbours as are here, as well as the many and great rivers, and excellent waters, most of which contain gold. In the trees and fruits and plants, there are great differences from those of Juana. In this, there are many spiceries, and great mines of gold and other metals. The people of this island, and of all the others that I have found and seen or not seen, all go naked, men and women, just as their mothers bring them forth; although some women cover a single place with the leaf of a plant, or a cotton something which they make for that purpose. They have no iron or steel, nor any weapons; nor are they fit thereunto; not because they be not a well-formed people and of fair stature, but that they are most wondrously timorous. They have no other weapons than the stems of reeds in their seeding state, on the end of which they fix little sharpened stakes. Even these, they dare not use; for many times has it happened that I sent two or three men ashore to some village to parley, and countless numbers of them sallied forth, but as soon as they saw those approach, they fled away in such wise that even a father would not wait for his son. And this was not because any hurt had ever been done to any of them:—on the contrary, at every headland where I have gone and been able to hold speech with them, I gave them of everything which I had, as well cloth as many other things, without accepting aught therefor; but such they are, incurably timid. It is true that since they have become more assured, and are losing that terror, they are artless and generous with what they have, to such a degree as no one would believe but he who had seen it. Of anything they have, if it be asked for, they never say no, but do rather invite the person to accept it, and show as much lovingness as though they would give their hearts. And whether it be a thing of value, or one of little worth, they are straightways content with whatsoever trifle of whatsoever kind may be given them in return for it. I forbade that anything so worthless as fragments of broken platters, and pieces of broken glass, and strap-buckles, should be given them; although when they were able to get such things they seemed to think they had the best jewel in the world, for it was the hap of a sailor to get, in exchange for a strap, gold to the weight of two and a half castellanos, and others much more for other things of far less value; while for new blancas they gave every thing they had, even though it were the worth of two or three gold castellanos, or one or two arrobas of spun cotton. They took even pieces of broken barrel-hoops, and gave whatever they had, like senseless brutes; insomuch that it seemed to me ill. I forbade it, and I gave gratuitously a thousand useful things that I carried, in order that they may conceive affection, and furthermore may be made Christians; for they are inclined to the love and service of their Highnesses and of all the Castilian nation, and they strive to combine in giving us things which they have in abundance, and of which we are in need. And they know no sect, or idolatry; save that they all believe that power and goodness are in the sky, and they believed very firmly that I, with these ships and crew, came from the sky; and in such opinion, they received me at every place where I landed, after they had lost their terror. And this comes not because they are ignorant; on the contrary, they are men of very subtle wit, who navigate all those seas, and who give a marvellously good account of everything—but because they never saw men wearing clothes or the like of our ships. And as soon as I arrived in the Indies, in the first island that I found, I took some of them by force, to the intent that they should learn our speech and give me information of what there was in those parts. And so it was, that very soon they understood us and we them, what by speech or what by signs; and those Indians have been of much service. To this day I carry them with me who are still of the opinion that I come from heaven, as appears from much conversation which they have had with me. And they were the first to proclaim it wherever I arrived; and the others went running from house to house and to the neighbouring villages, with loud cries of "Come! come to see the people from heaven!" Then, as soon as their minds were reassured about us, every one came, men as well as women, so that there remained none behind, big or little; and they

all brought something to eat and drink, which they gave with wondrous lovingness. They have in all the islands very many canoes, after the manner of
rowing-galleys, some larger, some smaller; and a good many are larger than
a galley of eighteen benches. They are not so wide, because they are made of
a single log of timber, but a galley could not keep up with them in rowing,
for their motion is a thing beyond belief. And with these, they navigate
through all those islands which are numberless, and ply their traffic. I have
seen some of those canoes with seventy and eighty men in them, each one
with his oar. In all those islands, I saw not much diversity in the looks of the
people, or in their manners and language; but they all understand each
other, which is a thing of singular towardness for what I hope their Highnesses will determine, as to making them conversant with our holy faith,
unto which they are well disposed. I have already told how I had gone a
hundred and seven leagues, in a straight line from West to East, along the
seacoast of the Island of Juana; according to which itinerary, I can declare
that that island is larger than England and Scotland combined; as, over and
above those hundred and seven leagues, there remains for me, on the western side, two provinces whereto I did not go—one of which they call Anan,
where the people are born with tails—which provinces cannot be less in
length than fifty or sixty leagues, according to what may be understood from
the Indians with me, who know all the islands. This other, Española, has a
greater circumference than the whole of Spain from Colibre in Catalunya, by
the seacoast, as far as Fuente Ravia in Biscay; since, along one of its four
sides, I went for a hundred and eighty-eight great leagues in a straight line
from West to East. This is a land to be desired,—and once seen, never to be
relinquished—in which—although, indeed, I have taken possession of them
all for their Highnesses, and all are more richly endowed than I have skill
and power to say, and I hold them all in the name of their Highnesses who
can dispose thereof as much and as completely as of the kingdoms of
Castile—in this Española, in the place most suitable and best for its proximi-
ty to the gold mines, and for traffic with the continent, as well on this side as
on the further side of the Great Can, where there will be great commerce and
profit, I took possession of a large town which I named the city of Navidad.
And I have made fortifications there, and a fort which by this time will have
been completely finished and I have left therein men enough for such a purpose, with arms and artillery, and provisions for more than a year, and a
boat, and a man who is master of all sea-craft for making others; and great
friendship with the King of that land, to such a degree that he prided himself
on calling and holding me as his brother. And even though his mind might
change towards attacking those men, neither he nor his people know what
arms are, and go naked. As I have already said, they are the most timorous
creatures there are in the world, so that the men who remain there are alone
sufficient to destroy all that land, and the island is without personal danger
for them if they know how to behave themselves. It seems to me that in all

those islands, the men are all content with a single wife; and to their chief or king they give as many as twenty. The women, it appears to me, do more work than the men. Nor have I been able to learn whether they held personal property, for it seemed to me that whatever one had, they all took shares of, especially of eatable things. Down to the present, I have not found in those islands any monstrous men, as many expected, but on the contrary all the people are very comely; nor are they black like those in Guinea, but have flowing hair; and they are not begotten where there is an excessive violence of the rays of the sun. It is true that the sun is there very strong, notwithstanding that it is twenty-six degrees distant from the equinoctial line. In those islands, where there are lofty mountains, the cold was very keen there, this winter; but they endure it by being accustomed thereto, and by the help of the meats which they eat with many and inordinately hot spices. Thus I have not found, nor had any information of monsters, except of an island which is here the second in the approach to the Indies, which is inhabited by a people whom, in all the islands, they regard as very ferocious, who eat human flesh. These have many canoes with which they run through all the islands of India, and plunder and take as much as they can. They are no more ill-shapen than the others, but have the custom of wearing their hair long, like women; and they use bows and arrows of the same reed-stems, with a point of wood at the top, for lack of iron which they have not. Amongst those other tribes who are excessively cowardly, these are ferocious; but I hold them as nothing more than the others. These are they who have to do with the women of Matremonio—which is the first island that is encountered in the passage from Spain to the Indies—in which there are no men. Those women practise no female usages, but have bows and arrows of reeds such as above mentioned; and they arm and cover themselves with plates of copper of which they have much. In another island, which they assure me is larger than Española, the people have no hair. In this, there is incalculable gold; and concerning these and the rest I bring Indians with me as witnesses. And in conclusion, to speak only of what has been done in this voyage, which has been so hastily performed, their Highnesses may see that I shall give them as much gold as they may need, with very little aid which their Highnesses will give me; spices and cotton at once, as much as their Highnesses will order to be shipped, and as much as they shall order to be shipped of mastic—which till now has never been found except in Greece, in the island of Xio, and the Seignory sells it for what it likes; and aloe-wood as much as they shall order to be shipped; and slaves as many as they shall order to be shipped—and these shall be from idolaters. And I believe that I have discovered rhubarb and cinnamon, and I shall find that the men whom I am leaving there will have discovered a thousand other things of value; as I made no delay at any point, so long as the wind gave me an opportunity of sailing, except only in the town of Navidad till I had left things safely arranged and well established. And in truth I should have done much more if the ships had served me as well as might reasonably have been expected. This is enough; and thanks to eternal God our Lord who gives to all those who walk His way, victory over things which seem impossible; and this was signally one such, for although men have talked or written of those lands, it was all by conjecture, without confirmation from eyesight, importing just so much that the hearers for the most part listened and judged that there was more fable in it than anything actual, however trifling. Since thus our Redeemer has given to our most illustrious King and Queen, and to their famous kingdoms, this victory in so high a matter, Christendom should take gladness therein and make great festivals, and give solemn thanks to the Holy Trinity for the great exaltation they shall have by the conversion of so many peoples to our Holy faith; and next for the temporal benefit which will bring hither refreshment and profit, not only to Spain, but to all Christians. This briefly, in accordance with the facts. Dated on the caravel, off the Canary Islands, the 15 February of the year 1493.

At your command,

The Admiral

Benvenuto Cellini

Personal recognition for their accomplishments was not a goal generally sought by artists during the Middle Ages; the architects and artisans who designed and decorated the great Gothic cathedrals of Western Europe remain, for the most part, unknown. The Renaissance introduced a marked change in this practice. We know, for example, that Michelangelo designed the great dome of St. Peter's in Rome and that just after a century later Bernini was responsible for the enormous colonnade that surrounds the piazza in front of the cathedral. The individual, proud of his achievements, wished them to be recognized and admired as his work. Certainly, this was true of Benvenuto Cellini (1500–1571), the Florentine goldsmith and sculptor, who considered all of his exploits worthy of public recognition. As he puts it at the beginning of his famous *Autobiography*, "All men . . . who have done anything of excellence, or which may properly resemble excellence, ought . . . to describe their life with their own hand. . . ."

The selection that follows is composed of excerpts from Cellini's long *Autobiography*. These do not attempt to give a full account of his life but rather to offer some insights into the kind of individual he was. They reveal him as having a complex and even contradictory character—kind but arrogant, loving but vengeful, sociable but irascible, honest but devious, generous but covetous, hard-headed but credulous. Throughout everything shines the egotism of a rampant, yet engaging, individualist.

Consider the following questions as you study the text below.

1. Based on your reading of Cellini's autobiography, describe the life of an artist in Renaissance Italy. How different was it from the life of an artist in the Middle Ages?

2. How important were patrons to Cellini's career? How much control did he have over the type, style, and details of the pieces he created?

The Autobiography of Benvenuto Cellini

Book First

I

All men of whatsoever quality they be, who have done anything of excellence, or which may properly resemble excellence, ought, if they are persons of truth and honesty, to describe their life with their own hand; but they
ought not to attempt so fine an enterprise till they have passed the age of
forty. This duty occurs to my own mind, now that I am traveling beyond the
term of fifty-eight years, and am in Florence, the city of my birth. Many un-
toward things can I remember, such as happen to all who live upon our
earth; and from those adversities I am now more free than at any previous
period of my career—nay, it seems to me that I enjoy greater content of soul
and health of body than ever I did in by-gone years. I can also bring to mind
some pleasant goods and some inestimable evils, which, when I turn my
thoughts backward, strike terror in me, and astonishment that I should have
reached this age of fifty-eight, wherein, thanks be to God, I am still travelling
prosperously forward.

II

It is true that men who have laboured with some show of excellence,
have already given knowledge of themselves to the world; and this alone
ought to suffice them; I mean the fact that they have proved their manhood
and achieved renown. Yet one must needs live like others; and so in a work
like this there will always be found occasion for natural bragging, which is of
divers kinds, and the first is that a man should let others know he draws his
lineage from persons of worth and most ancient origin.

I am called Benvenuto Cellini, son of Maestro Giovanni, son of Andrea,
son of Cristofano Cellini; my mother was Madonna Elisabetta, daughter to
Stefano Granacci; both parents citizens of Florence. It is found written in
chronicles made by our ancestors of Florence, men of old time and of credi-
bility, even as Giovanni Villani writes, that the city of Florence was evidently
built in imitation of the fair city of Rome; and certain remnants of the Colosseum and the Baths can yet be traced. These things are near Santa Croce. The
capital was where is now the Old Market. The Rotonda is entire, which was
made for the temple of Mars, and is now dedicated to our Saint John. That
thus it was, can very well be seen, and cannot be denied; but the said buildings are much smaller than those of Rome. He who caused them to be built,

Trans. J. A. Symonds.

they say, was Julius Caesar, in concert with some noble Romans, who, when Fiesole had been stormed and taken, raised a city in this place, and each of them took in hand to erect one of these notable edifices.

. . .

Thus then we find; and thus we believe that we are descended from a man of worth. Furthermore, we find that there are Cellinis of our stock in Ravenna, that most ancient town of Italy, where too are plenty of gentle folk. In Pisa also there are some, and I have discovered them in many parts of Christendom; and in this state also the breed exists, men devoted to the profession of arms; for not many years ago a young man, called Luca Cellini, a beardless youth, fought with a soldier of experience and a most valorous man, named Francesco da Vicorati, who had frequently fought before in single combat. This Luca, by his own valour, with sword in hand, overcame and slew him, with such bravery and stoutness that he moved the folk to wonder, who were expecting quite the contrary issue; so that I glory in tracing my descent from men of valour.

As for the trifling honours which I have gained for my house, under the well-known conditions of our present ways of living, and by means of my art, albeit the same are matters of no great moment, I will relate these in their proper time and place, taking much more pride in having been born humble and having laid some honourable foundation for my family, than if I had been born of great lineage and had stained or so overclouded that by my base qualities.

. . .

VII

. . .

When I reached the age of fifteen, I put myself, against my father's will, to the goldsmith's trade with a man called Antonio, son of Sandro, known commonly as Marcone the goldsmith. He was a most excellent craftsman and a very good fellow to boot, high-spirited and frank in all his ways. My father would not let him give me wages like the other apprentices; for having taken up the study of this art to please myself, he wished me to indulge my whim for drawing to the full. I did so willingly enough; and that honest master of mine took marvellous delight in my performances. He had an only son, a bastard, to whom he often gave his orders, in order to spare me. My liking for the art was so great, or, I may truly say, my natural bias, both one and the other, that in a few months I caught up the good, nay, the best young craftsmen in our business, and began to reap the fruits of my labours. I did not, however, neglect to gratify my good father from time to time by playing on the flute or cornet. Each time he heard me, I used to make his tears fall accompanied with deep-drawn sighs of satisfaction. My filial piety often made me give him that contentment, and induced me to pretend that I enjoyed the music too.

XII

When I had recovered my health, I returned to my old friend Marcone, the worthy goldsmith, who put me in the way of earning money, with which I helped my father and our household. About that time there came to Florence a sculptor named Piero Torrigiani; he arrived from England, where he had resided many years; and being intimate with my master, he daily visited his house; and when he saw my drawings and the things which I was making, he said: "I have come to Florence to enlist as many young men as I can; for I have undertaken to execute a great work for my king, and want some of my own Florentines to help me. Now your method of working and your designs are worthy rather of a sculptor than a goldsmith; and since I have to turn out a great piece of bronze, I will at the same time turn you into a rich and able artist." This man had a splendid person and a most arrogant spirit, with the air of a great soldier more than of a sculptor, especially in regard to his vehement gestures and his resonant voice, together with a habit he had of knitting his brows, enough to frighten any man of courage. He kept talking every day about his gallant feats among those beasts of Englishmen.

In course of conversation he happened to mention Michel Agnolo Buonarroti, led thereto by a drawing I had made from a cartoon[1] of the divinest painter. This cartoon was the first masterpiece which Michel Agnolo exhibited, in proof of his stupendous talents. He produced it in competition with another painter, Lionardo da Vinci, who also made a cartoon; and both were intended for the council-hall in the palace of the Signory. They represented the taking of Pisa by the Florentines; and our admirable Lionardo had chosen to depict a battle of horses, with the capture of some standards, in as divine a style as could possibly be imagined. Michel Agnolo in his cartoon portrayed a number of foot-soldiers, who, the season being summer, had gone to bathe in Arno. He drew them at the very moment the alarm is sounded, and the men all naked run to arms; so splendid in their action that nothing survives of ancient or of modern art which touches the same lofty point of excellence; and as I have already said, the design of the great Lionardo was itself most admirably beautiful. These two cartoons stood, one in the palace of the Medici, the other in the hall of the Pope. So long as they

---

[1][A preliminary sketch for a work of art to be executed later—*Ed.*]

remained intact, they were the school of the world. Though the divine Michel Agnolo in later life finished that great chapel of Pope Julius, he never rose half-way to the same pitch of power; his genius never afterwards attained to the force of those first studies.

XIII

Now let us return to Piero Torrigiani, who, with my drawing in his hand, spoke as follows: "This Buonarroti and I used, when we were boys, to go into the Church of the Carmine, to learn drawing from the chapel of Masaccio. It was Buonarroti's habit to banter all who were drawing there; and one day, among others, when he was annoying me, I got more angry than usual, and clenching my fist, gave him such a blow on the nose, that I felt bone and cartilage go down like biscuit beneath my knuckles; and this mark of mine he will carry with him to the grave." These words begat in me such hatred of the man, since I was always gazing at the masterpieces of the divine Michel Agnolo, that although I felt a wish to go with him to England, I now could never bear the sight of him.

All the while I was in Florence, I studied the noble manner of Michel Agnolo, and from this I have never deviated. About that time I contracted a close and familiar friendship with an amiable lad of my own age, who was also in the goldsmith's trade. He was called Francesco, son of Filippo, and grandson of Fra Lippo Lippi, that most excellent painter. Through intercourse together, such love grew up between us that, day or night, we never stayed apart. The house where he lived was still full of the fine studies which his father had made, bound up in several books of drawings by his hand, and taken from the best antiquities of Rome. The sight of these things filled me with passionate enthusiasm; and for two years or thereabouts we lived in intimacy. At that time I fashioned a silver bas-relief of the size of a little child's hand. It was intended for the clasp to a man's belt; for they were then worn as large as that. I carved on it a knot of leaves in the antique style, with figures of children and other masks of great beauty. This piece I made in the workshop of one Francesco Salimbene; and on its being exhibited to the trade, the goldsmiths praised me as the best young craftsman of their art.

There was one Giovan Battista, surnamed Il Tasso, a woodcarver, precisely of my own age, who one day said to me that if I was willing to go to Rome, he should be glad to join me. Now we had this conversation together immediately after dinner; and I being angry with my father for the same old reason of the music, said to Tasso: "You are a fellow of words, not deeds." He answered: "I too have come to anger with my mother; and if I had cash enough to take me to Rome, I would not turn back to lock the door of that wretched little workshop I call mine." To these words I replied that if that was all that kept him in Florence I had money enough in my pockets to bring us both to Rome. Talking thus and walking onwards, we found ourselves at the gate San Piero Gattolini without noticing that we had got there; whereupon I said: "Friend Tasso, this is God's doing that we have reached this gate without either you or me noticing that we were there; and now that I am here, it seems to me that I have finished half the journey." And so, being of one accord, we pursued our way together, saying "Oh, what will our old folks say this evening?" We then made an agreement not to think more about them till we reached Rome. So we tied our aprons behind our backs, and trudged almost in silence to Siena. When we arrived at Siena, Tasso said (for he had hurt his feet) that he would not go farther, and asked me to lend him money to get back. I made answer: "I should not have enough left to go forward; you ought indeed to have thought of this on leaving Florence; and if it is because of your feet that you shirk the journey, we will find a return horse for Rome, which will deprive you of the excuse." Accordingly I hired a horse; and seeing that he did not answer, I took my way toward the gate of Rome. When he knew that I was firmly resolved to go, muttering between his teeth, and limping as well as he could, he came on behind me very slowly and at a great distance. On reaching the gate, I felt pity for my comrade, and waited for him, and took him on the crupper, saying: "What would our friends speak of us tomorrow, if, having left for Rome, we had not pluck to get beyond Siena?" Then the good Tasso said I spoke the truth; and as he was a pleasant fellow, he began to laugh and sing; and in this way, always singing and laughing, we travelled the whole way to Rome. I had just nineteen years then, and so had the century. [*1519—Ed.*]

When we reached Rome, I put myself under a master who was known as Il Firenzuola. His name was Giovanni, and he came from Firenzuola in Lombardy, a most able craftsman in large vases and big plate of that kind. I showed him part of the model for the clasp which I had made in Florence at Salimbene's. It pleased him exceedingly; and turning to one of his journeymen, a Florentine called Giannotto Giannotti, who had been several years with him, he spoke as follows: "This fellow is one of the Florentines who know something, and you are one of those who know nothing." Then I recognised the man, and turned to speak with him; for before he went to Rome, we often went to draw together, and had been very intimate comrades. He was so put out by the words his master flung at him, that he said he did not recognise me or know who I was; whereupon I got angry, and cried out: "O Giannotto, you who were once my friend—for have we not been together in such and such places, and drawn, and ate, and drunk, and slept in company at your house in the country? I don't want you to bear witness on my behalf to this worthy man, your master, because I hope my hands are such that without aid from you they will declare what sort of a fellow I am."

XIV

When I had thus spoken, Firenzuola, who was a man of hot spirit and brave, turned to Giannotto, and said to him, "You vile rascal, aren't you ashamed to treat a man who has been so intimate a comrade with you in this way?" And with the same movement of quick feeling, he faced round and said to me: "Welcome to my workshop; and do as you have promised; let your hands declare what man you are."

He gave me a very fine piece of silver plate to work on for a cardinal. It was a little oblong box, copied from the porphyry sarcophagus before the door of the Rotonda. Beside what I copied, I enriched it with so many elegant masks of my invention, that my master went about showing it through the art, and boasting that so good a piece of work had been turned out from his shop. It was about half a cubit in size, and was so constructed as to serve for a salt-cellar at table. This was the first earning that I touched at Rome, and part of it I sent to assist my good father; the rest I kept for my own use, living upon it while I went about studying the antiquities of Rome, until my money failed, and I had to return to the shop for work. Battista del Tasso, my comrade, did not stay long in Rome, but went back to Florence.

After undertaking some new commissions, I took it into my head, as soon as I had finished them, to change my master; I had indeed been worried into doing so by a certain Milanese, called Pagolo Arsago. My first master, Firenzuola, had a great quarrel about this with Arsago, and abused him in my presence; whereupon I took up speech in defence of my new master. I said that I was born free, and free I meant to live, and that there was no reason to complain of him, far less of me, since some few crowns of wages were still due to me; also that I chose to go, like a free journeyman, where it pleased me, knowing I did wrong to no man. My new master then put in with his excuses, saying that he had not asked me to come, and that I should gratify him by returning to Firenzuola. To this I replied that I was not aware of wronging the latter in any way, and as I had completed his commissions, I chose to be my own master and not the man of others, and that he who wanted me must beg me of myself. Firenzuola cried: "I don't intend to beg you of yourself; I have done with you; don't show yourself again upon my premises." I reminded him of the money he owed me. He laughed me in the face; on which I said that if I knew how to use my tools in handicraft as well as he had seen, I could be quite as clever with my sword in claiming the just payment of my labour. While we were exchanging these words, an old man happened to come up, called Maestro Antonio, of San Marino. He was the chief among the Roman goldsmiths, and had been Firenzuola's master. Hearing what I had to say, which I took good care that he should understand, he immediately espoused my cause, and bade Firenzuola pay me. The dispute waxed warm, because Firenzuola was an admirable swordsman, far better than he was a goldsmith. Yet reason made itself heard; and I backed my cause with the same spirit, till I got myself paid. In course of time Firenzuola and I became friends, and at his request I stood godfather to one of his children.

XV

I went on working with Pagolo Arsago, and earned a good deal of money, the greater part of which I always sent to my good father. At the end of two years, upon my father's entreaty, I returned to Florence, and put myself once more under Francesco Salimbene, with whom I earned a great deal, and took continual pains to improve in my arts. I renewed my intimacy with Francesco di Filippo; and though I was too much given to pleasure, owing to that accursed music, I never neglected to devote some hours of the day or night to study. At that time I fashioned a silver heart's-key (*chiavaquore*), as it was then called. This was a girdle three inches broad, which used to be made for brides and was executed in half relief with some small figures in the round. It was a commission from a man called Raffaello Lapaccini. I was very badly paid; but the honour which it brought me was worth far more than the gain I might have justly made by it. Having at this time worked with many different persons in Florence, I had come to know some worthy men among the goldsmiths, as, for instance, Marcone, my first master; but I also met with others reputed honest, who did all they could to ruin me, and robbed me grossly. When I perceived this, I left their company, and held them for thieves and blackguards. One of the goldsmiths, called Giovanbattista Sogliani, kindly accommodated me with part of his shop, which stood at the side of the New Market near the Landi's bank. There I finished several pretty pieces, and made good gains, and was able to give my family much help. This roused the jealousy of the bad men among my former masters, who were called Salvadore and Michele Guasconti. In the guild of the goldsmiths they had three big shops, and drove a thriving trade. On becoming aware of their evil will against me, I complained to certain worthy fellows, and remarked that they ought to have been satisfied with the thieveries they practised on me under the cloak of hypocritical kindness. This coming to their ears, they threatened to make me sorely repent of such words; but I, who knew not what the colour of fear was, paid them little or no heed.

XVI

It chanced one day that I was leaning against a shop of one of these men, who called out to me, and began partly reproaching, partly bullying. I answered that had they done their duty by me, I should have spoken of them what one speaks of good and worthy men; but as they had done the contrary, they ought to complain of themselves and not of me. While I was standing there and talking, one of them, named Gherardo Guasconti, their cousin, having perhaps been put up to it by them, lay in wait till a beast of burden went by. It was a load of bricks. When the load reached me, Gherardo pushed it so violently on my body that I was very much hurt. Turning suddenly round and seeing him laughing, I struck him such a blow on the temple that he fell down, stunned, like one dead. Then I faced round to his cousins, and said: "That's the way to treat cowardly thieves of your sort"; and when they wanted to make a move upon me, trusting to their number, I, whose blood was now well up, laid hands to a little knife I had, and cried: "If one of you comes out of the shop, let the other run for the confessor, because the doctor will have nothing to do here." These words so frightened them that no one stirred to help their cousin. As soon as I had gone, the fathers and sons ran to the Eight, and declared that I had assaulted them in their shops with sword in hand, a thing which had never yet been seen in Florence. The magistrates had me summoned. I appeared before them; and they began to upbraid me and cry out upon me—partly, I think because they saw me in my cloak, while the others were dressed like citizens in mantle and hood; but also because my adversaries had been to the houses of those magistrates, and had talked with all of them in private, while I, inexperienced in such matters, had not spoken to any of them, trusting in the goodness of my cause. I said that, having received such outrage and insult from Gherardo, and in my fury having only given him a box on the ear, I did not think I deserved such a vehement reprimand.

. . .

XIX

[LATER]

At Siena I waited for the mail to Rome, which I afterwards joined; and when we passed the Paglia, we met a courier carrying news of the new Pope Clement VII. Upon my arrival in Rome, I went to work in the shop of the master-goldsmith Santi. He was dead; but a son of his carried on the business. He did not work himself, but entrusted all his commissions to a young man named Lucagnolo from Iesi, a country fellow, who while yet a child had come into Santi's service. This man was short but well proportioned, and was a more skilful craftsman than any one whom I had met with up to that time; remarkable for facility and excellent in design. He executed large plate only; that is to say, vases of the utmost beauty, basins, and such pieces. Having put myself to work there, I began to make some candelabra for the Bishop of Salamanca, a Spaniard. They were richly chased, so far as the sort of work admits. A pupil of Raffaello da Urbino called Gian Francesco, and commonly known as Il Fattore, was a painter of great ability; and being on terms of friendship with the Bishop, he introduced me to his favour, so that

I obtained many commissions from that prelate, and earned considerable sums of money.

During that time I went to draw sometimes in Michel Agnolo's chapel, and sometimes in the house of Agostino Chigi of Siena, which contained many incomparable paintings by the hand of that great master Raffaello. This I did on feast-days, because the house was then inhabited by Messer Gismondo, Agostino's brother. They plumed themselves exceedingly when they saw young men of my sort coming to study in their palaces. Gismondo's wife, noticing my frequent presence in that house—she was a lady as courteous as could be, and of surpassing beauty—came up to me one day, looked at my drawings, and asked me if I was a sculptor or a painter; to whom I said I was a goldsmith. She remarked that I drew too well for a goldsmith; and having made one of her waiting-maids bring a lily of the finest diamonds set in gold, she showed it to me, and bade me value it. I valued it at 800 crowns. Then she said that I had very nearly hit the mark, and asked me whether I felt capable of setting the stones really well. I said that I should much like to do so, and began before her eyes to make a little sketch for it, working all the better because of the pleasure I took in conversing with so lovely and agreeable a gentlewoman. When the sketch was finished, another Roman lady of great beauty joined us; she had been above, and now descending to the ground-floor, asked Madonna Porzia what she was doing there. She answered with a smile: "I am amusing myself by watching this worthy young man at his drawing; he is as good as he is handsome." I had by this time acquired a trifle of assurance, mixed, however, with some honest bashfulness; so I blushed and said: "Such as I am, lady, I shall ever be most ready to serve you." The gentlewoman, also slightly blushing, said: "You know well that I want you to serve me"; and reaching me the lily, told me to take it away; and gave me besides twenty golden crowns which she had in her bag, and added: "Set me the jewel after the fashion you have sketched, and keep for me the old gold in which it is now set." On this the Roman lady observed: "If I were in that young man's body, I should go off without asking leave." Madonna Porzia replied that virtues rarely are at home with vices, and that if I did such a thing, I should strongly belie my good looks of an honest man. Then turning round, she took the Roman lady's hand, and with a pleasant smile said: "Farewell Benvenuto." I stayed on a short while at the drawing I was making, which was a copy of a Jove by Raffaello. When I had finished it and left the house, I set myself to making a little model of wax, in order to show how the jewel would look when it was completed. This I took to Madonna Porzia, whom I found with the same Roman lady. Both of them were highly satisfied with my work, and treated me so kindly that, being somewhat emboldened, I promised the jewel should be twice as good as the model. Accordingly I set hand to it, and in twelve days I finished it in the form of a fleur-de-lys, as I have said above, ornamenting it with little masks, children, and animals, exquisitely enamelled, whereby the diamonds which formed the lily were more than doubled in effect.

XX

While I was working at this piece, Lucagnolo, of whose ability I have before spoken, showed considerable discontent, telling me over and over again that I might acquire far more profit and honour by helping him to execute large plate, as I had done at first. I made him answer that, whenever I chose, I should always be capable of working at great silver pieces; but that things like that on which I was now engaged were not commissioned every day; and beside their bringing no less honour than large silver plate, there was also more profit to be made by them. He laughed me in the face, and said: "Wait and see Benvenuto; for by the time that you have finished that work of yours, I will make haste to have finished this vase, which I took in hand when you did the jewel; and then experience shall teach you what profit I shall get from my vase, and what you will get from your ornament." I answered that I was very glad indeed to enter into such a competition with so good a craftsman as he was, because the end would show which of us was mistaken. Accordingly both the one and the other of us, with a scornful smile upon our lips, bent our head in grim earnest to the work, which both were now desirous of accomplishing; so that after about ten days, each had finished his undertaking with great delicacy and artistic skill.

Lucagnolo's was a huge silver piece, used at the table of Pope Clement, into which he flung away bits of bone and the rind of divers fruits, while eating; an object of ostentation rather than necessity. The vase was adorned with two fine handles, together with many masks, both small and great, and masses of lovely foliage, in as exquisite a style of elegance as could be imagined; and seeing which I said it was the most beautiful vase that ever I set eyes on. Thinking he had convinced me, Lucagnolo replied: "Your work seems to me no less beautiful, but we shall soon perceive the difference between the two." So he took his vase and carried it to the Pope, who was very well pleased with it, and ordered at once that he should be paid at the ordinary rate of such large plate. Meanwhile I carried mine to Madonna Porzia, who looked at it with astonishment, and told me I had far surpassed my promise. Then she bade me ask for my reward whatever I liked; for it seemed to her my desert was so great that if I craved a castle she could hardly recompense me; but since that was not in her hands to bestow, she added laughing that I must beg what lay within her power. I answered that the greatest reward I could desire for my labour was to have satisfied her ladyship. Then, smiling in my turn, and bowing to her, I took my leave, saying I wanted no reward but that. She turned to the Roman lady and said: "You see that the qualities we discerned in him are companied by virtues, and not vices." They both expressed their admiration, and then Madonna Porzio continued: "Friend Benvenuto, have you never heard it said that when the poor give to the rich, the devil laughs?" I replied: "Quite true! and yet, in the midst of all his troubles, I should like this time to see him laugh"; and as I took my leave, she said that this time she had no will to bestow on him that favour.

When I came back to the shop, Lucagnolo had the money for his vase in a paper packet; and on my arrival he cried out: "Come and compare the price of your jewel with the price of my plate." I said that he must leave things as they were till the next day, because I hoped that even as my work in its kind was not less excellent than his, so I should be able to show him quite an equal price for it.

XXI

On the day following, Madonna Porzia sent a major-domo of hers to my shop, who called me out, and putting into my hands a paper packet full of money from his lady, told me that she did not choose the devil should have his whole laugh out; by which she hinted that the money sent me was not the entire payment merited by my industry, and other messages were added worthy of so courteous a lady. Lucagnolo, who was burning to compare his packet with mine, burst into the shop, then in the presence of twelve journeymen and some neighbours, eager to behold the result of this competition, he seized his packet, scornfully exclaiming "Ou! Ou!" three or four times, while he poured his money on the counter with a great noise. They were twenty-five crowns in giulios; and he fancied that mine would be four or five crowns *di moneta*. I for my part, stunned and stifled by his cries, and by the looks and smiles of the bystanders, first peeped into my packet; then, after seeing that it contained nothing but gold, I retired to one end of the counter, and, keeping my eyes lowered and making no noise at all, I lifted it with both hands suddenly above my head, and emptied it like a mill hopper. My coin was twice as much as his; which caused the onlookers, who had fixed their eyes on me with some derision, to turn round suddenly to him and say: "Lucagnolo, Benvenuto's pieces, being all of gold and twice as many as yours, make a far finer effect." I thought for certain that, what with jealousy and what with shame, Lucagnolo would have fallen dead upon the spot; and though he took the third part of my gain, since I was a journeyman (for such is the custom of the trade, two-thirds fall to the workman and one-third to the masters of the shop), yet inconsiderate envy had more power in him than avarice: it ought indeed to have worked quite the other way, he being a peasant's son from Iesi. He cursed his art and those who taught it to him, vowing that thenceforth he would never work at large plate, but give his whole attention to those whoreson gewgaws, since they were so well paid. Equally enraged on my side, I answered that every bird sang its own note; that he talked after the fashion of the hovels he came from; but that I dared swear that I should succeed with ease in making his lubberly lumber, while he would never be successful in my whoreson gewgaws. Thus I flung off in a passion, telling him that I would soon show him that I spoke truth. The bystanders openly declared against him, holding him for a lout, as indeed he was, and me for a man, as I had proved myself.

XXII

Next day, I went to thank Madonna Porzia, and told her that her lady-ship had done the opposite of what she said she would; for that while I wanted to make the devil laugh, she had made him once more deny God. We both laughed pleasantly at this, and she gave me other commissions for fine and substantial work.

Meanwhile, I contrived, by means of a pupil of Raffaello da Urbino, to get an order from the Bishop of Salamanca for one of those great water-vessels called *acquereccia*, which are used for ornaments to place on side-boards. He wanted a pair made of equal size; and one of them he intrusted to Lucagnolo, the other to me. Giovan Francesco, the painter I have mentioned, gave us the design. Accordingly I set hand with marvellous good-will to this piece of plate, and was accommodated with a part of his workshop by a Milanese named Maestro Giovan Piero della Tacca. Having made my prepa-rations, I calculated how much money I should need for certain affairs of my own, and sent all the rest to assist my poor father.

It so happened that just when this was being paid to him in Florence, he stumbled upon one of those Radicals who were in the Eight at the time when I got into that little trouble there. It was the very man who had abused him so rudely, and who swore that I should certainly be sent into the country with the lances. Now this fellow had some sons of very bad morals and re-pute; wherefore my father said to him: "Misfortunes can happen to anybody, especially to men of choleric humour when they are in the right, even as it happened to my son; but let the rest of his life bear witness how virtuously I have brought him up. Would God, for your well-being, that your sons may act neither worse nor better towards you than mine do to me. God rendered me able to bring them up as I have done; and where my own power could not reach, 'twas He who rescued them, against your expectation, out of your violent hands." On leaving the man, he wrote me all this story, begging me for God's sake to practise music at times, in order that I might not lose the fine accomplishment which he had taught me with such trouble. The letter so overflowed with expressions of the tenderest fatherly affection, that I was moved to tears of filial piety, resolving before he died, to gratify him amply with regard to music. Thus God grants us those lawful blessings which we ask in prayer, nothing doubting.

XXIII

While I was pushing forward Salamanca's vase, I had only one little boy as help, whom I had taken at the entreaty of friends, and half against my own will, to be my workman. He was about fourteen years of age, bore the name of Paulino, and was son to a Roman burgess, who lived upon the in-come of his property. Paulino was the best-mannered, the most honest, and

the most beautiful boy I ever saw in my whole life. His modest ways and actions, together with his superlative beauty and his devotion to myself, bred
in me as great an affection for him as a man's breast can hold. This passionate love led me oftentimes to delight the lad with music; for I observed that
his marvellous features, which by complexion wore a tone of modest melancholy, brightened up, and when I took my cornet, broke into a smile so lovely and sweet, that I do not marvel at the silly stories which the Greeks have
written about the deities of heaven. Indeed, if my boy had lived in those
times, he would probably have turned their heads still more. He had a sister,
named Faustina, more beautiful, I verily believe, than that Faustina about
whom the old books gossip so. Sometimes he took me to their vineyard, and,
so far as I could judge, it struck me that Paulino's good father would have
welcomed me as a son-in-law. This affair led me to play more than I was
used to do.

It happened at that time that one Giangiacomo of Cesena, a musician in
the Pope's band, and a very excellent performer, sent word through Lorenzo,
the trumpeter of Lucca, who is now in our Duke's service, to inquire whether
I was inclined to help them at the Pope's Ferragosto, playing soprano with
my cornet in some motets of great beauty selected by them for that occasion.
Although I had the greatest desire to finish the vase I had begun, yet, since
music has a wondrous charm of its own, and also because I wished to please
my old father, I consented to join them. During eight days before the festival
we practised two hours a day together; then on the first of August we went
to the Belvedere, and while Pope Clement was at table, we played those
carefully studied motets so well that his Holiness protested he had never
heard music more sweetly executed or with better harmony of parts. He sent
for Giangiacomo, and asked him where and how he had procured so excellent a cornet for soprano, and inquired particularly who I was. Giangiacomo
told him my name in full. Whereupon the Pope said: "So, then, he is the son
of Maestro Giovanni?" On being assured I was, the Pope expressed his wish
to have me in his service with the other bandsmen. Giangiacomo replied:
"Most blessed Father, I cannot pretend for certain that you will get him, for
his profession, to which he devotes himself assiduously, is that of a goldsmith, and he works in it miraculously well, and earns by it far more than he
could do by playing." To this the Pope added: "I am the better inclined to
him now that I find him possessor of a talent more than I expected. See that
he obtains the same salary as the rest of you; and tell him from me to join my
service, and that I will find work enough by the day for him to do at his other
trade." Then stretching out his hand, he gave him a hundred golden crowns
of the Camera in a handkerchief, and said: "Divide these so that he may take
his share."

When Giangiacomo left the Pope, he came to us, and related in detail all
that the Pope had said, and after dividing the money between the eight of us,
and giving me my share, he said to me: "Now I am going to have you

inscribed among our company." I replied: "Let the day pass; tomorrow I will give my answer." When I left them, I went meditating whether I ought to accept the invitation, inasmuch as I could not but suffer if I abandoned the noble studies of my art. The following night my father appeared to me in a dream, and begged me with tears of tenderest affection, for God's love and his, to enter upon this engagement. Methought I answered that nothing would induce me to do so. In an instant he assumed so horrible an aspect as to frighten me out of my wits, and cried: "If you do not, you will have a father's curse; but if you do, may you be ever blessed by me!" When I awoke, I ran, for very fright, to have myself inscribed. Then I wrote to my old father, telling him the news, which so affected him with extreme joy that a sudden fit of illness took him, and well-nigh brought him to death's door. In his answer to my letter, he told me that he too had dreamed nearly the same as I had.

XXIV

Knowing now that I had gratified my father's honest wish, I began to think that everything would prosper with me to a glorious and honourable end. Accordingly, I set myself with indefatigable industry to the completion of the vase I had begun for Salamanca. That prelate was a very extraordinary man, extremely rich, but difficult to please. He sent daily to learn what I was doing; and when his messenger did not find me at home, he broke into fury, saying that he would take the work out of my hands and give it to others to finish. This came of my slavery to that accursed music. Still I laboured diligently night and day, until, when I had brought my work to a point when it could be exhibited, I submitted it to the inspection of the Bishop. This so increased his desire to see it finished, that I was sorry I had shown it. At the end of three months I had it ready, with little animals and foliage and masks, so beautiful as one could hope to see. No sooner was it done than I sent it by the hand of my workman, Paulino, to show that able artist Lucagnolo, of whom I have spoken above. Paulino, with the grace and beauty which belonged to him, spoke as follows: "Messer Lucagnolo, Benvenuto bids me say that he has sent to show you his promises and your lumber, expecting in return to see from you his gewgaws." This message given, Lucagnolo took up the vase, and carefully examined it; then he said to Paulino: "Fair boy, tell your master that he is a great and able artist, and that I beg him to be willing to have me for a friend, and not to engage in aught else." The mission of that virtuous and marvellous lad caused me the greatest joy; and then the vase was carried to Salamanca, who ordered it to be valued. Lucagnolo took part in the valuation, estimating and praising it far above my own opinion. Salamanca lifted up the vase, cried like a true Spaniard: "I swear by God that I will take as long in paying him as he has lagged in making it." When I heard this, I was exceedingly put out, and fell to cursing all Spain and every one who wished well to it.

Amongst other beautiful ornaments, this vase had a handle, made all of one piece, with most delicate mechanism, which, when a spring was touched, stood upright above the mouth of it. While the prelate was one day ostentatiously exhibiting my vase to certain Spanish gentlemen of his suite, it chanced that one of them, upon Monsignor's quitting the room, began roughly to work the handle, and as the gentle spring which moved it could not bear his loutish violence, it broke in his hand. Aware what mischief he had done, he begged the butler who had charge of the Bishop's plate to take it to the master who had made it, for him to mend, and promised to pay what price he asked, provided it was set to rights at once. So the vase came once more into my hands, and I promised to put it forthwith in order, which indeed I did. It was brought to me before dinner; and at twenty-two o'clock the man who brought it returned, all in a sweat, for he had run the whole way, Monsignor having again asked for it to show to certain other gentlemen. The butler, then, without giving me time to utter a word, cried: "Quick, quick, bring me the vase." I, who wanted to act at leisure and not to give it up to him, said that I did not mean to be so quick. The servingman got into such a rage that he made as though he would put one hand to his sword, while with the other he threatened to break the shop open. To this I put a stop at once with my own weapon, using therewith spirited language, and saying: "I am not going to give it to you! Go and tell Monsignor, your master, that I want the money for my work before I let it leave this shop." When the fellow saw he could not obtain it by swaggering, he fell to praying me, as one prays to the Cross, declaring that if I would only give it up, he would take care I should be paid. These words did not make me swerve from my purpose; but I kept on saying the same thing. At last, despairing of success, he swore to come with Spaniards enough to cut me in pieces. Then he took to his heels; while I, who inclined to believe partly in their murderous attack, resolved that I would defend myself with courage. So I got an admirable little gun ready, which I used for shooting game, and muttered to myself: "He who robs me of my property and labour may take my life, too, and welcome." While I was carrying on this debate in my own mind, a crowd of Spaniards arrived, led by their major-domo, who, with the headstrong rashness of his race, bade them go in and take the vase and give me a good beating. Hearing these words, I showed them the muzzle of my gun, and prepared to fire, and cried in a loud voice: "Renegade Jews, traitors, is it thus that one breaks into houses and shops in our city of Rome? Come as many of you thieves as like, an inch nearer to this wicket, and I'll blow all their brains out with my gun." Then I turned the muzzle toward their major-domo, and making as though I would discharge it, called out: "And you big thief, who are egging them on, I mean to kill you first." He clapped spurs to the jennet he was riding, and took flight headlong. The commotion we were making stirred up all the neighbours, who came crowding round, together with some Roman gentlemen who chanced to pass and cried: "Do but kill the renegades, and we will stand by you." These words had the effect of frightening the Spaniards in good earnest. They withdrew, and were compelled by the circumstances to relate the whole affair to Monsignor. Being a man of inordinate haughtiness, he rated the members of his household, both because they had engaged in such an act of violence, and also because, having begun, they had not gone through with it. At this juncture the painter, who had been concerned in the whole matter, came in, and the Bishop bade him go and tell me that if I did not bring the vase at once, he would make mincemeat of me; but if I brought it, he would pay its price down. These threats were so far from terrifying me, that I sent him words I was going immediately to lay my case before the Pope.

In the meantime, his anger and my fear subsided; whereupon, being guaranteed by some Roman gentlemen of high degree that the prelate would not harm me, and having assurance that I should be paid, I armed myself with a large poniard and my good coat of mail, and betook myself to his palace, where he had drawn up all his household. I entered, and Paulino followed with the silver vase. It was just like passing through the Zodiac, neither more nor less; for one of them had the face of the lion, another of the scorpion, a third of the crab. However, we passed onward to the presence of the rascally priest, who spouted out a torrent of such language as only priests and Spaniards have at their command. In return I never raised my eyes to look at him, nor answered word for word. That seemed to augment the fury of his anger; and causing paper to be put before me, he commanded me to write an acknowledgement to the effect that I had been amply satisfied and paid in full. Then I raised my head and said I should be very glad to do so when I had received the money. The Bishop's rage continued to rise; threats and recriminations were flung about; but at last the money was paid, and I wrote the receipt. Then I departed, glad at heart and in high spirits.

Desiderius Erasmus

The combination of Renaissance humanism with Christianity that characterized the northern Renaissance is exemplified most clearly in the writings of Erasmus of Rotterdam (1466–1536). Intensely aware of the shortcomings of the Catholic church of his day, Erasmus was nevertheless convinced that the elimination of these evils lay not in a rejection of Christianity but rather in a return to it. Believing that the Church had departed from the true teachings of its founder, he urged a reform of religious beliefs and practices based on a return to the gospel of the New Testament, to the "philosophy of Christ," as he called it. Erasmus felt that such a reform should be inaugurated and carried forward by the Church itself through a program of widespread education. He parted company with Martin Luther, unwilling to go along with Luther's insistence that gradual reform from within based on an appeal to reason was futile, and that the only solution lay in violent revolt against the Church. Although Erasmus refused to join the Protestant movement, he contributed significantly to the Reformation by appealing for a return to the original teachings of Christ and by directing pointed satires against abuses within the Church.

The selection that follows describes some of the more blatant abuses prevalent in the Church during the early sixteenth century. It consists of a conversation between a pious believer and his less gullible friend, in which the former relates his adventures during pilgrimages he has made to three holy sites: the shrine of Santiago de Compostella (in Spain), dedicated to St. James the Apostle; the shrine of our Lady of Walsingham (in eastern England), dedicated to the Virgin Mary; and the shrine of the martyr Thomas à Becket, at Canterbury, England. The dialogue was taken from Erasmus's book *The Colloquies*, first published in 1526. Erasmian irony is evident throughout the selection, sometimes in a gentle form in the asides of Menedemus (which Ogygius usually misunderstands) and once quite directly and forcefully, in his short speech near the end condemning the physical embellishment of the churches at the expense of the poor.

Consider the following questions as you study the text below.

1. What objections did Erasmus have to religious pilgrimages and the veneration of the saints? How would you explain the popularity of these forms of religious expression in the early sixteenth century?

2. What reforms did Erasmus advocate? Was he in favor of the abolition of the institutional church? Why or why not?

The Religious Pilgrimage

Menedemus, Ogygius

MEN.: What novelty is this? Don't I see my old neighbor Ogygius, that nobody has set their eyes on for six months? There was a report he was dead. It is he, or I'm mightily mistaken. I'll go up to him, and welcome him. Welcome Ogygius.

OGY.: And well met, Menedemus.

MEN.: From what part of the world have you come? For there was a melancholy report that you had taken a voyage to the Stygian shades.

OGY.: No, thank God, I never was better in all my life than I have been since I saw you last.

MEN.: And may you live always to confute such vain reports. But what strange dress is this? It is all set off with scalloped shells, full of images of lead and tin and chains of straw-work, and the cuffs are adorned with snakes' eggs instead of bracelets.[1]

OGY.: I have been to pay a visit to St. James at Compostella, and after that to the famous virgin on the other side of the water in England. This was rather a revisit for I had been to see her three years before.

MEN.: What! out of curiosity, I suppose?

OGY.: No, because of religion.

MEN.: That religion, I suppose, the Greek tongue taught you.

OGY.: My wife's mother had bound herself by a vow, that if her daughter should be delivered of a live male child, I should go to present my respects to St. James in person, and thank him for it.

MEN.: And did you salute the saint only in your own and your mother-in-law's name?

OGY.: No, in the name of the whole family.

MEN.: Truly I am persuaded your family would have been every bit as well, if you had never complimented him at all. But what answer did he make you when you thanked him?

OGY.: None at all; but on taking my present, he seemed to smile, and gave me a gentle nod and this scallop shell.

MEN.: But why does he rather give those than any thing else?

OGY.: Because he has plenty of them, the neighboring sea furnishing him with them.

---

[1][Scallop shells were worn by pilgrims to Santiago de Compostella; "snakes' eggs" are rosary beads—*Ed.*]

Trans. N. Bailey. Minor modifications have been made in the translation, mainly to modernize the language.

MEN.:   O gracious saint, that is both a midwife to women in labor, and hospitable to travellers too! But what new fashion of making vows is this, that one who does nothing himself, shall make a vow that another man shall keep? Suppose that you should tie yourself up by a vow that I should fast twice a week, if you should succeed in such and such an affair, do you think I'd perform what you had vowed?

OGY.:   I believe you would not although you had made the vow yourself: For you enjoy mocking saints. But it was my mother-in-law who made the vow and it was my duty to be obedient. You know the temper of women, and also my interest was at stake.

MEN.:   If you had not performed the vow, what risk would you have run?

OGY.:   I don't believe the saint could have laid an action at law against me; but he might in the future have stopped his ears at my petitions, or slily have brought some mischief or other upon my family—You know the humor of great persons.

MEN.:   Please tell me, how does the good St. James do?

OGY.:   Why truly, not so well by far as he used to.

MEN.:   What's the matter, has he grown old?

OGY.:   Trifler! You know saints never grow old. But because of this new opinion that has been spread through the world, he has not so many visits made to him as he used to have; and those that do come give him a bare salute, and either nothing at all, or little or nothing else; they say they can bestow their money to better purpose upon those that need it.

MEN.:   An impious opinion.

OGY.:   And this is the reason why this great apostle, who used to glitter with gold and jewels, now is only the block of wood that he is made of and has scarce a candle.

.   .   .

MEN.:   But what God carried you to England?

OGY.:   A very favorable wind; and I had made half a promise to the Virgin by the Sea, to pay her another visit within two or three years.

MEN.:   What did you go to ask for of her?

OGY.:   Nothing new; but those common matters, the health of my family, the increase of my fortune, a long and a happy life in this world, and eternal happiness in the next.

MEN.:   But could not our Virgin Mary have done as much for you here? She has a temple at Antwerp, much more magnificent than the one by the sea.

OGY.:   I won't deny that she is able, but one thing is bestowed in one place, and another thing in another; whether this be her pleasure merely, or whether she, being of a kind disposition, accommodates herself in this to our feelings.

MEN.:   I have often heard of James but please give me some account of the Virgin by the Sea.

OGY.:   I will do it as briefly as I can. Her name is very famous all over England; and you shall scarce find anybody in that island who thinks his affairs can prosper, unless he makes some present to that lady every year, greater or smaller, according to his means.

MEN.:   Where does she dwell?

OGY.:   Near the coast, upon the furthest part between the west and the north, about three miles from the sea; it is a town that depends chiefly on tourists. There is a college of canons there, to which the Latins have added the name of regulars, which are of a middle sort between monks and those canons called Seculars.

MEN.:   You tell me of amphibious creatures, such as the beavers are.

OGY.:   So are crocodiles too. But joking apart, I'll tell you briefly: In bad cases they are canons, in favorable cases they are monks.

MEN.:   You are speaking to me in riddles.

OGY.:   Why then I will give you a mathematical demonstration. If the Pope of Rome shall throw a thunder-bolt at all monks, then they'll all be canons; but if he will allow all monks to marry, then they'll all be monks.

MEN.:   These new favours, I wish they would take mine for one.

OGY.:   But to return to the point. This college has little to maintain it but the generosity of the Virgin; for all presents of value are reserved but any small change goes to support the flock and the head of it, who is called the Prior.

MEN.:   Are they men of good lives?

OGY.:   Not much wrong. They are richer in piety than in revenue. There is a neat church but the Virgin does not dwell in it herself; but has donated it in honor of her son. Her church is on the right-hand side of her son's.

MEN.:   Upon his right-hand side! Which way then does her son face?

OGY.:   That's well taken notice of. When he looks toward the west he has his mother on the right, and when he looks toward the east, she is on his left. But she does not dwell there, for the building is not finished. The doors and windows are all open and the wind blows through it, and not far off is a place where Oceanus the father of the winds resides.

MEN.:   That's too bad; where does she dwell then?

OGY.:   In that unfinished church that I spoke of there is a little boarded chapel, with a little door on each side to receive visitors. There's very little light in it but what comes from the tapers but the scent is very pleasant.

MEN.:   All these things conduce to religion.

OGY.:   Menedemus, if you saw the inside of it you would say it was the home of the saints, it is all so glittering with jewels, gold and silver.

MEN.:   You make me want to go too.

OGY.:   If you do, you will never repent of your journey there.

MEN.:   Is there any holy oil there?

OGY.:   Simpleton, that oil is only the sweat of saints in the sepulchres, such as Andrew, Catherine, etc. Mary was never buried.

MEN.:   I confess I made a mistake, but end your story.

OGY.:   That religion may spread itself the more widely some things are shewn at one place and some at another.

MEN.:   Also the donations may be larger, according to the old saying, "Many hands will carry off much plunder."

OGY.:   And there is always someone there, to show you what you want to see.

MEN.:   What, some of the canons?

OGY.:   No, no, they are not permitted, lest under the guise of religion they should prove irreligious and while they are serving the virgin lose their own virginity. Only in the inner chapel, which I call the Chamber of the holy Virgin, a canon stands at the altar.

MEN.:   What does he stand there for?

OGY.:   To receive and keep whatever is given.

MEN.:   *Must* people give?

OGY.:   No, but a certain religious modesty makes some give, when anyone is close by, who would not give a farthing if there were no witnesses; or they give more than otherwise they would give.

MEN.:   You describe human nature as I have experienced it myself.

OGY.:   There are some so devoted to the Holy Virgin that while they pretend to lay one gift on the altar, by a wonderful sleight of hand, they steal what another has laid down.

MEN.:   But if no one were around would the Virgin thunder at them?

OGY.:   Why should the Virgin do that, any more than God himself does, whom they are not afraid to rob and to break through the walls of the church to do so?

MEN.:   I can't tell which I admire most, the impious confidence of those wretches, or God's patience.

OGY.:   At the north side there is a gate, not of the church, don't mistake me, but of the wall that incloses the churchyard that has a very little wicket, as in the great gates of noblemen, so that whoever wants to get in must first venture breaking his shins, and afterwards crack his head too.

MEN.:   In truth, it would not be safe for a man to enter in against an enemy at such a little door.

OGY.:   You're right. But yet the verger told me that some time ago a knight on horseback, having escaped from his enemy, who followed him at his heels, got in through this wicket. The poor man, at the last moment commended himself to the holy Virgin nearest to him. He resolved to take sanctuary at her altar, if the gate had been open. So behold, something never heard of before, both man and horse suddenly appeared in the churchyard with his enemy left on the outside, stark mad at his disappointment.

MEN.:   And did he give you reason to believe so wonderful an escape?

OGY.:   Without doubt.

MEN.:   That was no easy matter to a man of your intelligence.

OGY.:   He showed me a plate of copper nailed on the door, that had the very image of this knight who was thus saved, dressed in the clothing then in fashion among the English, as we see in old pictures, which if they are drawn truly, mean that the barbers and dyers and weavers in those days had a hard time of it.

MEN.: Why so?

OGY.: Because he had a beard like a goat, and there was not a wrinkle in any of his clothes which were made so tight to his body that they made his body seem more slender. There was also another plate that showed an exact copy of the chapel on it.

MEN.: Then there was no doubt about the story.

OGY.: Under the little wicket there was an iron grate, no bigger than what a man on foot could just get in at. For it was not fit that any horse afterwards should tread on that place which the former knight had consecrated to the Virgin.

MEN.: And very good reason.

OGY.: From there towards the east there is another chapel full of wonders; I went. Another verger there received me. There we prayed a little and we were shewn the middle joint of a man's finger. I kissed it, and asked whose relic it was. He told me it was St. Peter's. What, said I, the Apostle? He said it was. I then noticed the size of the joint, which was large enough to be taken for that of a giant. Upon which I said that Peter must have been a huge man. At this one of the company began to laugh. I was very much annoyed, for if he had kept quiet the verger would have shewn us all the relics. However, we pacified him pretty well by giving him a few coins. In front of this little chapel stood a house. He told us that in the winter when everything was buried in snow, it was brought there from some place a great way off. Under this house there were two wells that were fed by a fountain full of water, consecrated to the holy Virgin. The water was very cold, and of help in curing pains in the head and stomach.

MEN.: If cold water will cure pains in the head and stomach, in time oil will quench fire.

OGY.: But, my good friend, you are hearing of something miraculous; for what miracle is there in cold water quenching thirst?

MEN.: That must be only part of this story.

OGY.: It was positively affirmed that this spring burst out of the ground suddenly, at the command of the holy Virgin. I, observing everything very carefully, asked him how many years ago it was that the little house was brought there. He said it had been there for some ages. But, said I, the walls don't seem to carry any marks of great age on them. He did not deny it. Nor these pillars, said I. He admitted that those had been set up recently. But this was obvious. Then, said I, the straw and reeds, the whole thatch roof seems not to have been so long laid. He agreed. Nor do these cross beams and rafters that hold up the roof seem to have been laid many years ago. He confessed they were not. Since there was no part of the cottage remaining, said I to him, how then can it be that this is the very cottage that was brought so far through the air?

MEN.:   Tell me, how did the sexton extricate himself from this difficulty?

OGY.:   He immediately showed us an old bear skin, tacked to a piece of timber, and almost laughed at us to our very faces, for not recognizing this as proof of the building's great age. So, being satisfied, and excusing our dulness of apprehension, we turned ourselves to the heavenly milk of the blessed Virgin.

MEN.:   O Mother like her Son! For as he has left us so much of his blood on earth, so she has left us so much of her milk that it is hard to believe that a woman who never had but one child should have so much, even though her child had never sucked a drop.

OGY.:   And they tell us the same stories about our Lord's cross, that is shewn both publicly and privately, in so many places that if all the fragments were gathered together, they would seem to be a full cargo for a large ship. And yet our lord himself carried the whole cross on his shoulders.

MEN.:   And don't you think this is wonderful?

OGY.:   It may be said to be an extraordinary thing, but not a wonderful one, because the Lord who enlarges these things at will is omnipotent.

MEN.:   You offer a very pious explanation of it, but I am afraid that a great many such things are forged for the sake of getting money.

OGY.:   I cannot think God would allow anyone to mock him like that.

MEN.:   But when both mother and son, father and spirit are robbed by sacrilegious persons, they don't seem to react at all to deter wicked persons, not even a nod or a stamp, so compassionate is the divine being.

OGY.:   This is true, but listen further. That milk is kept on the high altar, in which Christ is in the middle, and his mother, for the sake of respect, is at his right hand; for the milk represents the mother.

MEN.:   Why, can it be seen then?

OGY.:   It is preserved in a crystal glass.

MEN.:   Is it liquid then?

OGY.:   What do you talk of being liquid, when it has been put in more than 1500 years ago? It is so solid you would take it for beaten chalk, tempered with the white of an egg.

MEN.:   But why don't they shew it open?

OGY.:   So the milk of the virgin won't be defiled by the kisses of men.

MEN.:   You are right, for I believe there are some who put lips to it that are neither pure nor virgin ones.

OGY.:   As soon as the officer sees us, he quickly runs and puts on a surplice and a stole around his neck and falls down very devoutly and worships, and by and by gives us the holy milk to kiss. Then we prostrated ourselves at the lowest step of the altar, and having first paid our adoration to Christ, we applied ourselves to the virgin in the following prayer, which we had written before-hand for this very purpose:

"Virgin Mother, who hast merited to give suck to the Lord of heaven and earth, thy Son Jesus, from thy virgin breasts; we desire that being purified by his blood, we may arrive at that happy infant state of dove-like innocence, which being void of malice, fraud, and deceit, we may continually desire the milk of the evangelical doctrine, until it attains the level of a perfect man, and to the measure of the fulness of Christ, whose blessed society thou wilt enjoy for evermore, with the Father and the Holy Spirit. Amen."

MEN.:   Truly, a devout prayer. But what answer did she make?

OGY.:   If my eyes did not deceive me, they were both pleased; for the holy milk seemed to give a leap and the eucharist seemed to look somewhat brighter than usual. In the meantime the officer came to us, without speaking a word, and held out a kind of table, like the one the toll-takers on the bridges in Germany hold out to you.

MEN.:   I know, for I have often cursed those greedy tables when I travelled in Germany.

OGY.:   We laid down some pieces of money, which he presented to the Virgin. After this, through our interpreter (if I remember right) one Robert Aldridge, a well-spoken young man, and a great master of the English language, I enquired, as civilly as I could, what assurance he had that this was really the Virgin's milk. And truly, I desired to be sure of this, in order to stop the mouths of some impious persons, who like to scoff at all these things. The officer first contracted his brow without speaking a word so I asked the interpreter to put the same question to him again, but in the fairest manner possible; and he did it in so obliging a manner that if he had addressed himself to the mother herself in these terms, she would not have taken it amiss. But the officer, as if he were possessed, looked at us with astonishment and with a sort of horror, and, cursing our blasphemous question, said, "What need is there for such a question when you have an authentic record?" And he would have thrown us out as heretics, had not a few pence calmed him down.

MEN.:   How did you react then?

OGY.:   Just as if we had been stunned with a cudgel, or struck with thunder, we sneaked away, humbly begging his pardon for our impertinence. For so a man ought to do in holy matters. From there we went to the little chapel, the dwelling of the holy Virgin. On our way there, an expounder of sacred things, one of the minors, appears; he stares at us as if he wants to draw our pictures; and a little further on another meets us, staring at us in the same manner, and after him a third.

MEN.:   It may be they all wanted to draw your picture.

OGY.:   But I suspected something far different.

MEN.:   What did you imagine then?

OGY.:   That some sacrilegious person had stolen some of the virgin's vestments, and that I was suspected as the thief. Therefore, having entered the chapel, I addressed myself to the virgin mother with this short prayer:

"O thou who of all women art alone a mother and a virgin, the most happy of mothers and the purest of virgins, we that are impure do now come to visit and address ourselves to thee that are pure, and reverence thee with our poor offerings, such as they are. O that thy son would enable us to imitate thy most holy life, that we may deserve, by the grace of the Holy Spirit, to conceive the Lord Jesus in the most inward bowels of our minds and having once conceived him never to lose him. Amen."

So I kissed the altar, laid down some money, and withdrew.

MEN.:   Did the Virgin hear you? Did she give you any nod as a token that she had heard your prayer?

OGY.:   As I told you before, the light was dim, and she stood in the dark at the right side of the altar. And the rebuke of the former officer had made me so dejected that I did not dare to lift up my eyes again.

MEN.:   Then this adventure did not have a very happy conclusion?

OGY.:   On the contrary, the happiest of all.

MEN.:   Now you encourage me again; for, as your Homer says, "my heart had sunk into my breeches."

OGY.:   After lunch we returned to church again.

MEN.:   How did you dare to do that, being suspected of sacrilege?

OGY.:   Maybe I was but I did not suspect myself. A clear conscience fears nothing. I much wanted to see the record that the shewer of the relics had referred us to. After hunting a great while for it, we found it at last; but it was hung up so high that it took good eyes to read it and mine are none of the best, nor none of the worst. Therefore, not being willing wholly to trust to him in a matter of such importance, I went along with Aldrisius as he read it.

MEN.:   Well! and were all your doubts removed?

OGY.:   I was ashamed of myself that I should doubt of a matter that was made so plain before one's eyes, the name, the place, the order of the proceeding, in one word, there was nothing omitted. There was one William of Paris, a man of general piety, but more especially religious in getting together the relics of saints all over the earth. Having travelled over a great many countries and having everywhere diligently searched monasteries and churches, at last he arrived at Constantinople (for this William's brother was a bishop there). When he was preparing to return home, the bishop told him that there was a certain nun who had the virgin's milk and that he would be the happiest man in the world if he could possibly get any of it, either for love or money, or by any other means because all the relics he had hitherto collected were nothing compared to that sacred milk. Upon this, William never was at rest till he had obtained one half of this milk and having gotten this treasure thought himself richer than Croesus.

MEN.:   And very well he might, 'twas a thing so unexpected too.

OGY.:   He goes straight homeward but falls sick on the way.

MEN.:   O how little trust is to be put in human felicity, that it shall be either perfect or long-lived!

OGY.:   Finding himself in danger, he sends for a Frenchman, a faithful fellow-traveller, and makes him swear secrecy and then delivers the milk to him on this condition, that if he got home safe he should deposit that treasure on the altar of the holy virgin that is worshipped at Paris, in that noble church that has the river Seine on each side of it,[2] as if itself parted in reverence to the divinity of the virgin. To sum up the matter in few words, William was buried; the other rides post but he falls sick by the way and, thinking himself past recovery, he gives the milk to an Englishman that was his fellow-traveller, making him take a solemn oath that he would perform that which he himself was to have done. The one dies, the other takes it, and puts it upon the altar, in the presence of all the canons of the place, those that at that time were called regulars, as they are yet at St. Genoveve. He obtained half this milk from them and carried it into England and made a present of it to this place by the sea, his mind being moved to do so by a divine impulse.

MEN.:   Truly this story hangs together very well.

OGY.:   Even farther, so there might not be left the least room to doubt, the very names of the bishops were set down who were authorized to grant releases and indulgences to those who came to see the milk, according to the power given to them, but not without some donation.

MEN.:   And how far did that power extend?

OGY.:   For forty days.

MEN.:   But are there days in purgatory?

OGY.:   There certainly is time there.

MEN.:   But when they have disposed of this stock of forty days, have they no more to bestow?

OGY.:   No, for occasionally there arises something for them to bestow, and it's in this respect quite different from the tub of the Danaides. For though that is continually filling, but is always empty; in this, though you are continually drawing out, there is never less in the container.

MEN.:   But if the remission of forty days were given to a hundred thousand men, would everyone have so much?

OGY.:   Yes, so much.

MEN.:   And suppose that they who have received forty days in the morning should ask for forty days more at night, would they be able to supply them?

OGY.:   Yes, ten times over in an hour.

MEN.:   I wish I had such a container at home. I would not wish for above three pennies, if they might be doubled and tripled after that manner.

[2][Notre Dame de Paris—*Ed.*]

OGY.: You might as well wish to be turned into gold yourself, and as soon have had what you wished for. But to return to my story, there was one argument added, by a man of great piety and candor, which is, that though the virgin's milk, which is shewn in many other places, is indeed venerable enough, because it was scraped off from stone, yet this was more venerable than all the rest, because it was saved as it flowed from the virgin's breast, without touching the ground.

MEN.: But how do they know that?

OGY.: O! the nun at Constantinople who gave it to them said so.

MEN.: It may be she heard it from St. Bernard.

OGY.: I believe she did.

MEN.: He, when he was very old, had the joy to taste milk from the same nipple which the child Jesus sucked. So I wonder why he was not rather called "lactifluous" than "mellifluous." But why is that called the virgin's milk that did not flow from her breasts?

OGY.: That did flow from her breasts, but dropping on the stone she sat on while she was giving suck, it concreted and was, afterwards, by a miracle multiplied.

MEN.: Right. Go on.

OGY.: These things being finished, we were just on the point of going away; but walking about, and looking around us to see if there was anything worth taking notice of, the chapel officers came to us again, leering at us, pointing at us with their fingers, advancing on us, retreating, running backward and forward, nodding, as if they would have said something to us, if they had had courage enough to have done so.

MEN.: And weren't you afraid then?

OGY.: No, not at all: but I looked them full in the face very cheerfully, as if to say, speak and welcome. At length one of them came up to me and asked my name. I told him. He asked me if I was the person who two years ago set up a votive table in Hebrew letters? I told him I was.

MEN.: Can you write Hebrew, then?

OGY.: No, but they call everything Hebrew that they can't understand. But finally the protos-hysteros of the college came.

MEN.: What title is that? Have they not an abbot?

OGY.: No.

MEN.: Why not?

OGY.: Because they don't understand Hebrew.

MEN.: Have they no bishop?

OGY.: None at all.

MEN.: Why not?

OGY.: Because the virgin is so poor that she cannot afford to buy a staff and a mitre.

·   ·   ·

MEN.:   Come on, continue with what you have begun.
OGY.:   Afterwards he shewed me statues of gold and silver. This, says he, is solid gold, and this is only silver gilt. He told me the weight of every one, the price, and the name of the donor. Since I was so full of admiration at everything, and congratulated the virgin on being mistress of so much wealth, says the officer to me, inasmuch as I perceive you are so pious a spectator, I think I should not do fairly by you if I should conceal anything from you; therefore you shall see the greatest secrets the virgin has. And presently he takes out of a drawer from under the altar a world of admirable things, the details of which if I should enumerate them, the day would not be long enough, so that thus far the journey was a success for me. I fully satisfied my curiosity with fine sights and brought home with me this inestimable present—a pledge of the virgin's love, given me by herself.
MEN.:   Did you ever make trial of the powers of this piece of wood?
OGY.:   I have. Three or four days ago, when I was in an inn, I encountered a man stark mad, whom they were just going to put into chains. I put this piece of wood secretly under his pillow and he fell into a sound sleep and slept a long time, and when he rose in the morning he was as normal as ever.
MEN.:   Perhaps he was not mad but drunk, and sleep commonly cures that distemper.
OGY.:   Menedemus, since you love to joke use another subject. It is neither pious nor safe to joke about saints. In fact, the man himself told me, there was a woman who appeared to him in his sleep of an incomparable beauty, who held a cup to him to drink.
MEN.:   Hellebore, I believe.
OGY.:   That's uncertain; but this is certain, that the man recovered his reason.
MEN.:   Did you fail to visit Thomas, Archbishop of Canterbury?[3]
OGY.:   No, I did not. It is one of the most religious pilgrimages in the world.
MEN.:   I long to hear about it, if it won't be too much trouble for you.
OGY.:   It is so far from that, that you will oblige me in hearing of it. That part of England that looks towards Flanders and France is called Kent. Its main town is Canterbury. There are two monasteries in it that are almost contiguous and they are both Benedictine. That which bears the name of Augustine is the older of the two; that which is now called by the name of St. Thomas, seems to have been the seat of St. Thomas the Archbishop, where he had led his life with a few monks whom he chose for his companions, as now-a-days deans have their palaces near the church though separate from the houses of other canons. Long ago both bishops and canons were monks, as is apparent from the records.

[3][Thomas à Becket, who was assassinated in Canterbury Cathedral in 1170—*Ed.*]

But the church that is dedicated to St. Thomas[4] raises itself up towards heaven with such majesty that it strikes those who behold it at a great distance with religious awe and with its splendor makes the light of the neighboring palaces look dim and as it were obscures the place that was in old times the most celebrated for religion. There are two lofty towers which stand, as it were, bidding visitors welcome from afar off and a ring of bells that make the adjacent country echo far and wide with their rolling sound. In the south porch of the church stand three stone statues of men in armour, who with wicked hands murdered the holy man, with their given names, Tusci, Fusci, and Berti.

MEN.:   Why have such wicked men so much honor paid them?

OGY.:   They have the same honor paid them that is paid to Judas, Pilate, Caiaphas, and the band of wicked soldiers whose images you may see carved on stately altars. And their names are added so that no one later might speak well of them. They are set there in open sight, to be a warning to wicked courtiers, that no one may hereafter presume to lay his hand on either bishops or the possessions of the church. For these three ruffians went mad with horror after committing their crime nor would they have recovered if holy Thomas had not been begged for his help.

MEN.:   O the perpetual clemency of martyrs!

OGY.:   When you go in, a spacious majesty of place opens itself to you, which is free to everyone.

MEN.:   Is there nothing to be seen there?

OGY.:   Nothing but the bulk of the structure and some books chained to the pillars containing the Gospel of Nicodemus, and the sepulchre of—I can't tell who.

MEN.:   And what else?

OGY.:   Iron gates inclose the place called the choir, so that there's no entrance but the view is left open from one end of the church to the other. You ascend to this by a great many steps under which there is a vault that opens a passage to the north side. There they have a wooden altar, consecrated to the holy virgin; it is a very small one and remarkable for nothing except as a monument of antiquity, reproaching modern-day luxury. In that place the good man is reported to have taken his last leave of the virgin, when he was at the point of death. On the altar is the point of the sword, with which the top of the head of that good prelate was wounded, and some of his brains were beaten out, to make sure he died. We most religiously kissed the sacred rust of this weapon, out of love to the martyr. Leaving this place, we went down into a vault underground; there are two custodians there. The first thing they shew you is the skull of the martyr, as it was pierced; the

[4][Canterbury Cathedral—*Ed.*]

upper part is left open to be kissed; all the rest is covered over with silver. They also show you a leaden plate with the inscription, Thomas Acrensis. And there are hanging up the shirts of hair cloth, the girdles, and breeches, with which this prelate used to mortify his flesh, the very sight of which is enough to strike one with horror and to reproach the effeminacy and delicacy of our age.

MEN.: Also, perhaps, of the monks themselves.

OGY.: That I can neither affirm nor deny, nor does it signify much to me.

MEN.: You say right.

OGY.: From there we return to the choir. On the north side they open a private enclosure. It is incredible how many bones they brought out of it, skulls, chins, teeth, hands, fingers, whole arms, all which we having first adored, kissed; nor had there been any end of it, had it not been for one of my fellow-travellers, who indiscreetly interrupted the officer who was shewing them.

MEN.: Who was he?

OGY.: He was an Englishman, his name was Gratian Pullus, a man of learning and piety, but not so respectful of this part of religion as I could wish he were.

MEN.: I fancy he was a Wickliffite.[5]

OGY.: No, I believe he was not, though he had read his books; but I don't know where he got them.

MEN.: Did he make the officer angry?

OGY.: He took out an arm still having some bloody flesh on it and shewed a reluctance to kiss it and a sort of uneasiness in his countenance. And quickly the officer shut up all his relics again. After this we viewed the table of the altar and the ornaments and afterwards those things that were laid up under the altar. All was very rich; you would have said Midas and Croesus were beggars compared to them if you had beheld the great quantities of gold and silver.

MEN.: And was there no kissing here?

OGY.: No, but my mind was touched with other sorts of wishes.

MEN.: What were they?

OGY.: It made me to think I had no such relics in my own house.

MEN.: A sacrilegious wish!

OGY.: I confess it, and I humbly begged pardon of the saint before I set my foot out of the church. After this we were taken into the vestry. Good God! What a display of silk vestments was there, of golden candlesticks! There we saw also St. Thomas's pastoral staff. It looked like a cane plated over with silver; it weighed little, and was not decorated, and was no longer than up to one's waist.

MEN.: Wasn't there a cross on it.

[5][Follower of John Wycliffe, English religious reformer (1320?–1384)—*Ed.*]

OGY.:   I saw none: There was a gown shewn, made of silk, but coarse, and without jewels, and a handkerchief, still having plain marks of sweat and blood from the saint's neck. We readily kissed these memorials of frugality in olden times.

MEN.:   Are these shewn to everybody?

OGY.:   Certainly not, my good friend.

MEN.:   How then did you come to have such credit with them, that none of their secrets were concealed from you?

OGY.:   I had some acquaintance with the Reverend Prelate William Warham, the Archbishop, and he recommended me.

MEN.:   I have heard he was a man of great humanity.

OGY.:   Really, if you knew the man, you would take him for humanity itself. He was a man of such learning, such candor, and such piety that there was nothing lacking in him to make him a most accomplished prelate. From there we were conducted up higher for behind the high altar there is another ascent, as into another church. In a certain chapel we were shewn the whole face of the good man set in gold and adorned with jewels; but here an unexpected accident nearly ended our visit.

MEN.:   I wait sadly to hear what unfortunate matter this was.

OGY.:   My friend Gratian lost control of himself here. After a short prayer, he says to the custodian, good father, is it true, as I have heard, that Thomas, while he lived, was very generous to the poor? Very true, replies he, and began to relate a great many instances of his charity. Then, answers Gratian, I don't believe that generosity in him has changed, unless it be for the better. The officer agreed. Then, says he again, if this holy man was so liberal to the poor, when he was a poor man himself and stood in need of charity to support his own body, don't you think he would take it well now, when he is grown so rich and wants nothing, if some poor woman having a family of children at home ready to starve, or daughters in danger of being under a necessity to prostitute themselves for want of money, or a husband sick in bed and destitute of all comforts; if such a woman should ask his permission to make bold with some small portion of these vast riches, for the relief of her family, taking it either as by consent, or by gift, or by way of borrowing? The assistant making no answer to this, Gratian being a warm man, added, I am fully persuaded that the good man would be glad in his heart that when he is dead he could be able to relieve the necessities of the poor with his wealth. On this the custodian began to frown and purse his lips and to look upon us as if he would have eaten us up. I don't doubt but he would have spit in our faces and have thrown us out of the church, except that we had the archbishop's recommendation. I did pacify him to some extent with soft words, telling him that Gratian did not speak this from his heart but had an odd sense of humor. I also left a little money.

MEN.:   Indeed I very much approve of your piety. But I sometimes seriously question how they can possibly excuse themselves from being guilty of a fault, who consume such vast sums in building, beautifying, and enriching churches, setting no bound to their expenses. I agree that there ought to be a dignity in the sacred vestments and the vessels of a church, appropriate to the solemn service and would have the structure of it to have a certain air of majesty. But to what purpose are so many golden fonts, so many candlesticks, and so many images? To what purpose is such a profusion of expense on organs? Nor are they content with one pair. What signify those concerts of music, hired at so great an expense, when in the meantime our brothers and sisters, Christ's living temples, are ready to perish from hunger and thirst?

OGY.:   There is no man, either of piety or wisdom, but would wish for a moderation in these matters; but since this error proceeds from excessive piety, it deserves some approval, especially when we reflect on the contrary error of others, who rob churches rather than build them up. Churches are commonly endowed by great men and monarchs, who would employ the money worse in gambling or war. And moreover, if you take anything away from the church, in the first place it is called sacrilege and in the second place it closes the hands of those who had an inclination to give and, besides, it is a temptation to robbery. The churchmen are guardians of these things rather than masters of them. And lastly, I would rather see a church luxuriant with sacred furniture than as some of them are, naked and sordid, more like stables than churches.

MEN.:   But we read that the bishops of old were commended for selling the sacred vessels and relieving the poor with the money.

OGY.:   And so they are commended today but they are only commended; and I believe they neither have the power, nor the will, to follow this example.

MEN.:   But I interrupt your account. I now expect to hear the conclusion of your story.

OGY.:   Well, you shall have it and I'll be very brief. At this point, out comes the head of the college.

MEN.:   Who was he? the abbot of the place?

OGY.:   He wears a mitre and has the revenue of an abbot, he lacks nothing but the name. He is called the prior because the archbishop replaces the abbot. For in old time everyone who was an archbishop of that diocese was a monk.

MEN.:   It wouldn't matter if I was called a camel if I had the revenue of an abbot.

OGY.:   He seemed to me to be a godly and prudent man and not unacquainted with the scotch theology.[6] He opened the box in which the remainder of the holy man's body is said to rest.

---

[6][Apparently a reference to the medieval theologian John Duns Scotus (1265?–1308)—*Ed.*]

MEN.: Did you see the Bones?

OGY.: That is not permitted, nor can it be done without a ladder. But a wooden box covers a golden one, which when being lifted up with ropes reveals an inestimable treasure.

MEN.: What do you mean?

OGY.: Gold was the cheapest part. Everything sparkled and shined with very large and rare jewels, some of them bigger than a goose's egg. Some monks stood there with the greatest veneration. When the cover was taken off, we all worshipped. The prior, with a white wand, touched every stone one by one, telling us the name in French, the value of it, and who was the donor of it. The main stones were the presents of kings.

MEN.: He needed to have a good memory.

OGY.: You are right, and yet practice goes a great way, for he does this frequently. Then he carried us back into a vault. There the Virgin Mary has her residence; it is something dark and is doubly railed in and surrounded with iron bars.

MEN.: What is she afraid of?

OGY.: Nothing, I suppose, but thieves. And I never in my life saw anything more laden with riches.

MEN.: You tell me of riches in the dark.

OGY.: When candles were brought in, we saw more than a royal sight.

MEN.: What, does it go beyond the Virgin by the Sea in wealth?

OGY.: It appears to go far beyond that. What is concealed she knows best. These things are shewn to no one but great persons or special friends. In the end, we were returned to the vestry. There a chest covered with black leather was pulled out; it was set on the table and opened. They all fell down on their knees and worshipped.

MEN.: What was in it?

OGY.: Pieces of linen rags, a great many of them still retaining the marks of the snot. These were the rags, they say, that the holy man used to wipe the sweat off from his face and neck and the snot out of his nose, or any other such filth which human bodies are not free from. Here again my Gratian behaved himself none too well. For the gentle prior offered to him as an Englishman, an acquaintance, and a man of considerable authority, one of the rags for a present, thinking he had presented him with a very desirable gift. But Gratian unthankfully took it squeamishly in his fingers and laid it down with an air of contempt, making up his mouth at it as if he would have smacked it. For this was his habit, if anything came his way that he wanted to express his contempt for. I was both ashamed and afraid. Nevertheless the good prior, though aware of the insult, seemed to take no notice of it; and after he had civilly entertained us with a glass of wine, he dismissed us and we went back to London.

Martin Luther

To raise money to build St. Peter's Cathedral in Rome, the greatest monument of Renaissance art, Pope Leo X authorized the granting of papal indulgences in return for suitable donations to the Church. In 1517, one of the papal agents, a Dominican friar named John Tetzel, appeared in central Germany to grant these indulgences. Martin Luther (1483–1546), a professor at the University of Wittenberg, responded by posting on the door of the Castle Church a list of Ninety-Five Theses, in which he attacked the entire theory and practice of indulgences.

Although Tetzel's activities had set him off, Luther based his opposition to the Church on grounds far deeper than the problem of indulgences. Basically, the question centered in the salvation of people's souls. From his studies of St. Paul and St. Augustine, Luther, who was himself a Catholic monk, became convinced that since all people are utterly condemned and lost as a result of original sin, it is impossible for them to achieve salvation by any works of their own. Rather, salvation is the free gift of God's grace through faith. This doctrine of justification by faith rather than by works undercut the position of the Catholic Church, which maintained that since the works necessary to salvation (such as the sacraments) could be performed only with the aid of the priesthood, the Church provided the sole means to salvation. In place of the priestly hierarchy, Luther substituted the notion of the priesthood of all believers, an idea that was to become a cornerstone of Protestantism. In the selection that follows he defends his "heretical" views, largely through a vigorous attack on both the theology and the practices of the Church.

Consider the following questions as you study the text below.

1. Compare Luther's opinion of the Roman Catholic Church to that of Erasmus. On what would they have agreed? On what would they have disagreed?

2. What strategies did Luther use to make his arguments particularly appealing to the German nobility? Why did Luther believe that temporal authorities should have jurisdiction over the clergy within their realms?

An Open Letter to the Christian Nobility of the German Nation Concerning the Reform of the Christian Estate, 1520

TO HIS MOST ILLUSTRIOUS AND MIGHTY IMPERIAL MAJESTY, AND TO THE CHRISTIAN NOBILITY OF THE GERMAN NATION,

DOCTOR MARTIN LUTHER

Grace and power from God, Most illustrious Majesty, and most gracious and dear Lords.

It is not out of sheer forwardness or rashness that I, a single, poor man, have undertaken to address your worships. The distress and oppression which weigh down all the Estate of Christendom, especially of Germany, and which move not me alone, but everyone to cry out time and again, and to pray for help, have forced me even now to cry aloud that God may inspire some one with His Spirit to lend this suffering nation a helping hand. Ofttimes the councils have made some pretence at reformation, but their attempts have been cleverly hindered by the guile of certain men and things have gone from bad to worse. I now intend, by the help of God, to throw some light upon the wiles and wickedness of these men, to the end that when they are known, they may not henceforth be so hurtful and so great a hindrance. God has given us a noble youth to be our head and thereby has awakened great hopes of good in many hearts; wherefore it is meet that we should do our part and profitably use this time of grace.

In this whole matter the first and most important thing is that we take earnest heed not to enter on it trusting in great might or in human reason, even though all power in the world were ours; for God cannot and will not suffer a good work to be begun with trust in our own power or reason. Such works He crushes ruthlessly to earth, as it is written in the xxxiii Psalm, "There is no king saved by the multitude of an host: a mighty man is not delivered by much strength." On this account, I fear, it came to pass of old that the good Emperors Frederick I and II, and many other German emperors were shamefully oppressed and trodden under foot by the popes, although all the world feared them. It may be that they relied on their own might more than on God, and therefore they had to fall. In our own times, too, what was it that raised the bloodthirsty Julius II to such heights? Nothing else, I fear,

"An Open Letter to the Christian Nobility of the German Nation Concerning the Reform of the Christian Estate," trans. C. M. Jacobs, in *Works of Martin Luther* (Philadelphia: Muhlenberg Press, 1915), Vol. II, pp. 63–84. Courtesy of the Fortress Press.

except that France, the Germans, and Venice relied upon themselves. The children of Benjamin slew forty-two thousand Israelites because the latter relied on their own strength.

That it may not so fare with us and our noble young Emperor Charles, we must be sure that in this matter we are dealing not with men, but with the princes of hell, who can fill the world with war and bloodshed, but whom war and bloodshed do not overcome. We must go at this work despairing of physical force and humbly trusting God; we must seek God's help with earnest prayer, and fix our minds on nothing else than the misery and distress of suffering Christendom, without regard to the deserts of evil men. Otherwise we may start the game with great prospect of success, but when we get well into it the evil spirits will stir up such confusion that the whole world will swim in blood, and yet nothing will come of it. Let us act wisely, therefore, and in the fear of God. The more force we use, the greater our disaster if we do not act humbly and in God's fear. The popes and the Romans have hitherto been able, by the devil's help, to set kings at odds with one another, and they may well be able to do it again, if we proceed by our own might and cunning, without God's help.

I. THE THREE WALLS OF THE ROMANISTS

The Romanists, with great adroitness, have built three walls about them, behind which they have hitherto defended themselves in such wise that no one has been able to reform them; and this has been the cause of terrible corruption throughout all Christendom.

First, when pressed by the temporal power, they have made decrees and said that the temporal power has no jurisdiction over them, but, on the other hand, that the spiritual is above the temporal power. Second, when the attempt is made to reprove them out of the Scriptures, they raise the objection that the interpretation of the Scriptures belongs to no one except the pope. Third, if threatened with a council, they answer with the fable that no one can call a council but the pope.

In this wise they have slyly stolen from us our three rods, that they may go unpunished, and have ensconced themselves within the safe stronghold of these three walls, that they may practise all the knavery and wickedness which we now see. Even when they have been compelled to hold a council they have weakened its power in advance by previously binding the princes with an oath to let them remain as they are. Moreover, they have given the pope full authority over all the decisions of the council, so that it is all one whether there are many councils—except that they deceive us with puppet-shows and sham-battles. So terribly do they fear for their skin in a really free council! And they have intimidated kings and princes by making them believe it would be an offence against God not to obey them in all these knavish, crafty deceptions.

Now God help us, and give us one of the trumpets with which the walls of Jericho were overthrown, that we may blow down these walls of straw and paper, and may set free the Christian rods for the punishment of sin, bringing to light the craft and deceit of the devil, to the end that through punishment we may reform ourselves, and once more attain God's favor.

Against the first wall we will direct our first attack.

It is pure invention that pope, bishops, priests and monks are to be called the "spiritual estate"; princes, lords, artisans, and farmers the "temporal estate." That is indeed a fine bit of lying and hypocrisy. Yet no one should be frightened by it; and for this reason—*viz.*, that all Christians are truly of the "spiritual estate," and there is among them no difference at all but that of office, as Paul says in I Corinthians xii, We are all one body, yet every member has its own work, whereby it serves every other, all because we have one baptism, one Gospel, one faith, and are all alike Christians; for baptism, Gospel and faith alone make us "spiritual" and a Christian people.

But that a pope or a bishop anoints, confers, tonsures, ordains, consecrates, or prescribes dress unlike that of the laity,—this may make hypocrites, and graven images, but it never makes a Christian or "spiritual" man. Through baptism all of us are consecrated to the priesthood, as St. Peter says in I Peter ii, "Ye are a royal priesthood, a priestly kingdom," and the book of Revelation says, "Thou hast made us by Thy blood to be priests and kings." For if we had no higher consecration than pope or bishop gives, the consecration by pope or bishop would never make a priest, nor might anyone either say mass or preach a sermon or give absolution. Therefore when the bishop consecrates it is the same thing as if he, in the place and stead of the whole congregation, all of whom have like power, were to take one out of their number and charge him to use this power for the others; just as though ten brothers, all king's sons and equal heirs, were to choose one of themselves to rule the inheritance for them all,—they would all be kings and equal in power, though one of them would be charged with the duty of ruling.

To make it still clearer. If a little group of pious Christian laymen were taken captive and set down in a wilderness, and had among them no priest consecrated by a bishop, and if there in the wilderness they were to agree in choosing one of themselves, married or unmarried, and were to charge him with the office of baptising, saying mass, absolving and preaching, such a man would be as truly a priest as though all bishops and popes had consecrated him. That is why in cases of necessity any one can baptise and give absolution, which would be impossible unless we were all priests. This great grace and power of baptism and of the Christian Estate they have well-nigh destroyed and caused us to forget through the canon law. It was in the manner aforesaid that Christians in olden days chose from their number bishops and priests, who were afterwards confirmed by other bishops, without all the show which now obtains. It was thus that Sts. Augustine, Ambrose, and Cyprian became bishops.

Since, then, the temporal authorities are baptised with the same baptism and have the same faith and Gospel as we, we must grant that they are priests and bishops, and count their office one which has a proper and a useful place in the Christian community. For whoever comes out of the water of baptism can boast that he is already consecrated priest, bishop, and pope, though it is not seemly that every one should exercise the office. Nay, just because we are all in like manner priests, no one must put himself forward and undertake, without our consent and election, to do what is in the power of all of us. For what is common to all, no one dare take upon himself without the will and the commands of the community; and should it happen that one chosen for such an office were deposed for malfeasance, he would then be just what he was before he held office. Therefore a priest in Christendom is nothing else than an office-holder. While he is in office, he has precedence; when deposed, he is a peasant or a townsman like the rest. Beyond all doubt, then, a priest is no longer a priest when he is deposed. But now they have invented *characteres indelebiles*, and prate that a deposed priest is nevertheless something different from a mere layman. They even dream that a priest can never become a layman, or be anything else than a priest. All this is mere talk and man-made law.

From all this it follows that there is really no difference between laymen and priests, princes and bishops, "spirituals" and "temporals," as they call them, except that of office and work, but not of "estate"; for they are all of the same estate,—true priests, bishops, and popes,—though they are not all engaged in the same work, just as all priests and monks have not the same work. This is the teaching of St. Paul in Romans xii and I Corinthians xii, and of St. Peter in I Peter ii, as I have said above, *viz.*, that we are all one body of Christ, the Head, all members one of another. Christ has not two different bodies, one "temporal," the other "spiritual." He is one Head, and He has one body.

Therefore, just as those who are now called "spiritual"—priests, bishops or popes—are neither different from other Christians nor superior to them, except that they are charged with the administration of the Word of God and the sacraments, which is their work and office, so it is with the temporal authorities,—they bear sword and rod with which to punish the evil and to protect the good. A cobbler, a smith, a farmer, each has the work and office of his trade, and yet they are all alike consecrated priests and bishops, and every one by means of his own work or office must benefit and serve every other, that in this way many kinds of work may be done for the bodily and spiritual welfare of the community, even as all the members of the body serve one another.

See, now, how Christian is the decree which says that the temporal power is not above the "spiritual estate" and may not punish it. That is as much as to say that the hand shall lend no aid when the eye is suffering. Is it not unnatural, not to say unchristian, that one member should not help another and prevent its destruction? Verily, the more honorable the member, the more should the others help. I say then, since the temporal power is ordained of God to punish evildoers and to protect them that do well, it should therefore be left free to perform its office without hindrance through the whole body of Christendom without respect of persons, whether it affect pope, bishops, priests, monks, nuns or anybody else. For if the mere fact that the temporal power has a smaller place among the Christian offices than has the office of preachers or confessors, or of the clergy, then the tailors, cobblers, masons, carpenters, potboys, tapsters, farmers, and all the secular tradesmen, should also be prevented from providing pope, bishops, priests and monks with shoes, clothing, houses, meat and drink, and from paying them tribute. But if these laymen are allowed to do their work unhindered, what do the Roman scribes mean by their laws, with which they withdraw themselves from the jurisdiction of the temporal Christian power, only so that they may be free to do evil and to fulfill what St. Peter has said: "There shall be false teachers among you, and through covetousness shall they with feigned words make merchandise of you."

On this account the Christian temporal power should exercise its office without let or hindrance, regardless whether it be pope, bishop, or priest whom it affects; whoever is guilty, let him suffer. All that the canon law has said to the contrary is sheer invention of Roman presumption. For thus saith St. Paul to all Christians: "Let every soul (I take that to mean the pope's soul also) be subject unto the higher powers; for they bear not the sword in vain, but are the ministers of God for the punishment of evil-doers, and for the praise of them that do well." St. Peter also says: "Submit yourselves unto every ordinance of man for the Lord's sake, for so is the will of God." He has also prophesied that such men shall come as will despise the temporal authorities, and this has come to pass through the canon law.

So then, I think this first paper-wall is overthrown, since the temporal power has become a member of the body of Christendom, and is of the "spiritual estate," though its work is of a temporal nature. Therefore its work should extend freely and without hindrance to all the members of the whole body; it should punish and use force whenever guilt deserves or necessity demands, without regard to pope, bishops, and priests,—let them hurl threats and bans as much as they will.

This is why guilty priests, if they are surrendered to the temporal law, are first deprived of their priestly dignities, which would not be right unless the temporal sword had previously had authority over them by divine right.

Again, it is intolerable that in the canon law so much importance is attached to the freedom, life and property of the clergy, as though the laity were not also as spiritual and as good Christians as they, or did not belong to the Church. Why are your life and limb, your property and honor so free, and mine not? We are all alike Christians, and have baptism, faith, Spirit, and all things alike. If a priest is killed, the land is laid under interdict,—why not when a peasant is killed? Whence comes this great distinction between those who are equally Christians? Only from human laws and inventions!

Moreover, it can be no good spirit who has invented such exceptions and granted to sin such license and impunity. For if we are bound to strive against the works and words of the evil spirit, and to drive him out in whatever way we can, as Christ commands and His Apostles, ought we, then, to suffer it in silence when the pope or his satellites are bent on devilish words and works? Ought we for the sake of men to allow the suppression of divine commandments and truths which we have sworn in baptism to support with life and limb? Of a truth we should then have to answer for all the souls that would thereby be abandoned and led astray.

It must therefore have been the very prince of devils who said what is written in the canon law: "If the pope were so scandalously bad as to lead souls in crowds to the devil, yet he could not be deposed." On this accursed and devilish foundation they build at Rome, and think that we should let all the world go to the devil, rather than resist their knavery. If the fact that one man is set over others were sufficient reason why he should escape punishment, then no Christian could punish another, since Christ commands the lowliest and the least.

Where sin is, there is no escape from punishment; as St. Gregory also writes that we are indeed all equal, but guilt puts us in subjection one to another. Now we see how they whom God and the Apostles have made subject to the temporal sword deal with Christendom, depriving it of its liberty by their own wickedness, without warrant of Scripture. It is to be feared that this is a game of Antichrist or a sign that he is close at hand.

The second wall is still more flimsy and worthless. They wish to be the only Masters of the Holy Scriptures, even though in all their lives they learn nothing from them. They assume for themselves sole authority, and with insolent juggling of words they would persuade us that the pope, whether he be a bad man or a good man, cannot err in matters of faith; and yet they cannot prove a single letter of it. Hence it comes that so many heretical and unchristian, nay, even unnatural ordinances have a place in the canon law, of which, however, there is no present need to speak. For since they think that the Holy Spirit never leaves them, be they ever so unlearned and wicked, they make bold to decree whatever they will. And if it were true, where would be the need or use of the Holy Scriptures? Let us burn them, and be satisfied with the unlearned lords at Rome, who are possessed of the Holy Spirit,—although He can possess only pious hearts! Unless I had read it myself, I could not have believed that the devil would make such clumsy pretensions at Rome, and find a following.

But, not to fight them with mere words, we will quote the Scriptures. St. Paul says in I Corinthians xiv: "If to anyone something better is revealed, though he be sitting and listening to another in God's Word, then the first, who is speaking, shall hold his peace and give place." What would be the use

of this commandment, if we were only to believe him who does the talking or
who has the highest seat? Christ also says in John vi, that all Christians shall
be taught of God. Thus it may well happen that the pope and his followers
are wicked men, and no true Christians, not taught of God, not having true
understanding. On the other hand, an ordinary man may have true understanding; why then should we not follow him? Has not the pope erred many
times? Who would help Christendom when the pope errs, if we were not to
believe another, who had the Scriptures on his side, more than the pope?

Therefore it is a wickedly invented fable, and they cannot produce a
letter in defence of it, that the interpretation of Scripture or the confirmation
of its interpretation belongs to the pope alone. They have themselves
usurped this power; and although they allege that this power was given to
Peter when the keys were given to him, it is plain enough that the keys were
not given to Peter alone, but to the whole community. Moreover, the keys
were not ordained for doctrine or government, but only for the binding and
loosing of sin, and whatever further power of the keys they arrogate to
themselves is mere invention. But Christ's word to Peter, "I have prayed for
thee that thy faith fail not," cannot be applied to the pope, since the majority
of the popes have been without faith, as they must themselves confess. Besides, it is not only for Peter that Christ prayed, but also for all Apostles and
Christians, as he says in John xvii: "Father, I pray for those whom Thou has
given Me, and not for these only, but for all who believe on Me through their
word." Is not this clear enough?

Only think of it yourself! They must confess that there are pious Christians among us, who have the true faith, Spirit, understanding, word and
mind of Christ. Why, then, should we reject their word and understanding
and follow the pope, who has neither faith nor Spirit? That would be to deny
the whole faith and the Christian Church. Moreover, it is not the pope alone
who is always in the right, if the article of the Creed is correct: "I believe in
one holy Christian Church"; otherwise the prayer must run: "I believe in the
pope at Rome," and so reduce the Christian Church to one man,—which
would be nothing else than a devilish and hellish error.

Besides, if we are all priests, as was said above, and all have one faith,
one Gospel, one sacrament, why should we not also have the power to test
and judge what is correct or incorrect in matters of faith? What becomes of
the words of Paul in I Corinthians ii: "He that is spiritual judgeth all things,
yet he himself is judged of no man," and II Corinthians iv: "We have all the
same Spirit of faith"? Why, then, should not we perceive what squares with
faith and what does not, as well as does an unbelieving pope?

All these and many other texts should make us bold and free, and we
should not allow the Spirit of liberty, as Paul calls Him, to be frightened off
by the fabrications of the popes, but we ought to go boldly forward to test
all that they do or leave undone, according to our interpretation of the
Scriptures, which rests on faith, and compel them to follow not their own

interpretation, but the one that is better. In the olden days Abraham had to listen to his Sarah, although she was in more complete subjection to him than we are to anyone on earth. Balaam's ass, also, was wiser than the prophet himself. If God then spoke by an ass against a prophet, why should He not be able even now to speak by a righteous man against the pope? In like manner St. Paul rebukes St. Peter as a man in error. Therefore it behooves every Christian to espouse the cause of the faith, to understand and defend it, and to rebuke all errors.

The third wall falls of itself when the first two are down. For when the pope acts contrary to the Scriptures, it is our duty to stand by the Scriptures, to reprove him, and to constrain him, according to the word of Christ in Matthew xviii: "If thy brother sin against thee, go and tell it him between thee and him alone; if he hear thee not, then take with thee one or two more; if he hear them not, tell it to the Church; if he hear not the Church, consider him a heathen." Here every member is commanded to care for every other. How much rather should we do this when the member that does evil is a ruling member, and by his evil-doing is the cause of much harm and offence to the rest! But if I am to accuse him before the Church, I must bring the Church together.

They have no basis in Scripture for their contention that it belongs to the pope alone to call a council or confirm its actions; for this is based merely upon their own laws, which are valid only in so far as they are not injurious to Christendom or contrary to the laws of God. When the Pope deserves punishment, such laws go out of force, since it is injurious to Christendom not to punish him by means of a council.

Thus we read in Acts xv that it was not St. Peter who called the Apostolic Council, but the Apostles and elders. If, then, that right had belonged to St. Peter alone, the council would not have been a Christian council, but an heretical *conciliabulum*. Even the Council of Nicaea—the most famous of all—was neither called nor confirmed by the Bishop of Rome, but by the Emperor Constantine, and many other emperors after him did the like, yet these councils were the most Christian of all. But if the pope alone had the right to call councils, then all these councils must have been heretical. Moreover, if I consider the councils which the pope has created, I find that they have done nothing of special importance.

Therefore, when necessity demands, and the pope is an offence to Christendom, the first man who is able should, as a faithful member of the whole body, do what he can to bring about a truly free council. No one can do this so well as the temporal authorities, especially since now they also are fellow-Christians, fellow-priests, "fellow-spirituals," fellow-lords over all things, and whenever it is needful or profitable, they should give free course to the office and work in which God has put them above every man. Would it not be an unnatural thing, if a fire broke out in a city, and every body were to stand by and let it burn on and on and consume everything that could burn, for the sole reason that nobody had the authority of the burgomaster, or because, perhaps, the fire broke out in the burgomaster's house? In such case is it not the duty of every citizen to arouse and call the rest? How much more should this be done in the spiritual city of Christ, if a fire of offence breaks out, whether in the papal government, or anywhere else? In the same way, if the enemy attacks a city, he who first rouses the others deserves honour and thanks; why then should he not deserve honour who makes known the presence of the enemy from hell, and awakens the Christians, and calls them together?

But all their boasts of an authority which dare not be opposed amount to nothing after all. No one in Christendom has authority to do injury, or to forbid the resisting of injury. There is no authority in the Church save for edification. Therefore, if the pope were to use his authority to prevent the calling of a free council, and thus became a hindrance to the edification of the Church, we should have regard neither for him nor for his authority; and if he were to hurl his bans and thunderbolts, we should despise his conduct as that of a madman, and relying on God, hurl back the ban on him, and coerce him as best we could. For this presumptuous authority of his is nothing; he has no such authority; and he is quickly overthrown by a text of Scripture; for Paul says to the Corinthians: "God has given us authority not for the destruction, but for the edification of Christendom." Who is ready to overleap this text? It is only the power of the devil and of Antichrist which resists the things that serve for the edification of Christendom; it is, therefore, in no wise to be obeyed, but is to be opposed with life and goods and all our strength.

Even though a miracle were to be done in the pope's behalf against the temporal powers, or though someone were to be stricken with a plague—which they boast has sometimes happened—it should be considered only the work of the devil, because of the weakness of our faith in God. Christ Himself prophesied in Matthew xxiv: "There shall come in My Name false Christs and false prophets, and do signs and wonders, so as to deceive even the elect," and Paul says in II Thessalonians ii, that Antichrist shall, through the power of Satan, be mighty in lying wonders.

Let us, therefore, hold fast to this: No Christian authority can do anything against Christ; as St. Paul says, "We can do nothing against Christ, but for Christ." Whatever does aught against Christ is the power of Antichrist and of the devil, even though it were to rain and hail wonders and plagues. Wonders and plagues prove nothing, especially in these evil times, for which all the Scriptures prophesy false wonders. Therefore we must cling with firm faith to the words of God, and then the devil will cease from wonders.

Thus I hope that the false, lying terror with which the Romans have this long time made our conscience timid and stupid, has been allayed. They, like all of us, are subject to the temporal sword; they have no power to interpret the Scriptures by mere authority, without learning; they have no authority to prevent a council or, in sheer wantonness, to pledge it, bind it, or take away its liberty; but if they do this, they are in truth in the communion of Antichrist and of the devil, and have nothing at all of Christ except the name.

II. ABUSES TO BE DISCUSSED IN COUNCILS

We shall now look at the matters which should be discussed in the councils, and with which popes, cardinals, bishops, and all the scholars ought properly to be occupied day and night if they love Christ and His Church. But if they neglect this duty, then let the laity and the temporal authorities see to it, regardless of bans and thunders; for an unjust ban is better than ten just releases, and an unjust release worse than ten just bans. Let us, therefore, awake, dear Germans, and fear God rather than men, that we may not share the fate of all the poor souls who are so lamentably lost through the shameful and devilish rule of the Romans, in which the devil daily takes a larger and larger place—if indeed, it were possible that such a hellish rule could grow worse, a thing I can neither conceive nor believe.

1.   It is a horrible and frightful thing that the ruler of Christendom, who boasts himself vicar of Christ and successor of St. Peter, lives in such wordly splendor that in this regard no king nor emperor can equal or approach him, and that he who claims the title of "most holy" and "most spiritual" is more worldly than the world itself. He wears a triple crown, when the greatest kings wear but a single crown; if that is like the poverty of Christ and of St. Peter, then it is a new kind of likeness. When a word is said against it, they cry out "Heresy!" but that is because they do not wish to hear how unchristian and ungodly such a practice is. I think, however, that if the pope were with tears to pray to God he would have to lay aside these crowns, for our God can suffer no pride, and his office is nothing else than this,—daily to weep and pray for Christendom, and to set an example of all humility.

However that may be, this splendour of his is an offence, and the pope is bound on his soul's salvation to lay it aside, because St. Paul says, "Abstain from all outward shows, which give offence," and in Rom. xii, "We should provide good, not only in the sight of God, but also in the sight of all men." An ordinary bishop's crown would be enough for the pope; he should be greater than others in wisdom and holiness, and leave the crown of pride to Antichrist, as did his predecessors several centuries ago. They say he is a lord of the world; that is a lie; for Christ, Whose vicar and officer he boasts himself to be, said before Pilate, "My kingdom is not of this world," and no vicar's rule can go beyond his lord's. Moreover, he is not the vicar of the glorified, but of the crucified Christ, as Paul says, "I was willing to know nothing among you save Christ, and Him only as the Crucified"; and in Philippians ii, "So think of yourselves as ye see in Christ. Who emptied Himself and took upon Him the appearance of a servant"; and again in I

Corinthians i, "We preach Christ, the Crucified." Now they make the pope a vicar of the glorified Christ in heaven, and some of them have allowed the devil to rule them so completely that they have maintained that the pope is above the angels in heaven and has authority over them. These are indeed the very works of the very Antichrist.

2. What is the use in Christendom of these people who are called the cardinals? I shall tell you. Italy and Germany have many rich monasteries, foundations, benefices, and livings. No better way has been discovered to bring all these to Rome than by creating cardinals and giving them the bishoprics, monasteries, and prelacies, and so overthrowing the worship of God. For this reason we now see Italy a very wilderness—monasteries in ruins, bishoprics devoured, the prelacies and the revenues of all the churches drawn to Rome, cities decayed, land and people laid waste, because there is no more worship or preaching. Why? The cardinals must have the income. No Turk could have so devastated Italy and suppressed the worship of God.

Now that Italy is sucked dry, they come into Germany, and begin oh so gently. But let us beware, or Germany will soon become like Italy. Already we have some cardinals; what the Romans seek by that the "drunken Germans" are not to understand until we have not a bishopric, a monastery, a living, a benefice, a *heller* or a *pfennig* left. Antichrist must take the treasures of the earth, as it was prophesied. So it goes on. They skim the cream off the bishoprics, monasteries, and benefices, and because they do not yet venture to turn them all to shameful use, as they have done in Italy, they only practise for the present the sacred trickery of coupling together ten or twenty prelacies and taking a yearly portion from each of them, so as to make a tidy sum after all. The priory of Würzburg yields a thousand *gulden*; that of Bamberg, something; Mainz, Trier and the others, something more; and so from one to ten thousand *gulden* might be got together, in order that a cardinal might live at Rome like a rich king.

"After they are used to this, we will create thirty or forty cardinals in a day, and give to one Mount St. Michael at Bamberg and the bishopric of Würzburg to boot, hang on to these a few rich livings, until churches and cities are waste, and after that we will say, 'We are Christ's vicars and shepherds of Christ's sheep; the mad, drunken Germans must put up with it.' "

I advise, however, that the number of cardinals be reduced, or that the pope be made to keep them at his own expense. Twelve of them would be more than enough, and each of them might have an income of a thousand *gulden* a year. How comes it that we Germans must put up with such robbery and such extortion of our property, at the hands of the pope? If the Kingdom of France has prevented it, why do we Germans let them make such fools and apes of us? It would all be more bearable if in this way they only stole our property; but they lay waste the churches and rob Christ's sheep of their pious shepherds, and destroy the worship and the Word of God. Even if there were not a single cardinal, the Church would not go under. As it is they do nothing for the good of Christendom; they only wrangle about the incomes of bishoprics and prelacies, and that any robber could do.

3.   If ninety-nine parts of the papal court were done away and only the hundredth part allowed to remain, it would still be large enough to give decisions in matters of faith. Now, however, there is such a swarm of vermin yonder in Rome, all boasting that they are "papal," that there was nothing like it in Babylon. There are more than three thousand papal secretaries alone; who will count the other offices, when they are so many that they scarcely can be counted? And they all lie in wait for the prebends and benefices of Germany as wolves lie in wait for the sheep. I believe that Germany now gives much more to the pope at Rome than it gave in former times to the emperors. Indeed, some estimate that every year more than three hundred thousand *gulden* find their way from Germany to Rome, quite uselessly and fruitlessly; we get nothing for it but scorn and contempt. And yet we wonder that princes, nobles, cities, endowments, land, and people are impoverished! We should rather wonder that we still have anything to eat!

John Calvin

The success of Protestantism as an international reform movement was due largely to the work of a younger contemporary of Luther, the Frenchman John Calvin. Born Jean Cauvin in Picardy in 1509, Calvin went to Paris in 1523 to study first for a clerical and later for a legal career. While there he became acquainted with the writings of Luther, which were beginning to circulate through France at the time. His growing sympathy for the German "heresies" brought him to the attention of the authorities and he was forced to flee the country. He finally settled in the small city of Geneva, Switzerland. There he initiated one of the most remarkable social and political experiments of modern times. Under his leadership Geneva was organized as a theocratic state. The clergy assumed control not only of the political affairs of the city but of the moral life of its citizens as well.

From Geneva, which came to be known as the Protestant Rome, Calvinism spread throughout most of Europe, into Germany, Poland, Bohemia, Hungary, and the Low Countries. The French Huguenots were Calvinists, as were the Scottish Presbyterians and the English Puritans, who brought both the religious doctrines and the theocratic social organization of Calvin across the Atlantic to the colony of Massachusetts.

Calvin was not only a religious and social reformer but also one of the greatest of all Christian theologians. In his *Institutes of the Christian Religion*, which he first published at the age of twenty-seven, he reiterated and defended the Augustinian doctrine of original sin, with its implied notions of election, faith, and grace. On the subject of predestination, about which most theologians had spoken in muted tones, Calvin was quite explicit. God in his omnipotence has decreed from all eternity the ultimate destiny of every individual soul. We, guilty sinners, can do nothing to alter this divine decree; all that rests with us is to praise God's infinite grace if he has elected us for salvation or to accept his just condemnation if he has damned us to hell.

The selection from the *Institutes* that follows outlines the main features of Calvin's theology.

Consider the following questions as you study the text below.

1. How did Calvin see human nature? How did he explain Adam and Eve's fall from grace?

2. Why did Calvin believe that good works had no effect on an individual's salvation or damnation? According to Calvin, what, if anything, could an individual do to ensure salvation?

Institutes of the Christian Religion

DISCUSSION OF HUMAN NATURE AS CREATED, OF THE FACULTIES OF THE SOUL, OF THE IMAGE OF GOD, OF FREE WILL, AND OF THE ORIGINAL INTEGRITY OF MAN'S NATURE

We must now speak of the creation of man: not only because among all God's works here is the noblest and most remarkable example of his justice, wisdom, and goodness; but because, as we said at the beginning, we cannot have a clear and complete knowledge of God unless it is accompanied by a corresponding knowledge of ourselves. This knowledge of ourselves is twofold: namely, to know what we were like when we were first created and what our condition became after the fall of Adam. While it would be of little benefit to understand our creation unless we recognized in this sad ruin what our nature in its corruption and deformity is like, we shall nevertheless be content for the moment with the description of our originally upright nature. And to be sure, before we come to the miserable condition of man to which he is now subjected, it is worth-while to know what he was like when first created. Now we must guard against singling out only those natural evils of man, lest we seem to attribute them to the Author of nature. For in this excuse, impiety thinks it has sufficient defense, if it is able to claim that whatever defects it possesses have in some way proceeded from God. It does not hesitate, if it is reproved, to contend with God himself, and to impute to him the fault of which it is deservedly accused. And those who wish to seem to speak more reverently of the Godhead still willingly blame their depravity on nature, not realizing that they also, although more obscurely, insult God. For if any defect were proved to inhere in nature, this would bring reproach upon him.

Since, then, we see the flesh panting for every subterfuge by which it thinks that the blame for its own evils may in any way be diverted from itself to another, we must diligently oppose this evil intent. Therefore we must so deal with the calamity of mankind that we may cut off every shift, and may vindicate God's justice from every accusation. Afterward, in the proper place, we shall see how far away men are from the purity that was bestowed upon Adam. . . .

From *Calvin: Institutes of the Christian Religion*, LCC, Vols. XX and XXI, ed. John T. McNeill and trans. Ford Lewis Battles. Published simultaneously in the U.S.A. by The Westminister Press and in Great Britain by S.C.M. Press, Ltd., London. Copyright © 1960, by W. L. Jenkins. Used by permission.

In this integrity man by free will had the power, if he so willed, to attain eternal life. Here it would be out of place to raise the question of God's secret predestination because our present subject is not what can happen or not, but what man's nature was like. Therefore Adam could have stood if he wished, seeing that he fell solely by his own will. But it was because his will was capable of being bent to one side or the other, and was not given the constancy to persevere, that he fell so easily. Yet his choice of good and evil was free, and not that alone, but the highest rectitude was in his mind and will, and all the organic parts were rightly composed to obedience, until in destroying himself he corrupted his own blessings.

Hence the great obscurity faced by the philosophers, for they were seeking in a ruin for a building, and in scattered fragments for a well-knit structure. They held this principle, that man would not be a rational animal unless he possessed free choice of good and evil; also it entered their minds that the distinction between virtues and vices would be obliterated if man did not order his life by his own planning. Well reasoned so far—if there had been no change in man. But since this was hidden from them, it is no wonder they mix up heaven and earth! They, as professed disciples of Christ, are obviously playing the fool when, by compromising between the opinions of the philosophers and heavenly doctrine, so that these touch neither heaven nor earth, in man—who is lost and sunk down into spiritual destruction—they will seek after free choice. But these matters will be better dealt with in their proper place. Now we need bear only this in mind: man was far different at the first creation from his whole posterity, who, deriving their origin from him in his corrupted state, have contracted from him a hereditary taint. For, the individual parts of his soul were formed to uprightness, the soundness of his mind stood firm, and his will was free to choose the good. If anyone objects that his will was placed in an insecure position because its power was weak, his status should have availed to remove any excuse; nor was it reasonable for God to be constrained by the necessity of making a man who either could not or would not sin at all. Such a nature would, indeed, have been more excellent. But to quarrel with God on this precise point, as if he ought to have conferred this upon man, is more than iniquitous, inasmuch as it was in his own choice to give whatever he pleased. But the reason he did not sustain man by the virtue of perseverance lies hidden in his plan; sobriety is for us the part of wisdom. Man, indeed, received the ability provided he exercised the will; but he did not have the will to use his ability, for this exercising of the will would have been followed by the perseverance. Yet he is not excusable, for he received so much that he voluntarily brought about his own destruction; indeed, no necessity was imposed upon God of giving man other than a mediocre and even transitory will, that from man's Fall he might gather occasion for his own glory.

.   .   .

BY THE FALL AND REVOLT OF ADAM
THE WHOLE HUMAN RACE WAS DELIVERED
TO THE CURSE, AND DEGENERATED FROM ITS
ORIGINAL CONDITION; THE DOCTRINE OF ORIGINAL SIN

With good reason the ancient proverb strongly recommended knowledge of self to man. For if it is considered disgraceful for us not to know all that pertains to the business of human life, even more detestable is our ignorance of ourselves, by which, when making decisions in necessary matters, we miserably deceive and even blind ourselves!

But since this precept is so valuable, we ought more diligently to avoid applying it perversely. This, we observe, has happened to certain philosophers, who, while urging man to know himself, propose the goal of recognizing his own worth and excellence. And they would have him contemplate in himself nothing but what swells him with empty assurance and puffs him up with pride.

But knowledge of ourselves lies first in considering what we were given at creation and how generously God continues his favor toward us, in order to know how great our natural excellence would be if only it had remained unblemished; yet at the same time to bear in mind that there is in us nothing of our own, but that we hold on sufferance whatever God has bestowed upon us. Hence we are ever dependent on him. Secondly, to call to mind our miserable condition after Adam's fall; the awareness of which, when all our boasting and self-assurance are laid low, should truly humble us and overwhelm us with shame. In the beginning God fashioned us after his image that he might arouse our minds both to zeal for virtue and to meditation upon eternal life. Thus, in order that the great nobility of our race (which distinguishes us from brute beasts) may not be buried beneath our own dullness of wit, it behooves us to recognize that we have been endowed with reason and understanding so that, by leading a holy and upright life, we may press on to the appointed goal of blessed immortality.

But that primal worthiness cannot come to mind without the sorry spectacle of our foulness and dishonour presenting itself by way of contrast, since in the person of the first man we have fallen from our original condition. From this source arise abhorrence and displeasure with ourselves, as well as true humility; and thence is kindled a new zeal to seek God, in whom each of us may recover those good things which we have utterly and completely lost. ...

Because of what God so severely punished must have been no light sin but a detestable crime, we must consider what kind of sin there was in Adam's desertion that enkindled God's fearful vengeance against the whole of mankind. To regard Adam's sin as gluttonous intemperance (a common notion) is childish. As if the sum and head of all virtues lay in abstaining

solely from one fruit, when all sorts of desirable delights abounded everywhere; and not only abundance but also magnificent variety was at hand in
that blessed fruitfulness of earth!

We ought therefore to look more deeply. Adam was denied the tree of
the knowledge of good and evil to test his obedience and prove that he was
willingly under God's command. The very name of the tree shows the sole
purpose of the precept was to keep him content with his lot and to prevent
him from becoming puffed up with wicked lust. But the promise by which
he was bidden to hope for eternal life so long as he ate from the tree of life,
and conversely, the terrible threat of death once he tasted of the tree of
knowledge of good and evil, served to prove and exercise his faith. Hence it
is not hard to deduce by what means Adam provoked God's wrath upon
himself. Indeed, Augustine speaks rightly when he declares that pride was
the beginning of all evils. For if ambition had not raised man higher than
was meet and right, he could have remained in his original state.

But we must take a fuller definition from the nature of the temptation
which Moses describes. Since the woman through unfaithfulness was led
away from God's Word by the serpent's deceit, it is already clear that disobedience was the beginning of the Fall. This Paul also confirms, teaching
that all were lost through the disobedience of one man. Yet it is at the same
time to be noted that the first man revolted from God's authority, not only
because he was seized by Satan's blandishments, but also because, con-
temptuous of truth, he turned aside to falsehood. And surely, once we hold
God's Word in contempt, we shake off all reverence for him. For, unless we
listen attentively to him, his majesty will not dwell among us, nor his worship remain perfect. Unfaithfulness, then, was the root of the Fall. But
thereafter ambition and pride, together with ungratefulness, arose, because Adam by seeking more than was granted him shamefully spurned
God's great bounty, which had been lavished upon him. To have been
made in the likeness of God seemed a small matter to a son of earth unless
he also attained equality with God—a monstrous wickedness! If apostasy,
by which man withdraws from the authority of his Maker—indeed insolently shakes off his yoke—is a foul and detestable offense, it is vain to ex-
tenuate Adam's sin. Yet it was not simply apostasy, but was joined with
vile reproaches against God. These assented to Satan's slanders, which accused God of falsehood and envy and ill will. Lastly, faithlessness opened
the door to ambition, and ambition was indeed the mother of obstinate disobedience; as a result, men, having cast off the fear of God, threw themselves wherever lust carried them. Hence Bernard rightly teaches that the
door of salvation is opened to us when we receive the gospel today with
our ears, even as death was then admitted by those same windows when
they were opened to Satan. For Adam would never have dared oppose
God's authority unless he had disbelieved in God's Word. Here, indeed,
was the best bridle to control all passions: the thought that nothing is better

than to practice righteousness by obeying God's commandments; then, that the ultimate goal of the happy life is to be loved by him. Therefore Adam, carried away by the devil's blasphemies, as far as he was able extinguished the whole glory of God.

As it was the spiritual life of Adam to remain united and bound to his Maker, so estrangement from him was the death of his soul. Nor is it any wonder that he consigned his race to ruin by his rebellion when he perverted the whole order of nature in heaven and on earth. "All creatures," says Paul, "are groaning," "subject to corruption, not of their own will." If the cause is sought, there is no doubt that they are bearing part of the punishment deserved by man, for whose use they were created. Since, therefore, the curse, which goes about through all the regions of the world, flowed hither and yon from Adam's guilt, it is not unreasonable if it is spread to all his offspring. Therefore, after the heavenly image was obliterated in him, he was not the only one to suffer this punishment—that, in place of wisdom, virtue, holiness, truth, and justice, with which adornments he had been clad, there came forth the most filthy plagues, blindness, impotence, impurity, vanity, and injustice—but he also entangled and immersed his offspring in the same miseries.

This is the inherited corruption, which the church fathers termed "original sin," meaning by the word "sin" the depravation of a nature previously good and pure. There was much contention over this matter, inasmuch as nothing is farther from the usual view than for all to be made guilty by the guilt of one, and thus for sin to be made common. This seems to be the reason why the most ancient doctors of the church touched upon this subject so obscurely. At least they explained it less clearly than was fitting. Yet this timidity could not prevent Pelagius from rising up with the profane fiction that Adam sinned only to his own loss without harming his posterity. Through this subtlety Satan attempted to cover up the disease and thus to render it incurable. But when it was shown by the clear testimony of Scripture that sin was transmitted from the first man to all his posterity, Pelagius quibbled that it was transmitted through imitation, not propagation. Therefore, good men (and Augustine above the rest) labored to show us that we are corrupted not by derived wickedness, but that we bear inborn defect from our mother's womb. . . .

So that these remarks may not be made concerning an uncertain and unknown matter, let us define original sin. It is not my intention to investigate the several definitions proposed by various writers, but simply to bring forward the one that appears to me most in accordance with truth. Original sin, therefore, seems to be a hereditary depravity and corruption of our nature, diffused into all parts of the soul, which first makes us liable to God's wrath, then also brings forth in us those works which Scripture calls "works of the flesh." And that is properly what Paul often calls sin. The works that come forth from it—such as adulteries, fornications, thefts, hatreds, murders, carousings—he accordingly calls "fruit of sin," although they are also commonly called "sins" in Scripture, and even by Paul himself.

We must, therefore, distinctly note these two things. First, we are so vitiated and perverted in every part of our nature that by this great corruption we stand justly condemned and convicted before God, to whom nothing is acceptable but righteousness, innocence, and purity. And this is not liability for another's transgression. For, since it is said that we became subject to God's judgment through Adam's sin, we are to understand it not as if we, guiltless and undeserving, bore the guilt of his offense but in the sense that, since we through his transgression have become entangled in the curse, he is said to have made us guilty. Yet not only has punishment fallen upon us from Adam, but a contagion imparted by him resides in us, which justly deserves punishment. For this reason, Augustine, though he often calls sin "another's" to show more clearly that it is distributed among us through propagation, nevertheless declares at the same time that it is peculiar to each. And the apostle himself most eloquently testifies that "death has spread to all because all have sinned." That is, they have been enveloped in original sin and defiled by its stains. For that reason, even infants themselves, while they carry their condemnation along with them from the mother's womb, are guilty not of another's fault but of their own. For, even though the fruits of their iniquity have not yet come forth, they have the seed enclosed within them. Indeed, their whole nature is a seed of sin; hence it can be only hateful and abhorrent to God. From this it follows that it is rightly considered sin in God's sight, for without guilt there would be no accusation.

Then comes the second consideration: that this perversity never ceases in us, but continually bears new fruits—the works of the flesh that we have already described—just as a burning furnace gives forth flame and sparks, or water ceaselessly bubbles up from a spring. Thus those who have defined original sin as "the lack of the original righteousness, which ought to reside in us," although they comprehend in this definition the whole meaning of the term, have still not expressed effectively enough its power and energy. For our nature is not only destitute and empty of good, but so fertile and fruitful of every evil that it cannot be idle. . . .

MAN HAS NOW BEEN DEPRIVED OF FREEDOM OF CHOICE AND BOUND OVER TO MISERABLE SERVITUDE

We have now seen that the domination of sin, from the time it held the first man bound to itself, not only ranges among all mankind, but also completely occupies individual souls. It remains for us to investigate more closely whether we have been deprived of all freedom since we have been reduced to this servitude; and, if any particle of it still survives, how far its power extends. But in order that the truth of this question may be more readily apparent to us, I shall presently set a goal to which the whole argument should be directed. The best way to avoid error will be to consider the perils that threaten man on both sides. (1) When man is denied all uprightness, he immediately takes occasion for complacency from the fact; and, because he is said to have no ability to pursue righteousness on his own, he holds all such pursuit to be of no consequence, as if it did not pertain to him at all. (2) Nothing, however slight, can be credited to man without depriving God of his honour, and without man himself falling into ruin through brazen confidence. Augustine points out both these precipices.

Here, then, is the course that we must follow if we are to avoid crashing upon these rocks: when man has been taught that no good thing remains in his power, and that he is hedged about on all sides by most miserable necessity, in spite of this he should nevertheless be instructed to aspire to a good of which he is empty, to a freedom of which he has been deprived. In fact, he may thus be more sharply aroused from inactivity than if he were supposed that he was endowed with the highest virtues. Everyone sees how necessary this second point is. I observe that too many persons have doubts about the first point. For since this is an undoubted fact, that nothing of his own ought to be taken away from man, it ought to be clearly evident how important it is for him to be barred from false boasting. At the time when man was distinguished with the noblest marks of honor through God's beneficence, not even then was he permitted to boast about himself. How much more ought he now to humble himself, cast down as he has been—due to his own ungratefulness—from the loftiest glory into extreme disgrace! At that time, I say, when he had been advanced to the highest degree or honor, Scripture attributed nothing else to him than that he had been created in the image of God, thus suggesting that man was blessed, not because of his own actions, but by participation of God. What, therefore, now remains for man, bare and destitute of all glory, but to recognize God for whose beneficence he could not be grateful when he abounded with the riches of this grace; and at least, by confessing his own poverty, to glorify him in whom he did not previously glory in recognition of his own blessings?

Also, it is no less to our advantage than pertinent to God's glory that we be deprived of all credit for our wisdom and virtue. Thus those who bestow upon us anything beyond the truth add sacrilege to our ruin. When we are taught to wage our own war, we are but borne aloft on a reed stick, only to fall as soon as it breaks! Yet we flatter our strength unduly when we compare it even to a reed stick! For whatever vain men devise and babble concerning these matters is but smoke. . . .

If this be admitted, it will be indisputable that free will is not sufficient to enable man to do good works, unless he be helped by grace, indeed by special grace, which only the elect receive through regeneration. For I do not tarry over those fanatics who babble that grace is equally and indiscriminately distributed. But it has not yet been demonstrated whether man has been wholly deprived of all power to do good, or still has some power, though meager and weak; a power, indeed, that can do nothing of itself, but with the help of grace also does its part. The Master of the Sentences meant to settle this point when he taught: "We need two kinds of grace to render us capable of good works." He calls the first kind "operating," which ensures that we effectively will to do good. The second he calls "cooperating," which follows the good will as a help. The thing that displeases me about this division is that, while he attributes the effective desire for good to the grace of God, yet he hints that man by his very own nature somehow seeks after the good—though ineffectively. Thus Bernard declares the good will is God's work, yet concedes to man that of his own impulse he seeks this sort of good will. But this is far from Augustine's thought, from whom Peter Lombard pretended to have taken this distinction. The ambiguity in the second part offends me, for it has given rise to a perverted interpretation. They thought we cooperate with the assisting grace of God, because it is our right either to render it ineffectual by spurning the first grace, or to confirm it by obediently following it. This the author of the work *The Calling of the Gentiles* expresses as follows: "Those who employ the judgment of reason are free to forsake grace, so that not to have forsaken it is a meritorious act; and what could not be done without the co-operation of the Spirit is counted meritorious for those whose own will could not have accomplished it." I chose to note these two points in passing that you, my reader, may see how far I disagree with the sounder Schoolmen. I differ with the more recent Sophists to an even greater extent, as they are farther removed from antiquity. However, we at least understand from this division in what way they grant free will to man. For Lombard finally declares that we have free will, not in that we are equally capable of doing or thinking good and evil, but merely that we are freed from compulsion. According to Lombard, this freedom is not hindered, even if we be wicked and slaves of sin, and can do nothing but sin.

Man will then be spoken of as having this sort of free decision, not because he has free choice equally of good and evil, but because he acts wickedly by will, not by compulsion. Well put, indeed, but what purpose is served by labeling with a proud name such a slight thing? A noble freedom, indeed—for man not to be forced to serve sin, yet to be such a willing slave that his will is bound by the fetters of sin!

.   .   .

ETERNAL ELECTION, BY WHICH GOD HAS PREDESTINED SOME TO SALVATION, OTHERS TO DESTRUCTION

In actual fact, the covenant of life is not preached equally among all men, and among those to whom it is preached, it does not gain the same acceptance either constantly or in equal degree. In this diversity the wonderful depth of God's judgment is made known. For there is no doubt that this variety also serves the decision of God's eternal election. If it is plain that it comes to pass by God's bidding that salvation is freely offered to some while others are barred from access to it, at once great and difficult questions spring up, explicable only when reverent minds regard as settled what they may suitably hold concerning election and predestination. A baffling question this seems to many. For they think nothing more inconsistent than that out of the common multitude of men some should be predestined to salvation, others to destruction. But how mistakenly they entangle themselves will become clear in the following discussion. Besides, in the very darkness that frightens them not only is the usefulness of this doctrine made known but also its very sweet fruit. We shall never be clearly persuaded, as we ought to be, that our salvation flows from the well-spring of God's free mercy until we come to know his eternal election, which illuminates God's grace by this contrast: that he does not indiscriminately adopt all into the hope of salvation but gives to some what he denies to others.

How much the ignorance of this principle detracts from God's glory, how much it takes away from true humility, is well known. Yet Paul denies that this which needs so much to be known can be known unless God, utterly disregarding works, chooses those whom he has decreed within himself. "At the present time," he says, "a remnant has been saved according to the election of grace. But if it is by grace, it is no more of works; otherwise grace would no more be grace. But if it is of works, it is no more of grace; otherwise work would not be work." If—to make it clear that our salvation comes about solely from God's mere generosity—we must be called back to the course of election, those who wish to get rid of all this are obscuring as maliciously as they can what ought to have been gloriously and vociferously proclaimed, and they tear humility up by the very roots. Paul clearly testifies that, when the salvation of a remnant of the people is ascribed to the election of grace, then only is it acknowledged that God of his mere good pleasure preserves whom he will, and moreover that he pays no reward, since he can owe none.

They who shut the gates that no one may dare seek a taste of this doctrine wrong men no less than God. For neither will anything else suffice to make us humble as we ought to be nor shall we otherwise sincerely feel how much we are obliged to God. And as Christ teaches, here is our only ground for firmness and confidence: in order to free us of all fear and render us victorious amid so many dangers, snares, and mortal struggles, he promises that whatever the Father has entrusted into his keeping will be safe. From this we infer that all those who do not know that they are God's own will be miserable through constant fear. Hence, those who by being blind to the three benefits we have noted would wish the foundation of our salvation to be removed from our midst, very badly serve the interests of themselves and of all other believers. How is it that the church becomes manifest to us from this, when, as Bernard rightly teaches, "it could not otherwise be found or recognized among creatures, since it lies marvelously hidden . . . both within the bosom of a blessed predestination and within the mass of a miserable condemnation"?

But before I enter into the matter itself, I need to mention by way of preface two kinds of men.

Human curiosity renders the discussion of predestination, already somewhat difficult of itself, very confusing and even dangerous. No restraints can hold it back from wandering in forbidden bypaths and thrusting upward to the heights. If allowed, it will leave no secret to God that it will not search out and unravel. Since we see so many on all sides rushing into this audacity and impudence, among them certain men not otherwise bad, they should in due season be reminded of the measure of their duty in this regard.

First, then, let them remember that when they inquire into predestination they are penetrating the sacred precincts of divine wisdom. If anyone with carefree assurance breaks into this place, he will not succeed in satisfying his curiosity and he will enter a labyrinth from which he can find no exit. For it is not right for man unrestrainedly to search out things that the Lord has willed to be hid in himself, and to unfold from eternity itself the sublimest wisdom, which he would have us revere but not understand that through this also he should fill us with wonder. He has set forth by his Word the secrets of his will that he has decided to reveal to us. These he decided to reveal in so far as he foresaw that they would concern us and benefit us. . . .

Profane men, I admit, in the matter of predestination abruptly seize upon something to carp, rail, bark, or scoff at. But if their shamelessness deters us, we shall have to keep secret the chief doctrines of the faith, almost none of which they or their like leave untouched by blasphemy. An obstinate person would be no less insolently puffed up on hearing that within the essence of God there are three Persons than if he were told that God foresaw what would happen to man when he created him. And they will not refrain from guffaws when they are informed that but little more than five thousand years have passed since the creation of the universe, for they ask why God's power was idle and asleep for so long. Nothing, in short, can be brought forth that they do not assail with their mockery. Should we, to silence these blasphemies, forbear to speak of the deity of Son and Spirit? Must we pass over in silence the creation of the universe? No! God's truth is so powerful, both in this respect and in every other, that it has nothing to fear from the evil-speaking of wicked men.

So Augustine stoutly maintains in his little treatise *The Gift of Perseverance*. For we see that the false apostles could not make Paul ashamed by defaming and accusing his true doctrine. They say that this whole discussion is dangerous for godly minds—because it hinders exhortations, because it shakes faith, because it disturbs and terrifies the heart itself—but this is nonsense! Augustine admits that for these reasons he was frequently charged with preaching predestination too freely, but, as it was easy for him, he overwhelmingly refuted the charge. We, moreover, because many and various absurdities are obtruded at this point, have preferred to dispose of each in its own place. I desire only to have them generally admit that we should not investigate what the Lord has left hidden in secret, that we should not neglect what he has brought into the open, so that we may not be convicted of excessive curiosity on the one hand, or of excessive ingratitude on the other. For Augustine also skillfully expressed this idea; we can safely follow Scripture, which proceeds at the pace of a mother stooping to her child, so to speak, so as not to leave us behind in our weakness. But for those who are so cautious or fearful that they desire to bury predestination in order not to disturb weak souls—with what color will they cloak their arrogance when they accuse God indirectly of stupid thoughtlessness, as if he had not foreseen the peril that they feel they have wisely met? Whoever, then, heaps odium upon the doctrine of predestination openly reproaches of God, as if he had unadvisedly let slip something hurtful to the church.

No one who wishes to be thought religious dares simply deny predestination, by which God adopts some to hope of life, and sentences others to eternal death. But our opponents, especially those who make foreknowledge its cause, envelop it in numerous petty objections. We, indeed, place both doctrines in God, but we say that subjecting one to the other is absurd.

When we attribute foreknowledge to God, we mean that all things always were, and perpetually remain, under his eyes, so that to his knowledge there is nothing future or past, but all things are present. And they are present in such a way that he not only conceives them through ideas, as we have before us those things which our minds remember, but he truly looks upon them and discerns them as things placed before him. And this foreknowledge is extended throughout the universe to every creature. We call predestination God's eternal decree, by which he determined with himself what he willed to become of each man. For all are not created in equal condition; rather, eternal life is foreordained for some, eternal damnation for others. Therefore, as any man has been created to one or the other of these ends, we speak of him as predestined to life or to death. . . .

As Scripture, then, clearly shows, we say that God once established by his eternal and unchangeable plan those whom he long before determined once for all to receive into salvation, and those whom, on the other hand, he would devote to destruction. We assert that, with respect to the elect, this plan was founded upon his freely given mercy, without regard to human worth; but by his just and irreprehensible but incomprehensible judgment he has barred the door of life to those whom he has given over to damnation. Now among the elect we regard the call as a testimony of election. Then we hold justification another sign of its manifestation, until they come into the glory in which the fulfillment of that election lies. But as the Lord seals his elect by call and justification, so, by shutting off the reprobate from knowledge of his name or from the sanctification of his Spirit, he, as it were, reveals by these marks what sort of judgment awaits them.

The Counter-Reformation

The Counter-Reformation of the Catholic church—or the Catholic Refor-mation, as it is sometimes called—expressed itself in three main institu-tions: the Society of Jesus (usually called the Jesuits), the Inquisition (or Holy Office), and the Council of Trent. The Society of Jesus was founded by St. Ignatius of Loyola (1491–1556), an unlettered Spanish soldier who, as the result of a religious experience he underwent after being wounded in battle, resolved to become a "soldier of Christ." Once he had recov-ered, he set about educating himself, starting with elementary school and continuing through the University of Paris, where he began organizing the Jesuit order. Loyola's new society was established along military lines: an iron discipline demanded that each member show complete obe-dience to his immediate superiors and ultimately to his supreme com-mander, the pope. During the religious conflicts of the sixteenth and seventeenth centuries, the Jesuits were always to be found on the side of the papal forces, in opposition primarily to the Protestants but to Catholic liberals as well.

The Inquisition was an old organization developed by the Domini-can order in the thirteenth century primarily to combat the Albigensian heresy in southern France. It gained its greatest strength, however, in Spain. There it was used, particularly under the leadership of Torquema-da, as the prime agent in the suppression of heretics. After the Reforma-tion, the Inquisition joined forces with the Jesuits to combat the "Protestant heresy."

The Council of Trent, called originally by Pope Paul III in 1545, met at irregular intervals over a period of nearly twenty years under three dif-ferent popes in the northern Italian city of Trent. Although the council reaffirmed the central doctrines of the Catholic church against what it con-sidered to be the heretical views of Protestantism, it also called for the elimination of abuses that had crept into the church. The selection that fol-lows includes some of the more important decrees, concerning both doc-trine and practice, adopted by the council.

Consider the following questions as you study the text below.

1. Compare the understanding of original sin put forth by the Council of Trent with that of John Calvin. On what key points did the Council disagree with Calvin?

2. Compare the opinion on the veneration of the saints put forth by the Council of Trent with that of Erasmus. On what key points did the Council disagree with Erasmus?

The Canons and Decrees
of the Council of Trent

DECREE TOUCHING THE OPENING OF THE COUNCIL

Doth it please you,—unto the praise and glory of the holy and undivided Trinity, Father, and Son, and Holy Ghost; for the increase and exaltation of the Christian faith and religion; for the extirpation of heresies; for the peace and union of the Church; for the reformation of the Clergy and Christian people; for the depression and extinction of the enemies of the Christian name,—to decree and declare that the sacred and general council of Trent do begin, and hath begun?

They answered: It pleaseth us.

DECREE CONCERNING THE CANONICAL SCRIPTURES

The sacred and holy, oecumenical, and general Synod of Trent,—lawfully assembled in the Holy Ghost, the same three legates of the Apostolic See presiding therein,—keeping this always in view, that, errors being removed, the purity itself of the Gospel be preserved in the Church; which [Gospel], before promised through the prophets in the holy Scriptures, our Lord Jesus Christ, the Son of God, first promulgated with His own mouth, and then commanded to be preached by His Apostles to every creature, as the fountain of all, both saving truth, and moral discipline; and seeing clearly that this truth and books, and the unwritten traditions which, received by the Apostles from the mouth of Christ himself, or from the Apostles themselves, the Holy Ghost dictating, have come down even unto us, transmitted as it were from hand to hand; (the Synod) following the examples of the orthodox Fathers, receives and venerates with an equal affection of piety, and reverence, all the books both of the Old and the New Testament—seeing that one God is the author of both—as also the said traditions, as well those appertaining to faith as to morals, as having been dictated, either by Christ's own word of mouth, or by the Holy Ghost, and preserved in the Catholic Church by a continuous succession.

The Canons and Decrees of the Sacred and Oecumenical Council of Trent, trans. J. Waterworth.

DECREE CONCERNING THE EDITION,
AND THE USE, OF THE SACRED BOOKS

Moreover, the same sacred and holy Synod,—considering that no small utility may accrue to the Church of God, it if be made known which out of all the Latin editions, now in circulation, of the sacred books, is to be held as authentic,—ordains and declares, that the said old and vulgate edition, which, by the lengthened usage of so many ages, has been approved of in the Church, be, in public lectures, disputations, sermons and expositions, held as authentic; and that no one is to dare, or presume to reject it under any pre-text whatever.

Furthermore, in order to restrain petulant spirits, It decrees, that no one, relying on his own skill, shall,—in matters of faith, and of morals pertaining to the edification of Christian doctrine,—wrestling the sacred Scripture to his own senses, presume to interpret the said sacred Scripture contrary to that sense which holy mother Church,—whose it is to judge of the true sense and interpretation of the holy Scriptures,—hath held and doth hold;—or even contrary to the unanimous consent of the Fathers; even though such inter-pretations were never (intended) to be at any time published. . . .

DECREE CONCERNING ORIGINAL SIN

That our Catholic *faith, without which it is impossible to please God*, may, errors being purged away, continue in its own perfect and spotless integrity, and that the Christian people may not *be carried about with every wind of doctrine*; whereas that old serpent, the perpetual enemy of mankind, amongst the very many evils with which the Church of God is in these our times troubled, has also stirred up not only new, but even old, dissensions touching original sin, and the remedy thereof; the sacred and holy, oecu-menical and general Synod of Trent,—lawfully assembled in the Holy See presiding therein,—wishing now to come to the reclaiming of the erring, and the confirming of the wavering—following the testimonies of the sacred Scriptures, of the holy Fathers, or the most approved councils, and the judge-ment and consent of the Church itself, ordains, confesses, and declares these things touching the said original sin:

1.   If any one does not confess that the first man, Adam, when he had transgressed the commandment of God in Paradise, immediately lost the ho-liness and justice wherein he had been constituted; and that he incurred, through the offense of that prevarication, the wrath and indignation of God, and consequently death, with which God had previously threatened him, and, together with death, captivity under his power who thenceforth *had the empire of death, that is to say, the devil*, and that the entire Adam, through that offence of prevarication, was changed, in body and soul, for the worse; let him be anathema.

2.   If any one asserts, that the prevarication of Adam injured himself alone, and not his posterity; and that the holiness and justice, received of God, which he lost, he lost for himself alone, and not for us also; or that he, being defiled by the sin of disobedience, has only transfused death, and pains of the body, into the whole human race, but not sin also, which is the death of the soul; let him be anathema:—whereas he contradicts the apostle who says; *by one man sin entered into the world, and by sin death, and so death passed upon all men, in whom all have sinned.*

3.   If any one asserts, that this sin of Adam,—which in its origin is one, and being transfused into all by propagation, not by imitation, is in each one as his own,—is taken away either by the powers of human nature, or by any other remedy than the merit of the *one mediator, our Lord Jesus Christ, who hath reconciled us to God in his own blood, made unto us justice, sanctification, and redemption*; or if he denies that the said merit of Jesus Christ is applied, both to adults and to infants, by the sacrament of baptism rightly administered in the form of the Church; let him be anathema: *For there is no other name under heaven given to men, whereby we must be saved.* Whence that voice; *Behold the lamb of God, behold him who taketh away the sins of the world*; and that other; *As many as have been baptized, have put on Christ.*

.   .   .

THAT A RASH PRESUMPTUOUSNESS IN THE MATTER OF PREDESTINATION IS TO BE AVOIDED

No one, moreover, so long as he is in this mortal life, ought so far to presume as regards the secret mystery of divine predestination, as to determine for certain that he is assuredly in the number of the predestinate; as if it were true, that he that is justified, either cannot sin any more, or, if he do sin, that he ought to promise himself an assured repentance; for except by special revelation, it cannot be known whom God hath chosen unto Himself.

.   .   .

ON THE SACRAMENTS IN GENERAL

Canon I. If any one saith, that the sacraments of the New Law were not all instituted by Jesus Christ, our Lord; or, that they are more, or less, than seven, to wit, Baptism, Confirmation, the Eucharist, Penance, Extreme Unction, Order, and Matrimony; or even that any one of these seven is not truly and properly a sacrament; let him be anathema.

Canon II. If any one saith, that these said sacraments of the New Law do not differ from the sacraments of the Old Law, save that the ceremonies are different, and different the outward rites; let him be anathema.

Canon III. If any one saith, that these seven sacraments are in such wise equal to each other, as that one is not in any way more worthy than another; let him be anathema.

Canon IV. If any one saith, that the sacraments of the New Law are not necessary unto salvation, but superfluous; and that, without them, or without the desire thereof, men obtain of God, through faith alone, the grace of justification;—though all (the sacraments) are not indeed necessary for every individual; let him be anathema.

Canon V. If any one saith, that these sacraments were instituted for the sake of nourishing faith alone; let him be anathema.

Canon VI. If any one saith, that the sacraments of the New Law do not contain the grace which they signify; or, that they do not confer that grace on those who do not place an obstacle thereunto; as though they were merely outward signs of grace or justice received through faith, and certain marks of the Christian profession, whereby believers are distinguished amongst men from unbelievers; let him be anathema.

Canon VII. If any one saith, that grace, as far as God's part is concerned, is not given through the said sacraments, always, and to all men, even though they receive them rightly, but (only) sometimes, and to some persons; let him be anathema.

Canon VIII. If any one saith, that by the said sacraments of the New Law grace is not conferred through the act performed, but that faith alone in the divine promise suffices for the obtaining of grace; let him be anathema.

Canon IX. If any one saith, that, in the three sacraments, Baptism, to wit, Confirmation, and Order, there is not imprinted in the soul a character, that is, a certain spiritual and indelible sign, on account of which they cannot be repeated; let him be anathema.

Canon X. If any one saith, that all Christians have power to administer the word, and all the sacraments; let him be anathema.

Canon XI. If any one saith, that, in ministers, when they effect, and confer the sacraments, there is not required the intention at least of doing what the Church does; let him be anathema.

Canon XII. If any one saith, that a minister, being in mortal sin,—if so be that he observe all the essentials which belong to the effecting, or conferring of, the sacrament,—neither effects, nor confers the sacrament; let him be anathema.

Canon XIII. If any one saith, that the received and approved rites of the Catholic Church, wont to be used in the solemn administration of the sacraments, may be condemned, or without sin be omitted at pleasure by the ministers, or be changed, by every pastor of the churches, into other new ones; let him be anathema.

. . .

ON THE REAL PRESENCE OF OUR LORD
JESUS CHRIST IN THE MOST HOLY
SACRAMENT OF THE EUCHARIST

In the first place, the holy Synod teaches, and openly and simply professes, that, in the august sacrament of the holy Eucharist, after the consecration of the bread and wine, our Lord Jesus Christ, true God and man, is truly, really, and substantially contained under the species of those sensible things. For neither are these things mutually repugnant,—that our Saviour Himself always sitteth at the right hand of the Father in heaven, according to the natural mode of existing, and that, nevertheless, He be, in many other places, sacramentally present to us in his own substance, by a manner of existing, which, though we can scarcely express it in words, yet can we, by the understanding illuminated by faith, conceive, and we ought most firmly to believe, to be possible unto God: for thus all our forefathers, as many as were in the true Church of Christ, who have treated of his most holy Sacrament have most openly professed, that our Redeemer instituted this so admirable a sacrament at the last supper, when, after the blessing of the bread and wine, He testified, in express and clear words, that He gave them His own very Body, and His own Blood; words which,—recorded by the holy Evangelists, and afterwards repeated by Saint Paul, whereas they carry with them that proper and most manifest meaning in which they were understood by the Fathers,—it is indeed a crime the most unworthy that they should be wrested, by certain contentious and wicked men, to fictitious and imaginary tropes, whereby the verity of the flesh and blood of Christ is denied, contrary to the universal sense of the Church, which, as *the pillar and ground of truth*, has detested, as satanical, these inventions devised by impious men; she recognising, with a mind ever grateful and unforgetting, this most excellent benefit of Christ.

. . .

ON THE MOST HOLY SACRAMENT OF THE EUCHARIST

Canon I. If any one denieth, that, in the sacrament of the most holy Eucharist, are contained truly, really, and substantially, the body and blood together with the soul and divinity of our Lord Jesus Christ, and consequently the whole Christ; but saith that He is only therein as in a sign, or in figure, or virtue; let him be anathema.

Canon II. If any one saith, that, in the sacred and holy sacrament of the Eucharist, the substance of the bread and wine remains conjointly with the body and blood of our Lord Jesus Christ, and denieth that wonderful and singular conversion of the whole substance of the bread into the Body, and of the whole substance of the wine into the Blood—the species only of the bread and wine remaining—which conversion indeed the Catholic Church most aptly calls Transubstantiation; let him be anathema.

.   .   .

Canon IX. If any one denieth, that all and each of Christ's faithful of both sexes are bound, when they have attained to years of discretion, to communicate every year, at least at Easter, in accordance with the precept of the holy Mother Church; let him be anathema.

.   .   .

Canon XI. If any one saith, that faith alone is a sufficient preparation for receiving the sacrament of the most holy Eucharist; let him be anathema. And for fear lest so great a sacrament may be received unworthily, and so unto death and condemnation, this holy Synod ordains and declares, that sacramental confession, when a confessor may be had, is of necessity to be made beforehand, by those whose conscience is burthened with mortal sin, how contrite even soever they may think themselves. But if any one shall presume to teach, preach, or obstinately to assert, or even in public disputation to defend the contrary, he shall be thereupon excommunicated.

.   .   .

ON THE ECCLESIASTICAL HIERARCHY, AND ON ORDINATION

But, forasmuch as in the sacrament of Order, as also in Baptism, and Confirmation, a character is imprinted, which can neither be effaced nor taken away; the holy Synod with reason condemns the opinion of those, who assert that the priests of the New Testament have only a temporary power; and that those who have once been rightly ordained, can again become laymen, if they do not exercise the ministry of the word of God. And if any one affirm, that all Christians indiscriminately are priests of the New Testament, or that they are all mutually endowed with an equal spiritual power, he clearly does nothing but confound the ecclesiastical hierarchy, which is *as an army set in array*; as if, contrary to the doctrine of blessed Paul, *all were apostles, all prophets, all evangelists, all pastors, all doctors.* Wherefore, the holy Synod declares that, besides the other ecclesiastical degrees, bishops, who have succeeded to the place of the apostles, principally belong to this hierarchical order; that they are *placed*, as the same apostle says *by the Holy Ghost, to rule the Church of God*; that they are superior to priests; administer the sacrament of Confirmation; ordain the ministers of the Church; and that they can perform very many other things; over which functions others of an inferior order have no power. Furthermore, the sacred and holy Synod teaches, that, in the ordination of bishops, priests, and of the other orders, neither the consent, nor vocation, nor authority, whether of the people, or of any civil power or magistrate whatsoever, is required in such wise as that, without this, the ordination is invalid; yea rather doth It decree, that all those who, being only called and instituted by the people, or by the civil power and magistrate, ascend to the exercise of these ministrations, and those who of their own rashness assume them to themselves, are not ministers of the Church, but are to be looked upon as *thieves and robbers, who have not entered by the door*. These are the things which it hath seemed good to the sacred Synod to teach the faithful of Christ, in general terms, touching the sacrament of Order.

. . .

ON THE SACRAMENT OF MATRIMONY

. . .

Canon IX. If anyone saith, that clerics constituted in sacred orders or Regulars, who have solemnly professed chastity, are able to contract marriage, and that being contracted it is valid, notwithstanding the ecclesiastical law, or vow; and that the contrary is nothing else than to condemn marriage; and, that all who do not feel that they have the gift of chastity, even though they have made a vow thereof, may contract marriage; let him be anathema; seeing that God refuses not that gift to those who ask for it rightly, neither does *He suffer us to be tempted above that which we are able*.

Canon X. If any one saith, that the marriage state is to be placed above the state of virginity, or of celibacy, and that it is not better and more blessed to remain in virginity, or in celibacy, than to be united in matrimony; let him be anathema.

. . .

ON THE INVOCATION, VENERATION, AND RELICS, OF SAINTS, AND ON SACRED IMAGES

The holy Synod enjoins on all bishops, and others who sustain the office and charge of teaching, that, agreeably to the usage of the Catholic and Apostolic Church, received from the primitive times of the Christian religion, and agreeably to the consent of the holy Fathers, and to the decrees of sacred Councils, they especially instruct the faithful diligently concerning the intercession and invocation of saints; the honour (paid) to relics; and the legitimate use of images: teaching them, that the saints, who reign together with Christ, offer up their own prayers to God for men; that it is good and useful suppliantly to invoke them, and to have recourse to their prayers, aid, (and) help for obtaining benefits from God, through His Son, Jesus Christ our Lord, who is our alone Redeemer and Saviour; but that they think impiously, who deny that the saints, who enjoy eternal happiness in heaven, are to be invocated; or who assert either that they do not pray for men; or, that the invocation of them to pray for each of us even in particular, is idolatry: or that it is repugnant to the word of God; and is opposed to the honour of the *one mediator of God and men, Christ Jesus*; or, that it is foolish to supplicate, vocally, or mentally, those who reign in heaven. Also, that the holy bodies of holy martyrs, and of others now living with Christ—which bodies were the living members of Christ, and *the temple of the Holy Ghost*, and which are by Him to be raised unto eternal life, and to be glorified—are to be venerated by the faithful; through which (bodies) many benefits are bestowed by God on men; so that they who affirm that veneration and honour are not due to the relics of saints; or, that these, and other sacred monuments, are uselessly honoured by the faithful; and that the places dedicated to the memories of the saints are in vain visited with the view of obtaining their aid; are wholly to be condemned, as the Church has already long since condemned, and now also condemns them.

Moreover, that the images of Christ, of the Virgin Mother of God, and of the other saints, are to be had and retained particularly in temples, and that due honour and veneration are to be given them; not that any divinity, or virtue, is believed to be in them, on account of which they are to be worshipped; or that anything is to be asked of them; or, that trust is to be reposed in images, as was of old done by the Gentiles who placed their hope in idols; but because the honour which is shown them is referred to the prototypes which those images represent; in such wise that by the images which we kiss, and before which we uncover the head, and prostrate ourselves, we adore Christ; and we venerate the saints, whose similitude they bear: as by the decrees of Councils, and especially of the second Synod of Nicaea, has been defined against the opponents of images.

. . .

CARDINALS AND ALL PRELATES OF THE CHURCHES SHALL BE CONTENT WITH MODEST FURNITURE AND A FRUGAL TABLE: THEY SHALL NOT ENRICH THEIR RELATIVES OR DOMESTICS OUT OF THE PROPERTY OF THE CHURCH

It is to be wished, that those who undertake the office of a bishop should understand what their portion is; and comprehend that they are called, not to their own convenience, not to riches or luxury, but to labours and cares for the glory of God. For it is not to be doubted, that the rest of the faithful also will be more easily excited to religion and innocence, if they shall see those who are set over them, not fixing their thoughts on the things of this world, but on the salvation of souls, and on their heavenly country. Wherefore the holy Synod, being minded that these things are of the greatest importance toward restoring ecclesiastical discipline, admonishes all bishops, that, often meditating thereon, they show themselves conformable to their office, by their actual deeds, and the actions of their lives; which is a kind of perpetual sermon; but above all that they so order their whole conversation, as that others may thence be able to derive examples of frugality, modesty, continency, and of that holy humility which so much recommends us to God.

Wherefore, after the example of our fathers in the Council of Carthage, it not only orders that bishops be content with modest furniture, and a frugal table and diet, but that they also give heed that in the rest of their manner of living, and in their whole house, there be nothing seen that is alien from this holy institution, and which does not manifest simplicity, zeal toward God, and a contempt of vanities. Also, it wholly forbids them to strive to enrich their own kindred or domestics out of the revenues of the church: seeing that even the canons of the Apostles forbid them to give to their kindred the property of the church, which belongs to God: but if their kindred be poor, let them distribute to them thereof as poor, but not misapply, or waste, it for their sakes: yea, the holy Synod with the utmost earnestness, admonishes them completely to lay aside all this human and carnal affection toward brothers, nephews, and kindred, which is the seed-plot of many evils in the Church. And what has been said of bishops, the same is not only to be observed by all who hold ecclesiastical benefices, whether Secular or Regular, each according to the nature of his rank, but the Synod decrees that it also regards the cardinals of the holy Roman Church; for whereas, upon their advice to the most holy Roman Pontiff, the administration of the universal Church depends, it would seem to be a shame, if they did not at the same time shine so pre-eminent in virtue and in the discipline of their lives, as deservedly to draw upon themselves the eyes of all men.

.   .   .

DECREE CONCERNING INDULGENCES

Whereas the power of conferring Indulgences was granted by Christ to the Church; and she has, even in the most ancient times, used the said power, delivered unto her of God; the sacred holy Synod teaches, and enjoins, that the use of Indulgences, for the Christian people most salutary, and approved of by the authority of sacred Councils, is to be retained in the Church; and It condemns with anathema those who either assert, that they are useless; or who deny that there is in the Church the power of granting them. In granting them, however, It desires that, in accordance with the ancient and approved custom in the Church, moderation be observed; lest, by excessive facility, ecclesiastical discipline be enervated. And being desirous that the abuses which have crept therein, and by occasion of which this honourable name of Indulgences is blasphemed by heretics, be amended and corrected, It ordains generally by this decree, that all evil gains for the obtaining thereof, —whence a most prolific cause of abuses amongst the

Christian people has been derived,—be wholly abolished. But as regards the other abuses which have proceeded from superstition, ignorance, irreverence, or from whatsoever other source, since, by reason of the manifold corruptions in the places and provinces where the said abuses are committed, they cannot conveniently be specially prohibited; it commands all bishops, diligently to collect, each in his own church, all abuses of this nature, and to report them in the first provincial Synod; that, after having been reviewed by the opinions of the other bishops also, they may forthwith be referred to the Sovereign Roman Pontiff, by whose authority and prudence that which may be expedient for the universal Church will be ordained; that thus the gift of holy Indulgences may be dispensed to all the faithful, piously, holily, and incorruptly.